THE WOMAN QUESTION IN FRANCE, 1400–1870

This is a revolutionary reinterpretation of the French past from the early fifteenth century to the establishment of the Third Republic, focused on public challenges and defenses of masculine hierarchy in relations between women and men. Karen Offen surveys heated exchanges around women's "influence"; their exclusion from "authority"; the increasing prominence of biomedical thinking and population issues; concerns about education, intellect, and the sexual politics of knowledge; and the politics of women's work. Initially, the majority of commentators were literate and influential men. However, as more and more women attained literacy, they too began to analyze their situation in print and to contest men's claims about who women were and should be and what they should be restrained from doing, and why. As urban print culture exploded and revolutionary ideas of "equality" fuelled women's claims for emancipation, this question resonated throughout francophone Europe and, ultimately, across the seas.

KAREN OFFEN (Ph.D., Stanford University) is a historian and independent scholar affiliated as a Senior Scholar with the Michelle R. Clayman Institute for Gender Research at Stanford University in California.

THE WOMAN QUESTION IN FRANCE, 1400–1870

KAREN OFFEN

CAMBRIDGE
UNIVERSITY PRESS

CAMBRIDGE
UNIVERSITY PRESS

University Printing House, Cambridge CB2 8BS, United Kingdom

One Liberty Plaza, 20th Floor, New York, NY 10006, USA

477 Williamstown Road, Port Melbourne, VIC 3207, Australia

4843/24, 2nd Floor, Ansari Road, Daryaganj, Delhi – 110002, India

79 Anson Road, #06–04/06, Singapore 079906

Cambridge University Press is part of the University of Cambridge.

It furthers the University's mission by disseminating knowledge in the pursuit of
education, learning, and research at the highest international levels of excellence.

www.cambridge.org
Information on this title: www.cambridge.org/9781107188082
DOI: 10.1017/9781316946367

© Karen Offen 2017

First published 2017

Printed in the United Kingdom by Clays, St Ives plc

A catalogue record for this publication is available from the British Library.

Library of Congress Cataloging-in-Publication Data
NAMES: Offen, Karen., author.
TITLE: The woman question in France, 1400-1870 / Karen Offen.
DESCRIPTION: Cambridge, United Kingdom ; New York, NY : Cambridge University Press, 2017. |
Includes bibliographical references and index.
IDENTIFIERS: LCCN 2017004386 | ISBN 9781107188082 (Hardback : alkaline paper)
SUBJECTS: LCSH: Women–France–History. | Women–France–Social conditions. |
Women–Political activity–France–History. | Sex role–France–History. |
France–History. | France–Social conditions. |
France–Politics and government.
CLASSIFICATION: LCC HQ1613 .O34 2017 | DDC 305.40944–dc23
LC record available at https://lccn.loc.gov/2017004386

ISBN 978-1-107-18808-2 Hardback

I dedicate this volume to my ever supportive husband of fifty-plus years, George R. Offen. Without his unflagging encouragement and sustaining belief in the promise of my historical scholarship (or at least his respect for my pursuit of the missing voices), this book would never have been completed. I thank him, first, for offering to carry my books, then for discovering the existence of the Bibliothèque Marguerite Durand in Paris, for sharing the journey and helping to raise our daughters while I was excavating sources in the archives and libraries, and especially for being, in my eyes at least, the kindest and most considerate male-feminist lover, companionate spouse, and adventure travel companion a woman could ever wish for.

Contents

Preface

> Writing about French history, especially as an outsider, is not an
> enterprise for the faint-hearted.
>
> Siân Reynolds, 1996

This volume and its companion volume, *Debating the Woman Question in
the French Third Republic, 1870–1920*, represent the results of an empirical,
detailed work of scholarship, the product of a life's work. This volume
provides *reconnaissance*, documenting the emergence and development of a
cluster of themes in the debates (written and published in French) on the
woman question that span roughly 450 years. These themes and the
manner in which they are articulated reveal the particularities of the status
of French women (both single and married) and the peculiarities of the
surrounding culture, particularities and peculiarities that provoke and
inform controversies over the woman question under the French monarchies and in neighboring Francophone lands. I have written it with
general readers in mind as well as those with expertise in French history.

One unusual feature of this volume is that it breaks with conventional
political chronology by bridging the French Revolution as well as several
other early nineteenth-century efforts to contest monarchical rule. What
I intend here is to provide a history of a debate that spans what French
historians refer to as "ruptures" even as it contributes to our appreciation of
a monarchical "longue durée" that includes the First Empire of Napoléon,
the Bourbon Restoration, the July Monarchy, and the Second Empire of
Napoléon III. The debates on the woman question are tightly tied to the
contestation of authoritarian government and the repeated attempts to
achieve some form of democratic rule under a republic. Thus, this volume
should not be seen as a mere prologue to the ensuing debates on the
woman question during the French Third Republic, which provides a
more hospitable model of government but attempts to sink its roots in a
turbulent and rapidly evolving economic and cultural context.

Indeed, my point in elaborating at length on the important themes in the debates over the earlier four centuries (prior to, during, and following the Revolution through the Second Empire) is grounded in the realization that *no aspect of the debates on the woman question actually began with the Third Republic*. This volume demonstrates, evidence in hand, that the woman question debates (in manuscript and ultimately in print forms) were underway in French-speaking lands for centuries prior to the Revolution and, also, that they would gain both amplitude and magnitude as they benefitted from – and incorporated – the ultimately revolutionary vocabulary of liberty, equality, and justice, within a framework provided by the enormous political, economic, social, and cultural changes of the late eighteenth and early nineteenth centuries that extended throughout western and central Europe. Scholars of early modernity and the Enlightenment know about the earlier debates, but they rarely connect their findings to developments in the nineteenth and twentieth centuries. Nor do scholars of gender politics during the French Revolution follow the debates into the nineteenth century. Conversely, historians of the Third Republic (and later) do not, for the most part, make the connections of these debates in the early modern or immediate post-revolutionary period. Thus, the seven chapters in this volume will serve to bring the "modernists" up to speed on the development of the themes over time and will demonstrate the continuities that transcend customary historical periodization. They will also facilitate the understanding of the tight connections to the earlier periods for those whose knowledge is concentrated on the Third Republic (and its successor regimes). Above all, this approach will highlight the finding that these debates are extremely political and that they seem to recur in every generation.

Following the proclamation of the Republic in September 1870 and the Paris Commune, the amplification of the debates during the first fifty years of the French Third Republic, will be addressed in my companion volume (mentioned earlier) by paying far closer attention to chronological and contextual developments, for which we have far more evidence than we do for the earlier centuries about the participants in the debates and more insight into how the debates actually proceed. The themes developed in this volume will, however, enable readers to situate the later developments within a far longer time period (what the French call the *longue durée*).

I have drawn from and built on key arguments made in my own earlier publications for material to repurpose here, but no chapter in this volume (except for Chapter 5 on the politics of women's history, which has been reworked and expanded) reprints the substance of an earlier published article. Wherever appropriate, I have acknowledged my borrowings in the bibliographical footnotes, on the presumption that I need no "permission" from other publishers to utilize my own work in a modified form. This book has no formal bibliography; however, the footnotes are both bibliographical and historiographical and both primary and secondary sources are cited in order of publication rather than alphabetically. I have tried to make the references as complete, explicit, and transparent as possible, so that others can easily access the evidence if they so desire and verify (or dispute) the conclusions I have reached. I have resisted the urge to quote from secondary sources, and have attempted to track down the original documents or their facsimiles.

This seemingly unending debate on the woman question is nothing less than a contest over the politics of knowledge, one in which the knowledge base has long been male-centered. Indeed, this book provides a case study in what we now call "the sexual politics of knowledge." It takes some doing for women and their associates sympathetic to women's rights to make a dent in, and eventually, to begin contributing to and finally, significantly inflecting, expanding, and "gendering" that knowledge base. As the narrative proceeds, I make a point of not anticipating what comes next but try to situate the action (and thus, the readers) in the moment; this is accomplished by paying careful attention to verb tenses, and in some cases the use of the future conditional. Generally speaking, I prefer to let theoretical insights proceed from the abundant evidence that I have unearthed (there is still much more evidence awaiting discovery), rather than imposing one or another theoretical "lens" on the reading of that evidence. Finally, all translations from the French are mine, unless otherwise attributed in the notes.

Acknowledgments

This book, like my earlier publication *European Feminisms* and the volume that will complement this one, is a synthetic work of interpretative history grounded in primary sources. Such work is possible only by building on the earlier contributions and insights of my many colleagues in French and European history, literature, art, and culture, by revisiting their sources and supplementing them with my own discoveries, and by weaving the whole into a fresh fabric. Rather than thanking them here individually (you know who you are) for their contributions and insights, or relegating such recognition to the chapter footnotes (as one manuscript reviewer suggested), I have chosen to acknowledge their work (and that of other "authorities") in the body of the text. This strategy indicates not only that I have read their books and articles but also that I have taken into account their findings and observations. By thus acknowledging the scholars whose research and insights has contributed greatly to the foundation for my book, I also demonstrate what a major contribution their practice of women's and gender history has made to reorienting the discipline of history more generally – and, in particular, to reconceptualizing French (and Francophone) history from a gendered perspective. No one should doubt that this book is grounded in decades of collaborative, collegial feminist scholarship.

I have not neglected "quarrels" or disagreements with other historians in the text. I prefer to think of such disagreements as legitimate debates about interpretation. It is, of course, also possible to relegate these to the footnotes, but I think that engaging readers in the ongoing conversations about interpretations of evidence remains a critical component of the best practice of historical writing, and that highlighting the occasions where historians differ should not be avoided.

I do want to acknowledge the financial support for this project, through research fellowships and awards from the National Endowment for the

Humanities, the Rockefeller Foundation, and the John Simon Guggenheim Memorial Foundation, as well as the moral support provided by my decades-long affiliation with the Michelle R. Clayman Institute for Gender Research (established as the Institute for Research on Women) at Stanford University. Moreover, without the most helpful librarians and curators at Stanford's Green Library and Hoover Library (as well as a sprinkling of smaller campus libraries, including the medical school library), and the directors and staff of numerous libraries and archives in France, Belgium, and Switzerland, I could not have located and consulted so many primary sources over the years. Thank you so much for your help!

I am deeply grateful to both the anonymous readers (for the press) for the detailed attention they have given to my chapters. These heroic colleagues went over my manuscript in detail. Their suggestions for improving the final version are deeply appreciated. The extended attention and care of these colleagues (and other friends and associates over the years) is a priceless gift. I would especially like to thank the staff at Cambridge University Press, beginning with Lewis Bateman, who initially took on my book(s) before his retirement in May 2016 and who selected the two anonymous readers. I also thank Michael Watson at Cambridge University Press's UK office for shepherding both books through the publication process. Thanks go to the production crew, beginning with Robert Judkins at Cambridge University Press, to Divya Arjunan of SPI Global, and to Julia Ter Maat in Singapore for her careful copyediting. I also appreciate the great care with which Robert Swanson at Arc Indexing, Inc., prepared the index for this volume.

Reconnaissance

Voices from the French Debates on the Woman Question, 1400–1870

Just the sight of this book [by Matheolus] ... made me wonder how it happened that so many different men – and learned men among them – have been and are so inclined to express both in speaking and in their treatises and writings so many wicked insults about women and their behavior.

Christine de Pizan
Le Livre de la Cité des dames / The Book of the City of Ladies (1405)

* * *

If we had permitted our women to make the laws and to write History, what tragic and hideous narratives women would have been able to write about the unmentionable wickedness of their unworthy males.

Henri Corneille Agrippa de Nettesheim
Sur la noblesse et l'excellence du sexe féminin ... (1529, 1537)

* * *

To promote a woman to bear rule, superiority, dominion, or empire above any realm, nation, or city, is repugnant to nature; contumely [*an insult*] to God, a thing most contrary to his revealed will and approved ordinance; and finally, it is the subversion of good order, of all equity and justice.

John Knox
The First Blast of the Trumpet against the Monstrous Regiment of Women (1558)

* * *

Happy you are, Reader, if you do not belong to this sex, which has been deprived of liberty and kept from all benefits; which has also been excluded from all virtues and barred from obligations, offices, and public functions: in a word, deprived of power.

Marie LeJars de Gournay
Grief des dames (1626)

* * *

If I wore chains that could be broken, they would have been broken long ago. . . . Under what conditions can liberty be found? From birth we are not only the slaves of our parents but of custom and fashion. . . . We are not given even the freedom to choose our masters, since we are often married against our inclination . . . Ambition is useless to us and our heritage is obedience.

Madeleine de Scudéry
Clélie, Histoire Romaine, Book II (1660)

* * *

In all that which is taught to Women, do we see any thing that tends to solid instruction? It seems on the contrary, that men have agreed on this sort of education, on purpose to abase their courage, darken their mind, and to fill it only with vanity, and fopperies; there to stifle all the seeds of Vertue, and Knowledge, to render useless all the dispositions which they might have to great things, and to take from them the desire of perfecting themselves, as well as we by depriving them of the means.

François Poullain de la Barre
De l'Égalité des deux sexes (1673)

* * *

[W]oman was specifically made to please man. If man ought to please her in turn, the necessity is less direct. His merit lies in his power; he pleases simply because he is strong. I grant you this is not the law of love; but it is the law of nature, which is older than love itself. . . . The whole education of women ought to be relative to men.

Jean-Jacques Rousseau
Émile, ou De l'éducation (1762)

* * *

The representatives should have absolutely the same interests as those represented; therefore women should only be represented by women. . . . Why is it that the law is not the same for both? Why does one sex have everything and the other nothing?

Madame B* B****
Cahier des Doléances et Réclamations de Femmes (1789)

* * *

Either no individual of the human race has genuine rights, or else all have the same; and he who votes against the right of another, whatever the religion, the colour, or sex of that other, has henceforth abjured his own.

Marie-Jean-Antoine-Nicolas de Caritat, marquis de Condorcet
Sur l'Admission des femmes au droit de cité (1790)

* * *

Man, are you capable of being just? It is a woman who asks you this question; at least you will not deny her this right. Tell me! Who has given you the sovereign authority to oppress my sex?

Olympe de Gouges
Les Droits de la femme (1791)

* * *

Citoyennes, it is as Christians and mothers that women must demand the rank that belongs to them in the church, the state, and the family. . . . It is especially this sacred function as mother, which some insist is incompatible with the exercise of a citizen's rights, that imposes on woman the duty of watching over the future of her children and confers on her the right to intervene in all the activities not only of civil life but of political life as well.

Jeanne Deroin
"Mission de la femme" (1849)

* * *

The eighteenth century proclaimed the rights of man, the nineteenth will proclaim the right of woman.

Victor Hugo
"Sur la Tombe de Louise Jullien" (1853)

* * *

Through labor, also, does woman claim to conquer her civil rights. ... To exclude woman from active occupations in order to confine her to the cares of the household is to attempt an impossibility, to close the way to progress, and to replace woman beneath the yoke of man ... it is in human nature to rule and domineer over those whom we provide with their daily bread.

Jenny P. d'Héricourt
La Femme affranchie (1860) / *A Woman's Philosophy of Woman, or Woman Affranchised* (1864)

* * *

Equal to man before God, before the law woman is in a state of dependence from which she alone can extricate herself.

Eugénie Niboyet
Le vrai livre des femmes (1863)

* * *

[T]he present state of our society demonstrates that under the misleading names of liberty and equality woman is held back in deplorable inferiority and excluded from employments that were formerly guaranteed her by both legislation and custom.

Julie-Victoire Daubié
La Femme pauvre au XIXe siècle (1866)

* * *

After having reflected a great deal on the destiny of women in all times and in every nation, I have come to the conclusion that every man ought to say to every woman, instead of *bonjour –Pardon!* for the strongest have made the laws.

Alfred de Vigny
Journal d'une poëte 1867 (quote from 1844)

* * *

Women's inferiority is not a natural fact, we repeat, it is a human invention, a social fiction.

Maria Deraismes
"La Femme et le droit" (1868)

* * *

Woman is neither a slave nor a queen nor an idol. She is a human being like yourselves; like you, she has a right to autonomy. ... By denying woman the right to work, you degrade her; you put her under man's yoke and deliver her over to man's good pleasure. By ceasing to make her a worker, you deprive her of her liberty and, thereby, of her responsibility ... , so that she will no longer be a free and intelligent creature, but merely a reflection, a small part of her husband. ... It is work alone that makes independence possible and without which there is no dignity.

Paule Mink
"Le Travail des femmes" (1868)

* * *

One thing we may be certain of—that what is contrary to women's nature to do, they never will be made to do by simply giving their nature free play. The anxiety of mankind to interfere in behalf of nature, for fear lest nature should not succeed in effecting its purpose, is an altogether unnecessary solicitude. What women by nature cannot do, it is quite superfluous to forbid them from doing. ... I should like to hear somebody openly enunciating the doctrine ... "It is necessary to society that women should marry and produce children. They will not do so unless they are compelled. Therefore it is necessary to compel them." The merits of the case would then be clearly defined.

John Stuart Mill
On the Subjection of Women / L'Assujetissement des Femmes (1869)

* * *

Confronting the Women Question
in French History
A General Introduction

The very eruption of a "woman question," as the controversy over the relations of the sexes in society was long called in France, can be read as evidence of a serious sociopolitical problem, of contestation over what I am calling the "sexual balance of power." Studies of the balance of power, as posed by earlier generations of historians, envisaged only international or intranational struggles by male elites for political dominance; even as these studies expanded to consider class conflict, they took for granted (and said nothing about) the sexual imbalance of power within the societies they were discussing.

Women's history has changed all this, not only by excavating and highlighting women's lived experiences but also by confronting historians with the centrality of the politics of gender as a subject worthy of historical scrutiny. Once one has begun to consider the past by examining its gender politics, it is impossible to revert to more conventional ways of viewing it.

The significance of studying public debates as a means of interpreting different understandings of a situation in the past cannot be overestimated. This was rarely possible before the advent of print culture. As the eminent historian Natalie Zemon Davis has acknowledged: "To me an important entry into a period is through its arguments and debates, the unresolved questions that keep being tossed about, the issues on which a consensus seems impossible. Central conflicts or axial debates are great markers or signposts for a period. ... Central disagreements are a good way to characterize a society or a time period."[1] No disagreement was more central to French society over time than that over the "proper" relations of the sexes. Studying the debates on the "woman question" in its depth and breadth confirms the truth of the statement by historian Melissa Feinberg, who proposed in 2012 (concerning debates over sexuality and morality),

---

[1] As quoted in Natalie Zemon Davis, *A Passion for History: Conversations with Denis Crouzet* (Kirksville, MO: Truman State University Press, 2010), p. 84.

that they "lead us to wonder whether it is not the existence of the debate itself that is central to the modern condition."[2]

Debates on the woman question throw into relief the instability and shifting character of the balance of power between the sexes; it reveals a series of legal and institutional efforts by men as a group (or at least elite, literate men as a group purporting to represent the rest) to control, dominate, and subordinate women as a group, but it also allows us to uncover women's efforts (accompanied by the efforts of their male advocates) to contest such hegemonic claims. Precisely because the continuing efforts to reconfigure the situation of women inevitably imply reconfiguring the situation of men, these very efforts to redress the balance on women's behalf challenged a broad spectrum of received and imposed ideas, both religious and secular, about the "proper" (God or nature ordained) relationship of males and females to one another, to their children and their elders, to property and economic life, to organized religion, and to the state. The woman question, in short, was sociopolitical dynamite.

For six centuries the woman question has occupied a central position in the political debates of the French state and its educated elite. Yet, until the emergence of women's history as a child of the contemporary women's movement, professional historians of France, female or male, scarcely acknowledged the existence of this issue, much less its political significance. If anything, scholars considered it a "mere" literary debate – "*une querelle des femmes.*" In France, as elsewhere, inquiry into the history of the woman question reveals both a parable of progress and a chronicle of frustration. Understanding the form this controversy took and the range of issues it encompassed is of crucial significance for understanding the development of contemporary French society. Indeed, the controversy lays bare the centrality of sexual politics, the significance of gender issues in forging a conscious national identity and in constructing a secular state, a state in which men initially claimed all positions of authority and shaped new laws governing even the most personal aspects of human existence in dialogue with – and in opposition to – the imperial claims of Roman Catholicism. This secular thrust, which was particularly pronounced in the French case, makes Western European state formation distinctive, a sharp contrast to developments in other states where organized religious authorities, Islamic and Confucian in particular, continued to monopolize the regulation of personal relations well into the twentieth century.

---

[2] Melissa Feinberg, "Sexuality, Morality, and Single Women in Fin-de-Siècle Central Europe," *Journal of Women's History*, 24:3 (Fall 2012), 181.

The relative success of secular resistance to organized theocracies in the West (notably the shattering of Christian unity and, in particular, the fragmentation of faith brought on by the Protestant reformers) early on created a space in which such issues could be openly debated.

The richness of the French historical record – its printed record – allows us to examine the woman question controversy over these six centuries. Indeed, few nations, east or west, can boast of such long-term visibility of women and disputes about gender.[3] It bears underscoring that many of the earliest, most eloquent, and influential defenders of women's cause in early modern Europe – both men and women – wrote in a French cultural context: Christine de Pizan, the Italian-born humanist writing at the court of Charles VI; Marie le Jars de Gournay, the *fille adoptive* of Michel de Montaigne; François Poullain de la Barre, Cartesian philosopher and Protestant convert; Marie-Jean-Nicolas Caritat, marquis de Condorcet, celebrated philosopher and mathematician.

France also provides a consistent and unusually rich record of women playing highly visible roles in public life, both at court and beyond. As Voltaire pointedly observed in his second dedicatory letter to *Zaïre*, addressed in the 1730s to the newly appointed British ambassador to the Sublime Porte, "Society depends on women. All the peoples that have the misfortune to keep them locked up are unsociable."[4] His remarks serve to underscore the fact that French women of the upper classes were never successfully sequestered, as was the case in so many other cultures, both Christian and Muslim, bordering the Mediterranean. France was exceptional among the European monarchies in deliberately excluding women from succession to the throne, but at court, one can point to a series of women who as regents or royal mistresses were extremely influential, though technically illegitimate, political players in the monarchies of early

---

[3] My colleague Gisela Bock insists that the debates on the woman question were pan-European from the outset, a claim that I do not dispute; I would only point out the salient fact that in France these debates began decades earlier than in England, Spain, the Italian city-states, or the German states, and that the debates in the French language had an arguably significant influence beyond the kingdom's borders. See *Die europaeische Querelle des Femmes: Geschlechter-debatten seit dem 15. Jahrhundert*, ed. Gisela Bock & Margarete Zimmermann. Special issue of *Querelles:Jahrbuch für Frauenforschung 1997* (Stuttgart: J. B. Metzler, 1997), and Gisela Bock, *Women in European History*, transl. Allison Brown (Oxford: Blackwell, 2002), esp. chapter 1. In my book *European Feminisms, 1700–1950: A Political History* (Stanford, CA: Stanford University Press, 2000), I provide examples of how the texts from the French debates traveled throughout Europe from the eighteenth century on, influencing the woman question debates from Scandinavia to Spain, and from Russia to the Ottoman Empire and beyond.

[4] Voltaire, "A M. le Chevalier Falkener (Séconde épitre dédicatoire)," in *Zaïre: Tragédie en cinq actes* (1736), *Oeuvres complètes de Voltaire*, vol. 1: Théatre (Paris, 1877), p. 551.

modern France: Diane de Poitiers, Catherine de Médicis, Madame de Montespan, Madame de Pompadour are among the most famous, though by no means the only ones.

Women's visibility and significance in French society was not restricted to the court nobility, where their patronage was essential to advancement; it was considerably more widespread. As the English feminist Mary Wollstonecraft observed in her *History of the French Revolution* (1794), "From the enjoyment of more freedom than the women of other parts of the world, those of France have acquired more independence of spirit than any other."[5] Among the wealthier classes, some dowried urban women from propertied families found relative personal freedom in marriage after severely constrained girlhoods. Other women, single or widowed, founded important religious orders. Women played a major role, one long acknowledged by scholars, in the development of French literary culture and manners. They were poets and writers and artists; they pioneered the French novel. A few established influential salons. They began to appear in theatrical productions in the seventeenth century. Urban women of the artisan class took part in an astonishing number of commercially and culturally important activities; in the course of these activities, they articulated a remarkably explicit consciousness of their societal prerogatives and dignity as women. And they had no compunctions about defending both. As Madame de Beaumur, editor of the *Journal des Dames*, retorted to a male critic of her publication in 1762: "I love this sex, I am jealous to uphold its honor and its rights."[6] Based on evidence of this sort, it is possible to argue that this very visibility of women and the cultural significance attributed to them stimulated and heightened consciousness about and concern over the relationship of the sexes and underscored its fundamental importance for sociopolitical organization, not only in France but far beyond its borders.[7]

Indeed, the historical study of women in France – and of French ideas about the woman question – offers a thought-provoking counterpoint to that of English-speaking societies, where women's subordination was constructed according to different designs. Today's postmodern industrialized France is the product of reshaping an old monarchical, Roman Catholic Christian, military–agrarian society, which in its turn overlaid

---

[5] Mary Wollstonecraft, *An Historical and Moral View of the Origin and Progress of the French Revolution and the Effect It Has Produced in Europe* (1794; 2nd ed., 1795), intro. by Janet M. Todd (New York: Scholar's Facsimiles & Reprints, 1974), pp. 425–426.

[6] Madame de Beaumur, "Avant-Propos," *Journal des Dames* (March 1762), 224.

[7] See Offen, *European Feminisms*.

and attempted to displace earlier pagan cultures in which the cult of the maternal, fertility rites, and magical practices abounded. Since the twelfth century, debate about the sexes has been hammered out in the dominant culture from an amalgam of Christian and neo-Platonic ideas, embedded in the chivalric tradition. It has been tempered by the ideological reformulations that, during the sixteenth and seventeenth centuries, accompanied the challenges of civic humanism and the reappropriation and adaptation of Roman law, the Protestant reformation, the Catholic counterreformation and, during the seventeenth and eighteenth centuries, by aggressive monarchical centralization and state-building efforts, the articulation of resistance to these efforts, the rise of market capitalism, colonial expansion, the European Enlightenment, and, not least, the upheaval of the French Revolution. All this, before industrialization (both the mechanization and centralization of manufacturing) and rampant commodification began to have much impact.

It bears insisting that this was no silent process. The debate on the woman question surfaced in recorded form in virtually every century of French history since late medieval times. Both manuscript sources and the abundant fruits of the development of printing attest to its presence.[8] With near-predictable regularity, in moments of political, economic, and social stress, the woman question, like a figure from a resplendent mechanical clock, strutted forth to disrupt the discourse of men who presumed to reshape or restructure society, to speak in terms of "universal man" without taking women into account or by deliberately denigrating or marginalizing them. The sources attest to the raising of the woman question wherever there have been petitioners for justice, seeking relief from what they considered to be ill treatment based on dissenting religious convictions, lack of rank, race, or (more recently) socioeconomic class. Since the seventeenth century, claims to emancipate women have been embedded in the repeated challenges to the authority of priests, kings, and fathers, and to slavery, to which they compared women's situation in institutionalized marriage.[9] They have accompanied virtually all efforts to offset the development of a "heartless" capitalist economic system and the

---

[8] The debates on the woman question take place in what Jürgen Habermas has famously called *Öffentlichkeit* – best translated as "public space." Indeed, they would hardly be possible without; "public space" is the "battleground."

[9] See Karen Offen, "How (and Why) the Analogy of Marriage with Slavery Provided the Springboard for Women's Rights Demands in France, 1640–1848," in *Women's Rights and Transatlantic Antislavery in the Era of Emancipation*, ed. Kathryn Kish Sklar & James Brewer Stewart (New Haven: Yale University Press, 2007), pp. 57–81.

effects of a "soulless" materialism, and more recently, to seek "liberation" from all "oppressions," whether economic, political, sexual, or psychic.

During the French Revolution of 1789–1795, however, the institutional formalities governing the sociopolitical relationship of the sexes were subjected to abrupt and detailed attempts at reconstruction in a secular context. This was a significant turning point (if not exactly a "beginning"). After an initial spurt of liberalizing legislation, which among other things invested single adult women with full property rights, including equal inheritance, men of all social classes were quickly reauthorized by the authors of Napoléon's Civil Code to wield a quasi-absolute legal authority – as husbands and fathers – over their wives and children. In the law, "public" and "private" spheres were explicitly delineated in terms of male/female dualism. Indeed (as was also the case elsewhere), insistence on such distinctions and on "social roles" seemed to offer men a concrete way of contending with the apparent chaos and disorder of the revolutionary period. By the mid-nineteenth century, the principle of democratic rule had triumphed (at least temporarily): by granting the vote to all adult men, the leaders of the Second Republic extended to each male a share of political authority in the nation, a right continued under the Third Republic. Maria Deraismes was not alone in arguing pointedly that "in France, male supremacy is the last aristocracy."[10] Even though French women were deliberately excluded from formal political life by this decision, they would be continually credited with wielding enormous "influence" over male decision-making. Symbolically, this all-male republic – and women's ostensible influence over it – would be represented by an allegorical woman, the goddess of liberty, who acquired the popular nickname of "Marianne."[11]

Throughout the nineteenth century French moralists and reformers would insist – as was also the case in other countries of Europe and in the United States – that in a properly ordered society, a complete and complementary sexual division of labor should prevail, even when they

---

[10] From a speech by Maria Deraismes, 14 January 1882, in her *Oeuvres complètes*, vol. 2 (Paris, 1895), p. 283. In fact, the expression *"aristocratie masculine"* appears in 1789, following the Declaration of the Rights of Man, in the *Requête des dames à l'Assemblée nationale*. This latter tract, first republished by Amédée Lefaure, *Le Socialisme pendant la Révolution française, 1789–1798* (Paris, 2nd ed., 1867), can now be consulted in a reprint edition of women's revolutionary texts, *Les Femmes dans la Révolution française*, présentés par Albert Soboul, 2 vols. (Paris: EDHIS, 1982), 1, doc. 19, and in partial English translation in Offen, *European Feminisms*, pp. 54–55.

[11] See Maurice Agulhon, *Marianne into Battle: Republican Imagery and Symbolism in France, 1789–1880*, tr. Janet Lloyd (Cambridge, UK, & New York: Cambridge University Press, 1981; orig. publ. in French as *Marianne au combat* (Paris: Flammarion, 1979).

objected to women's thoroughgoing subordination to men through the institution of marriage. Authors of prescriptive literature encouraged marriage for all, with men in charge of political (and increasingly) of economic affairs and women in the home, keeping house and tending children. Some refer to this as the doctrine of "separate spheres," but I think it is more accurate to talk about this sexual division of labor in terms of public and domestic spaces, and, further, to acknowledge that controversies arose concerning the "political" and "economic" value of domesticity and its associated tasks.

Such prescriptions did not mesh with the extant reality, which was a good deal more fluid. Many French men and women remained single. Not only did women continue to be a visible yet extralegal force, but they were far from successfully contained in male-headed households. Some 30 percent of all adult Frenchwomen, including a surprising proportion of married women, were employed in the workforce, adding their hard-earned *sous* to the overall family economy. Rural peasant women and urban working-class women drudged away at labor that could be judged harsh even by comparison to the field labor of black slaves in the antebellum American South. Religious orders, reestablished following the Revolution, attracted hundreds of thousands of women. In the course of the century, the French birth rate fell more dramatically, earlier, further, than that of any other Western nation while infant mortality rates remained scandalously high as thousands of urban-born infants were sent away by their mothers into the countryside to be raised – or buried – by rural wet nurses. In the cities and large towns, abortion and child abandonment, or infanticide by indigent mothers, came to be viewed as major social problems; venereal diseases rampaged through the population and government-licensed prostitution flourished, even as the rate of sex crimes committed by men against women rose.

But this was not all. By the 1890s French women's rights activists would introduce the terms "féminisme" and "féministe" to the European political vocabulary and by 1900 these terms would become common currency throughout the Western world. Feminists in France proposed a far different vision of society and the sociopolitical relations of the sexes, one in which women were free and equal, one in which women had rights *as women*, as embodied *female* individuals, as sexed human beings, at once different and equal, and one in which women could be present and well-represented in every sector of society, thereby restoring equilibrium in the sexual balance of power. These French women and their allies insisted on a renegotiation of what political theorist Carole Pateman has astutely baptized the "sexual contract," a contract made by men for men, a contract women had had no role in negotiating.[12] But in the period this volume addresses, these terms had not yet come into use.

Scope and Approach

When I began research for this book over forty years ago, the study of women's history by academically trained historians was in its infancy even in the United States and in France it seemed to be virtually uncharted terrain.[13] Retrieval of the most basic information was required, and I intended simply to discover whether there had ever been a movement for women's emancipation in France during the later nineteenth century. At that point I had been studying French history intensively for ten years without having run across any scholarly discussion of it! Having discovered during my investigations of the Third Republic press that there was indeed such a movement, I was intrigued initially by questions of national character and psychology: I hoped to determine whether there was any specifically French "cultural configuration" (to use the anthropologist Ruth Benedict's term)[14] that would distinguish agitation on behalf of women's rights there from contemporaneous agitation in the United States or England.

As I proceeded, I became increasingly certain that even as the debate on the woman question developed in an international context there were indeed elements that seemed specific to French culture, elements that

---

[12] Carole Pateman, *The Sexual Contract* (Stanford: Stanford University Press, 1988).

[13] A popular genre of women's history, generally of the sensationalist type (e.g., secrets of the boudoir), has long existed in France, but the investigation of French women's history by scholars also dates further than is usually recognized, though it had to be rediscovered by academic historians in the 1970s (see Chapter 6 in this volume). Today important scholarship on French women's history is being produced not only in France but in the English-speaking world. To date the results remain underutilized (when not actively resisted) by other historians, including those who profess interest in *mentalités*, demography, and family history, not to mention practitioners of political and economic history. Much remains to be done to bring women – and gender-sensitive analysis – into the mainstream of historical writing about France. For recent assessments, see Françoise Thébaud, *Écrire l'histoire des femmes* (Fontenay/St.Cloud: ENS-Sèvres, 1998); Thébaud, "Écrire l'histoire des femmes: Parcours historiographique, débats méthodologiques et rapports avec les institutions," in *Écrire l'Histoire des Femmes en Europe du Sud: XIXe-XXe Siècles/ Writing Women's History in Southern Europe, 19th-20th Centuries*, ed. Gisela Bock & Anne Cova (Lisbon: Celta Editora, 2003), pp. 97–115; and Françoise Thébaud, *Écrire l'histoire des femmes et du genre* (Fontenay/St. Cloud: ENS-Sèvres, 2007). For overviews, see the review essays by Karen Offen, "French Women's History: Retrospect (1789–1940) and Prospect," *French Historical Studies* 26:4 (Fall 2003), 727–767, and Jean Elisabeth Pedersen, "French Feminisms, 1848–1949," *French Historical Studies* 37:4 (Fall 2014), 663–687.

[14] Ruth Benedict, *Patterns of Culture* (Boston: Houghton Mifflin, 1959; orig. publ. by Houghton Mifflin, 1934), p. 60.

profoundly shaped the ways in which the controversy on the woman question was framed and argued, along with the sociopolitical context within which any deliberate actions to enhance women's civil and political status in that nation could be taken.[15] The presentation and analysis of these elements constitute the content of this volume.

These elements, I found, included (first and foremost) the extraordinary sociopolitical significance, or "influence," overtly attributed to women by men and by other women – and which provoked their formal and repeated exclusion by men from political authority since the end of the sixteenth century. This latter phenonemon in particular is one that bridges the transition from the old regime to the republics, from an agrarian society to an industrial one. But although this attribution of power and influence to women (and women's acknowledgement and celebration of it) had regularly been remarked upon, and the concomitant exclusion of women from authority, neither had ever been properly problematized as an historical issue, nor had the two been adequately linked. These two elements will be discussed in the first two chapters.

The third distinctive element, to be discussed in Chapter 3, is the strategic political importance accorded to biomedical thinking in French society as Catholic theological justifications for gender arrangements were challenged and reconceptualized by secular, even anticlerical thinkers, many of whom were physicians, and the close relationship of such thinking to French notions of hierarchy, authority, and order. A fourth element, related closely to the third and first, is the political and ideological emphasis on educated motherhood that paradoxically accompanied a precipitous nineteenth-century drop in the French birth rate and emerged from the intersection of the debate on population with that on woman question. This element will be presented in Chapter 4.

A fifth and final element of this cultural configuration concerns some of the peculiar traits of French republican national identity during its formative period, especially in its legal, educational, and economic aspects. These traits flow from its political heritage, drawing initially on a predominantly Roman tradition of masculine identification with the republic, yet permeated by the ostensibly gender-free liberal and ostensibly "universal" ideals of the Revolution, tinged by a ferocious anticlericalism that opposed the

---

[15] My inquiry proceeds from the same premises as those of Pierre Bourdieu – though as a historian I prefer the term *context* to Bourdieu's notion of *habitus*. The objective seems the same, however – to make visible those things that in France are taken entirely for granted and thereby to situate published discussion of the woman question and its discussants. A fish swimming in a fish bowl, or in the sea, does not notice that its medium is water.

universal imperialism of the Roman Catholic Church. During the years of the Third Republic, France would find itself in an international political context in which it was bordered to the east by a newly unified, highly authoritarian, militaristic, and "masculinist" monarchical state, which in 1870 had defeated the French imperial armies and subsequently would make much of France's "femininity." This context promoted the development of standing citizen armies and great navies, in a competitively masculinized international political environment shaped increasingly by resurgent imperial expansion abroad and labor unrest at home.

These five elements both contributed to and would set limits on the extent to which the sexual balance of power could be tilted a bit more in women's favor, especially during the first five decades of the Third Republic (1870–1920), which will be addressed in a subsequent volume, *Debating the Woman Question in the French Third Republic, 1870–1920*. The national distinctiveness of these factors and the ways in which they shaped the debates on the woman question only became apparent as I engaged in a project that continually threatened to (and finally did) mushroom into a full-fledged comparative and gendered analysis of Western thought.[16]

The argument that follows is framed with reference to my dissatisfaction with the gender blindness that characterized most earlier historical writing about France, which culminated in Simone de Beauvoir's claim, in her now-classic work *Le Deuxième Sexe* (1949) that women had no history of their own.[17] I address this problem in Chapter 6, on the politics of women's history in France. In some sense this entire project on unearthing and analyzing the debates on the woman question in France can be considered a "prequel" and a rebuttal of Beauvoir's claim. My argument is also framed in response to my discomfort with attempts by my own generation of Anglophone feminist scholars, particularly in some related disciplines, to theorize generally about women's situation solely on the basis of Anglo-American evidence – or to view it through the distorting lens of their contemporary preconceptions and preoccupations.

---

[16] A framework for such a study undergirds the interpretative documentary collection, *Women, the Family, and Freedom: The Debate in Documents, 1750–1950*, ed. Susan Groag Bell & Karen Offen (Stanford: Stanford University Press, 1983), 2 vols. Henceforth, *WFF*, vol. 1. Offen's *European Feminisms* lays out a comparative analysis of feminisms.

[17] Simone de Beauvoir, *Le Deuxième Sexe* (Paris: Gallimard, 1949), vol. 1, pp. 173–174. Feminist historians in Europe have since critiqued Beauvoir's presentation of history: see in particular the essays by Claudia Opitz and Karin Hausen in *Simone de Beauvoir: Le Deuxième Sexe. Le livre fondateur du féminisme moderne en situation*, ed. Ingrid Galster (Paris: Honoré Champion Editeur, 2004). Additionally, I have critiqued Beauvoir's presentation of her French feminist predecessors in "History, Memory, and Simone de Beauvoir," unpublished address at Vassar College, April 2009.

With respect to the historiography, I should note that I began my project looking exclusively at the Third Republic. As research progressed, two types of issues emerged: chronological and comparative. First, I realized that the story could not begin in 1870 or 1880, or even in 1800; abundant evidence made it clear that married women's abysmal status in the Civil Code of 1804 was no "beginning," but rather the conclusion of an earlier struggle, the tracing of which took me back to the sixteenth century and well before, but the echoes of which would mark the centuries that followed. I recognized a need, though one I long resisted, to explore the *longue durée*. As I attempted to reconstruct and unpack this earlier story, and to ponder its subsequent effect, I realized that certain explanatory schemes devised in recent women's history and feminist theory, notably those concerned with chronology, did not hold up for the French case. It seemed ridiculous, for example, to speak – as many feminists today continue to do – in terms of "first wave" and "second wave" feminism; these terms might work to loosely describe organizational, or "movement" efforts, but they fall short when it comes to encompassing the many earlier pre-organizational phases of the French debates on the woman question.

Second, I was reinforced in my conviction that what needed to be addressed was not France's "universality" but rather its cultural exceptionality in a comparative European context. Nothing could be taken for granted. The "problem" of women's power and influence took a particular shape in France from the sixteenth century on, within in a more general context of secularization, formation of a nation/state, emerging political theory and justificatory history, and, in particular, the explosive spread of print culture. Earlier historians had worked over all these topics in extremely helpful ways, but only rarely with reference to their gendered dimensions.

Nor did the theoretical frameworks developed by feminist and post-structuralist scholars in other areas assist in clarifying the developments I was uncovering in the French case. Of particular concern were the following, mentioned here in the order I encountered them: first, the a-historicity exhibited in the 1970s debates among feminist cultural anthropologists, beginning with Sherry B. Ortner's influential essay, "Is Female to Male as Nature Is to Culture?" (1974) on the nature/culture dichotomy as then embodied in the work of Claude Lévi-Strauss.[18] In second place

[18] Sherry B. Ortner, "Is Female to Male as Nature is to Culture," in *Woman, Culture, and Society*, ed. Michelle Zimbalist Rosaldo & Louise Lamphere (Stanford, CA: Stanford University Press, 1974), pp. 67–87.

came the more general insufficiency of Marxist-feminist analysis to provide a framework for understanding the seeming paradox of women's high status coupled with severe civil and political constraints in a French context that predates industrialization; third, the lack of attention given to gender issues in pre-revolutionary history or political theory until very recently (this has since been remedied to a considerable degree by the varied and significant contributions of Jim Collins, Christine Fauré, Dena Goodman, Daniel Gordon, Sarah Hanley, Joan B. Landes, Sarah C. Maza, and Éliane Viennot and her associates in the SIEFAR) to debates about the development of the so-called public sphere and citizenship in Europe, but particularly in France; fourth, the insistent Anglo-centrism and a-historicity (as well as the peak-hopping tendencies) of much influential work in the history of Anglophone political theory (including the otherwise brilliant feminist analyses of Carole Pateman and Jean Bethke Elshtain)[19]; and fifth, the insistently male bias of such French theorists as Michel Foucault, whose otherwise very influential theories about sexuality, power, and social control never adequately took either women or the express issue of the gender of *authority* into account.

Terminology

Historians have been summoned in recent years to heighten their sensitivity to their own use of language and terminology. Consequently, before embarking on a discussion of these peculiarly French historical elements, I want to say a few words about the use of several terms that I will be employing in this book: "the woman question," "woman," "gender," "feminism" and "feminist," "misogyny," "bourgeois" and "bourgeoisie," and "sociopolitical." It is my intention to alert readers to the political implications of these terms as well as to their historical baggage, to explain my own usage at the outset, and then to employ the terms as consistently as possible throughout the book.

---

[19] My discontent with the aforementioned constraints that hamper political theorists was only reinforced by attending a conference in memory of Susan Moller Okin, held at Stanford University in early February 2005, in the course of which most of the leading feminist political theorists in the United States addressed Okin's contributions. See the conference volume *Toward a Humanist Justice: The Political Philosophy of Susan Moller Okin*, ed. Debra Satz & Rob Reich (New York: Oxford University Press, 2009). A more recent study, focused on women as political philosophers in early modern Europe, is *A History of Women's Political Thought in Europe, 1400–1700* by Jacqueline Broad & Karen Green (Cambridge, UK: Cambridge University Press, 2009).

Some readers may already be troubled by my use of the term, "the woman question." The British scholar Dale Spender (among others) has argued that to speak of "the woman question" is to scapegoat women, to displace the issue. She views the term as indicative of the extent to which men have controlled sociopolitical discourse.[20] Her criticism requires a response.

The term, "the woman question," was widely used during the nineteenth century by many European writers, both women and men, to describe the complex totality of issues raised for women and for men by women's subordinate status.[21] Unlike the term "feminism" (of which more shortly), the "woman question" encompasses the arguments both for and against change in women's position relative to that of men, and from perspectives that encompass the entire spectrum of political discourse from Right to Left, from reactionary to revolutionary; this term was by no means the monopoly of socialist critics, although in the later nineteenth century they also claimed it. It suggested then, as it does now, the magnitude of the challenge posed to the existing institutions designed by men, and to male-dominated discourse, by demands for the emancipation of women. I think it is meaningful to employ it here in that sense, a sense that at once acknowledges the displacement of which Spender complains but also demonstrates its political importance.

From a historian's perspective, the woman question is itself analytically interesting precisely because of what the displacement allows us to see. For historians of women, the very fact that men have so often articulated their reaction to a variety of social stresses by discussing women, gives us insight into the historical *problématique* of phallogocentric thinking.[22] Since the birth of print, the repeated and well-documented eruptions of the woman question in Western thought provide us with unparalleled insights into

---

[20] Dale Spender, *Women of Ideas and What Men Have Done to Them* (London & Boston: Routledge & Kegan Paul, 1982), p. 44.

[21] The first use I have found of the term *"la question des femmes"* in France is by Jenny P. d'Héricourt, in her 1856 article "M. Proudhon et la question des femmes," *Revue philosophique et religieuse*, 6, n° 21 (December 1856), 5–15. It was subsequently used by the educator Marie Pape-Carpantier in her series, "La Question des femmes," *L'Économiste français*, nᵒˢ 22–30 (25 January through 25 March 1863). Louis Blanc and Alexandre Dumas *fils* both spoke of *"la question des femmes"* in 1872 publications. *Le Petit Parisien* featured a series of articles on *"la question des femmes"* during the spring of 1879. Theodore Stanton subsequently consecrated the term in English usage with his book, *The Woman Question in Europe* (New York: G. P. Putnam's Sons, 1884). In German, the first use of the term I have encountered is Karl Bücher, *Die Frauenfrage im Mittelalter* (Tübingen: H. Laupp, 1882).

[22] The expression "phallogocentric" comes from France, with particular reference to feminist criticism of the neo-Freudian psychoanalytic theories of Jacques Lacan. The French semiotician Roland Barthès expresses the thought differently by insisting on "woman" as a signifier in male discourses. One could also simply say "male-centered."

situations of disequilibrium in the power relationship of the sexes within complex societies. Indeed, the woman question, with its focus on women's relatively disadvantaged sociopolitical status, offers us a window into the heart of a politics of gender, the evidence for which is more often hidden than not, yet which, like the better-documented politics of religion, race, and class, are issues of central importance to the historian who would hope to comprehend the processes of sociopolitical change at their most elemental level. No question cuts so deep into the fundamental values of a culture as the woman question, because the male–female relationship is surely the most basic (because of its procreative potential), often the most problematic and infuriating human relationship, yet it is still envisioned by people in most organized societies as the most potentially satisfying and mutually beneficial relationship that can exist among human beings. In a highly centralized, order-conscious society such as France, this relationship strikes to the heart of sociopolitical organization – the organization of "the family" in relation to the state, and the changing constraints that have been (and continue to be) placed on the personal freedom of individuals (men and women) in the interests of societal survival.

Another troublesome term is the French term "la femme," or "Woman" in the singular. Today such usage is criticized by some as reductionist or "essentialist"; today's vanguard feminist theorists prefer to speak of "women" in the plural, suggesting the diversity of behaviors, attitudes, and social types that exist – and have long existed – among women, while other post-feminist critics would prefer to deconstruct the term completely.[23] Yet, curiously, this ostensible reductionism, this focus on "woman" also lies squarely at the base of a historical female consciousness that cannot be so easily dismissed. In nineteenth-century discourse, both male and female writers, including pro-woman writers, referred to "*la femme*" as a collective entity in the singular rather than in the plural.[24] By so doing, writers of both sexes acknowledged the one overriding,

[23] See, for example, "Variations on Common Themes," *Feminist Questions/ Questions Féministes*, 1:1 (Summer 1980), 3–21; and Sylvie Chaperon, "Femme: Objet non-identifié; analyse épistémologique du féminisme," *Le Temps modernes*, n° 487 (February 1987), 85–95. In the late 1980s, Denise Riley would take up such arguments; see her *"Am I That Name?": Feminism and the Category "Women" in History* (Minneapolis, MN: University of Minnesota Press, 1988). See also Elizabeth V. Spelman, *Inessential Woman: Problems of Exclusion in Feminist Thought* (Boston: Beacon Press, 1988), and, for a rebuttal, Liz Stanley, "Recovering *Women* in History from Feminist Deconstruction," *Women's Studies International Forum*, 13:1–2 (1990), 151–157.

[24] Already in 1863 Marie Pape-Carpantier made a point of using "les femmes" rather than "la femme," even as she insisted on women's solidarity across class and other boundaries (see n. 21). Earlier, Mary Wollstonecraft made this distinction in her *Vindication* (1792).

unifying factor that has been apparent since the dawn of time: women bear children, following on sexual consorting with men. In the *Dictionnnaire générale de la langue française* published in the late nineteenth century by Hatzfeld and Darmesteter, for example, "la femme" in the human species is defined simply as "a person of the sex that is organized to conceive and give birth."[25] This is not to say that they all do so, or that giving birth is all they *should* do. Yet, by virtue of this primal physiological "fact," "woman" came to constitute a "class" in European positive law, particularly as it pertained to their status in marriage. Nineteenth-century writers clearly recognized that the assignment of sex at birth had profound social consequences, precisely because of women's unique role as childbearers. Both women and men accepted this, even as they interpreted its sociopolitical significance differently. They used the term "*la femme*" to describe this reality in the singular. In this book I will speak of "women" when I discuss the varieties of experience among women, but when I am referring to the nineteenth-century French discourse, I will employ the term "woman" whenever discussion of the source material demands it.

This brings us to the term "gender," used today to express the categorical social construction of difference between the sexes. For several decades European scholars, indeed even contemporary French feminist commentators, would claim that the term "gender" is a twentieth-century American invention, one that is virtually untranslatable even by the French word "genre."[26] In the course of my own investigations of early modern France, however, I have located numerous instances of the term *genre* being used specifically to designate social constructions of sexual difference – not least in the *Encyclopédie*, in the writings of Madame d'Épinay (who speaks of human beings of the *genre masculin* and *genre féminin*, specifying

---

[25] See, for example, in the 1850s and 1860s, Jenny P. d'Héricourt, *La Femme affranchie* (Brussels: A. Lacroix, Van Meenen et Cie, 1860); André Léo, *La Femme et les moeurs* (Paris: Au journal Le Droit de femmes 1869); Olympe Audouard, *La Femme dans le mariage, la séparation et le divorce* (Paris: E. Dentu, 1870). A. Hatzfeldt, A. Darmesteter, & A. Thomas, *Dictionnaire général de la langue française*, 2 vols. (Paris, 1890–1893), s.v. "Femme."

[26] See, in particular, treatments of this issue by Gisela Bock and Yvonne Hirdman in *Writing Women's History: International Perspectives*, ed. Karen Offen, Ruth Roach Pierson, & Jane Rendall (London: Macmillan, & Bloomington: Indiana University Press, 1991). For a French response, see the explanatory note accompanying the translation of Eleanor Maccoby's article, "Gender as a Social Category" (1988) as "Le Sexe, Catégorie sociale," *Actes de la recherche en sciences sociales*, n° 83 (June 1990), 16. See also Mona Ozouf, *Les Mots des femmes: Essai sur la singularité française* (Paris: Fayard, 1995), in English as *Women's Words: Essay on French Singularity*, translated by Jane Marie Todd (Chicago: The University of Chicago Press, 1997); in chapter 10, Ozouf exhibits a serious misunderstanding of feminisms in the United States, as well as of the history of women in her own country.

that she is not talking about grammar), and in several revolutionary pamphlets detailing French women's demands addressed to the National Assembly in 1789.[27] This usage ought not to be entirely surprising, given the long-standing insistence of the French on cultural constructions more generally; what surprises is that today's French scholars should have lost sight of the originality and historicity of this indigenous contribution.[28] In this book, I will speak of "the sexes" to connote male and female, and will use the term gender when I discuss the sociopolitical constructions of "masculine" and "feminine" that pervade the French debate on the woman question, as indeed it does elsewhere as well.

The fourth set of problematic terms, "*féminisme*" and "*féministe*," did not enter popular usage in France until the 1890s, although they predate this period by a decade or two. I have set forth elsewhere the origins of these words (which cannot be attributed to Charles Fourier, as some have subsequently claimed) and their early usage and have offered a historically based definition.[29] What is important to note here is that in surveying the history of feminism in Europe across centuries and cultures, two distinct approaches or arguments on behalf of the equality of the sexes and ending women's subordination, representing two distinct sociopolitical positions, can be identified. The tradition I have baptized "relational feminism" insists on sexual difference and male–female complementarity, and gives precedence to societal claims over (or in tandem with) claims for individual self-definition and autonomous (i.e., not dependent) action by members of either sex. "Individualist feminism" on the other hand, which the French long perceived as an Anglo-American import, appeared to discount sexual difference, to emphasize the "abstract" individual, and to make claims for individual autonomy and equal rights in terms that few French

---

[27] See the *Encylopédie, ou, Dictionnaire raisonné des sciences, des arts et des métiers*, vol. 7 (FO-GY), s.v. "Genre" in particular with respect to the distinction between the sexes in grammar. See also Mme d'Épinay's clarifications in her *Conversations d'Émilie* (1776; orig. publ. 1774), p. 11: "Quand je dis *l'homme*, j'entens toutes les créatures humaines; quand je dis *un homme*, je désigne seulement alors une créature humaine du genre masculin, & quand je dis *une femme*, je désigne une créature humaine du genre féminin." See also *Requête des dames à l'Assemblée Nationale* (1789), referenced in n. 10.

[28] See my articles, "Le gender est-il une invention américaine?" in *CLIO: Histoire, Femmes et Sociétés*, n° 24 (2006), 291–304, and "Before Beauvoir, before Butler: 'Genre' and 'Gender' in France and the Anglo-American World," in "*On ne naît pas femme; on le devient*":*The Life of a Sentence*, ed. Bonnie Mann & Martina Ferrari (New York: Oxford University Press, in press).

[29] On the deployment of these words in France between 1870 and 1900, and the concepts of "relational" and "individualist" feminism, see Karen Offen, "Sur les origines des mots 'féminisme' et 'féministe'," *Revue d'Histoire Moderne et Contemporaine*, 34:3 (July–September 1987), 492–496; revised and expanded English version in *Feminist Issues*, 8:2 (Fall 1988), 45–51.

commentators would deem acceptable. In nineteenth-century France, the relational current dominated discussion of women's emancipation (though purely individualist arguments do appear from time to time), and "women's rights," or "rights for women," rather than "equal rights," provided the keywords for discussion.[30] Our contemporary pseudo-dichotomy "equality versus difference" only came into play in the later nineteenth century, in the context of debates over protective legislation for women workers.[31] For the most part, French women's rights advocates insisted on equality-in-difference, and would make a point that positing equality for women did not signify identity (except in a strict legal sense) with men.

"Misogyny," or woman-hating, is another term that requires comment. It is important for our purposes to understand what does and does not constitute misogyny in the French context. In recent scholarship the term has all too often been used loosely and pejoratively to brand any male participant in the woman question debate who placed emphasis on sexual difference or on separate but equal "spheres." In the light of what we now know about the preponderance of relational feminist arguments in the nineteenth century, it seems difficult to believe that such an emphasis could automatically qualify someone as a misogynist. Such a judgment must rest on what else a writer is saying about women, and in what tone. Misogyny must be gauged with an eye open to the elemental psychological reality of fear of and/or overtly expressed contempt for women, not merely the asymmetrical positioning that could be characterized as "male chauvinism."[32] Seen in this way, it is possible to qualify as misogynists the

---

[30] See Karen Offen, "Defining Feminism: A Comparative Historical Approach," *Signs: Journal of Women in Culture and Society*, 14:1 (Fall 1988), 119–157.

[31] See my article, "Reflections on National Specificities in Continental European Feminisms," *University College Galway Women's Studies Centre Review* (Ireland), 3 (1995), 53–61, and the brilliant response to the "equality-versus-difference" dichotomy by Anna G. Jónasdóttir & Drude von der Fehr, "Introduction: Ambiguous Times – Contested Spaces in the Politics, Organization and Identities of Gender," in *Is There a Nordic Feminism?*, ed. Drude von der Fehr, Bente Rosenbeck, & Anna G. Jónasdóttir (London: UCL Press, 1998), pp. 1–18.

[32] The classic psychoanalytic texts in English on men's fear of women include H. R. Hays, *The Dangerous Sex: The Myth of Feminine Evil* (New York: Putnam's Sons, 1964); R. E. L. Masters and Eduard Lea, *The Anti-Sex: The Belief in the Natural Inferiority of Women. Studies in Male Frustration and Sexual Conflict* (New York: Julian Press, 1964); Karl Stern, *The Flight from Woman* (New York: Farrar, Straus & Giroux, 1965); and Wolfgang Lederer, *The Fear of Women* (New York: Grune & Stratton, 1968). See also Joseph Carman Smith, *The Neurotic Foundations of Social Order: Psychoanalytic Roots of Patriarchy* (New York: New York University Press, 1990). French participants in this discussion include Maurice Godelier, "The Origins of Male Domination," *New Left Review*, n° 127 (May–June 1981), 3–17, which leans heavily on the work of American anthropologist Eleanor Leacock, and Pierre Bourdieu, *La Domination masculine* (Paris: Seuil, 1998); in English as *Masculine Domination* (Cambridge, UK: Polity Press, 2001). My own understanding of male fear has been deeply informed by the work of anthropologist Peggy Reeves Sanday, *Female*

nineteenth-century social critics Pierre-Joseph Proudhon and Gustave LeBon, whose overt hostility toward women with intellectual or professional pretensions so pervades the texts in which they argued that all women were inferior to all men. However, Ernest Legouvé, Edouard Laboulaye, and Émile de Girardin, all of whom evidenced a deep respect for women and advocated major reforms on their behalf, cannot be called misogynists, even though they too insisted on the sociopolitical consequences of sexual difference and sometimes advocated a limited degree of hierarchy in marriage as a principle of societal order.

Furthermore, the words *"bourgeois"* and *"bourgeoisie"* require clarification. Historically, in French, the terms simply express the concept of city dweller, an inhabitant of the town (*bourg*) as opposed to the countryside. But they are also tied to notions of private property (particularly landed property) and the learned professions (what the Germans call *Bildungsburgertum*). In the sociopolitical parlance of the pre-revolutionary order, the

Power and Male Dominance: On the Origins of Sexual Equality (Cambridge, UK: Cambridge University Press, 1981).

    Not surprisingly, France also offers one of the best-documented, if not the oldest, traditions of misogynistic iconography in the Western world; see Laure Beaumont-Maïllet, *La Guerre des sexes, XVe-XIXe siècles: les albums du cabinet des estampes de la Bibliothèque Nationale* (Paris: Albin Michel, 1984), and Sara F. Matthews Grieco, *Ange ou Diablesse: La Représentation de la femme au XVIe siècle* (Paris: Flammarion, 1991). Jean Delumeau draws brilliantly on Lederer's work to illuminate the French case in *La Peur en Occident (XIV-XVIIIe siècles): Une cité assiégé* (Paris: Fayard, 1978; in English as *Sin and Fear*, New York, 1990); see especially chapters 10–12 on the fear of women and witches. See also Jeanne Calo, *La Création de la femme chez Michelet* (Paris, 1975), p. 135, who also distinguishes nicely between antifeminism and misogyny. But see also the critiques of misogyny by Eva Figes, *Patriarchal Attitudes: Women in Society* (London: Faber, 1970), and Adrienne Rich, "Compulsory Heterosexuality and Lesbian Existence," *Signs*, 5:4 (Summer, 1980), 631–660. Rich wryly suggests (643) that male fear is rooted not in fear of women's ostensibly insatiable sexuality, as male writers in the psychoanalytic tradition have insisted, but rather in the concern (plaintively voiced by Jean-Jacques Rousseau) that women might become indifferent to them. Such criticism raises important questions about the historical construction of masculinity in European societies. For provocative introductions to evidence about the reconstruction of masculinity in a nineteenth-century French context, see Peter N. Stearns, *Be a Man: Males in Modern Society* (New York: Holmes & Meier, 1979); Annelise Maugue, *L'Identité masculine en crise au tournant du siècle* (Paris: Rivages, 1987); and Robert A. Nye's excellent study, *Masculinity and Male Codes of Honor in Modern France* (Oxford: Oxford University Press, 1993). See also Neil Hertz, "Medusa's Head: Male Hysteria under Political Pressure," *Representations*, 4 (Fall 1983), 27–54; Susanna Barrows, *Distorting Mirrors: Visions of the Crowd in Late Nineteenth Century France* (New Haven, CT: Yale University Press, 1981); and Peter Gay, *The Bourgeois Experience: Victoria to Freud*, 5 vols. (New York: Oxford University Press and W. W. Norton, 1984–1998), vol. 1, pp. 33ff. More recently, see Angus McLaren, *The Trials of Masculinity: Policing Sexual Boundaries, 1870–1930* (Chicago: University of Chicago Press, 1997) and *Hommes et Masculinités, de 1789 à nos jours: contributions à l'histoire du genre et de la sexualité en France*, ed. Regis Revenin, préface de Alain Corbin (Paris: Éditions Autrement, 2007). The "problem" of masculinity was not new to the nineteenth century; for the earlier period, see the essays in *High Anxiety: Masculinity in Crisis in Early Modern France*, ed. Kathleen P. Long (Kirksville, MO: Truman State University Press, 2002).

bourgeoisie was part of the Third Estate, distinct from the clergy and the nobility. The Goncourt brothers would characterize the eighteenth-century bourgeoisie as "that floating order, without precise boundaries, that borders on *le peuple* by its labor, and on the nobility by its affluence."[33] Moreover, the term bourgeois is also attached to a certain lifestyle and to various associated virtues of piety, morality, and hard work (though never manual labor) and a style of self-presentation and correct behavior that developed in opposition to the perceived licence, debauchery, luxury, and vice of the eighteenth-century aristocracy during the Regency and the reign of Louis XV.[34] With the abolition of the three orders and their privileges in the French Revolution, the distinctions between the bourgeoisie and nobility would become fuzzier, particularly as very wealthy commoners, investing in land, appropriated some aspects of the former aristocratic lifestyle and some families of the former nobility of robe and sword adopted habits of bourgeois austerity; clearly, the so-called triumph of the bourgeoisie had multiple and often contradictory ramifications. Some scholarly studies of nineteenth-century bourgeois families have focused on evidence from account books and personal financial or notarial records.[35] Others have turned to an examination of childrearing practices and family life, and to the study of kinship practices and behaviors.[36] In

[33] Edmond & Jules de Goncourt, *La Femme au XVIIIe siècle* (Paris: F. Didot frères, fils et Cie, 1862), pp. 254–255.

[34] See Elinor Barber, *The Bourgeoisie in 18th Century France* (Princeton, NJ: Princeton University Press, 1955), pp. 78–81; and Pierre Goubert, *The Ancien Regime* (New York: Harper & Row, 1974), chapter 10: "Bourgeois and Bourgeoises," pp. 232–260. See also Alfred Cobban, "The 'Middle-Class' in France, 1815–1848," *French Historical Studies*, 5:1 (Spring 1967), reprinted in Alfred Cobban, *France Since the Revolution* (London: Cape, 1970), pp. 7–21; and Alain Decaux, *Histoire des Françaises* (Paris: Perrin, 1972), vol. 2, chapters 3, 4, and 6. See also Christine Adams, *A Taste for Comfort and Status: A Bourgeois Family in Eighteenth-Century France* (University Park, PA: Pennsylvania State University Press, 2000). I have always been impressed by Theodore Zeldin's provocative deconstruction of the bourgeoisie; see Theodore Zeldin, *France, 1848–1945. Vol. 1: Ambition, Love, and Politics* (Oxford, UK: Oxford University Press, 1973), esp. chapter 1: "The Pretensions of the Bourgeoisie." Sarah C. Maza has deconstructed the notion still further in *The Myth of the French Bourgeoisie: An Essay on the Social Imaginary 1750–1850* (Cambridge, MA: Harvard University Press, 2003). None of this erudite analysis seems to have impacted the common understandings or general (even polemical) usage of these terms.

[35] Viz., Marguerite Perrot, *La Mode de vie des familles bourgeoises, 1873–1953* (Paris: A. Colin, 1961), and Adeline Daumard, *Les Bourgeois de Paris au XIXe siècle* (Paris: Flammarion, 1970). See especially chapter 5: "Femmes" in Daumard, in which the author, while acknowledging the state of utter legal dependence in which married women found themselves, insists on the importance of women's exercise of indirect influence as a compensating factor.

[36] Here the work of Philippe Ariès, notably his *Centuries of Childhood: A Social History of Family Life* (New York: Vintage, 1962; orig. publ. in French, 1960), can be credited with stimulating the growth of an entire scholarly subfield in family history. See also Jesse R. Pitts, "Continuity and Change in Bourgeois France," in *In Search of France: The Economy, Society, and Political System in the Twentieth*

France sociologists frequently distinguish among the *grande bourgeoisie*, the *classes moyennes*, and the *petit bourgeoisie*.[37]

However, these seemingly descriptive terms have long carried a political charge. We cannot ignore the fact that in twentieth-century political discourse the terms "bourgeois" and "bourgeoisie" resonate with polemical overtones. In the course of the nineteenth century, "bourgeois" became a pejorative epithet in the polemics of Marxist-socialists of both sexes, a word to be pronounced disparagingly by those who wished to be politically correct by identifying with the working class, and onto which could be displaced a variety of repudiated behavioral characteristics ranging from material greed and insensitivity to the problems of social inferiors to hypocrisy, false consciousness, and sexual repression. In the Manicheaen rhetoric of class struggle, only the proletariat could shine forth as the model of virtuous behavior for the future – the "good guys" – while the bourgeoisie represented "the bad guys" who were ultimately destined to lose. For over a hundred years this party-line approach continued to mark the scholarship emanating from nations where an official Marxist-Leninist line prevailed. Only in the wake of *glasnost* has this practice, which was used particularly to denigrate feminists and their aspirations, begun to lose its political charge.[38]

Western scholarship in the last twenty years evidences considerable movement away from such oversimplification. With respect to historical scholarship on modern France, one has only to point to the brilliant deconstruction of "*la bourgeoisie*" by Theodore Zeldin in his massive study, *France, 1848–1945*.[39] Raising the issue of gender in her study, *Ladies of the*

Century, ed. Stanley Hoffmann et al. (Cambridge, MA: Harvard University Press, 1963), esp. pp. 249–254.

[37] In the 1920s and 1930s, sociologists quarreled over and dissected these class subdistinctions; see Edmond Goblot, *La Barrière et le niveau: étude sociologique sur la bourgeoisie française* (Paris: F. Alcan, 1925; new ed., Paris: Presses Universitaires de France, 1967; 3rd ed. PUF, 2010); and for a criticism of Goblot, Louise-Marie Ferré, *Les Classes sociales dans la France contemporaine* (Paris: J. Vrin, 1934; St. Leger-en-Yvelines, chez l'auteur, distrib. by Hachette, 1936). See also Joseph Aynard, *La Bourgeoisie française: essai de psychologie* (Paris: Perrin, 1934). For more recent attempts to illuminate the class problem, see the distinctions made by Paul-Henry Chombart de Lauwe in the conference volume, *Sociologie comparée de la famille contemporaine* (Paris: CNRS, 1955), p. 155; and Robert L. Hoffman, *Revolutionary Justice: The Social and Political Theory of P.-J. Proudhon* (Urbana, IL: University of Illinois Press, 1972), p. 311, n. 3. There is, of course, also an important historical literature on the problem of social classes and the French Revolution during the 1960s and early 1970s, which ultimately culminated in dethroning the previously hegemonic Marxist interpretation of the revolution.

[38] See Marilyn J. Boxer, "Rethinking the Socialist Construction and International Career of the Concept 'Bourgeois Feminism'," *American Historical Review*, 112:1 (February 2007), 131–158.

[39] See Zeldin, *France, 1848–1945*, vol. 1, chapter 1, and Eugen Weber, *Peasants into Frenchmen: The Modernization of Rural France, 1870–1914* (Stanford, CA: Stanford University Press, 1976), pp. 236–237.

Leisure Class, my colleague Bonnie G. Smith ably addressed the question: "What is a bourgeois woman?" Her ethnological approach detailed the ways in which increasing wealth offered some nineteenth-century French women opportunities to carve out a separate space of reproduction, domestic life, and religion, which they themselves controlled and within which they articulated values that were often diametrically opposed to those of the men of their own families and class.[40] Despite such advances in our understanding, other scholars continue to use the term "bourgeois" loosely and censoriously.[41] Historian Sarah Maza has even questioned its very being.[42]

In this book (and in its sequel) I will attempt to use the term "bourgeois" with restraint and without pejorative intent. It will refer descriptively to persons, most of whom belonged to the urban educated and professional classes, who participated in the published debates on the woman question. As concerns those debates, there were both progressive and neotraditionalist elements within this bourgeoisie and these will be so designated. In nineteenth-century France, there is no monolithic class-related position on the social relation of the sexes. And appearances could be deceptive. Properly gloved and hatted "ladies" and well-turned out "gentlemen" could be revolutionaries on the woman question, while women and men of the proletariat could staunchly defend and uphold conventional, even reactionary views about male dominance in the family and society. Indeed, aristocrats could also be found on both sides of the debate.

Finally, readers may have already noticed my repeated use of the term "sociopolitical." Like my colleague Lynn Hunt, I employ this word deliberately to challenge the arbitrary yet time-honored distinction between "political" and "social" concerns, which has enjoyed such hegemony in European thought that for a long time it remained unquestioned even by the political theorists and historians who studied it.[43] I take issue with the condescending gallantry of those writers who, like the anonymous English

---

[40] Bonnie G. Smith, *Ladies of the Leisure Class: The Bourgeoises of Northern France in the Nineteenth Century* (Princeton, NJ: Princeton University Press, 1981). See also the more recent ethnological work on the French bourgeoisie by Béatrix LeWita, *Ni Vue ni connue: Approches ethnographique de la culture bourgeoise* (Paris: Editions de la Maison des sciences de l'homme, 1988).

[41] The usage of Elizabeth Fox-Genovese is troublesome in this respect. See her article, "The Ideological Bases of Domestic Economy: The Representation of Women and the Family in the Age of Expansion," in Elizabeth Fox-Genovese & Eugene Genovese, *Fruits of Merchant Capital* (New York: Oxford University Press, 1983), pp. 299–336.

[42] Maza, The *Myth of the French Bourgeoisie.*

[43] See Lynn Hunt, editor's introduction to *Eroticism and the Body Politic* (Baltimore: Johns Hopkins University Press, 1991), p. 6.

editorialist of *Common Sense*, would "lay aside politics" to discuss views about ladies.[44] We now understand that "discussing ladies" *was* politics. The term sociopolitical captures the contested and negotiated character of all societal organization, including governments and the relations between the sexes, in modern times. "Politics" has encompassed, and continues to encompass, far more than affairs of state.

* * * * *

The five themes, or elements, laid out in this volume will be examined in a subsequent volume for their specific development during the French Third Republic. That volume will be organized by chronological slices (1871–1889, 1890–1900, 1901–1914, and 1914–1920) with subsections devoted to each element, followed by an epilogue.

---

[44] Leader in *Common Sense, or the Englishmen's Journal*, n° 135 (September 1739), as quoted by Gerald M. MacLean in his introduction to François Poullain de La Barre's *The Woman as Good as the Man; or The Equality of Both Sexes* (Detroit: Wayne State University Press, 1988), p. 27.

CHAPTER I

Querying Women's Power and Influence in French Culture

It is a peculiar and quite remarkable fact of French civilization that long before the revolutionary era, educated French writers identified women with culture, not with nature. Indeed, one of the most striking features of French history since the Renaissance is the enormous cultural power and influence that men publicly attributed to women – and, what is more, that women claimed for themselves. The most superficial rendering of this concern is embodied in the popular French cliché *cherchez la femme*, which could carry both positive and negative charges. "Men make the laws," it was commonly said before the Revolution, "but women shape the morals."[1] The implication of this oft-repeated observation was that morals were the more important of the two. In his celebrated story *Paul et Virginie* (1788), the educational writer Bernardin de Saint-Pierre argued that "women have contributed more than the *philosophes* to form and reform the nations. . . . They lay the first foundations of natural law" through their contributions as mother, comforters, inventors of everything agreeable. He perceived women as the bridge between nature and culture: "You are the flowers of life . . . You civilize the human race . . . You are the Queens of our beliefs and of our moral order."[2] But women's power could also have malevolent consequences, as Pierre Choderlos de Laclos tried to demonstrate in his four-volume 1782 novel, *Les Liaisons dangereuses.*[3]

---

[1] See the exchange between Adélaide and Bayard ("Les hommes font les lois"/ "Les femmes font les moeurs") in Guibert's play, *Le Connétable de Bourbon* (1769), in Jacques-Antoine-Hippolyte Guibert, *Oeuvres dramatiques de Guibert . . . publié par sa veuve* (Paris, 1822), vol. 10, p. 22.

[2] Jacques-Henri Bernardin de Saint-Pierre, introduction to *Paul et Virginie* (orig. publ. 1787/1788). English transl. from the 1806 ed. in Ludmilla Jordanova, *Sexual Visions: Images of Gender in Science and Medicine between the Eighteenth and Twentieth Centuries* (Madison: University of Wisconsin Press, 1989), p. 34.

[3] Pierre Choderlos de Laclos, *Les Liaisons dangeueuses.* 4 vols. (Paris: Durand Neveu, 1782). This novel, with its wicked, scheming main character Madame de Morteuil is, like Bernardin de Saint-Pierre's *Paul et Virginie*, still in print today.

After the Revolution, male cultural critics as diverse as the radical utopian Charles Fourier and the Catholic counterrevolutionary monarchist Louis de Bonald pointed to women's status as the *primary* index of a nation's civilization.[4] In 1825, the literary critic and writer Charles Nodier (later elected to the Académie Française) observed that "women's power seems to diminish as democracy rises," and concluded that "political liberty seems to be incompatible with the power of women."[5] In 1828 the writer Fanny Burnier Mongellaz entitled her two-volume work *De l'influence des femmes sur les moeurs et les destinées des nations, sur leurs familles et la société.*[6] Early in the July Monarchy, Prosper Enfantin and his Saint-Simonian companions set out for Egypt in search of the female Messiah, and Nodier (commenting in 1833 on the emerging current to emancipate women spearheaded by the Saint-Simonians and the women writing for *La Femme libre*) hesitated; in his mind, any progress women made in their social position would make them lose "the inappreciable advantage of protection and love that they owe to their organic delicateness, to their long and delicious childhood, to their legal minority." In Nodier's view, women's superiority in Western morals was based squarely on their physical inferiority; "if they were not weak they would never have been so powerful," he remarked. "Christianity and chivalry, which found them to be slaves, made them sovereign." He preferred the influence of women "as angels and divinities" to women free to compete in the world of men.[7] Alexis de Tocqueville investigated the condition of women in the United States and reported back in his study of *Democracy in America*, insisting on the freedom of American young women, but also on the strict sexual division of labor into public and domestic responsibilities.[8] In the 1840s the philosopher (and former secretary to the comte de Saint-Simon)

---

[4] The celebrated statement by Charles Fourier to the effect that "Social progress and historic changes occur by virtue of the progress of women toward liberty, and decadence of the social order occurs as the result of a decrease in the liberty of women," in his *Théorie des quatre mouvements* (1808) is foreshadowed by similar language in the works of well-known eighteenth-century writers, including John Millar (1771) in Scotland and A.-L. Thomas (1772) in France.

[5] Charles Nodier, "De l'influence des femmes dans un gouvernement représentatif," published in J.-A. Ségur, *Les Femmes, leur condition et leur influence dans l'ordre social, chez les différents peuples anciens et modernes* (Paris, 1825), 2nd ed., vol. 4, quotes, pp. 228, 243.

[6] Fanny Burnier Mongellaz, *De l'influence des femmes sur les moeurs et les destinées des nations, sur leurs familles et la société.* 2 vols. (Paris: Chez L. G. Michaud et chez Delaunay, 1828; 2nd ed. 1831).

[7] Charles Nodier, "La femme libre, ou de l'émancipation des femmes," *L'Europe littéraire: journal de la littérature nationale et étrangère*, n° 2 (March 1833), 11–12; quotes all 11. Consulted at Beineke Library, Yale University, 25 October 2001.

[8] See Alexis de Tocqueville, *Democracy in America*, vol. 2 (New York: Vintage, 1959; orig. publ. 1840), pp. 222–225.

Auguste Comte envisioned the worship of woman as a central tenet of his new "religion of humanity."[9] The historian Jules Michelet went so far as to enshrine "woman" (*la femme*) as the very engine of history. One does not find this kind of talk in many other world cultures.

The ongoing public debate over women's power and influence is central to understanding the woman question as a pivotal element in the politics of French culture. Yet contemporary scholars, unlike their predecessors, have long sidestepped the "problem" of French women's cultural influence. Recent historiography on women and culture has focused more on culture in the ethnographic (or artistic) sense.[10] Here I want to turn the spotlight back on the politics of French high culture and to focus it specifically on this debate over women's cultural power and influence. In the following chapter, I will show how this discussion relates to the issue of political authority.

The Social and Cultural Construction of Sex in France

Even as women in France were identified with culture, the historical record also reveals a series of concerted efforts made over centuries by educated Frenchmen to break, contain, channel, and control their influence. Well before the Revolution, France had become a veritable laboratory not only for the celebration and denigration of women, but also for conscious efforts to structure and restructure the sociopolitical implications of sexual

---

[9] See Auguste Comte, *Système de politique positive* (Paris, 1848); cf. Comte, "The Influence of Positivism upon Women," in his *A General View of Positivism*, transl. J. H. Bridges (London, 1875; rep't ed., Stanford University Press, n.d.); see doc. 63 in *WFF*, vol. 1.

[10] An important statement by French scholars on the issue of women's culture and power in ethno-historical perspective is Cécile Dauphin, Arlette Farge, Geneviève Fraisse, Christiane Klapisch-Zuber, Rose-Marie Lagrave, Michelle Perrot, Pierrette Pézerat, Yannick Ripa, Pauline Schmitt-Pantel, & Danièle Voldman, "Culture et pouvoir des femmes: Essai d'historiographie," *Annales: Économies, Sociétés, Civilisations* (March–April 1986), n° 2, 271–293. This article has since been published in English in the *Journal of Women's History*, 1:1 (Spring 1989), 63–88, and a revised translation appeared in *Writing Women's History: International Perspectives*, ed. Karen Offen, Ruth Roach Pierson, & Jane Rendall (London: Macmillan, 1991, & Bloomington: Indiana University Press, 1991), pp. 107–133. "Culture" in this essay is understood in a purely anthropological sense.

In an important corrective effort to insist on the eighteenth-century tradition of identifying women with Culture (rather than with Nature), see Jane Rendall's pathbreaking essay "The Enlightenment and the Nature of Women," in Rendall, *The Origins of Modern Feminism* (New York: Schocken, 1984), which focuses on the influential histories of women by the Scottish Enlightenment writers. In the same vein, see Sylvia Tomaselli, "The Enlightenment Debate on Women," *History Workshop*, n° 20 (Autumn 1985), 101–124. See also Dena Goodman's essay, "Governing the Republic of Letters: The Politics of Culture in the French Enlightenment," *History of European Ideas*, 13:3 (1991), 183–199, which explores the gender politics of the salon.

difference, or what we now call "gender."[11] Literary historians have attributed much importance to the courtly love tradition as a vehicle for
emphasizing the centrality of women in medieval France.[12] The later
quarrel over the so-called *précieuses*, and the playwright Molière's humor-
ous denigration of the *précieuses ridicules* and the *femmes savantes* has
been repeatedly chronicled and deftly deconstructed.[13] Historians such as
Carolyn Lougee have insisted on the importance in the early seventeenth
century of Neo-Platonism as a counterweight to the asceticism of Christian
tradition in reasserting the centrality of women and heterosexual human
love. Lougee demonstrated early on how the woman question in that
century was central to a major debate about the sociopolitical order and
how the shaping of women's education, as embodied by Archbishop
Fénelon's influential *Treatise on the Education of Daughters* (1687), became
a key element in a project to reform French society from the top down.[14]
In a study of literary misogyny in the seventeenth century, Pierre Darmon
has abundantly documented the intensity and perversity of men's literary
response to women's influence; Christine Fauré has demonstrated the
extent to which it shaped French political theory, and Arlette Farge has
examined its manifestations in the more popular stories of the *Bibliothèque
Bleue*.[15] Sarah Hanley has posited the "engendering of the state" itself
during this period.[16] Literary historian Joan DeJean has demonstrated that

---

[11] See the discussion concerning the term "gender" in this volume's general introduction, and in my
two articles cited there.

[12] See the sophisticated analyses by Georges Duby, *The Knight, the Lady and the Priest*, transl. by
Barbara Bray (New York, 1983; orig. publ. in French, 1981), and Penny Schine Gold, *The Lady and
the Virgin: Image, Attitude and Experience in Twelfth-Century France* (Chicago: University of
Chicago Press, 1985).

[13] See Eva Avigdor, *Coquettes et précieuses* (Paris: A.-G. Nizet, 1982), and Domna Stanton's exposé of
the literary politics of *préciosité*, "The Fiction of Préciosité and the Fear of Women," *Yale French
Studies*, n° 62 (1981), 107–134.

[14] Carolyn C. Lougee, *Le Paradis des femmes* (Princeton, NJ: Princeton University Press, 1976),
pp. 34–40.

[15] Pierre Darmon, *Mythologie de la femme dans l'Ancienne France* (Paris: Seuil, 1983); Arlette Farge,
"L'Homme et la femme: un conflit qui traverse la Bibliothèque bleue," introduction to *Le Miroir des
femmes* (Paris: Montalba,1982), pp. 11–81; Laure Beaumont-Maillet, *La Guerre des sexes, XVe-XIXe
siècles: les albums du Cabinet des Estampes de la Bibliothèque Nationale* (Paris: Albin Michel, 1984);
and especially Christine Fauré, *La Démocratie sans les femmes* (Paris: Presses Universitaires de France,
1985), now in English transl. as *Democracy without Women* (Bloomington: Indiana University
Press, 1991).

[16] See the following essays by Sarah Hanley, "Engendering the State: Family Formation and State
Building in Early Modern France," *French Historical Studies*, 16:1 (Spring 1989), 4–27; "Social Sites
of Political Practice in France: Lawsuits, Civil Rights, and the Separation of Power in Domestic and
State Government, 1500–1800," *American Historical Review*, 102:1 (Feb. 1997), 27–52; "'The
Jurisprudence of the Arrêts': Marital Union, Civil Society, and State Formation in France,
1550–1650," *Law and History Review*, 21:1 (Spring 2003), 1–40; and "The Family, the State, and

women writers embedded a devastating critique of institutional marriage at the very heart of the seventeenth-century novel, which they in fact invented, while Nancy K. Miller has shown that the most important eighteenth-century novels written by men had women's stories at the heart of their narratives.[17] Historian Dena Goodman has documented the erosion of women's approaches to spelling and grammar as the all-male Académie Française took charge of consolidating the French language and, in particular, giving precedence to the "masculine" in grammar.[18] Historians of women in nineteenth-century France have repeatedly pointed out the prejudicial legal situation of French wives under the 1804 Civil Code, correctly emphasizing the stark reassertion of legal control by husbands over the persons and properties of wives.[19] But they have rarely made explicit why the jurists, the physicians, and the moralists thought it so necessary to emphasize and empower the masculine.

With this pervasive historical current of repeated acknowledgement of women's power and influence, post-revolutionary nineteenth-century Frenchmen resumed work on the project of attempting to control it through a deliberate process of reconstructing gender. As we will see in the subsequent volume, the leaders of the Third Republic, like their predecessors, would also formulate very specific views on the subject of how women's influence in France should be channeled and contained. They invested heavily in the promotion of sexual dimorphism (or sexual stratification), at once ideological and institutional, that was meant to

the Law in Seventeenth- and Eighteenth-Century France: The Political Ideology of Male Right versus an Early Theory of Natural Rights," *Journal of Modern History*, 78:2 (June 2006), 289–332.

For an important analytic demonstration of seventeenth-century aristocratic women exercising power, see Sharon Kettering, "The Patronage Power of Early Modern French Noblewomen," *The Historical Journal*, 32:4 (1989), 817–841.

[17] Joan DeJean, *Tender Geographies: Women and the Origins of the Novel in France* (New York: Columbia University Press, 1991) and Nancy K. Miller, *The Heroine's Text: Readings in the French and English Novel, 1722–1782* (New York: Columbia University Press). Miller argues (xi) that the real audience for these novels was male, and that the underlying ideology "codes feminity [sic] in paradigms of sexual vulnerability." For a scathing analysis of how the achievements of seventeenth-century literary women were deformed and denigrated in subsequent male historiography, see Faith E. Beasley, *Salons, History, and the Creation of Seventeenth-Century France* (Aldershot: Ashgate, 2006). See also the review of Beasley's book and the author's response on *H-France*, vol. 33 & vol. 34 (both 2007).

[18] See Dena Goodman, "L'ortografe des dames: Gender and Language in the Old Regime," *French Historical Studies*, 25:2 (Spring 2002), 191–223.

[19] See Theodore Zeldin, *France, 1848–1945* (Oxford, UK: Oxford University Press, 1973), vol. 1; James F. McMillan, *Housewife or Harlot: The Place of Women in French Society, 1870–1940* (New York: St. Martin's Press, 1981); and Patrick Kay Bidelman, *Pariahs Stand Up!: The Founding of the Liberal Feminist Movement in France, 1858–1889* (Westport, CT: Greenwood Press, 1982). See this volume's Chapter 2 on "Assessing the Problem of Women and Political Authority in French History."

culminate in a set of sharply separate, yet complementary – though asymmetrical and hierarchically organized – spaces for women and for men.[20] That such ambitious schemes never entirely succeeded may itself be tribute to the power of women's influence, and to French women's ability to subvert and divert such plans toward their own ends.

Probing Women's Power and Influence

Given the importance of this project for controlling women's power and influence, it is necessary to understand what was meant by "the influence of women" in French culture. Of what was this influence perceived to consist? How did it operate? In what ways did it manifest itself in the French debate on the woman question, both in the monarchies of early modern France and during the Revolution? What would be its significance for rethinking women's situation in the wake of the Revolution and for shaping the campaigns of the organized women's rights movement that blossomed during the Third Republic? How did contemporaries, male and female, frame their approaches to this issue?

The tantalizing and oft-quoted discussion of women's influence provoked by the Goncourt brothers in the 1860s reveals multiple dimensions of the issue. In *Woman in the Eighteenth Century* (1862), Edmond and Jules de Goncourt penned a florid and undoubtedly exaggerated rhetorical portrait of women's influence on eighteenth-century political life.[21]

> Woman was the governing principle, the directing reason and the commanding voice of the eighteenth century. She was the universal and fatal cause, the origin of events, the source of things. She presided over Time, like the Fortune of her History. Nothing escaped her; within her grasp she held the King and France, the will of the sovereign and the authority of public opinion – everything! She gave orders at Court, she was mistress in her home. She held the revolutions of alliances and political systems, peace

[20] See Jennifer Heuer & Anne Verjus, "L'invention de la sphère domestique au sortir de la Révolution," *Annales Historique de la Révolution française*, (2002, n° 1), 1–28. See also Suzanne Desan's study, *The Family on Trial in Revolutionary France* (Berkeley & Los Angeles: University of California Press, 2004). Note that I prefer to speak of spaces, not "spheres," although "spheres" will appear here and there in this book when I am quoting others.

[21] Edmond & Jules de Goncourt, *The Woman of the Eighteenth Century*, transl. Jacques Le Clercq and Ralph Roeder (New York: Minton, Balck & Company, 1927; orig. publ. in French, 1862), pp. 243–244. But see also Julia Kavanagh, *Woman in France during the Eighteenth Century*, 2 vols. (New York: G. P. Putnam's Sons, 1893); this book was originally published in 1850 in London and in Philadelphia – that is, prior to the Goncourt work. Kavanagh insists (vol. 1, p. 4) on elite women's enormous power in the old regime and scolds earlier historians for "never fully or willingly acknowledg[ing] its existence."

and war, the literature, the arts and the fashions of the eighteenth century, as well as its destinies, in the folds of her gown; she bent them to her whim or to her passions.

This was not read by nineteenth-century contemporaries as pure hyperbole. Such extravagant historical arguments resonated – and no doubt refracted the anxieties of the French male public to whom they were primarily addressed. At that very time, Napoléon III had committed French troops to support Piedmontese forces in their war against Austria, following his liaison with the elegant Comtesse de Castiglione, who had been sent to France expressly to acquire that support by the Piedmontese prime minister – her cousin Camillo di Benso, comte de Cavour. The enemies of Empress Eugénie could credibly, though erroneously, depict her as the *machina ex dea* of the clerical party and the mistress of "distaff diplomacy." Thus, the subtext of the Goncourt brothers' argument implied a warning for the future of the Second Empire itself, based on the ominous shadow of women's influence and the blame assigned to it for the fall of the *ancien régime*.[22]

There could be no doubt that a hundred years earlier, prior to the Revolution, certain clever women had played extraordinary roles in court politics as well as in urban high culture. The brothers Goncourt may have exaggerated the phenomenon, but they did not invent it. It is significant that the celebrated eighteenth-century political philosopher Montesquieu (sensitized by his reading of François Poullain de la Barre's 1673 treatise on the equality of the sexes) had elaborated on women's role in his *Spirit of the Laws* and had provoked other civic-minded men to look critically at the phenomenon.[23] Rousseau wrote, in his epistolary novel *Julie, or the New Heloise* (1761),[24] that

[22] Nancy Nichols Barker concluded that the charges brought against Eugénie for intruding into political affairs were unfounded. See her *Distaff Diplomacy: The Empress Eugénie and the Foreign Policy of the Second Empire* (Austin: University of Texas Press, 1967). Many of these slanders are rehearsed again by Victoire Bidegain, "L'origine d'une réputation: l'image de l'impératrice Eugénie dans la société française du Second Empire (1853–1870)," in *Femmes dans la Cité, 1815–1871*, ed. Alain Corbin, Jacqueline Lalouette, & Michèle Riot-Sarcey (Paris: Creaphis, 1997), 57–67.

[23] See Montesquieu, *Spirit of the Laws* (originally published 1748); Condorcet, *Lettres d'un bourgeois de New Haven à un citoyen de Virginie* (1787), in *Oeuvres de Condorcet*, ed. A. Condorcet O'Connor & F. Arago, 12 vols. (Paris: Firmin-Didot, 1847–1849), vol. 9 (1847), p. 20. On Poullain's influence on Montesquieu's earlier *Lettres persanes*, see Bernard Magné, "Une Source de la Lettre persane XXXVIII ?," *Revue d'histoire littéraire de la France*, vol. 68 (1968): 407–414. The definitive study of Poullain de la Barre is Siep Stuurman, *François Poullain de la Barre and the Invention of Modern Equality* (Cambridge, MA: Harvard University Press, 2004).

[24] J.-J. Rousseau, *Julie, ou la Nouvelle Heloise* (1761), part II, letter 21. From vol. 2 of the 1823 edition (Paris: chez Mme Veuve Dabo, 1823), pp. 27–28.

> French gallantry has given women a universal power. ... Everything
> depends on them; nothing gets done except by them or for them. ... In
> many matters [*dans les affaires*] they have a natural ascendance, even over
> their husbands, for obtaining what they want, not because they are hus-
> bands, but because they are men, and it is understood that a man will never
> refuse anything to any woman, even his own wife.

The marquis de Condorcet complained in the late 1780s that women
would probably be angry with his own offer of "mere" civic equality, since
they were so enthralled by Rousseau, who had acknowledged their empire
over men (even as he attempted to curb it).[25]

Foreigners also commented on the topic of French women's influence.
Writing about the same time as Condorcet, the American minister to
France, Thomas Jefferson, informed General George Washington in
strongly disapproving terms of the extent of Frenchwomen's *de facto*
political power, a judgment seconded by Alexander Hamilton.[26] The
American emissary Gouverneur Morris wrote in his diary, upon arriving
in France in the spring of 1789, "We are in the land of women. ... they
enjoy an almost unlimited power and seem to take extreme pleasure in it."
But, he added, "I am not sure that the country is the better off for it."[27]

The Americans' opinion was evidently shared by many of the French
revolutionary legislators of the 1790s. After four full years of effort to
demand their rights, interspersed by several years of diatribes against their
participation by the Parisian and provincial press, in late 1793 French
women found themselves banned from political activity by the Jacobin
government. Indeed, one early twentieth-century historian of French
feminism suggested that many of the French revolutionary leaders, like
Jefferson, "were not far from thinking that Woman was the cause of all the
faults of the tyrants," and just as centuries earlier the fathers of the Church
had blamed women for the fall of Man, so the fathers of the Revolution

[25] Condorcet, *Lettres d'un bourgeois de New Haven à un citoyen de Virginie, sur l'inutilité de partager le pouvoir législatif entre plusieurs corps* (1787); reprinted in *Oeuvres de Condorcet*, vol. 9 (1847), p. 20.
[26] Jefferson to General Washington, Paris, 4 December 1788. Orig. publ. in Thomas Jefferson, *Memoir, Correspondance, and Miscellanies*, ed. Thomas Jefferson Randolph, vol. 2 (Charlottesville, 1829), pp. 406–407. See also Alexander Hamilton's comparable expression of concern in *The Federalist* (letter nº 6, 14 November 1787), ed., with introd. & notes, Jacob E. Cooke (Middletown, CT: Wesleyan University Press, 1961), pp. 29–30. Jefferson's opinion on the necessity of excluding women from politics (along with children and slaves) was expressed even more firmly in his 1816 letter to Samuel Kerchival, later published in *Memoir, Correspondence, and Miscellanies, from the Papers of Thomas Jefferson*, vol. 4, p. 295.
[27] Quoted in French in Jean-Jacques Fiechter, *Un Diplomate américaine sous la Terreur; les années européennes de Gouverneur Morris, 1789–1798* (Paris: Fayard, 1983), p. 55. The Morris diaries, at the Library of Congress, have never been published.

held women accountable for the "fall of France."[28] Indeed, a closer analysis of the debate on the woman question in France prior to the revolution offers ample evidence for interpreting the undermining of women's situation in French law, capped by the Civil Code, as the consequence of a deliberate campaign by male jurists to curb women's powerful yet wholly illegitimate influence in political life.

Sexuality, Sensuality, Beauty, and Charm

What were the perceived bases of French women's power and influence? Among eighteenth-century male writers, Jean-Jacques Rousseau offered perhaps the most candid insight into the principal source of women's influence. To him, it lay purely and simply in men's inability to resist women's seductiveness, their power of sexual attraction. Like the fathers of the Church, whose doctrines Rousseau professed to despise, he perceived women as rapacious temptresses. Indeed, he preached male control and female modesty as a means of protecting men and preventing their sexual powers from being overtaxed by women. "Women," wrote Rousseau in his educational treatise *Émile* (1762),[29]

> so easily stir men's senses and awaken in the bottom of their hearts the remains of an almost extinct desire that if there were some unhappy climate on this earth where philosophy had introduced this custom, especially in warm countries where more women than men are born, the men tyrannized over by the women would at last become their victims and would be dragged to their deaths without ever being able to defend themselves.

But, he added ominously, "When the time comes that women are no longer concerned with men's well-being, men will no longer be good for anything at all."

Reason, Rousseau argued, was the tool God gave to man not only to regulate his own unlimited desires but *to control women and thereby to*

---

[28] Léon Abensour, *Le Problème féministe* (Paris: Radot, 1927), p. 75. The most extreme example is provided by the virulent attacks on Marie-Antoinette during the revolution; these are analyzed by Chantal Thomas, *La Reine scélérate: Marie-Antoinette dans les pamphlets* (Paris: Seuil, 1989); Elizabeth Colwill, "Just Another Citoyenne? Marie-Antoinette on Trial, 1790–1793," *History Workshop*, n° 28 (Autumn 1989), 63–87; and Lynn Hunt, "The Many Bodies of Marie Antoinette: Political Pornography and the Problem of the Feminine in the French Revolution," in *Eroticism and the Body Politic*, ed. Lynn Hunt (Baltimore & London: Johns Hopkins University Press, 1991), pp. 108–130. A nineteenth-century example is Edouard de Beaumont, *L'Épée et les femmes* (Paris, 1881; in English as *The Sword and Womankind*, New York: Panurge Press, 1929), which blames men's "emasculation" on women's intrigues and men's abandonment of the sword as a weapon of war.

[29] From J.-J. Rousseau, *Émile*, as retranslated in *WFF*, vol. 1, doc. 10, p. 45.

ensure that women remained preoccupied with men's well-being. "Woman was specifically made to please man," he insisted. This was, on Rousseau's part, a deliberate assertion, not an assumption. It was prescriptive, not descriptive. His point could not have been more politically explicit. No French writer, even in the nineteenth century, would ever underrate (or attempt to neutralize by denying) the power of female sexuality and seductiveness in the way that Dr. William Acton and others effectively did in the English context.[30]

Twentieth-century academic historians, until very recently, had systematically skirted discussion of the sensual bases of women's influence, despite the force of the evidence that attests to its importance.[31] Another way of approaching this question is to consider the historical significance of women's beauty, as historian Christine Adams is doing. Writing about Thérésia Cabarrus, later Madame Tallien, whose contribution to ending the Terror through her influence on Tallien has become the stuff of legend ("Notre Dame de Thermidor") and whose importance during the Directory was underscored by all observers, Adams asks readers to take seriously the sheer aesthetic appeal that gave some women celebrity status and underpinned not only their social influence but also their political influence, as in Madame Tallien's case. When beauty was coupled with a self-consciousness of the positive work beauty and fashion could do by influencing men to behave in high-minded and generous ways, it could and seemingly did sometimes work miracles.[32] Even Napoléon was for a time influenced by her charms, but later banished her from court and even from contact with her former best friend Josephine Beauharnais, who as Napoléon's wife became Empress.

But neither sensuality nor beauty was the sole factor underpinning women's power and influence. A second aspect of Frenchwomen's influence was underscored by the Goncourt brothers' contemporary, the historian Jules Michelet, who inadvertently emphasized the importance of kinship networks and relative age at marriage to women's empowerment. In his book, *La Femme* (1859), Michelet would offer counsel to young men

---

[30] See the much-discussed characterization of women's ostensible "lack of sexual feeling" by the British physician, William Acton, *The Functions and Disorders of the Reproductive Organs* (1857), reprinted in *Victorian Women*, eds. Erna Olafson Hellerstein, Leslie Parker Hume, & Karen Offen (Stanford, CA: Stanford University Press, 1981), doc. 37 (ii), pp. 177–179. I return to this issue in Chapter 3.

[31] See Arthur Mitzman, "Michelet and the Republican Mission, 1868–70: The Policing of Eros," *Journal of the History of Sexuality*, 3:1 (1992), 1–32.

[32] See Christine Adams, "Venus of the Capitol': Madame Tallien and the Politics of Beauty under the Directory," *French Historical Studies*, 37:4 (Fall 2014), 599–629.

concerning the choice of wives. His advice is revealing. Significantly, he urged them to choose much younger women with no families of their own. Only thus could a woman be molded by her husband to suit his express wishes.[33] Only thus could he play Pygmalion. Michelet was as suspicious of women who had been trained by other women as of those who were under the influence of priests. Clearly, Michelet considered that women who were in close contact with kin networks, female networks, or who were close in age to their husbands might neither be pliable nor obedient – nor interested exclusively in a husband's well-being. In order to assert male authority in the household, Michelet's ideal scheme for the husband, men must isolate women in order to dominate them; only then could men securely worship them. Implicit in his argument was the fear that a woman who was a man's peer – or who had access to networks outside her own doors – would dominate him![34] In short, to Michelet, women's freedom meant men's ruin.

The Goncourt brothers also offered a third explanation. Discounting women's charms, they insisted that the power of women in France derived from their [emotional] intelligence. Women, they believed, possessed an uncanny insight into human nature, an instinctive intelligence (we would call it "women's intuition") that allowed them to develop strategic skill at managing men.[35] This point would be constantly underscored by women writers as well; for example, the Anglo-French journalist Claire de Pratz, in her 1912 book *France from Within*, reported that "Her [a woman's] power lies exclusively in what men call her womanly charm, which in reality is her intense faculty for the sympathetic assimilation of the ideas and even the passions and emotions of others."[36] Earlier she had underscored that "France is a woman's country. The Frenchman is devoted to the cult of

[33] Jules Michelet, *La Femme*, as reprinted in *WFF*, vol. 1, doc. 97, p. 340. The fascination of some notable male writers, perhaps inspired by the Pygmalion myth, with discovering and shaping the *jeune fille sauvage* dates from at least 1755; see the *Histoire d'une jeune fille sauvage, trouvée dans les bois à l'age de dix ans, publiés par Madame H...t, (1751) . . . suivi de documents annexes et présenté par Franck Tinland* (Bordeaux: Duclos, 1970). In *France from Within* (London & New York: Hodder & Stoughton, 1912), Claire de Pratz also speaks to this issue of men's desire to "form" their younger wives.

[34] Such fears were evidently commonplace in French peasant societies; see Martine Segalen, *Mari et femme dans la société paysanne* (Paris: Flammarion, 1980), pp. 149–152. A similar point is made concerning the power of women in French urban working-class families by Michelle Perrot, "De la Nourrice à l'employée: Travaux de femmes dans la France du XIXe siècle," *Le Mouvement social*, n° 105 (October–December 1978), 4.

[35] Goncourt & Goncourt, *Woman*, chapter 9: "The Domination and Intelligence of Woman," esp. pp. 246–248.

[36] De Pratz, *France from Within*, p. 163.

Woman. He adores *la femme*, and he is more than nine-tenths convinced that she is the better half of humanity. In his home life, as in his business – be that what it may – he consults his wife upon every detail, and the Frenchman's most intimate counsellor [sic] and friend is always his wife, mother or sister."[37] Was this too much of a good thing?

The poet Gérard de Nerval, translator of Goethe's *Faust* and seeker of the "Eternal Feminine," offered a fourth, and complementary explanation, concerning male insecurity, in his *Voyage en Orient* (1851):[38]

> Yes, let us be young in Europe as long as we can, but go to spend our old age in the Orient, the country of men worthy of the name, the land of the patriarchs. In Europe, where our institutions have suppressed physical strength, woman has become too powerful. With all that power of seduction, of ruse, of perseverance and persuasion with which heaven has endowed her, the woman of our own countries has become socially the equal of man, and this was more than was necessary to ensure that he should inevitably and eternally become her victim.

Emerging from this somewhat random cluster of widely read male and female authors is a multifaceted acknowledgement of women's influence, no element of which in any way treats women as negligible or oppressed creatures. In these men's eyes, women were empowered not only by their sexual attractiveness, but also by their kin networks, their innate emotional as well as rational intelligence, and their associations with other women, which all but rendered superfluous men's advantage of physical strength. Taken together, these insights, particularly those of the male writers, provide us with a searing portrait of masculine psychological insecurity in face of the fearsome specter of unbridled female power. Historian Joan Landes has remarked that "the structures of modern republican politics can be construed as part of an elaborate defense against women's power and public presence."[39] The evidence I have accumulated attests to the fact that such elaborate defenses were being constructed and reconstructed under the successive monarchies, centuries before the advent of modern republican politics. There is nothing particularly "republican" about male anxieties, though it could be said that male anxieties in the French context have sometimes exploded in acutely aggressive forms.

---

[37] Claire de Pratz, "French Women and English Women," *Votes for Women* (February 1908), 64.

[38] Gerard de Nerval, *Voyage en Orient* (Paris: Charpentier, 1851); as translated in *The Women of Cairo: Scenes of Life in the Orient*, vol. 2 (New York: Harcourt, Brace and Company, 1930), p. 36. Nerval's musings seem to have been stimulated by his purchase of a young, and presumably docile, slave girl.

[39] Joan B. Landes, *Women and the Public Sphere in the Age of the French Revolution* (Ithaca, NY: Cornell University Press, 1988), pp. 203–204.

Those French men who did worry about female power and influence continually felt the necessity of taking exceptional measures to assert their manly authority in a situation in which they perceived themselves as "merely" legally dominant. With the combined forces of law, prescription, and custom – and physical strength – behind them, it is highly illuminating to recognize that such men remained insecure, still obsessively worried about controlling women. Must all women be inevitably seen as "daughters of Eve"? Must woman, then, remain a "muse" or a "madonna" in order to render herself less threatening to the male of the species?[40] Was the "woman question," ultimately, a Man Problem, an unresolvable problem of male identity and anxieties about masculinity?[41] Is the entire debate on the woman question simply evidence of repeated efforts to stabilize male gender identity by imposing limits or constraints on troubling, invasive female "other," as contemporary cultural theorists might put it?

French Women Acknowledge and Applaud Women's Influence

And here I turn to the examination of women's words on this subject. What I find remarkable is that French women, not least the feminists among them, were equally assertive about the significance of women's influence and recognized the necessity of channeling it to constructive use through better education. Mongellaz was by no means the only one to develop this theme. In the 1833 prospectus for her publication, *Le Conseiller des Femmes* [Women's Counselor], the Saint-Simonian and women's rights advocate Éugénie Niboyet likewise insisted on the power of women's influence, despite their de facto political powerlessness; in 1849 the feminist activist Jeanne Deroin made a similar point.[42] The feminist novelist and essayist André Léo (Léodile Béra, veuve Champseix) underscored the point again in 1869, when she wrote that women's "influence, though difficult to pin down in ordinary times, nevertheless exists. The heart of the matter is to know whether this influence should be instinctive or cultivated, ... whether it should be exercised in broad daylight or in the shadows." And in Hubertine Auclert's pro-suffrage

---

[40] See Stéphane Michaud, *Muse et madone: Visages de la femme de la Révolution française aux apparitions de Lourdes* (Paris: Seuil, 1985).

[41] See my article, "Is the 'Woman Question' Really the 'Man Problem'?" in *Confronting Modernity in Fin-de-Siecle France: Bodies, Minds and Gender*, ed. Christopher E. Forth & Elinor Accampo (London: Palgrave/Macmillan, 2010), pp. 43–62.

[42] Éugénie Niboyet, "Prospectus," *Le Conseiller des Femmes*, (1 October 1833), 2; Jeanne Deroin, "Mission de la femme," *L'Opinion des Femmes*, (28 January 1849) (see *WFF*, vol. 1, doc. 77, p. 261).

newspaper, *La Citoyenne*, the masthead subheading asserted that "Woman is one of the driving forces [*forces vives*] of France that has been neglected for all too long."[43]

The remarks of female observers from neighboring countries in the late nineteenth and early twentieth centuries also reflect the continuing fascination with this theme of women's power and influence in French culture. One recurrent refrain in the commentaries of contemporary British and American writers on the woman question during the Third Republic is that the actual position of married women in French society was dramatically better than that of their Anglo-American counterparts, despite their clearly subordinate status in French civil and political law. In 1908, for instance, the British writer Violet Stuart Wortley pointed out that "though legally [French] women occupy a much inferior status to men, in practice they constitute the superior sex. They are the 'power behind the throne,' and both in the family and in business relations undoubtedly enjoy greater consideration than English women. There are unwritten laws in their favor."[44] Exactly what these "unwritten laws" were Wortley never specified. Around 1916, Emmeline Pankhurst, the militant English suffragette, remarked to a younger French colleague that what she perceived as the hesitancy of French feminism (relative to the action-packed and controversial suffrage campaigns of the Women's Social and Political Union in Britain) could be explained by the fact that French women already had influence and knew it.[45] Such observations were repeatedly offered by outside observers to explain why feminist agitation had been less militant in France around the turn of the century than in England.

Moreover, it seemed that not all French men were as worried about women's influence as Gerard de Nerval and his associates; the number of male-feminists in France was slowly but constantly expanding. By 1909, the German reformer Käthe Schirmacher could write that in France "for political reasons, the women's rights movement is supported by men to a degree not noticeable in any other country."[46] Schirmacher's observations were seconded by Claire de Pratz, who would remark in 1912: "I have been

[43] André Léo, *La Femme et les moeurs: liberté ou monarchie* (Paris: Au Journal *Le Droit des Femmes*, 1869), p. 7; Auclert's paper, *La Citoyenne*, issues of the late 1880s.
[44] Violet Stuart Wortley, "Feminism in England and France," *The National Review*, 51 (March–April 1908), 793–794.
[45] Reported by Louli Milhaud Sanua, *Figures féminines, 1909–1939* (Paris: Lib. Beaufils, 1946), pp. 37–38.
[46] Käthe Schirmacher, *The Modern Woman's Rights Movement: A Historical Survey*, transl. Carl Conrad Eckhardt (2nd German edn., 1909; New York, 1912; reprint edn., New York, 1971), pp. 181–182. The secretary-general of the Conseil National des Femmes Françaises, Ghénia Avril de Sainte-Croix,

interested to learn from long and continued personal investigation that most of our greater representative men – politicians, writers, artists, and thinkers of all kinds – are entirely feminist in their views."[47] Indeed, such explanations seemed self-evident to contemporaries; no further elaboration was deemed necessary. What requires historical explanation, then, is the seemingly yawning chasm that existed in France between prescriptions for controlling women, whether in law or moral stricture, and the imputed power and influence women continued to enjoy in nineteenth-century French society despite their undisputed formal subordination in marriage.[48]

Indeed, acknowledgement of women's influence and power in French society remains explicit to this day at various levels of society, and it is perhaps still more visible to observers from other cultures than to the French themselves. One does not have to look back exclusively to queens and royal favorites, or to the *merveilleuses* of the Directory, or at women's important contributions to French high culture as writers, painters, musicians, actresses, singers, journalists, and so forth, or even confine oneself to looking at urban centers to find compelling evidence of women's talent and achievements and of their sense of importance, influence, and power.

Ethnographers Explore Women's Influence in the French Countryside

Research since the 1970s in French village anthropology and ethnography by feminist scholars elucidates the question of women's influence and men's anxieties from another angle and in a distinctively different time and social class milieu. One instance is provided by Lucienne Roubin's analysis of the *chambrettes*, or men's clubs of Provençal village society, a society that was still (during the 1960s) highly sex-segregated in the routines of daily life. These clubs, which have a long history, serve as "a constant and concrete indication of the existence of male society and emphasize the distance separating it from female society."[49] The

would also insist on this point; see her article, "Les Françaises dans les grandes sociétés féminines internationales," *La Revue* (1 November 1915), 456–460.

[47] De Pratz, *France from Within*, p. 169.

[48] This point seems to be entirely missed by James F. McMillan in his survey *France and Women, 1789–1914: Gender, Society and Politics* (London: Routledge, 1998), which dwells on women's disempowerment and mostly male prescriptions about how women should be and should be controlled, rather than the remarkable story of what women in France thought and did and how they fought back against male domination.

[49] Lucienne Roubin, "Espace masculin, espace féminin en communauté provençale," *Annales: É.S.C.*, 25 (1970), 537–560; in English, "Male Space and Female Space within the Provençal Community,"

articulated need village men felt to separate themselves, even escape, from the world of women reveals what seems to be a psychic necessity to enforce physical boundaries between the sexes. In a parallel investigation of a small Provençal village, the American anthropologist Rayna [Rapp] Reiter reported that the women of the village perceived their own sphere, centered around the household where they were indisputably in command, to be more powerful than that of the men. Unlike the men's more public networks, which were supra-familial, professional, and collegial, women's networks were centered around kin and the village itself. Reiter also points out that however powerful a woman perceived herself to be in the village setting, once she left it and encountered the strictures of formal, male-centered political and economic institutions, she would discover quickly how circumscribed her power actually was.[50]

The research of another American ethnologist, Susan Carol Rogers, has also addressed the relationship between formalized male forms of power and the more diffuse female power, focusing on one village in Lorraine. In one study, Rogers has pointed to the ways in which (in this village) both sexes colluded in acting out a "myth" of male dominance, despite the discernable evidence that women, because they controlled household activities in that setting, actually wielded great power and influence over the men.[51] In a historical study of women's changing roles in the families of wealthy nineteenth-century Catholic industrial families in the Nord (northwest France) over three generations, Bonnie Smith also probed the extent of female power and influence. Like Reiter and Rogers, she

---

in *Rural Society in France: Selections from the Annales: Économies, Sociétés, Civilisations*, ed. Robert Forster & Orest Ranum (Baltimore: Johns Hopkins University Press, 1977), pp. 152–180. See also Maurice Agulhon, *Le Cercle dans la France bourgeoise, 1810–1848* (Paris: A. Colin, 1977), p. 53.

[50] Rayna R. Reiter, "Men and Women in the South of France: Public and Private Domains," in *Toward an Anthropology of Women*, ed. Rayna R. Reiter (New York: Monthly Review Press, 1975), pp. 252–282. See also Segalen, *Mari et femme* (see n. 34).

[51] Susan Carol Rogers, "Female Forms of Power and the Myth of Male Dominance: A Model of Female/Male Interaction in Peasant Society," *American Ethnologist*, 2:4 (November 1975), 727–756. See also Rogers, "Woman's Place: A Critical Review of Anthropological Theory," *Comparative Studies in Society and History*, 20:1 (January 1978), 123–162, for a critique of the assumptions about male domination in British and American ethnological literature, and Segalen's comparable critique of the French folklorists' interpretation of the discourse on male authority, *Mari et femme*, pp. 167–183.

For a very important cross-cultural exploration of the origins of sexual inequality, see Peggy Reeves Sanday, *Female Power and Male Dominance* (Cambridge, UK: Cambridge University Press, 1981); see also Eleanor Leacock, *Myths of Male Dominance* (New York: Monthly Review Press, 1981). Both historical and anthropological evidence suggests that in at least some other regions of France, male dominance was no myth; see Susan Carol Rogers, "Gender in Southwestern France: The Myth of Male Dominance Revisited," *Anthropology*, 9:1–2 (1985), 65–86. Cf. also Pierre Bourdieu, *Masculine Domination* (Cambridge, UK: Polity Press, 2001).

demonstrated that although the women's internal household world was elaborated in terms of great significance, sharp limits were nevertheless imposed on their power and influence by the increasingly expansive male-dominated political world outside the household.[52] These are admittedly discrete samplings, but taken together, they reveal a more general pattern.

Conversely, a group of women historians in France has criticized certain aspects of this ethnologically centered scholarship, charging that its authors sidestep or obscure issues of sexual politics – the power relations and hierarchies of values. They have called for closer examination of women's informal power, for studies of the dynamics of conflict, tensions, even violence, with an eye to the ways in which the power attributed to women in the household may actually be "compensatory," based on domination of women over other younger or less privileged women.[53] This remains an important agenda for research, calling for novel types of evidence. Yet it should not excuse historians from examining more easily accessible printed sources that lie, neglected, in the public record. What I find particularly intriguing about the history of the woman question, especially in the nineteenth century, is the way in which both men and women deliberately elaborated and manipulated the notions of women's power and influence to achieve particular political effects.

The Politics of Gender in France

What we are all talking about, in fact, in diverse vocabularies and from diverse disciplinary perspectives, is the politics of gender in France. And this politics of gender has a long though diversely documented past. As I have suggested in the General Introduction to this book (among other publications), for centuries the French themselves have understood gender as being socially constructed; this insight is by no means exclusive to late twentieth-century feminist scholars. Why else did the French concern themselves so seriously with the overall "education" (not merely "instruction" or schooling but also gender upbringing) of girls and boys?

One of the principal claims made throughout centuries of French cultural criticism (and reiterated by such male Enlightenment figures as Poullain de la Barre, Montesquieu, the chevalier de Jaucourt, the baron d'Holbach, and Helvétius (and not least, the cross-dressing chevalier

[52] Bonnie G. Smith, *Ladies of the Leisure Class: The Bourgeoises of Northern France in the Nineteenth Century* (Princeton, NJ: Princeton University Press, 1981).
[53] See Dauphin et al., "Culture et pouvoir des femmes" (n. 10).

d'Éon, who read all these works) was that women's ostensible inferiority to men was entirely attributable to their inadequate education, by which they meant the combination of instruction and upbringing. Indeed, in the eighteenth century, this became a favorite theme of Enlightenment writers: It so aggravated Rousseau that he rejected the blame, retorting: "And since when is it men who concern themselves with the education of girls? Who is preventing the mothers from raising them as they please?"[54] Was he responding perhaps to the feisty Madame de Beaumer, editor of the *Journal des Dames*, who charged in March 1762 (the same year in which Rousseau published *Émile*): "If we have not been raised up in the sciences as you have, it is you who are the guilty ones." Madame d'Épinay, commenting on A.-L. Thomas's influential *Essay on the Character, Manners, and Genius of Women in Different Ages* (1772), observed that Thomas "constantly attributes to nature what we have obviously acquired from education and institutions."[55] She went on to speak specifically about "*genre masculin*" and "*genre féminin*," stipulating that she was not referring to grammar. Essay contests addressing the question of women's education and upbringing proliferated during the 1770s and 1780s.[56] The great writer Madame de Staël insisted on the importance of institutions and education in the shaping of women.[57] She, like her predecessors, understood that gender roles were socially constructed, or as it was formulated in the French vocabulary of the time, "nature" had to be shaped, to make it acceptable to "culture."[58] Leaving aside, for a subsequent chapter

---

[54] In *Émile*, book V, in *WFF*, vol. 1, doc. 10.

[55] Mme de Beaumer, in *WFF*, vol. 1, doc. 2; Letter from Mme d'Épinay to the abbé Galiani, 14 March 1772; first published by Benedetto Croce, "Una lettera inedita della signora d'Épinay e il 'Dialogue sur les femmes' dell'abate Galiani," in *Mélanges d'histoire littéraire générale et comparée, offerts à Fernand Baldensperger*, 2 vols. (Paris: H. Champion, 1930), vol. 1, p. 178. Mme d'Épinay's text has been reprinted in A.L. Thomas, Diderot, Madame d'Épinay, *Qu'est-ce qu'une femme?, un débat, préfacé par Elisabeth Badinter* (Paris: P.O.L., 1989).

[56] Among these were the competitions sponsored by the Academy of Besançon in 1776 and by the Academy of Châlons-sur-Marne in 1783.

[57] Mme de Staël, *De la littérature* (1800), in *Oeuvres complètes de Mme la Baronne de Staël*, vol. 4 (Paris, 1820), p. 472.

[58] On the nature/culture dualism in French thought, see Maurice Bloch & Jean H. Bloch, "Women and the Dialectics of Nature in Eighteenth-Century French Thought," in *Nature, Culture, and Gender*, ed. Carol MacCormack & Marilyn Strathern (Cambridge, UK: Cambridge University Press, 1980), pp. 25–41. For a critique of its translation into the work of Claude Lévi-Strauss and other influential anthropologists, see Penelope Brown & Ludmilla J. Jordanova, "Oppressive Dichotomies: The Nature/Culture Debate," in *Women in Society: Interdisciplinary Essays*, ed. Cambridge Women's Studies Group (London: Virago, 1981), pp. 224–241. The politics of biomedical constructions of women and "nature" will be further explored in Chapter 3, this volume.

For an astute overview of recent debates in anthropology provoked by feminist criticism, see Louise Lamphere, "Feminism and Anthropology: The Struggle to Reshape our Thinking about

(Chapter 3), a discussion of what "nature" entailed as concerned women and the family in France, let me offer several examples of the way in which nineteenth-century (i.e., post-revolutionary) male writers addressed "gender" as a cultural construct.

In his sardonic book *Physiologie de mariage* (1829), Honoré de Balzac asserted that only a small proportion of the female sex in France were in fact truly "women." "A woman," he wrote, "is a rare variety of the human race, and her principal characteristics are due to the special care men have bestowed upon its cultivation – thanks to the power of money and the moral fervor of civilization." Moreover, Balzac argued, "Love is her religion; she thinks how to please the one she loves," and "The species is in fine at once the queen of the world and the slave of passion."[59] Such men claimed to define, in short, what a "woman" was.

One particular experiment in the sociopolitical construction of gender that gained great notoriety in the counterrevolutionary nineteenth century was the production, among Christian families of the upper and upper-middle classes, of the much-celebrated type of the "*ingenue*" or "*jeune fille bien elevée*," known variously as the *demoiselle* or the *oie blanche* (white goose). This social type, which according to its champion – the historian Paule Constant – originated in the fifteenth century, "belonged to a Christian, elitist and sexist society which, through her, attained perfection." Such a young girl was raised as a saint, a pure soul, while the young man was raised as a hero. Constant deems this *jeune fille* as "*la forme parfaite de la feminité*," a daughter who becomes the chef d'oeuvre of the mother.[60] The *ingenue* was most valued when pure, innocent, trained to submission and dependence by suppressing all prospects of developing a strong personality prior to marriage; she was, in short, the naïve virgin, applauded by many members of the wealthiest and most leisured classes, and by those who aspired to join them. She was also, in effect, an art form, a luxury product made for men. The model seems to have been devised specifically to thwart, or at least to delay, the blossoming of womanly power and influence, and concomitantly awareness of the potency of female sexuality – at least until the rude awakening of marriage and copulation.

In 1880, Guy de Maupassant, critical of the emerging campaign for women's rights and its supporters, would insist that men should [continue

---

Gender," in *The Impact of Feminist Research in the Academy*, ed. Christie Farnham (Bloomington: Indiana University Press, 1987), pp. 11–33.

[59] Honoré de Balzac, *Physiologie du mariage* (Paris, 1829), as transl. in *The Works of Honoré de Balzac*, ed. William P. Trent, vols. 33–34 (New York, n.d.), pp. 23–24.

[60] See Paule Constant, *Un monde à l'usage des demoiselles* (Paris: Gallimard, 1987), quotes, pp. 359, 14.

to] demand that women be "the charm and luxury of their existence." "When woman demands her rights, let us accord her only one: the right to please."[61] However, the committed revolutionary Louise Michel never understood why, intelligence being in rather short supply, one would want to cripple the intelligence of any creature, remarking that "Little girls are brought up in foolishness and are expressly disarmed so that men can deceive them more easily. That is what men want. It is precisely as if someone threw you into the water after having forbidden you to learn to swim or even after having tied your arms and legs."[62] Some thirty years later, in a post-war essay, the novelist Colette Yver would describe the self-same *jeune fille bien élevée*: "Their personalities had been worked like metal. Their excellent education had made them up just as cosmetics make up a face." "They were raised, in short, for men."[63] In effect, these artificial creations would become sacrificial lambs on the altar of French masculine hegemony, as feminist critics who espoused a far different, more self-empowering education for girls would point out.

What seems most appalling to twenty-first century critics about the model of the *jeune fille bien élevée* is undoubtedly the fact that so many other women – mothers, grandmothers, aunts, directors of convent schools – colluded in producing this product, ostensibly pleasing to God, but in fact designed and designated for men's pleasure and rule – "the right to please." Indeed, much as in the case of Chinese foot binding or female genital circumcision in Africa, the fact of female collusion (or was it merely acquiescence) in the education of these "white geese" is inescapable. Even so, there were not a few women who managed to escape or who were "improperly" or "inadequately" socialized to this model, Louise Michel among them. A small number of such women became leading writers, such as George Sand, who (perhaps because her antecedents were not middle class) was allowed to run free as a girl. Clémence Royer would become a great scientific observer, denouncing the sexual politics of knowledge. Others, such as Maria Deraismes, Hubertine Auclert, and

---

[61] Guy de Maupassant, "La Lysistrata moderne," *Le Gaulois*, 30 December 1880; reprinted in his *Oeuvres complètes*, vol. 16 (Paris, 1968), pp. 71–74; quote, 73.

[62] Louise Michel, *The Red Virgin: Memoirs of Louise Michel*, ed. & transl. by Bullitt Lowry & Elizabeth Ellington Gunter (University, AL: University of Alabama Press, 1981), pp. 140–141; in the French edition, *Mémoires de Louise Michel* (Paris: F. Roy, 1886), p. 107.

[63] Colette Yver, "Jeunes filles bien élevées, jeunes filles mal élevées," *Le Correspondant* (10 December 1919), 995, 1000. A second such construct was the woman made entirely for "love" where "love" was merely a synonym for sex. Another, broader notion of "love," which revolved around the love of others (*agape*) can be explored in the works of the poet Marceline Desbordes-Valmore; see the publications of Marc Bertrand and the website www.desbordes-valmore.net.

Nelly Roussel would become activists in movements for sociopolitical change, spearheading the women's movement of the Third Republic. There were also other ways, even within a household, in which such innocence could be subverted, as Émile Zola pointed out in his novel *Pot-Bouille* (1882), when he composed a scene in which the maidservant seduced the *jeune fille* and taught her the secrets of lesbian love![64] In a society in which gender was considered manipulable, and women's influence an acknowledged fact, systemic education for women could be seen both as the key to their control and to their emancipation.

The Mother-Educator Model

From the seventeenth century on, a second and competing approach to the shaping of gender roles emerged, a role that went hand-in-glove with the critique of court society and aristocratic decadence, and also fostered civic involvement. This was the model of *la mère-éducatrice*, the secular mother-educator or civic mother.

This mother-educator model took on increasing political importance among progressive reformers (from bishop Fénelon's *Treatise on the Education of Daughters* on) who were bent on *national* reform, and it blossomed in the wake of the French Revolution. Its retrospective importance lies in its strategic insistence on the positive life-giving, nurturing qualities of motherhood, and on their sociopolitical significance; it was, in fact, a supreme reply to the misogynistic literature of early modern France, in which (as Arlette Farge has pointed out) women were constantly associated by male writers with death and motherhood was never mentioned.[65] Yet

[64] See Susan Yates article, "The Enemy Within: The Maid in the Nineteenth Century French Novel," in *France: Politics, Society, Culture and International Relations. Papers from the Seventh George Rudé Seminar in French History and Civilisation, The University of Sydney, 21–23 July 1990*, ed. Robert Aldrich (Sydney: Department of Economic History, University of Sydney, 1990).

[65] Several American historians of France have explored the sex-role prescriptions encapsulated in early nineteenth-century children's stories, especially stories about girls or young women written by women for the guidance of girls. See Ann Ilan Alter, "Women Are Made, not Born: Making Bourgeois Girls into Women, France 1830–1870" (Ph.D. dissertation, Rutgers University, 1980); and Laura S. Strumingher, *What Were Little Girls and Boys Made Of? Primary Education in Rural France, 1830–1880* (Albany, NY: SUNY Press, 1983). Of special interest for this period is the general study encompassing girls' education by Barbara Corrado Pope, "Mothers and Daughters in Early Nineteenth-Century Paris" (Ph.D. dissertation, Columbia University, 1981); Marie-Françoise Lévy, *Des mères en filles; l'éducation des françaises 1850–1880* (Paris: Calmann-Lévy, 1984); Cécile Dauphin, "The Construction of Femininity in the Epistolary Manuals of Nineteenth-Century France," *The Journal of Women's Studies* (Calcutta), 1:1 (April–September 1996), 37–60; and Constant, *Monde a l'usage des demoiselles*, cited in n. 60. For attempts to subvert these messages, see the discussion on the 1860s–1870s educational reformers, especially Clarisse Coignet, in Chapter 4.

this oppositional political character of the mother-educator model has been completely overlooked by such contemporary critics as Elisabeth Badinter, who in her writings on motherhood points only to the limitations imposed on women's autonomy by the assertion that all women possessed a "maternal instinct."[66]

In the eighteenth and nineteenth centuries, however, the mother-educator model can be said to have incorporated a substantial measure of pro-woman thought (putting mothers in charge of children's education instead of fathers was already a decisive promotion), and it incorporated a sociopolitical role assignment, not a strictly subservient domestic one. In the post-revolutionary early nineteenth century the model was widely touted by writers of both sexes, including Catholic monarchists, Protestants, and secular republicans. In fact there was virtual unanimity among republicans that the "education" of women, both in the sense of character formation and formal instruction, must become a central concern of secular French society and the nation, precisely *because* of women's cultural importance and influence, which must not be left to manipulation and exploitation by the Church.

Partisans of the mother-educator model exhorted women to exert their power and influence over every member of the next generation. This was certainly an advance on the notion of the "white goose," the young woman shaped solely for love – and man's enchantment. Moreover, in the revolutionary context, it promised women a quasi-public role, as long as her power and influence was contained within the immediate family. In its feminist form, the mother-educator model proved to be very empowering for women; in its antifeminist form, however, it did not sustain any promise of a woman's existence as an autonomous being, or as an independent political or social actor outside the family.

Some advocates of women's emancipation would ultimately argue that women's motherliness and educational role *should* be turned outward toward educating and reshaping the entire society, to the development of a republican woman – as distinct from the mother-educator. In 1856, the redoubtable Jenny P. d'Héricourt argued that "All social vices are the product of feminine influence, from which it is impossible to escape.

For a study of gender messages in the school textbooks of the Third Republic, see the important articles and book of Linda L. Clark, especially *Schooling the Daughters of Marianne: Textbooks and the Socialization of Girls in Modern French Primary Schools* (Albany, NY: SUNY Press, 1984).

[66] Elisabeth Badinter, *L'Amour en plus: Histoire de l'amour maternel (XVIIe – XXe siecle)* (Paris: Flammarion, 1980); translated as *Mother Love, Myth and Reality: Motherhood in Modern History* (New York: Macmillan, 1981).

The sole remedy for healing these vices is to render women's influence as salutary as it [has been], generally speaking, pernicious, and for that woman must be given her place at the side of man in political life [*la cité*], in marriage, and at work."[67] Jenny d'Héricourt and many others recognized that French men's deliberate attempts (over several centuries) to exclude their powerful, influential women from *political authority* was not inadvertent; it constituted a fundamental problem in the development of French society and culture, one that historians of France, Europe and the West more generally can no longer sweep under the rug.

---

[67] Jenny P. d'Héricourt, "De l'Émancipation civile des femmes," *La Ragione*, n° 82 (10 May 1856), 60–64; quote, 63. See also her subsequent article, "Le Parce Que de l'émancipation civile des femmes, " *La Ragione*, n° 84 (24 May 1856), 86–90 [Ed.: italic emphasis is in the text].

CHAPTER 2

Assessing the Problem of Women and Political Authority in French History

When Edith Cresson was appointed prime minister of France in May 1992 by President François Mitterrand, a new era seemed to have opened in French political life. No society in the Western world had declaimed so insistently about women's power and influence, yet no nation-state proved so reluctant to allow women access to political rights, much less to positions of political authority (that is to say, to power in its most formal sense of governance), or to support them in its exercise. The French case offers a fascinating study of the historical construction of a seeming incompatibility of women and politics that stubbornly continues to inform political life under the Fifth Republic, to the point where the very terms *la femme politique* or *les femmes politiques* (to cite the title of Laure Adler's 1993 book) still seemed awash in contradictions.[1] France, like Britain, was "a state riddled by resistance to political women."[2] Only with the feminist campaign for parity in the 1990s, and Segolene Royal's nearly successful campaign for president of the Republic in 2007–2008, has this notion been frontally challenged. It has not been laid to rest.

The standard story usually opens with the issue of woman suffrage, which was placed on the agenda in 1789 and enacted only in 1944. Typically, the first question that comes to mind – at least in the English-speaking world – is "why did it take so long for women in France to obtain the vote?" In the Francophone world, and among English-speaking political theorists as well, recent discussion has been framed in terms of the concepts of power (*pouvoir*), equality (*égalité*), or democracy (*démocratie*). Although the question is well-intentioned and these prevailing concepts have multiple connotations, they deflect our attention from the specific problem manifested in the historical record. Attempts to exclude women

---

[1] Laure Adler, *Les Femmes politiques* (Paris: Seuil, 1993).
[2] The expression is from Margot C. Finn's review of Brian Harrison's *Prudent Revolutionaries* in the *Journal of Modern History*, 63:3 (September 1991), 571.

from political authority in France did not begin with the "Declaration of the Rights of Man" or the "universal subject" or the advent of "democracy" or even with the closing of the revolutionary women's clubs by the Jacobins in 1793; they stem from a far more venerable tradition. The vote is only one aspect of a far deeper, centuries-old French male anxiety about women's wielding of political authority.

This chapter surveys evidence that encompasses five centuries of explicit efforts to preserve the exercise of political authority for men. Here I deliberately shift the emphasis from the abstract concepts of power and democracy to the more concrete notion of political authority. I thereby seek to insist on the importance of the politics of gender for understanding the political, intellectual, and cultural history of France – and francophone Europe – over the *longue durée* by documenting the extent to which concerns about gender became embedded at the very core of French notions about governance and rule, thus building on and supplementing Sarah Hanley's insistence on the centrality of gender and "gender contraries" in the construction of the French state.[3]

The notions of "power" and "influence" (examined in Chapter 1) are not synonymous with political authority. Indeed, the structural reality that underlay the continuing French preoccupation with women's influence and power in culture was the formal exclusion of women from affairs of state and their severe legal subordination in marriage. It is impossible to properly appreciate the intensity of the later debate on the woman question in nineteenth- and twentieth-century France, during its experiments with democratic forms of government, without some historical understanding of how women's status in French civil and political law came to be so disadvantageous. One cannot grasp the extent of women's

---

[3] For an important reinterpretation of French state construction highlighting the role of "gender contraries," see Sarah Hanley, "Family and State in Early Modern France: The Marriage Pact," in *Connecting Spheres: Women in the Western World, 1500 to the Present,* ed. Marilyn J. Boxer & Jean Quataert (New York: Oxford University Press, 1987), pp. 53–63; "Engendering the State: Family Formation and State Building in Early Modern France," *French Historical Studies,* 16:1 (Spring 1989), 4–27; "Social Sites of Political Practice in France: Lawsuits, Civil Rights, and the Separation of Power in Domestic and State Government, 1500–1800," *American Historical Review,* 102:1 (February 1997), 27–52; "'The Jurisprudence of the Arrêts': Marital Union, Civil Society, and State Formation in France, 1550–1650," *Law and History Review,* 21:1 (Spring 2003), 1–40; and "The Family, the State, and the Law in Seventeenth- and Eighteenth-Century France: The Political Ideology of Male Right versus an Early Theory of Natural Rights," *Journal of Modern History,* 78:2 (June 2006), 289–332. See also her article on the Salic Law in the *Encyclopédie politique et historique des femmes,* ed. Christine Fauré (Paris: Presses Universitaires de France, 1997, pp. 11–30; 2nd ed., revue et corrigée, 1997; English edition, London: Routledge, 2000) and Hanley's introduction to *Les Droits des femmes et la loi Salique* (Paris: Indigo & côté-femmes, 1994), pp. 7–18.

subordination in those laws without some knowledge of the prior sequence of political events, and in particular the immediate context for the theoretical arguments that led to their enactment. First, we will consider the better-known consequences of the revolutionary years for women, then examine some of the earlier, underlying historical conditioning factors.

The Subordination of Wives to Husbandly Authority in the French Civil Code (1804)

Of fundamental importance for the post-revolutionary period were the new, man-made, secular laws that governed marriage and the family with virtually no changes from 1804 until the reforms of 1938 and 1965. The legal status of married women in French law from the early nineteenth to the mid-twentieth century was no longer regulated by the Church but by the Napoleonic Code of 1804.[4] In these new laws, adult women

---

[4] The 1804 Civil Code is available in many editions. The laws regulating marriage and its contingent property relationships are located in Book I, Title V: "On Marriage," especially in chapter 6 (Arts. 212–226; the section read aloud at the civil marriage ceremony), and in Book III: "Of Marriage Contracts and of the Respective Rights of Husband and Wife." The standard English translation of the Code for the period under consideration here is Henry Cachard, *The French Civil Code, with the Various Amendments Thereto, as in Force on March 15, 1895* (London: Stevens and Sons, Ltd., 1895). A revised edition of Cachard's translation appeared in 1930. A helpful bibliography on various matters covered in the Code prior to 1930 can be found in *Guide to the Law and Legal Literature of France*, prepared for the Library of Congress by George Wilfred Stumberg (Washington, 1931). Those who wish to explore the Code, its construction, and its application in greater detail will, of course, consult *Discussions du Code Civil dans le Conseil d'Etat, précédées des articles correspondants du texte et du projet*, ed. Michel-Louis-Étienne Regnaud de Saint-Jean d'Angely, L Jouanneau, C Jouanneau, Solon Jouanneau, and Jean-Baptiste Delaporte, 3 vols. (Paris: Demonville, 1805–1808); Jacques de Maleville, *Analyse raisonnée de la discussion du Code civil au Conseil d'État*. 4 vols. 3rd ed. (Paris, 1822), and Victor-Alexis-Désiré Dalloz, *Jurisprudence générale: Répértoire méthodique et alphabétique de législation, de doctrine et de jurisprudence*. New ed., 44 vols. (Paris, 1845–1873) and its *Supplément*, 19 vols. (1887–1897).

An authoritative older historical overview of the development of French matrimonial law for the pre-1914 period is Charles Lefebvre, *Histoire du droit matrimonial français*, 3 vols. in 5 (Paris: L. Larose & L. Tenin, 1906–1923), esp. vol. 3: *Le droit des gens mariés* (1908). Lefebvre, a professor of matrimonial law at the Paris Law Faculty, was an authority on pre-Revolutionary customary law. He was an outspoken critic of separate property regimes, including the dowry (derived from Roman Law), and a staunch partisan of the "true" community property regime in marriage, which he believed to represent a "more French" concept of marriage as an association of equals. He criticized the impact of Roman law for adversely affecting the emergence of a more equitable marriage law in France. Lefebvre's analysis is also available in a more condensed form, as a series of lectures delivered to American students in 1919, in *La Famille en France, dans le droit et dans les moeurs* (Paris: M. Giard, 1920). Other useful accounts for this period include Jules Basdevant, *Des Rapports de l'église et de l'état dans la législation du mariage du Concile de Trente au Code civil*, thèse, Faculté de Droit, Université de Paris (Paris: Société de Recueil général des lois et des arrêts et du Journal du Palais, 1900); Paul Viollet, *Histoire du droit civil français* (Paris: L. Larose & L. Tenin, 1905; reissued 1966, Aalen: Scientica-Verlag); and Julien Bonnecase, *La Philosophie du Code Napoléon appliquée au droit de*

irrespective of social class were first divided into two groups, the married and the unmarried. Married women were treated as a class, distinct from and subordinate to the class of men, and every member of this class of women was subordinated to what the French called *puissance du mari*, or the power (I prefer to translate *puissance* as "authority") of the husband. In what follows we will be discussing primarily the subordinate situation of women in marriage. But first the new legal situation of single women must be briefly presented.

In 1791 the revolutionary government had granted single adult women, like sons (both from age 25), full exercise of property rights and a limited number of other civil rights. But because the lawmakers established a sharp separation at that time between *civil* (property) rights and *civic* (political) rights, even these single women were denied political rights (these being treated as *offices viriles* in the old Roman legal sense). This situation was confirmed following the establishment of universal manhood suffrage in 1848.[5] Procedurally, however, these civil rights were more difficult to exercise than it might appear. In order to engage either in property transactions or court actions, single adult women (including widows) had repeatedly to provide up-to-date evidence, certified by the police (or their informal precinct agents, the concierges, who kept tabs on the tenants in each apartment building), that they were not married (and not, therefore, under *puissance du mari*). This could be an infuriating and humiliating process as the labor leader and feminist Jeanne Bouvier found out, when she tried to get a loan against an earlier investment she had made: the credit agent insisted on seeing a certificate of singleness from her concierge to prove that she was unmarried [*célibataire*] and therefore empowered as a

famille; ses destinées dans le droit civil contemporain, 2nd ed., rev. and augmented (Paris: E. de Boccard, 1928).

A good shorter treatment in French of women's status in the Civil Code is Louis Delzons, "Les Lois des femmes," *Revue des Deux Mondes* (15 November 1906), 402–436, and Delzons, *La Famille française et son évolution* (Paris: A. Colin, 1913). For a brief survey in English, see H.D. Lewis, "The Legal Status of Women in Nineteenth-Century France," *Journal of European Studies*, 10:3 (September 1980), 178–188.

[5] Jean Portemer, "Le Statut de la femme en France, depuis la réformation des coutumes jusqu'à la rédaction du Code civil," in *Recueils de la Société Jean Bodin*, vol. 12 (1959), p. 453, notes the exceptionality of young independent single women in France before the eighteenth century. Such women, he notes, were not covered by existing law because ordinarily most were either married off or placed in convents before the age of 25. The civil (but not civic or political) empowerment of single women in 1791 is ably discussed by Elisabeth Guibert-Sledziewski, "Naissance de la femme civile," *La Pensée*, n° 238 (March–April 1984), 34–48; and "La Femme: objet de la Révolution," *Annales historiques de la Révolution française*, n° 267 (January–March 1987), 1–16.

single woman to engage in such a financial transaction.[6] This was but one documented case that has come down to us.

In drafting the 1804 Code, male jurists had deliberately enshrined male authority in marriage over the persons and property of wives and children. The nineteenth-century French model of the family as both a political and social institution was conjugal (not multigenerational), hierarchical, and authoritarian; it prescribed male dominance and female dependence in the name of the "laws of nature." It invested all husbands with what can only be called modestly modified patriarchal powers: the notorious Article 213 of the Code prescribed that men owed protection to wives in exchange for their obedience.[7] Article 214 stipulated that a wife had to live

---

[6] See Jeanne Bouvier, "Comment je suis devenue féministe" in *Mes Mémoires: Une syndicaliste féministe, 1876–1935*, ed. Daniel Armogathe with Maïté Albistur (Paris: Maspero, 1983), p. 244.

[7] This was enshrined in Article 213 of the Civil Code: "A husband owes protection to his wife; a wife obedience to her husband." See Lefebvre, *La Famille en France*, chapters 5–6. See also the following works by historians: Robert Mandrou, *Introduction à la France moderne: essai de psychologie historique* (Paris, 1961); François Lebrun, *La Vie conjugale sous l'Ancien régime* (Paris: A. Colin, 1975); and Jean-Louis Flandrin, *Families in Former Times: Kinship, Household and Sexuality* (Cambridge, UK: Cambridge University Press, 1979; orig. publ. in French, 1976).

In French usage, the term "patriarchal" generally refers to the powers of the multigenerational households (stem families) headed by the eldest male; this usage was confirmed by Frédéric Le Play and his school of reformers in the 1860s and 1870s (see the discussion in Chapter 7 in this volume). By "modified patriarchal powers," I mean here the authority invested in the husband in the conjugal family unit, sometimes consisting only of spouses and children, though this was still sometimes enlarged to include domestic servants and single related dependents. It was this *puissance maritale* and *puissance paternelle* applied to the conjugal family form that was reinforced by royal legislation extending the powers of the husband/father over wife and children during the seventeenth and eighteenth centuries. It is important to recognize that *puissance paternelle* did not adhere exclusively to males; in the absence of the husband/father, *puissance paternelle* could be officially vested in the wife/mother. See Lefebvre, *La Famille en France*, chapter 8. The English language notion of "deputy husband" nicely captures this distinction.

On the successful institutionalization of male legal authority in the marital family in early modern France, see Pierre Petot & André Vandenbossche, "Le Statut de la femme dans les pays coutumiers français du XIIIe au XVIIe siècle," *Recueils, Société Jean Bodin*, vol. 12 (1959), pp. 243–254, esp. p. 244; Paul Ourliac, "L'Évolution de la condition de la femme en droit français," *Annales de la Faculté de droit de Toulouse*, 14 (1966), 43–71; and the testimony of Mandrou, *France moderne*, pp. 112–21, and Lebrun, *Vie conjugale*, pp. 78–84. For custom and the accompanying religious prescriptions, see Flandrin, *Families in Former Times*, pp. 118–129. See also James F. Traer, *Marriage and the Family in Eighteenth-Century France* (Ithaca, NY: Cornell University Press, 1980). On women's issues generally, see the still unsurpassed study of Léon Abensour, *La Femme et le féminisme avant la Révolution* (Paris: E. Leroux, 1923; reprinted 1977).

For comparison with the Anglo-American tradition, see Ruth H. Bloch, "Untangling the Roots of Modern Sex Roles: A Survey of Four Centuries of Change," *Signs: Journal of Women in Culture and Society*, 4:2 (Winter 1978), 236–252; and Mary Beth Norton, "The Evolution of White Women's Experience," *American Historical Review*, 89:3 (June 1984), 593–619. Norton provides an excellent discussion of British political theory in her book *Founding Mothers and Fathers: Gendered Power and the Forming of American Society* (New York: Knopf, 1996). See also Ruth H. Bloch, *Gender and Morality in Anglo-American Culture 1650–1800* (Berkeley & Los Angeles: University of California Press, 2003).

with her husband, and in return, he would supply her needs "according to his means and condition."

Most French couples married under the legal regime of community of property between husbands and wives, with husbands formally in charge of administering or disposing of any assets that came to the couple. This was the normative marital regime, especially for those who embarked upon marriage with few or no assets. But it was not exclusively a regime for the poor. Under the community regime as constructed by the French, these married women were, like their English counterparts under *couverture*, "civilly dead," sharing this dubious distinction with minors, criminals, and the insane. Needless to say, wives could suffer grievously from abuses of male authority under this construction of the community property system.[8]

In the newly codified law, there were, however, two other marital property regimes that could be – and often were – established by marriage contract: separation of property and the dowry regime. Propertied families with daughters generally opted for one or the other. Couverture did not apply here.

Before the revolution, the dowry regime had been the prevailing practice in the Midi, the provinces of southern France where multigenerational families were more the norm than further north. The dowry regime was particularly favored by wealthy families concerned about greedy and

---

[8] In contrast, recent scholarship in English and American law reveals that the English law of *couverture*, dating from the thirteenth century, was slowly being eroded from the late sixteenth century on both by practice and statute in favor of limited vesting of property rights for married women. The American colonies experienced considerable erosion during the later eighteenth century. See the excellent analyses by Richard H. Chused, "Married Women's Property Law, 1800–1850," *Georgetown Law Journal*, 7:5 (June 1983), 1359–1425, esp. 1384–1397, and Mary Lynn Salmon, *Women and the Law of Property in Early America* (Chapel Hill: University of North Carolina Press, 1986).

For the British case, see Susan Staves, *Married Women's Separate Property in England, 1660–1833* (Cambridge, MA: Harvard University Press, 1990). For changes in the British law from 1837 on, and the important reforms of 1870 and 1882, see Erna Reiss, *Rights and Duties of Englishwomen: A Study in Law and Public Opinion* (Manchester, UK: Sherratt & Hughes, 1934), and Lee Holcombe, *Wives and Property: Reform of the Married Women's Property Law in Nineteenth-Century England* (Toronto: University of Toronto Press, 1982). The attack on *couverture* in England was led by Barbara Leigh Smith (Bodichon), who published *A Brief Summary in Plain Language of the Most Important Laws Concerning Women, Together with a Few Observations Thereon* (1854), and Lord Brougham, a reforming peer who introduced the first Married Women's Property Bill in the House of Lords in 1857. See Caroline Cornwallis, "The Property of Married Women," *Westminster Review*, 66 (October 1856), 331–360, which also reprints the women's petition to Parliament of March 1856 and discusses the Law Amendment Society's report. Also of interest are the articles by Susan Moller Okin, "Patriarchy and Married Women's Property in England: Questions on Some Current Views," *Eighteenth-Century Studies*, 17:2 (Winter 1983–1984), 121–138, and Amy Louise Erickson, "Possession – and the Other One-Tenth of the Law: Assessing Women's Ownership and Economic Roles in Early Modern England," *Women's History Review*, 16:3 (July 2007), 369–385.

unethical financial dealings by their daughters' husbands, and anxious to keep landed assets in their own families.[9] Dowries generally consisted of inalienable income-producing property (most often land producing agricultural revenues) vested in the wife; Article 1540 of the Civil Code stipulated that dowry was "the property that the wife brought to the husband in order to support the charges of the marriage." There seemed to be some contradiction between this provision and Article 214 of the new Code, which stipulated that husbands were expected to supply wives' needs. Women did retain some control over property under this dowry regime. Though administered by the husband, for instance, dowry property could never be sold or mortgaged; the intent was to vest management in the husband and to pass the property on intact to the couple's children. Wives whose husbands misadministered their dowries had the right to sue in court for *séparation de biens* and for restoration of their dowries (Article 1563). Moreover, women married under this regime could control other property vested in their name as *biens paraphernaux*, or peripheral goods (see Article 1547ff.), which could provide them with some degree of financial (and therefore, personal) independence.[10]

The legal regime of separate property, the second option available through a marriage contract, did allow married women to own and manage their own property and revenues, both those brought to the marriage and those acquired afterward, outside marital control (Articles 1536–1539, 1449–1450). A wife was still subjected to certain legal restrictions on the sale or mortgaging of her properties (Article 217). Under this regime both spouses were obligated to contribute to the expenses of the marriage. This was the regime preferred by the families of women who were engaged in commerce or professional occupations in their own right. It would subsequently be proposed as a general solution for all married women by late nineteenth-century reformers such as Jeanne-E. Schmahl, no doubt influenced by the example of the Married Women's Property Laws that had recently been enacted in England and the United States. Legal separation of marital property (along with bed and board) by court order

---

[9] Civil Code, Title V, Chapter 3, Book 3, Arts. 1540–1581. For additional background, see A. Eyquem, *Le Régime dotal: son histoire, son évolution, et ses transformations au XIXe siècle* (Paris: Marchal & Billard, 1903).

[10] Jules Michelet insisted on the relative independence and influence French women acquired from the dowry regime, compared with English or German women, who were, "so to speak, . . . absorbed in the husband." See his *Woman/La Femme* (New York: Carleton, 1873; orig. publ. Paris: Hachette, 1859), pp. 16–17. Note also Edouard Chantpie's attack on the dowry in 1860, in the name of ensuring women's moral perfection; Chantpie, *La Figure féminine au XIXe siècle: l'esprit de la dot* (Paris: Amyot, 1861).

also provided a means of relative economic independence for unhappily married women in an age of indissoluble marriage.[11]

Civil divorce had been legalized in France during the Revolution and was maintained in the 1804 Code, but lawmakers abrogated it in 1816, under the Bourbon Restoration, in response to pressure from neo-traditionalist Catholics. Despite repeated demands and campaigns, French legislators resisted reestablishing civil divorce until 1884, and then approved it only on limited grounds.[12] Efforts to broaden the grounds for civil divorce would continue well into the twentieth century.

French commentators have long affirmed that the inferior position of Frenchwomen in the law was tempered by their superior status in *moeurs*, that is to say, their exercise of women's "indirect" influence. Expressions of this belief were pervasive, as we have indicated earlier.[13] The fact remains, nevertheless, that in nineteenth-century French civil law married women (with the exception of those who had opted for separate property regimes) were effectively a disenfranchised class, though less severely so than English wives, whose very legal persons were absorbed (prior to 1880) by those of their husbands.

Much has been written about the 1804 Civil Code and its treatment of married women, both by legal scholars and by advocates of revision.[14] What bears underscoring here is that the subordination of married women in the community property regime enshrined in the 1804 Code was neither accidental nor inadvertent. It was a direct consequence of a long power struggle between two male-dominated hierarchies – the Roman Catholic Church and the French Monarchy – for control of the institution of marriage itself, and for leverage over family heads and their dependents. The Code was, in effect, the culmination of a movement that began during the sixteenth century to bolster the legal authority of the individual male head of household and to attempt to exclude women from succession to landed property (and other transmissible forms of property) and the political rights that had been vested in it in feudal practice. In seventeenth-century France, husbands (not fathers, as claimed by Roland Mousnier) gained authority over the *person* as well as over the *property* of

---

[11] See Lefebvre, *La Famille en France*, chapter 6. Civil divorce, initiated during the Revolution and maintained by Napoléon, was outlawed in France from 1816 until 1884.

[12] On divorce see Roderick Phillips, *Putting Asunder: A History of Divorce in Western Society* (Cambridge, UK: Cambridge University Press, 1988), esp. chapters 5 and 11, and, for a differing view, Theresa McBride, "Public Authority and Private Lives: Divorce after the French Revolution," *French Historical Studies*, 17:3 (Spring 1992), 747–768.

[13] See Chapter 1 in this volume.   [14] See the works cited in n. 4 and n. 7.

wives.[15] Husbands were becoming legally armed to displace clan or house-hold chieftains as the agents of the state, subject also to the state's control. From the standpoint of women's legal history, the Napoleonic Code can be viewed as the capstone to a process of transformative erosion in medieval women's legal status that was tightly intertwined with the efforts of king and the *parlements* to rationalize French society, to favor the male-headed conjugal family at the expense of kinship ties by reinforcing husbandly (and, following from that, paternal) authority, to constrain antisocial behavior by "dependent" individuals and, above all, to confirm the authority of the French state over men and their dependents even as it assured their allegiance.[16] In her provocative article, "Engendering the State," the historian Sarah Hanley has baptized this "the family-state compact." The reality of the so-called rise of "bourgeois individualism," which the compact fostered, was that it was deliberately exclusive to men.[17]

An earlier generation of French legal historians downplayed, even as they acknowledged, the impact of these specific changes in women's status. The overall importance of secularizing the institution of marriage was clearly uppermost in their minds. The French legal scholar Pierre Petot argued in the 1950s that the renaissance of Roman law in sixteenth-century France had only the effect of reinforcing what was already a formal inequality of the sexes established in the interest of the male, even as the Catholic Church was making efforts to improve women's situation in marriage (notably through measures adopted in the interest of the bride and groom during the Council of Trent, according to which the presence of the priest alone and the consent of the parties to the marriage alone – not parental consent – sufficed to validate a marriage). Petot's colleague, Jean Portemer, insisted on the primacy of "family" interests and asserted therefore that this legislation was not unfavorable to women *as women*; indeed, in one article, he pointed out how incidental the measures con-cerning women were in the broader scheme of things, though in a more

[15] Contrary to Roland Mousnier's claims, in *La Famille, l'enfant, et l'éducation en France et en Grande-Bretagne du XVf au XVIIf siècle*, 3 vols. (Paris: Centre de documentation universitaire, 1975), vol. 1, pp. 120 and 149–156. Compare Portemer, "Statut de la femme en France," p. 454, and Lefebvre, *La Famille en France*, n. 4.

[16] That interest in reinforcing paternal authority, as well as marital authority, was significant in this period is suggested by the essay contest themes of 1799–1802 in the Institut National de France, second section. See Martin S. Staum, "Images of Paternal Power: Intellectuals and Social Change in the French National Institute," *Canadian Journal of History*, 17:3 (December 1982), 425–445.

[17] This point is also underscored by Michèle Bordeaux, "Droit et femmes seules: les pièges de la discrimination," in *Madame ou Mademoiselle? Itinéraires de la solitude féminine 18e - 20e siècle*, ed. Arlette Farge & Christiane Klapisch-Zuber (Paris: Arthaud-Montalba, 1984), pp. 19–57, esp. pp. 22–26. See also Hanley (n. 3).

extensive study he too underscored the extent to which changes in the laws (from the reformation of customs on) tended to confirm (and to rationalize) the power of husbands over wives.[18] Portemer's attitude can be placed in the camp of those who think restricting women's independence is "for their own good" and essential to family cohesion.

A new generation of feminist scholars of Western political and legal theory, inspired by the pioneering work of Sàrah Hanley and Eliane Viennot, challenges such perspectives, arguing that such developments were far from "incidental" or of secondary importance. They deny that these measures were for women's own good.[19] Indeed, they are uncovering abundant evidence that concern about controlling women was, in fact, on the minds of many men among the ruling classes (not all of whom could be considered *bourgeois*). Feminist historians are meanwhile rediscovering the variety of ways in which literate and articulate seventeenth- and eighteenth-century women, from Marie Le Jars de Gournay and Gabrielle Suchon to Olympe de Gouges and Fanny Raoul, challenged such initiatives. The issue of controlling women, and eliminating them from positions of authority, was addressed explicitly, though not always at great length, in the works of virtually every major figure (and many minor figures) in the development of Western political theory. For these male theorists and polemicists, redefining woman's "place" (and restating the case for their subordination to men) according to the dictates of "natural law," rather than on theological grounds, was a central rather than a

---

[18] See Pierre Petot, "La Famille en France sous l'ancien régime," *Sociologie comparée de la famille contemporaine* (Paris, 1955): 9–14; see also the two articles by Jean Portemer, "Statut de la femme en France" (n. 3), and Portemer, "La Femme dans la législation royale des deux derniers siècles de l'ancien régime," *Études d'histoire du droit privé, offertes à Pierre Petot* (Paris: Librairie générale de droit et de jurisprudence, 1959), 441–454. More recently, see Portemer, "Réflexions sur les pouvoirs de la femme selon le droit français au XVIIe siècle," *XVIIe siècle*, n° 144 (July–September 1984), 189–202.

For a thoroughly neo-traditionalist twentieth-century interpretation, see Jean Derruppé, "L'Évolution du droit français de la famille, du début du siècle à la guerre de 1939," in *Renouveau des idées sur la famille*, ed. Robert Prigent (Paris: Presses Universitaires de France, 1954), pp. 149–160. Derruppé argues (p. 149) that: "The legislator can . . . preserve the family from the disagregation that menaces it due to economic and social evolution."

[19] Of primary importance here is the recent two-volume magnum opus by Éliane Viennot, *La France, les femmes et le pouvoir*, vol. 1: *L'invention de la loi salique (Ve-XVIe siècle)* (Paris: Perrin, 2006) and vol. 2: *Les résistances de la société (XVIIe – XVIIIe siècle)* (Paris: Perrin, 2008) as well as the three volumes of articles published by SIEFAR (Publications de l'Université de Saint-Étienne), including *Revisiter la « querelle des femmes ». Discours sur l'égalité/inégalité des sexes, de 1400 à 1600*, ed. Armel Dubois-Nayt, Nicole Dufournaud, & Anne Paupert (2013); *Revisiter la « querelle des femmes ». Discours sur l'égalité/inégalité des sexes, de 1600 à 1750*, ed. Daniele Haase-Dubosc & Marie-Élisabeth Henneau (2013); and *Revisiter la « querelle des femmes ». Discours sur l'égalité/inégalité des sexes, de 1750 aux lendemains de la Révolution*, ed. Eliane Viennot, with Nicole Pellegrin (2012).

secondary preoccupation. In France, the works of such diverse seventeenth-century writers as Cardin Le Bret, author of *De la Souveraineté du Roy* (1632), and the legist Jean Domat, author of *Les Lois civiles dans leur ordre naturel* (1689–1694), offer support for this perspective.[20]

Unfortunately, the most significant recent English-language feminist critiques of western political theory have continued to focus on the development of contract theory in the British tradition, beginning with John Locke in the late seventeenth century; Rousseau, Hegel, and Marx offer the only Continental flavor in what is a dominantly Anglo-American pudding.[21] The evidence now emerging on the French case substantiates my initial suspicion that to begin the search for the determinant period in the modern politics of gender with Locke (or to focus on the public/private debate in British and American history since 1800, as others have done) is to take up the search in the wrong time and place. The experience of France in the early modern period demands a more extensive reanalysis by feminist scholars, as does its interaction with the British tradition.[22] In what follows, I will touch briefly on the highlights of the French theoretical and practical justifications for women's subordinate position in the

[20] Le Bret (Cardin), sieur de Vély, *De la Souveraineté du Roy* (Paris, 1632); Jean Domat, *Les Lois civiles dans leur ordre naturel -- le droit public et legum delectus*, 3 vols. (Paris, 1689–1694). On these political writers, see Christine Fauré, *La Démocratie sans les femmes: Essai sur le libéralisme en France* (Paris: Presses Universitaires de France, 1985). An English translation of this important study, *Democracy Without the Women*, was published in 1991 by Indiana University Press. See also the various articles, "Femme," in Diderot's *Encyclopédie*, vol. 6 (Paris, 1756).

[21] I am thinking particularly of the nonetheless valuable contributions of Susan Moller Okin, *Women in Western Political Thought* (Princeton, NJ: Princeton University Press, 1979); the essays in *The Sexism of Social and Political Theory*, ed. Lorenne M. G. Clark & Lynda Lange (Toronto: University of Toronto Press, 1979); Jean Bethke Elshtain, *Public Man, Private Woman: Women in Social and Political Thought* (Princeton, NJ: Princeton University Press, 1981); Linda J. Nicholson, *Gender and History* (New York: Columbia University Press, 1986); and Carole Pateman, *The Sexual Contract* (Stanford, CA: Stanford University Press, 1988).

Also important (though uneven for my purposes) are the essays of Elizabeth Fox-Genovese, including "Property and Patriarchy in Classical Bourgeois Political Theory," *Radical History Review*, 4:2–3 (Spring-Summer 1977), 36–59, and "The Ideological Bases of Domestic Economy: The Representation of Women and the Family in the Age of Expansion," in Elizabeth Fox-Genovese & Eugene Genovese, *Fruits of Merchant Capital* (New York: Oxford University Press, 1983), pp. 299–336 (notes, pp. 442–447).

[22] In English, only the studies of Nannerl O. Keohane, *Philosophy and the State in France: The Renaissance to the Enlightenment* (Princeton, NJ: Princeton University Press, 1980) and Carolyn C. Lougee, *Le Paradis des femmes: Women, Salons, and Social Stratification in Seventeenth-Century France* (Princeton, NJ: Princeton University Press, 1976) focus specifically on the French case, though not on the legal developments we are discussing here. Lougee does not refer to sixteenth-century developments at all. An important corrective is Fauré, *Démocratie sans les femmes*, cited in n. 20. See also the suggestive essays by historians Marilyn J. Boxer & Jean H. Quataert, "Women in the Age of Religious Upheaval and Political Centralization," in *Connecting Spheres: Women in the Western World*, cited in n. 3.

laws of marriage and in relation to the state from the late sixteenth century through 1848, in order to demonstrate the lines of continuity.

Disputing Female Rule, or "Gynecocracy," in Sixteenth- and Seventeenth-Century Europe

The learned Henri Corneille Agrippa de Nettesheim declared Woman queen of the universe with the world God created as her palace. Woman was superior to man, he claimed, because she was God's penultimate creation.[23] Other men, and especially elite men in France, did not envision woman's place that way. Far from it. A particularly consequential theoretical contribution to French thinking about the political and legal status of women in early modern times was articulated in 1577 by the political philosopher Jean Bodin (1530–1596). Bodin advocated order and state supremacy to counter the impending anarchy of his admittedly turbulent era. In his *Six Livres de la République* [Six Books of the Republic], Bodin invoked the combined authority of Aristotle, Biblical scripture, and the old Roman law, with its insistence on public and private spheres, to set forth explicitly what he believed to be the optimal arrangement for the sexes in the family and in society – the subordination of women and their eviction from positions of political authority.[24]

It is of great consequence for the future of women in political life that Bodin framed his arguments amidst an ongoing controversy in the European world over monarchical rule and succession by women. During the previous hundred years many women had ruled in various kingdoms and duchies in Europe, including Isabella of Castille, who co-ruled the Kingdom of Spain with her husband Ferdinand of Aragon, Isabella's daughter Joanna who inherited the kingdom of Castille, and Margaret of Austria who served several terms as regent of the Netherlands in the early sixteenth century. But in 1553, controversy over women's rule would escalate when the Catholic Mary Tudor, then married to Phillip II of Spain, succeeded her Protestant father Henry VIII and her brother Edward VI as Mary I,

---

[23] Henri Corneille Agrippa de Nettesheim, *Sur la noblesse et l'excellence du sexe féminin, de sa prééminence sur l'autre sexe* (1537). Préface de Marie-Josèphe Dhavernas (Paris: côté-femmes éditions, 1990), pp. 40–41.

[24] Jean Bodin, *Les Six Livres de la République* (Paris, 1577). Available in English as *Six Books of the Commonwealth*, abridged and translated by M. J. Tooley (New York: Macmillan, 1955). Constance Jordan reports that Bodin's work did not appear in English translation until 1606, after the death of Elizabeth I; see her article, "Women's Rule in Sixteenth-Century British Political Thought," *Renaissance Quarterly*, 40:3 (Autumn 1987), 421–451.

queen of England. Her vicious persecutions of English Protestants provoked the Scottish Calvinist reformer John Knox (c. 1514–1572) to publish
(anonymously, in Geneva, in 1558, where he had recently been made a
citizen) his *First Blast of the Trumpet against the Monstrous Regiment of
Women*, in which he raged venomously and vindictively for some forty-five
pages against female rule, objecting that it was prohibited by God and the
Bible as well as by Nature.[25] "To promote a woman to bear rule, superiority, dominion or empire above any realm, nation or city is repugnant to
nature, contumely [insulting] to God, a thing most contrarious to His
revealed will and approved ordinance, and finally it is the subversion of
good order, of all equity and justice." He cited every ancient Biblical and
Church antifeminist authority known to him (from Genesis to St. Paul,
Tertullian and Chrystostom) in support his claims of women's inferiority
to men and the impossibility of their rule, and he branded Mary I as
Jezebel and the instrument of Satan. What was more, he concluded with a
call to arms, urging the male nobility to overthrow such a "monster." As
Knox's biographer Rosalind K. Marshall remarks, this last claim was most
"startlingly controversial and Knox knew it." The impact of this final
argument in European court and religious circles cannot be overestimated;
even John Calvin and Martin Luther had not gone that far; a call for rising
up against one's prince was revolutionary, but targeting the sex of the
"prince" was even more so. Indeed, Knox's Protestant associates were
scandalized by his audacity and intemperance, and Mary I promptly
"issued a proclamation against the importing of heretical and seditious
books into England."[26]

Knox's "Blast" upset not only the ailing Mary Tudor and her immediate
successor, Elizabeth I, but also the French-born and very well-connected
Marie de Guise, who had long acted as Queen Regent for her now-
adolescent daughter Mary, Queen of Scots, who was now also queen
consort of France, having just married (24 April 1558) the French dauphin
François II. Thus, Knox's "Blast" would have immediate consequences for
the French kingdom. Following the untimely death of the dauphin and the
"deposition" of her French mother as regent, the young, very Catholic, and
very Frenchified Mary returned to Scotland to claim her throne.

---

[25] John Knox, *The First Blast of the Trumpet Against the Monstrous Regiment of Women* (Geneva, 1558).
I have consulted the 1895 English edition, edited by Constable & Co., London. Another
authoritative edition can be consulted in *The Political Writings of John Knox: The First Blast of the
Trumpet ... and Other Selected Works* (Washington, DC: Folger Shakespeare Library, & London:
Associated University Presses, 1985).

[26] Rosalind K. Marshall, *John Knox* (Edinburgh: Birlinn Ltd., 2008; 2013), pp. 110, 115.

Immediately after her arrival in mid-August 1560 and her royal entry to Edinburgh on 2 September, she summoned John Knox (who had also returned to Scotland, where he had been named minister of the prominent and now Protestant St. Giles Church) to her palace where she confronted him directly over his "blast."[27] The controversy over rule by women had not only become inextricably entangled in Protestant–Catholic contestation but also a disruptive element in Franco–English–Scottish foreign relations.

By the time Jean Bodin published his *Six Books* in 1577, controversy over the reign of queens had not abated. Elizabeth I had firmly installed her rule in England, and her cousin Mary Queen of Scots had become her political prisoner (although Mary's execution did not take place until 1587).[28] In France, Catherine de Médicis, the widow of Henri II, ruled as queen mother, periodically acting as regent for her remaining sons. She was implicated in the massacre of French Protestant leaders on St. Barthelemy's Day in 1572. What was more, the Infanta Isabella (born 1566), daughter of Philip II of Spain and his third wife, Elisabeth de Valois (this Elisabeth was the daughter of Henri II and Catherine de Médicis), had also emerged as a potential claimant for the French throne, should none of Catherine and Henri II's sons survive.[29] To those who opposed female rule, the "female threat" seemed to run on unabated. Not surprisingly, then, there is a remarkable resemblance and continuity in anxiety level and tone from the arguments against female rule by John Knox in 1558 to Jean Bodin's 1577 aggressive arguments for male rule, and the subsequent restatement of the case in the tract entitled *Patriarchia* by the British aristocrat Sir Robert Filmer, which in turn would stimulate John Locke's response in his celebrated *Second Treatise*.[30]

[27] See Marshall, *John Knox*, chapter 8, for a lively account of this confrontation. See also Amanda Shephard, *Gender and Authority in Sixteen-Century England: The Knox Debate* (Keele, Staffordshire: Ryburn Publishers, 1994), and the exhibition catalog for *Mary, Queen of Scots 'In my end is my beginning'* (Edinburgh: National Museum of Scotland, 2013), with text by Rosalind K. Marshall.

[28] A manuscript (in two copies), now in the British Library, entitled "A Dutifull Defense of the Lawful Regiment of Women" by Lord Henry Howard, refutes John Knox's "Blast." The author indicated that in 1577 a councilor of Elizabeth I had asked him to compose such a counterargument; it was actually written c. 1590 but never published. See Amanda Shephard, "Henry Howard and the Lawful Regiment of Women," *History of Political Thought*, 12:4 (Winter 1991), 589–603.

[29] Thanks to Sarah Hanley for the information on the Infanta Isabella; see her introduction to *Les Droits des femmes et la loi Salique*, cited in n. 3.

[30] Bodin's thought has been established as having a major influence on Sir Robert Filmer, whose much-discussed *Patriarcha* (drafted and privately circulated in the 1630s; published 1680) spurred John Locke to write the first of his two pathbreaking treatises on civil government (1698). On the Bodin–Locke connection, see Peter Laslett's introductions to Filmer and Locke, in *Patriarcha and Other Political Works of Sir Robert Filmer* (Oxford: Oxford University Press, 1949), pp. 27–28, and

Bodin would postulate that the French royal succession should proceed neither by election nor via the female line, but by strict hereditary succession in the male line. "Gynecocracy," or female rule, he asserted, was "directly contrary to the laws of nature as well as to the laws of God."[31] He argued aggressively that:

> Nature has endowed men with strength, foresight, pugnacity, authority, but has deprived women of these qualities. Moreover the law of God explicitly enjoins that the woman should be subject, not only in matters concerning law and government, but within each particular family. The most terrible of maledictions uttered against the enemy was that they might have women to rule over them. Even the civil law forbids to women all charges and offices proper to men, such as judging, pleading, and such-like acts. This is not only because of their lack of prudence, but also because vigorous action is contrary to the sex, and to the natural modesty and reserve of women.

John Locke, *Two Treatises of Government; A Critical Edition with Introduction and Apparatus Criticus* by Peter Laslett, ed. (2nd ed., London: Cambridge University Press, 1967). Useful reassessments of Bodin's position on the woman question include Preston King, "Bodin on Female Rule," in appendix to King, *The Ideology of Order: A Comparative Analysis of Jean Bodin and Thomas Hobbes* (New York: Barnes & Noble, 1974), 289–290, and Pierre-Louis Vaillancourt, "Bodin et le pouvoir politique des femmes," in *Jean Bodin: Actes du Colloque interdisciplinaire d'Angers, 24 au 27 Mai 1984*, 2 vols. (Angers: Presses de l'Université d'Angers, 1985), vol. 1, pp. 63–74. See also Ginevra Conti Odorisio, *La Famille et l'État dans la République de Jean Bodin* (Paris: L'Harmattan, 2007; translated from Italian).

The conduct of Catherine de Médicis as regent and queen mother, particularly the controversy over her alleged responsibility for the 1572 St. Bartholomew's Day Massacre, looms large as background for Bodin's views. Two other important contributions to the debate were the anonymous tract, attributed to the printer Henri Estienne and others, *Discours merveilleux de la vie, actions et déportements de Cathérine de Médicis, Royne Mère* (1578), and David Chambers, "Discours de la succession des femmes aux possessions de leurs parens, & aux publics gouvernemens," in *Histoire abbregée de tous les Roys de France, Angleterre et Ecosse, mise en ordre par forme d'Harmonie* (Paris, 1579).

For a scholarly assessment of the demonization of the queen mother in subsequent historical writing, see Nicola Mary Sutherland, "Catherine de Medici: The Legend of the Wicked Italian Queen," in her volume, *Princes, Politics and Religion, 1547–1589* (London: Hambledon Press, 1984), pp. 237–248; and Elaine Kruse, "The Blood-Stained Hands of Catherine de Médicis," in *Political Rhetoric, Power, and Renaissance Women*, ed. Carole Levin & Patricia Sullivan (Albany: SUNY Press, 1995), pp. 139–155. More recent studies include Leonie Frieda, *Catherine de Medici: Renaissance Queen of France* (London: Weidenfeld & Nicolson, 2003) and Thierry Wanegffelen, *Catherine de Médicis: Le pouvoir au féminin* (Paris: Payot, 2005). Most recently, see the balanced reevaluation of Catherine de Médicis as queen mother and regent by Kathleen Wellman in *Queens and Mistresses of Renaissance France* (New Haven: Yale University Press, 2013), pp. 225–273.

[31] Bodin, *Six Books*, p. 203. The final sentence reads in French: "La Loy a défendu à la femme toutes les charges et offices propres aux hommes comme de juger, postuler – non pas seulement par faute de prudence – mais d'autant que les actions viriles sont contraires au sexe et à la pudeur et pudicité féminines." From Jean Bodin, *Six Livres de la République* (1576), VI, 5, p. 718. Preston King, *Ideology of Order*, p. 290, thus summed up Bodin's position: "Female rule offends male dignity."

Bodin's formulation encapsulated and restated an argument that would be reelaborated and reasserted in various forms, especially in France, for the next three hundred years. It could be summarized thus: Public business, that is, politics, is men's business. Women must be kept out of men's business, and under men's control for their own good. Men, of course, were asserted to be the sole arbiters of defining men's business as well as women's place. In the event that Biblical arguments proved insufficient, it seemed that the "laws of nature" could provide suitable cover for what were, in fact, the laws of men.

On 28 June 1593, in support of the succession of Henri de Navarre (following the demise of the last living son of Henri II and Catherine de Médicis), the Parlement of Paris confirmed as "public law" the principle of male right (as Sarah Hanley describes it), formally excluding women and their progeny from the succession, as a fundamental underpinning of the French monarchy.[32] Women could, nevertheless, continue to serve as regents, by virtue of their derivative status as mothers of kings, an exception that was repeatedly invoked by reforming commentators to insist on women's capacity to wear the crown in their own right – as well as to ground subsequent political claims based on the authority of motherhood.[33]

Although objections and counterarguments to Bodin's unequivocal stipulations were forthcoming from writers ranging from David Chambers

[32] Parlement de Paris, Edict of 28 June 1593. See Vaillancourt, "Bodin et le pouvoir politique," pp. 70–71, and Fauré, *Démocratie sans les femmes*, p. 176. On the Salic Law problem, see Paul-Marie Viollet, "Comment les femmes ont été exclues en France de la succession à la couronne," *Mémoires de l'Académie des inscriptions et belles-lettres*, 34: pt. 2 (1893), 125–178, and in his multivolume study, "Exclusion des femmes et de leur descendance," in his *Histoire des Institutions politiques et administratives de la France*, vol. 2 (Paris: L. Larose, 1898), pp. 55–86. I will discuss the immediate political importance of Viollet's work for late nineteenth-century feminists in my subsequent volume. More recently, see John Milton Potter, "The Development and Significance of the Salic Law of the French," *English Historical Review*, 52, n° 106 (April 1937), 235–253; and especially Ralph E. Giesey, "The Juristic Basis of Dynastic Right to the French Throne," *Transactions of the American Philosophical Society*, n.s. 51, pt. 5 (1961), esp. 11–12, 17–22. See also Laurent Theis, "Le Trône de France interdit aux femmes," *L'Histoire*, n° 160 (November 1992), 16–22, and Sarah Hanley, "Uneasy States: The Political Uses of Gender Contraries to Legitimate Male Right and Establish Female Exclusion from Government in Family and State, 1200–1800," paper presented at IFRWH Bielefeld conference, April 1993, as well as her introduction to *Les Droits des femmes et la loi Salique*.

[33] See, in particular, David Chambers, "Discours" (cited in n. 30); Marie Le Jars de Gournay, *Grief des Dames* (Paris, 1626; reprinted 1989); François Poullain de la Barre, *The Woman as Good as the Man; or the Equality of Both Sexes*, transl. by A. L. (1677), edited with an introduction by Gerald M. MacLean (Detroit: Wayne State University Press, 1988), p. 123, and Voltaire's articles, "Femme" and "Loi Salique," in his *Dictionnaire philosophique* (1764), in his *Oeuvres complètes* (Paris: chez Th. Desoer, 1817), vol. 14. Of course, Montesquieu's *Esprit des lois* also figures prominently in this debate.

(who defended women's rule in 1579) to the French *philosophe* Voltaire in the 1760s (who thought the so-called Salic Law exclusion of women was simply silly), such arguments found constant reinforcement during the seventeenth century by cumulative contributions in French and English legal and political theory, as well as in a broader public discourse on the woman question, known to history as the *querelle des femmes*.[34] In mid-eighteenth century France these arguments were reencapsulated in the works of such influential legal writers as the jurist Robert Pothier.

Today, the best-remembered political theorist of the eighteenth century is, of course, another citizen of Geneva – Jean-Jacques Rousseau – whose views on women's subordination and their influence (particularly in his enormously influential *Julie, or the New Heloise* and *Émile*, both published in the early 1760s) have been endlessly rehearsed by historians of women and political theorists alike and will not be repeated here.[35] But Rousseau

[34] For commentary, see P.-C. Timbal, "L'Esprit du droit privé au XVIIe siècle," *Dix-Septième Siècle Revue*, n°s 58–59 (1963), 30–39; Petot and Vandenbossche, "Statut de la femme," *passim*.

For analyses of the literature on the "*querelle des femmes*" see Gustave Fagniez, *La Femme et la société française dans la première moitié du XVIIe siècle* (Paris: Librairie universitaire J. Gamber, 1929); Gustave Reynier, *La Femme au XVIIe siècle, ses ennemis et ses défenseurs* (Paris: J. Tallandier, 1929); and more recently, the diverse approaches of Paulette Bascou-Bance, "La Condition des femmes en France et le progrès des idées féministes du XVIe au XVIIIe siècle," *L'Information historique*, 28:4 (September 1966), 139–144; Marc Angenot, *Les Champions des femmes: examen du discours sur la supériorité des femmes, 1400–1800* (Montreal: Presses de l'Université de Québec, 1977); Ian Maclean, *Woman Triumphant: Feminism in French Literature, 1610–1652* (Oxford, UK: Clarendon Press, 1977); Pierre Darmon, *Mythologie de la femme dans l'Ancienne France* (Paris: Éditions du Seuil, 1983). Important recent feminist reinterpretations bearing on the *querelle* include Constance Jordan, *Renaissance Feminism: Literary Texts and Political Models* (Ithaca, NY: Cornell University Press, 1990); Joan DeJean, *Tender Geographies: Women and the Origins of the Novel in France* (New York: Columbia University Press, 1991); and Erica Harth, *Cartesian Women: Versions and Subversions of Rational Discourse in the Old Regime* (Ithaca, NY: Cornell University Press, 1992).

[35] Recent interpretations include Victor G. Wexler, "Made for Man's Delight: Rousseau as Antifeminist," *American Historical Review*, 81:2 (April 1976), 266–291; Jean-Louis Lecercle, "La Femme selon Rousseau," in *Jean-Jacques Rousseau: Quatre Études*, ed. Jean Starobinski et al. (Neuchâtel: A la Baconnière; Paris: Payot, 1978); Susan Moller Okin, *Women in Western Political Thought* (Princeton, NJ: Princeton University Press, 1979), part 3; Maurice Bloch & Jean H. Bloch, "Women and the Dialectics of Nature in Eighteenth-Century French Thought," in *Nature, Culture, and Gender*, ed. Carol MacCormack & Marilyn Strathern (Cambridge, UK, & New York: Cambridge University Press, 1980); Nannerl O. Keohane, "'But for Her Sex . . .': The Domestication of Sophie," *Revue de l'Université d'Ottawa*, 49:3–4 (1980), 390–400; Joel Schwartz, *The Sexual Politics of Jean-Jacques Rousseau* (Chicago: University of Chicago Press, 1984); Barbara Corrado Pope, "The Influence of Rousseau's Ideology of Domesticity," in *Connecting Spheres*, ed. Boxer & Quataert, pp. 136–145; and Paul Thomas, "Jean-Jacques Rousseau, Sexist?," *Feminist Studies*, 17:2 (Summer 1991), 195–217. On women readers' responses to Rousseau, see Mary Seidman Trouille, *Sexual Politics in the Enlightenment: Women Writers Read Rousseau* (Albany: SUNY Press, 1997). See also Penny Weiss, *Gendered Community: Rousseau, Sex, and Politics* (New York: New York University Press, 1993), and Jennifer J. Popiel, *Rousseau's Daughters Domesticity, Education, and Autonomy in Modern France* (University Presses of New England, 2008).

had company. Historians outside the field of legal history have accorded far too little attention to Robert Pothier's subsequent and related arguments concerning the power of husbands over the person and possessions of wives, particularly in his important treatises, *Traité de la puissance maritale* (1774) and *Traité de la puissance du mari sur la personne et les biens de la femme* (1779). Only in the last several decades have Pothier's contributions – which again reasserted as necessary the legal subordination of wives – been acknowledged by many scholars to be as important for the subsequent development of French family law as those of his somewhat younger British contemporary, Sir William Blackstone, for English and American law.[36] It suffices to underscore that Pothier's views would have a determinate influence on the men who drafted the notorious French Civil Code, whereas Rousseau's broader arguments for controlling women influenced the post-revolutionary climate of opinion in which such a Code could be enacted.

Revolutionary Resistance to According Political Authority to Women

Agitation on behalf of reforms in women's position in French law, incorporating demands for specific rights and entitlements, was part and parcel of the attack on arbitrary privilege that emerged in the course of the French Revolution. Yet even as the juridical privileges of caste as institutionalized in noble and non-noble orders – social stratification by accident of birth – was abolished in the revolutionary France of 1789; male privilege (*l'aristocratie masculine*, in the words of one revolutionary petition) would remain intact. Indeed, the very day following the National Assembly's proclamation of the Declaration of the Rights of Man, that body reaffirmed the fraudulent Salic Law principle (now "public law") that excluded women from succession to the French throne.[37] This act had both immediate and long-term significance, since the eldest child of Louis XVI and Marie-Antoinette was a girl, Marie-Thérèse-Charlotte de France, known as the Princesse Royale (born in 1778, she survived the Revolution and became the ward of her uncle, later Louis XVIII, who carefully controlled her

---

[36] Pothier's collected works are available in at least two nineteenth-century editions, published in 1834 and 1861 respectively. See also Abensour, *Femme et féminisme*; André-Jean Arnaud, *Les Origines doctrinales du Code civil français* (Paris, 1969); and Rodolfo Batiza, *Domat, Pothier, and the Code Napoléon; Some Observations Concerning the Actual Sources of the French Civil Code* (n.p., 1973).

[37] Christine Fauré makes much of the timing of this exclusion; see her *Democracy Without Women*, pp. 108–109.

movements and destiny).[38] It is in this context that one must understand the radicalism of the remarkable theoretical contributions to women's emancipation by the Marquis de Condorcet, who on the grounds of *reason* repeatedly insisted that women were entitled, like men, to full political rights, including suffrage and representation.[39] The controversy had shifted from agitation over the royal succession to the gender of citizenship, but the underlying principle was the same – the inclusion or exclusion of women from political authority.

During the early years of the French Revolution the question of whether women should enjoy equal political rights with men remained unanswered. The Declaration of the Rights of Man in 1789 left the question open, even as it incorporated a clause on public utility that provided an escape hatch from adherence to absolute principle when it came to women. Meanwhile, documents from 1789 and 1790 expressed multiple claims for basing women's claims for citizenship on their status as mothers. It was not until 1791, with the promulgation of the first revolutionary Constitution that women were formally barred from the exercise of political rights, and (by Talleyrand) from education for citizenship in the name of that very principle of public utility; it was in this context that the controversial Olympe de Gouges drafted her *Déclaration des Droits de la Femme et Citoyenne* and the Englishwoman Mary Wollstonecraft (a friend of Thomas Paine and critic of Edmund Burke), who attentively followed reports of the revolutionary events in Paris, framed her *Vindication of the Rights of Woman* as a direct response to Talleyrand.[40] Despite the

---

[38] See Roger Langeron, *Madame Royale: La Fille de Marie-Antoinette* (Paris: Hachette, 1958). A new account of this girl's fate is Susan Nagel, *Marie-Thérèse: The Fate of Marie Antoinette's Daughter* (New York: Bloomsbury, 2008). A recent Ph.D. dissertation (Universite de Paris I) is Hélène Becquet, "Royauté, royalismes et révolution: Marie-Thérèse-Charlotte de France (1778–1851)."

[39] The prospect of woman suffrage had first been raised by Condorcet in his treatise, *Sur l'Admission des femmes au droit du cité* (*Journal de la Société de 1789* [1790]); in John Morley's 1870 English translation, reprinted in *WFF*, vol. 1, doc. 24. On the Revolution's dismissal of the notion of political rights for women, see Portemer, "Statut de la femme," 477–482 and 488–489. See Bordeaux, "Droit et femmes seules," p. 20, for analysis of the pertinent wording in the constitutions of 1791, 1793, and 1795. On other aspects of women's exclusion from citizenship, see Olwen Hufton, *Women and the Limits of Citizenship in the French Revolution* (Toronto: University of Toronto Press, 1992).

[40] For a complete English translation of De Gouges's "Declaration," see *WFF*, vol. 1, doc. 26. Wollstonecraft's *Vindication* is widely reprinted – and analyzed. Important recent analytical publications in English are: Virginia Sapiro, *A Vindication of Political Virtue: The Political Theory of Mary Wollstonecraft* (Chicago: University of Chicago Press, 1992), and *A Vindication of the Rights of Woman: Mary Wollstonecraft*, ed. & introd. Eileen Hunt Botting (Princeton, NJ: Princeton University Press, 2014).

For further information on the militant women revolutionaries and women's participation in the revolution, see *Les Femmes et la Révolution 1789–1794*, ed. Paule Duhet (Paris: Julliard, 1971); Jane

influential arguments of Condorcet and others for women's full-fledged citizenship, many revolutionary men bitterly contested and finally rejected such claims.[41]

Instead, these revolutionary gentlemen (with only a few notable exceptions) insisted on the separation in French law between *civil* rights of property and *civic* (or political) rights. Even as the revolutionary government granted property rights to single adult women, these were detached from political rights, which were effectively construed as male privileges.[42] These privileges not only became untouchable; they were ultimately reinforced by the revolutionaries, this time with arguments framed (conveniently) in the name of so-called natural law. Although in 1793 the lawyer and delegate to the Convention, Jean-Jacques Régis de Cambacérès (1753–1824), proposed a code to the National Convention that was far less restrictive of women's situation in marriage than any preceding French law, it was never adopted.[43] In the meantime the Jacobins, who had

---

Abray, "Feminism in the French Revolution," *American Historical Review*, 80:1 (February 1975), 43–62; Louis Devance, "Le Féminisme pendant la Révolution française," *Annales Historiques de la Révolution Française*, n° 229 (July–September 1977), 341–376; *Women in Revolutionary Paris, 1789–1795*, ed. Darline Gay Levy, Harriet Branson Applewhite, & Mary Durham Johnson (Urbana, IL: University of Illinois Press, 1979); *Les Femmes dans la révolution française*, ed. Albert Soboul, 2 vols. (Paris: EDHIS, 1982); Darline Gay Levy & Harriet Branson Applewhite, "Women and Political Revolution in Paris," in *Becoming Visible: Women in European History*, ed. Renate Bridenthal, Claudia Koonz, & Susan Stuard (2nd ed., Boston: Houghton Mifflin, 1987), 279–306; Dominique Godineau, *Citoyennes tricoteuses: les femmes du peuple à Paris pendant la révolution française* (Paris: Alinea, 1988); and, for a comparative view, my chapter 3 on the French Revolutionary period in *European Feminisms*. The most influential nineteenth-century study is Jules Michelet, *Les Femmes de la Révolution* (Paris, 1854; reprinted, 1988). On Olympe de Gouges, see the definitive study by Olivier Blanc, *Olympe de Gouges* (Paris: Syros, 1981; rev. ed., 1989) and his expanded study, *Marie-Olympe de Gouges: Une humaniste à la fin du XVIIIe siècle* (Paris: Éditions René Viénet, 2003). For another interpretation, see Joan Wallach Scott, "French Feminists and the Rights of 'Man': Olympe de Gouge's Declarations," *History Workshop*, n° 28 (Autumn 1988), 1–21, and the pertinent chapter in her book, *Only Paradoxes to Offer: French Feminists and the Rights of Man* (Cambridge, MA: Harvard University Press, 1996): in French as *La Citoyenne paradoxale: Les féministes françaises et les droits de l'homme* (Paris: Albin Michel, 1998).

[41] The issue of citizenship for women is ably explored in Dominique Godineau, "Autour du mot citoyenne," *Mots*, n° 16 (March 1988), 91–110, and in her *Citoyennes tricoteuses*. See also Anne Soprani, *La Révolution et les femmes de 1789 à 1796* (Paris: MA Editions, 1988); Annette Rosa, *Citoyennes: les femmes et la Révolution française* (Paris: Messidor, 1988); and Hufton, *Women and the Limits of Citizenship*. See also Candice E. Proctor, *Women, Equality and the French Revolution* (Westport, CT: Greenwood Press, 1990). For a review of French and English-language work on women and the revolution (inspired by the bicentennial of the French Revolution), in which the issue of citizenship figures prominently, see Karen Offen, "The New Sexual Politics of French Revolutionary Historiography," *French Historical Studies*, 16:4 (Fall 1990), 909–922.

[42] On the separation of civil and political rights, see the articles by Guibert-Sledziewski, cited in n. 5.

[43] See the report of Cambacérès in the Convention, 9 August 1793, *Archives parlementaires*, sér. 1, vol. 70, pp. 551–554.

celebrated the Rights of Man with such enthusiasm, had consolidated their power. Not unlike certain of their predecessors, two centuries earlier, they were ruthless advocates of public order, fearful of anarchy, and utterly opposed to active participation (much less the exercise of authority) by women in public life. At the height of the Terror late in 1793, therefore, the Committee of Public Safety moved against "disorderly" women, decreeing the abolition of the revolutionary women's clubs, guillotining a select yet very disparate sample of highly visible and "political" women, including the queen, Madame Roland, and the outspoken Olympe de Gouges, and offered this advice to the women of the new French republic:[44]

> Women, do you wish to be republicans? Then love, follow, and teach the laws that remind your husband and children to exercise their rights. Be the glorifiers of the striking actions they can accomplish for *la patrie*, because these witness in your own favor; be simple in your dress, work hard in your household; never attend the popular assemblies with the idea of speaking up, but rather with the idea that your presence there will sometimes encourage your children. Then *la patrie* will bless you, for you will have really done for it what it has the right to expect of you.

Less than a decade later, under the Empire, the principle of exclusive male succession would be reaffirmed by Napoléon I (*Sénatus-consulte organique du 28 floreal An 12* [18 May 1804]). "The imperial dignity is hereditary in the direct natural and legitimate descendance of Napoléon Bonaparte, from male to male, by order of primogeniture, and to the perpetual exclusion of women and their descendants."[45]

Even though the monarchy was gone and a republic substituted in its place, the change in label had little significance when it came to reinforcing and defending masculine authority. Pro-woman optimists such as Charles Theremin, author of *De la Condition des femmes dans les républiques* (1799), thought that women's status should and must improve under a republic, especially in terms of education and opportunities to participate in public life. He viewed women and men as morally equal and physically complementary, and he advocated marriages of inclination over arranged marriages; even so he nevertheless stipulated that the husband should serve

---

[44] *Gazette Nationale, ou Le Moniteur universel*, n° 59, Nonidi 29 Brumaire, l'an II (Mardi, 19 November 1793, vieux style), p. 450.

[45] Sénatus-consulte organique du 28 floréal an 12, Title II: De l'hérédité. *Gazette Nationale, ou le Moniteur universel*, n° 240, Dimanche, 30 Floreal an 12 de la République (20 Mai 1804), p. 1086. Reprinted in *Constitutions et documents politiques*, ed. Maurice Duverger (Paris: Presses Universitaires de France, 1966), p. 79.

as political representative of the republican family.[46] "Husband and wife
are but a single political person and can never be anything else, although
they may be two civil persons." And he added that "One vote counts for
two: the woman's vote is virtually included in her husband's vote." In his
view, there was no need for separate political status for women, at least as
wives, since they were "virtually" represented. This perspective would have
a long life during the early nineteenth century, as Anne Verjus has
demonstrated.[47] Even the poet Constance Pipelet (later Constance de
Salm) applauded Theremin's ideas, but others would prove less liberal.[48]

A few women writers could already see the handwriting on the wall and
objected vociferously to more forceful attempts to exclude women from
public life. A case in point is provided by the extremely lucid and
pessimistic remarks by Fanny Raoul in 1801:[49]

> What is political society? It is that which conserves civil society. It is, if
> I dare to say it thus, the watchdog that civil society has established for the
> defense of its rights and to prevent their invasion. Now, if women amount
> to nothing in civil society, as I have proved, it is mistaken to say that
> political society is made for them; they can neither defend nor conserve
> their rights because they have none. It is not for this that they are excluded,
> but if one is excluded from this society *by the sole reason that it is made for
> them*, men should also be excluded because it is evidently made for them.

And Fanny Raoul continued:

> To whom has been given the exercise of civil responsibilities? To men.
> Who has been assured the rights of property? Men (for it cannot be said
> that women enjoy these rights; those who are *en puissance de maris*, to use
> the ridiculous and tyrannical language of the law, cannot dispose of their
> property without the husband's consent. Now there is no real property
> when one hasn't the freedom to dispose of it, because it is in this very act
> that the right exists; thus, it is only an illusory right for women). To whom
> has been given the right and privileges of paternity? To men. For whom has
> liberty and equality been established? Again, for men. In sum, everything is

---

[46] See Le citoyen (Charles) Theremin, *De la Condition des femmes dans les républiques* (Paris: Chez
Laran, an VII, [1799]), especially p. 11. Both subsequent quotations are on p. 59.

[47] For an important reinterpretation, which argues that in fact French women were not wholly
excluded from voting during the property-based electoral regimes of the early nineteenth century,
see Anne Verjus's *Le Cens de la famille: Les femmes et le vote, 1789–1848* (Paris: Belin, 2002).

[48] Constance D. T. Pipelet, *Rapport sur un ouvrage du Cen [citoyen] Theremin, intitulé De la condition
des femmes dans une République, lu par l'auteur à la soixante et unième séance publique du Lycée des
Arts, au 24 pluviôse an VIII, imprimé par l'ordre de la société* (Paris: Imprimerie de Gille, 1800).
Consulted on Gallica, Bibliothèque Nationale du France, 14 March 2013.

[49] F. R. (Fanny Raoul), *Opinion d'une femme sur les femmes* (Paris: Impr. de Giguet, An IX – 1801),
pp. 67–68.

by them or for them; it is therefore for them also, and for them alone, that political society has been made; women have no part in it.

Drafting the Civil Code of 1804

Since the sixteenth and throughout the eighteenth century French jurists had attempted unsuccessfully to consolidate France's mixed heritage of written and customary law into a unified secular legal system. The latter phases of the Revolution gave them the chance to complete this massive work. In the process the learned authors of the Code Napoléon would institutionalize this exclusion of married women (and mothers) from civic life by deliberately vesting all public familial authority in husbands (and fathers). These men gave legal sanction to the sentiment many shared with Jean-Jacques Rousseau: that a decent woman's "dignity is in leading a retired life; her glory is in the esteem of her husband; her pleasures are in the happiness of her family."[50] They neglected to add to this prescription the implicit coda . . . "or else!"

As First Consul, Napoléon Bonaparte (1769–1821) would take it upon himself to effect the codification of French law, with the assistance of Cambacérès (who had risen to Second Consul, with Napoléon, and then served as Minister of Justice) and a coterie of renowned jurists that included Portalis, Tronchet, Bigot-Préameneu, and Maleville. As concerned marriage, the Civil Code enacted in 1804 was a clear retreat from the non-interventionist approach proposed earlier to the Convention by Cambacérès. This Code synthesized the more conservative elements of Enlightenment analysis of woman's place, building on a series of recently elaborated biomedical arguments that served to bolster natural law theory, with the First Consul's own convictions of the political necessity of maintaining male guardianship over wives.

During the debates on this section of the Code, Napoléon himself presided over the sessions in the *Conseil d'État* and took an active part in the debates. He personally insisted on the article (subsequently Article 213 of the Code) stipulating that husbands owed protection to their wives, in exchange for which wives owed obedience to their husbands. When one

---

[50] From *Émile*, Book V, Pt. 2, as retranslated in *WFF*, vol. I, doc. 10. See also Ruth Graham, "Rousseau's Sexism Revolutionized," in *Woman in the 18th Century and Other Essays*, ed. Paul Fritz & Richard Morton (Toronto: Hakkert, & Sarasota, FL: S. Stevens, 1976), pp. 127–139; and Carol Blum, *Rousseau and the Republic of Virtue: The Language of Politics in the French Revolution* (Ithaca, NY: Cornell University Press, 1986).

member of the *Conseil d'État* inquired whether obedience had ever been imposed by law, Napoléon replied (and his words have been reported to us by the *conseiller d'État*, A. Thibaudeau) that the angel had said as much to Adam and Eve:[51]

> The word used to be said in Latin during the marriage service and the women did not understand it, at any rate not in Paris, where women believe that they have a perfect right to do just as they please. . . . Ought we not to add that the wife is not free to see people of whom the husband disapproves?

Napoléon had his way, but this compellingly authoritarian phrasing of the ostensibly revolutionary law laid it open to subsequent criticism of precisely the same kind that had been used in the early days of the Revolution by representatives of the Third Estate against the privileges of the nobility. Indeed, challenges to "male aristocracy" would increase throughout the nineteenth and early twentieth centuries.

Napoléon Bonaparte shared with many other male citizens of the new republic (not least the earlier Jacobins) a common admiration for the culture of Roman antiquity and for the Roman-inspired hierarchical and authoritarian approach to organizing gender relations. The neoclassical monuments raised to celebrate the military victories of Napoléon's armies were complemented by a legal monument destined to confirm the victory of a new secular patriarchy, with husbands (and to a lesser extent, fathers) as agents of the state, empowered by it but also subject to its control. It is in this sense that historian Jacques Donzelot is correct in insisting on a *police des familles.*[52]

The jurists who drafted the new Civil Code acknowledged the existence of women as individuals in theory, but as quickly subsumed this existence in the interest of the family and the state. Once again the "public utility" escape clause would triumph. In his 1803 report to the *Conseil d'État*, Portalis framed the legal organization of marriage squarely in terms of the right of the strongest:[53]

> Families are the seed-bed of the state, and families are formed by marriage. . . . The preference or equality of the two sexes has long been

[51] Napoléon's remarks were reported by A.-C. Thibaudeau, *Bonaparte and the Consulate*, transl. and ed. by G. K. Fortescue (New York: Macmillan, 1908; originally published in Paris: Ponthieu, 1827), p. 185. See also René Savatier, *L'Art de faire les lois: Bonaparte et le Code civil* (Paris: Dalloz, 1927).

[52] Jacques Donzelot, *La Police des familles* (Paris: Éditions du minuit, 1977); in English as *The Policing of Families*, transl. Robert Hurley (New York: Pantheon, 1979).

[53] Jean Portalis, "Exposé des motifs – Mariage – Titre V, projet du Code Civil." Procès-verbal du Conseil d'État, 10 March 1803, as republished in *Archives parlementaires*, 2nd série, vol. 7 (Paris, 1866), pp. 491, 502.

disputed. Nothing is more vain than these disputes. . . . They [the sexes] are equal in some things and incomparable in others. . . . It is not laws but nature itself that determines the lot of the two sexes. Woman needs protection because she is weaker; man is freer because he is stronger. It is not in our injustice but in their natural vocation that women must seek the principle of the more austere duties which are imposed on them for their own greater advantage and for the benefit of society.

Portalis and his colleagues expressed similar views in somewhat different terms the following year, in their "Preliminary Discourse" to the penultimate version of the Code Napoléon:[54]

Civil laws should intervene between spouses, between fathers and children; they should regulate family government. We have sought the plan of this government in nature. Marital authority is founded on the necessity of giving the preponderant voice, in a society of two individuals, to one of the associates, and on the preeminence of the sex to which this advantage is attributed. . . . It is by means of the little fatherland [*la petite patrie*], the family, that one becomes attached to the large one; good fathers, good husbands, and good sons make good citizens.

With the adoption of the Civil Code, the notion was confirmed in French law that marriage must be hierarchical, that the "strong" must rule the "weak," and that the place of wives and mothers must "naturally" be subordinate. Roman precedents were also invoked to reinforce the separation of the sexes, especially the juxtaposition of the *public* role of men with the *private* role of women in the republican state, or as the French preferred to designate these distinct spaces (or spheres) throughout the nineteenth century, *forum* versus *foyer*. In this mode of discourse also, public life – which was then defined primarily as *political* life – was explicitly reserved to male heads of households.[55] Public authority must be in male hands. This critical distinction between the respective roles of the sexes based in "nature," bolstered variously by a combination of antecedents from antiquity and appeals to biblical prescription (similar to those invoked by John Knox and Jean Bodin), and reinforced by and

---

[54] Jean Portalis et al., "Discours préliminaire prononcé lors de la présentation du projet de la commission du gouvernement," (1804) in *Recueil complèt des travaux préparatoires du Code civil*, ed. P.-A. Fenet (Paris, 1836), vol. 1, pp. 486, 522.
[55] See Louis-Gabriel-Ambroise, vicomte de Bonald, "De l'éducation de la femme," in *Législation primitive considérée ... par les seules lumières de la raison* (1802), in *Oeuvres complètes de M. de Bonald ... publiés par M. l'abbé Migne*. 3 vols. (Paris: J.-P. Migne, 1859), vol. 1, pp. 1398–1402; Joseph-Marie, comte de Maistre, *Les Soirées de Saint Petersbourg: ou Entretiens sur le gouvernement temporel de la providence* (Paris: La Colombe, 1960; orig. publ. 1821), pp. 93–94. For English translations of pertinent sections, see *WFF*, vol. 1, docs. 21, 42, 45.

coupled with contemporary medical authority and the notion of public utility to the state, set the parameters for subsequent discussion of women's secondary and higher education and participation in the liberal professions, as well as of women's economic role. Of necessity, it also shaped the discourse within which women framed their subsequent claims to serve on juries, to be admitted to the bar, and, of course, to exercise the right of suffrage – in short, to wield public authority.[56]

Continuing Debates on the Gender of Political Authority

It should surprise no one to learn that the debate over the subordination of wives in French law did not cease with the promulgation of the Civil Code. One era had ended, but another was beginning, and this era would be marked by a serious, long-sustained, if often interrupted, campaign for the legal emancipation of French women, or put differently, for women's legal rights. Women in France did not sit abjectly by as male authority was consolidated. Only a few years passed before specific articles of the Code concerning women's subjection in marriage and the Code's underlying philosophy of familial relations began to encounter overt criticism, including the charge that marriage as structured by the Code was just another form of legalized prostitution. By the 1830s, much of the French agitation for women's rights was directed squarely at the Civil Code and its adverse consequences for married women. This attack comprehended both the widely publicized critique of the Saint-Simonians under Prosper Enfantin and the legal critique mounted in the early novels of George Sand (pseud. Aurore Dupin, baronne Dudevant; 1804–1876), notably *Indiana* (1832), in the women's rights press of the 1830s, particularly *La Gazette des Femmes*, and in the theater and drama of the July Monarchy, especially in the works of the celebrated writer Victor Hugo (1802–1885), who would continue to champion expanded rights for women well into the Third Republic.[57]

[56] See Karen Offen, "Women, Citizenship, and Suffrage with a French Twist, 1789–1993," in *Suffrage and Beyond: International Feminist Perspectives*, ed. Caroline Daley & Melanie Nolan (Auckland, NZ: University of Auckland Press; London: Virago, & New York: New York University Press, 1994), pp. 151–170.

[57] See especially Sand's novel *Indiana* (Paris: J. P. Rorot & H. Dupuy, 1832). Sand's novels played a key role in arousing women's sense of grievance against their legal status not only in France but throughout Europe, including Scandinavia, the German states, Poland, and Russia. See *WFF*, vol. 1, for further references concerning Sand's pan-European influence. See Kathryn J. Crecelius, *Family Romances: George Sand's Early Novels* (Bloomington: Indiana University Press., 1987), and Whitney Walton, *Eve's Proud Descendants: Four Women Writers and Republican Politics in Nineteenth-Century France* (Stanford, CA: Stanford University Press, 2000).

By 1848 the brief for revision of the Code on behalf of the rights of women was fully developed in the critiques of enlightened reformers of both sexes as well as in those of more radical social critics. The most extreme libertarian (or anarchist) position centered on the concept of "free union" (as opposed to formalized marriage) and the assertion of an individual's absolute right (for men and women alike) to choose a mate without regard for considerations of family, rank, property, or state interference. Such critics opposed the notion of social control, whether by church or state, over matrimony. Adherents of the less iconoclastic moderate position, however, upheld that the institution of marriage did have considerable value; these persons, however, argued for major revisions of many specific articles of the Code to upgrade the legal rights of married women within the existing family structure. It is, wrote Sand in 1848, "a detestable error in our legislation that makes women dependent on men's cupidity and marriage a condition of eternal minority." Most young girls would never marry, she insisted, if they had the least notion of the civil laws governing marriage. She pointed to the hypocrisy of those "conservators of the old order" who so emphatically insisted on the rights of family and property when "the marriage pact they so admire and advocate absolutely destroys the property rights of an entire sex."[58] The time was ripe, Sand argued, for "civil equality, equality in marriage, equality in the family"; most people, she believed, would support such civil rights for married women. However, the active participation of women in political life was another matter; she considered the hour for this change had not yet arrived.[59] Her opinion was widely shared.

The venerable studies of July Monarchy reform literature by D. O. Evans remain useful: see especially Evans, *Le Drame moderne à l'époque romantique (1827–1850)* (Paris: Éditions de la Vie universitaire, 1927), and *Le Roman social sous la Monarchie de Juillet* (Paris: Presses Universitaires de France, 1930). See also Laure Adler, *A l'Aube du féminisme: les premières journalistes* (Paris: Payot, 1979), especially for the list of women's periodicals published between 1830 and 1847, in appendix, pp. 215–219. On the *Gazette des Femmes*, see Marie-Louise Puech, "Le Mystère de la Gazette des Femmes," *La Grande Revue*, 147, n° 3 (March 1935), 39–76. On the *Journal des Femmes*, see Evelyne Sullerot, *Histoire de la presse féminine en France, des origines à 1848* (Paris: A. Colin, 1966), chapter 12. An illuminating literary study of the Code is Marie-Henriette Faillie, *La Femme et le Code civil dans "La Comédie Humaine" d'Honoré de Balzac* (Paris: M. Didier, 1968).

[58] Sand, "Lettre aux Membres du comité central" (Paris, mid-April 1848), n° 3910, in *Correspondance de George Sand*, ed. Georges Lubin, vol. 8 (Paris: Garnier, 1964), pp. 400–408; first published posthumously in Sand, *Souvenirs et idées*, 2nd ed. (Paris: Calmann-Lévy, 1904). In *George Sand: Politique et polemiques* (Paris: Imprimerie nationale editions, 1997), Michelle Perrot indicates (p. 533) that the posthumous 1904 version, published by Sand's daughter, actually combined two separate texts.

[59] Sand, "Lettre aux Membres," *Correspondance*, p. 406.

Another important advocate of significant reforms in women's civil status was Ernest Legouvé (1807–1903). In his long article, "Femmes," prepared for Pierre Leroux's *Encyclopédie nouvelle*, and subsequently expanded in his *Histoire morale des femmes* (1849), he called for a wide range of reforms, including a law on seduction, removal of the interdict on paternity suits, a higher minimum age for girls before they could marry, the right of engaged women to participate in the drafting of their marriage contracts, extensive civil and property rights for married women, and legal empowerment for mothers, both married and unmarried, in important decisions concerning their own children.[60] Most male-feminist writers of the mid-nineteenth century would subsequently endorse Legouvé's list of reforms. But no such reforms would be achieved during the Second Republic or the Second Empire nor for many decades thereafter. The stream of articles published in *Le Droit des Femmes*, beginning in 1869 and subsequently summarized in Léon Richer's *Code des femmes* (1883), would but restate a case that had been made repeatedly by several generations of reformers, female and male.

But, in an era where property requirements continued to underlay male political rights, the issues of civil and political rights remained inextricably entangled. The revolutionary legislators had, as has been mentioned, separated civil (or property) rights from civic (or political) rights, enabling them to grant property rights to unmarried adult women even as they denied them to wives subject to the community property regime. With the restoration of the monarchy in 1814 (and until 1848) France would return to an electoral system based on property holding, but which would exclude all women (including otherwise qualified single women and propertied widows) from exercising a *direct* vote.[61]

1848: "Universal" Manhood Suffrage and Its Implications for Women

All that changed during the revolutionary days of February and March 1848 when the new Provisional Government, following the abdication of Louis Philippe, instituted universal *manhood* suffrage. It is here that the story of "democracy without women" really begins. The challenge of

---

[60] *Encyclopédie nouvelle*, s.v. "Femmes," vol. 5, pp. 211–232*** (triple pagination). See Karen Offen, "Ernest Legouvé and the Doctrine of 'Equality in Difference' for Women: A Case Study of Male Feminism in Nineteenth-Century French Thought," *Journal of Modern History*, 58:2 (June 1986), 452–484.

[61] On the indirect vote available to propertied women, see Verjus, *Cens de la famille*, cited in n. 47.

political rights for women and their eligibility for office was then directly raised and refused.[62] In February, even before the new electoral law was promulgated, Pauline Roland (a single woman, the intrepid mother of four) tried unsuccessfully to register to vote in the municipality of Bous-sac.[63] In early March, the Provisional Government set the terms for elections to the National Assembly. "*Tous les français*" over the age of 21 could vote; all property qualifications for the vote were abolished.[64] This

[62] The historiography on the woman question in 1848 is of mixed value depending on the emphases and degree of documentation; more often than not, the precise chronology as concerns the development of debate on the woman question is scrambled or left vague. The best account in English is Claire G. Moses, *French Feminism in the 19th Century* (Albany, NY: SUNY Press, 1984), chapter 6. See also Laura S. Strumingher, "The Struggle for Unity among Parisian Women: The *Voix des Femmes*," *History of European Ideas*, 11 (1989), 273–285, and S. Joan Moon, "Woman as Agent of Social Change: Woman's Rights during the Second French Republic," in *Views of Women's Lives in Western Tradition*, ed. F. R. Keller (Lewiston, NY: E. Mellen, 1990), 323–359. In French, see especially Michèle Riot-Sarcey, *La Démocratie à l'épreuve des femmes: Trois figures critiques du pouvoir 1830–1848* (Paris: Albin Michel, 1994). More recently, see the articles by Riot-Sarcey and myself in *1848: Actes du colloque international du cent cinquantenaire, tenu à l'Assemblée nationale à Paris, les 23–25 février 1998*, ed. Jean-Luc Mayaud (Paris: Société d'histoire de la révolution de 1848 et des révolutions du XIXe siècle & Créaphis, 2002), pp. 29–45, and my English-language account (which includes the principal documents in French and in English translation), "Women and the Question of 'Universal' Suffrage in 1848: A Transatlantic Comparison of Suffragist Rhetoric," *NWSA Journal*, 11:1 (Spring 1999), 150–177. In what follows, I have drawn particularly on these two articles, in which I returned to the sources and reconstructed afresh the chronological progression of the 1848 debates over women's civil and political rights.

Older but still insightful studies in French include Jules Tixerant, *Le Féminisme à l'époque de 1848 dans l'ordre politique et dans l'ordre économique* (Paris: Giard & Brière, 1908); Léon Abensour, *Le Féminisme sous le règne de Louis-Philippe et en 1848* (Paris: Plon-Nourrit, 1913); Marguerite Thibert, *Le Féminisme dans le socialisme français de 1830 à 1850* (Paris: M. Giard, 1926); and Edith Thomas, *Les Femmes de 1848* (Paris: Presses Universitaires de France, 1948). A more recent generation of French scholars has reexamined the period from the standpoint of "representation," "discourse," and identity formation: important contributions include Geneviève Fraisse, "Les femmes libres de 48, moralisme et féminisme," *Les Révoltes logiques*, n° 1 (1975), 23–50; Louis Devance, "Femme, famille, travail et morale sexuelle dans l'idéologie de 1848," *Romantisme*, n°s 13–14 (1976), 79–103; and Michèle Riot-Sarcey, "La Conscience féministe des femmes de 1848: Jeanne Deroin et Désirée Gay," in *Un Fabuleux destin, Flora Tristan: Actes du Premier Colloque International Flora Tristan, Dijon, 3 et 4 mars 1984* (Dijon: Éditions universitaires de Dijon, 1985), pp. 157–165. See also Stéphane Michaud, *Muse et madone: Visages de la femme de la Révolution française aux apparitions de Lourdes* (Paris: Seuil, 1985), and the essays in Stéphane Michaud, ed., *Flora Tristan, George Sand, Pauline Roland: Les Femmes et l'invention d'une nouvelle morale, 1830–1848* (Paris: Créaphis, 1994).

[63] On Roland's attempt to register as a voter, see Edith Thomas, *Pauline Roland: Socialisme et féminisme au XIXe siècle* (Paris: M. Rivière, 1956), p. 108.

[64] Decree of 5 March 1848, convoking the National Assembly. See the report from the *Annual Register* for 1848 in *Documents in the Political History of the European Continent 1815–1939*, ed. G. A. Kertesz (Oxford: Clarendon Press, 1968), doc. 37. The language "*tous les français*," qualified by "*jouissant de leurs droits civils et politiques*," was continued in the Constitution of 4 November 1848 (Art. 26) and in the electoral law of 15 March 1849.

Opinions on the gender indicated by "*tous les français*" differed. Referring to later efforts to argue the case for ambiguity in the language of the electoral law, Jules Tixerant insisted that in 1848 this wording "les français" carried no ambiguity; "*tous les français*," as qualified in the decree,

in itself was admittedly a daring and revolutionary step. But it was far from "universal," even though it increased the size of the electorate by a factor of 40.

Did the phrase *tous les Français* actually mean men only? *"Les français"* had been known, in other official documents such as the Penal Code, to mean "all the French," comprising both women and men. The gender terminology itself was clearly equivocal. But known precedent was less equivocal. During the Great Revolution, male privilege had been deliberately preserved in matters of defining citizenship, despite (or, perhaps more accurately, in the face of) the demands of Condorcet and others.[65] Nor were the French alone in taking such steps; in 1807 New Jersey lawmakers had closed a loophole in their electoral laws that had allowed women to vote, and subsequently, the British Parliament, in the famous Reform Bill of 1832 (which extended the vote to a far broader constituency of property holders), deliberately qualified the franchise by adding the word "men." From that time forth arguments for suffrage reform in Great Britain revolved not only around the better-known issue of further eliminating property requirements but also around changing the language of the law to read "persons" or adding "and women".[66]

The Provisional Government in Paris wasted no time clarifying the intent of the 1848 law. In the proclamation accompanying the decree, it was stated that: "The provisional electoral law that we have made is the

constitution, and subsequent law, unequivocally meant men. See Tixerant, *Féminisme à l'époque de 1848*, pp. 75–76. This did not deter several late nineteenth-century feminists from going to court in the 1880s to test the law.

[65] On the eighteenth-century evolution of the French meaning of *citoyen* from practicing Catholic to a secular, property-based notion identified with the nation (and against the clergy), see Jeffrey Merrick, "Conscience and Citizenship in Eighteenth-Century France," *Eighteenth-Century Studies*, 21:1 (Fall 1987), 48–70. On definitions of "citizenship" as male during the Revolution of 1789–1795, see Fauré, *Démocratie*, chapter 5, esp. pp. 184–185; Godineau, "Autour du mot," and William H. Sewell, Jr., "Le Citoyen/la Citoyenne: activity, passivity, and the revolutionary concept of citizenship," in *The Political Culture of the French Revolution*, ed. Colin Lucas (Oxford: Pergamon Press, 1988), 105–123; and the other works cited in notes 40 and 41; more recently, see Charlotte Wells, *Law and Citizenship in Early Modern France* (Baltimore: The Johns Hopkins University Press, 1994), and Jennifer Ngaire Heuer, *The Family and the Nation: Gender and Citizenship in Revolutionary France, 1789–1830* (Ithaca, NY: Cornell University Press, 2006).

[66] See Judith Apter Klinghoffer and Lois Elkis, "'The Petticoat Electors': Women's Suffrage in New Jersey, 1776–1807," *Journal of the Early Republic*, 12:2 (Summer 1992), 159–194. For Britain, see "An Act (2 William IV, c. 45) to Amend the Representation of the People in England and Wales, 7 June 1832," in *English Historical Documents*, ed. David C. Douglas, vol. 11 (1783–1832), ed. A. Aspinall & E. Anthony Smith (London: Eyre & Spottiswood, 1959), doc. 303, articles XIX and XX. See also John Stuart Mill's 1867 speech before the House of Commons, 20 May 1867; reprinted in *WFF*, vol. 1, doc. 135. Mill's amendment was voted down and the Second Reform Act, doubling the size of the male electorate by amending the property qualification, became law in August 1867. English women did, however, obtain the vote at the municipal level.

most expansive that has ever, among any people on the earth, called on the people to exercise the supreme right of man, his own sovereignty. The election belongs to everyone without exception.... . Every Frenchman [*Français*] of mature age [*en âge viril*] has political citizenship.... . The law is equal and absolute for all."[67] Most contemporaries understood exactly whom this language was intended to exclude.

In consequence, a small group of Parisian women raised their voices in protest. Calling themselves the Committee for Women's Rights, they queried why women had been forgotten. On 22 March these women presented their petition to the Provisional Government.[68] The mayor of Paris, Armand Marrast, explained to them that the current government could only extend the existing situation, since women had never held political rights. On this count he was dead wrong; legal scholars at the time knew perfectly well that in the Middle Ages property-holding noble French-women had often voted in the provincial estates, even winning the approval of Pope Innocent IV; in the late seventeenth century, Madame de Sévigné had voted in the estates of Brittany; indeed, such noblewomen had voted (admittedly by proxy) for representatives to the Estates-General in 1789, a precedent invoked by some women of the Third Estate.[69] But Marrast insisted that only the National Assembly, to be elected the following month, could ratify such a sweeping break with what he claimed to be the precedent.

But the matter did not end there. The claims raised by the women struck at the heart of what men then claimed were "universal" republican ideological principles. During the latter days of March and early April the issue of civil and political rights for women remained on the agenda. It was hotly debated in the press and in the clubs; even the bitter ridicule, satire, and merciless caricatures (published in the irreverent *Le Charivari*) were signs that the issue had touched a vital nerve among progressive men.[70] It could

---

[67] Explanation of the Electoral Provisions by the Provisional Government, *La Commune de Paris*, n° 10 (18 March 1848).

[68] An account of this initiative (led by a Mme Bourgeois) and the women's reception at the *Hôtel de Ville* is given in the brochure, *Les Femmes électeurs et éligibles* (Paris, 1848); partially reprinted in *Le Grief des femmes*, ed. Maïté Albistur & Daniel Armogathe, vol. 1 (Paris: Hier et Demain, 1978), pp. 280–281. This incident was reported in the article, "Les Femmes à l'oeuvre," *La Voix des Femmes*, n° 6 (26 March 1848).

[69] See Edouard Laboulaye, *Recherches sur la condition civile et politique des femmes, depuis les Romains jusqu'à nos jours* (Paris: A. Durand, 1843), who underscored that under the feudal system political power was vested in the fief, irrespective of the sex of the fiefholder. This book was well-known, having won a major prize from the *Académie des Sciences morales et politiques*; see Chapter 5 for discussion of its significance for the history of women.

[70] See Cillie Rentmeister, *Frauenbewegung in der Karikatur des 19. Jahrhunderts* (Berlin: Frauenbuchvertrieb, 1974), a small exhibit catalogue that reproduces many of the Daumier

not be ignored; it would not go away. For example, at the Icarians' *Société Fraternelle Centrale* (the one revolutionary club that welcomed women's participation), following a sympathetic speech by Étienne Cabet, the issue was put on the agenda for further study – and then indefinitely postponed.[71] Women were excluded from the lists of electors, and after several delays the Provisional Government scheduled the elections for the Constituent Assembly (which would decide on the electoral law) for 23 April.

As the question of political rights for women hung in abeyance, many women argued publicly against their exclusion from the republican electorate. None argued more eloquently than Jeanne Deroin (1805–1894) and the women of the new all-woman periodical, *La Voix des Femmes*, edited by Eugénie Niboyet (1796–1883). It was during this stressful period that French women elaborated their best case for the necessity of their full participation in civil and political life on the grounds of what Ernest Legouvé would subsequently baptize "equality in difference."

In the issue of 27 March, *La Voix des Femmes* published an editorial that called for "*Égalité complète, égalité vraie,*" for women to be both voters and candidates. In this same issue appeared Jeanne Deroin's vigorous editorial, "*Aux Citoyens français,*" in which she argued that "the motives that led our fathers to exclude women from all participation in the governance of the State are no longer valid." How could women be "left with only obligations to fulfill, without being given the rights of citizens?" "Are they to become the helots of your new Republic?" Must women obey laws and pay property taxes without any say about either? As a minimum, Deroin insisted that women must have some representatives, even if they had to be elected by men alone.[72]

drawings from *Le Charivari*, and H. Daumier, *Lib Women: Bluestockings and Socialist Women* (Paris & New York: Leon Amiel, n.d.). See also Laura S. Strumingher, "The Vésuviennes: Images of Women Warriors in 1848 and Their Significance for French History," *History of European Ideas*, 8:4–5 (1987), 451–488 (illustrated). Most of the "Vésuvienne" drawings appeared initially in *Le Charivari*.

71 The issue of women's rights, both civil and political, was brought to Etienne Cabet's club, the *Société Fraternelle Centrale*, in late March. See Cabet's sympathetic but cautious speech, of 29 March, in *Société Fraternelle Centrale. 6e discours du Citoyen Cabet, sur les élections* (Paris, 1848), esp. pp. 10–12. See also the subsequent "Adresse au Citoyen Cabet" from the women of *La Voix des Femmes*, signed by Eugénie Niboyet and Jeanne Deroin (published in *La Voix des Femmes*, n° 11 [31 March 1848] and in *Le Populaire*, 2 April 1848), and the address of the *Société pour l'Émancipation des Femmes* (no date), signed by Vierjole Longueville, présidente, and Félix Lamb (pseud. of Jenny P. d'Héricourt), *Le Populaire*, 9 April 1848. Cabet's subsequent antifeminist agenda, hostile to women's suffrage and even to wifely independence is scrupulously documented in Diana M. Garno, "Gender Dilemmas: 'Equality' and 'Rights' for Icarian Women," *Utopian Studies*, 6:2 (1995), 52–72.

72 See Jeanne Deroin, "Aux Citoyens français!," *La Voix des Femmes*, n° 7 (27 March 1848); transl. KO, in *WFF*, vol. 1, doc. 70; quote, p. 247. On Deroin, see Moses, *French Feminism*, chapter 6; my analysis in "The Theory and Practice of Feminism in Nineteenth-Century Europe," in *Becoming*

The Parisian women also aspired to candidacy for office for members of their sex. It was in this context that *La Voix des Femmes* put forward the candidacy of George Sand. Given Sand's feelings about the difficulties of political life for women under the civil laws to which they were subject in marriage (and we should remember that Sand, although legally separated, was still technically a married woman under French law), it was logical (though politically disappointing to some, both at the time and since) that she abruptly turned down all offers of candidacy.[73] Although she was known to be extremely active behind the scenes during the Provisional Government's tenure, she was reluctant to place herself in violation of the law.

Following the initial postponement of the elections, the Parisian women continued their campaign. Jeanne Deroin published another editorial in the issue of 10 April, addressed to "those who misunderstand us," in which she defended the concept of equal rights for all, insisted that such rights implied no repudiation of women's familial obligations (a recurring obsession of antisuffragists), and underscored that the social individual is composed of man and woman together (a Saint-Simonian claim that in fact echoed Olympe de Gouges's claim that the nation consisted of the union of man and woman).[74] The next day *La Voix des Femmes* addressed an editorial to the Provisional Government's minister of the Interior, Alexandre Ledru-Rollin, arguing that the women wanted to be *bonnes citoyennes* and claiming their rights "in the name of our duties" in the family as mothers. Clearly Ledru-Rollin and his colleagues had placed them on the defensive, as was evident in one telling allusion to the sexual politics of the earlier revolution: "We know the difference between Théroigne de Méricourt," the women insisted, "and Madame [Manon] Roland."[75]

Acknowledging that a final decision on electoral qualifications would have to await the election of a Constituent Assembly, these women nevertheless persevered. In a subsequent petition to the members of the

---

Visible, (2nd ed., Boston: Houghton Mifflin, 1987), pp. 348–350, and the articles by Fraisse, Devance, and Riot-Sarcey, cited in n. 62.

73 Sand's refusal to be a candidate has rarely been treated either sympathetically or contextually by some recent feminist scholars, who view her stand on this issue as a betrayal of her feminist "sisters" at *La Voix des Femmes,* and hence "politically incorrect." Her letter is reprinted in *La Voix des Femmes,* n° 19 (10 April 1848). Niboyet and her colleagues subsequently made it clear that their cause had no need of Sand as its figurehead. See *George Sand: Politique et polémiques,* cited in n. 58, for Sand's documents.

74 Jeanne Deroin, "A Ceux qui nous meconnaissent," *La Voix des Femmes,* n° 19 (10 April 1848).

75 "A M. Ledru-Rollin," *La Voix des Femmes,* n° 20 (11 April 1848).

Provisional Government, they backed away from their earlier, more comprehensive claims, pressing instead for full civil rights for all women – and political rights for single adult women and widows only. What seems striking in retrospect is that these women were so well-informed politically; they had mastered the republican rhetoric of liberty, equality, fraternity, and justice. They knew the law. This petition in particular was eloquently argued, appealing to all the noble sentiments of the century. These women cleverly invoked national pride – the representation of France as the very mother country of civilization – a nation that should, in effect, lead the world on the path of liberty, a liberty that would fully include women.[76]

Observers outside France were watching the French revolutionary experiment closely. Emma Willard, a pioneer educator of American girls who had important connections in France including the venerable revolutionary general Lafayette, summed up the situation in her published April 1848 letter to Dupont de l'Eure, one of the senior members of the Provisional Government. Her observations are worth quoting at length, since they not only echo to a considerable degree the rhetoric of the editorialists in *La Voix des Femmes*, but also invoke the notion of French women's power and influence, to which we have earlier alluded: [77]

> There is then a power of female influence constantly at work in society. The wise politician should consider this power and in constructing the machinery of government he should not only guard against its becoming an opposing force, but he should provide a machinery by means of which it will aid to propel the political train in the right direction. If the subject of female rights and influence was at all under the discerning ken of the great and liberal minds of France who are planning the future good of the world, this call on their attention would not now have been made; but we infer that such is not the case. The *men* of France are called upon to come forward, and by their representatives frame a constitution which they will thus be pledged to support. *All* the men are called. The slaves too are kindly

[76] "Petition des femmes aux Membres du Gouvernement provisoire de la République française," *La Voix des Femmes*, n° 35 (28 April 1848); also reprinted in *Le Grief des femmes*, vol. 1 pp. 284–286.

[77] Emma Willard's letter to Dupont de l'Eure, dated April 1848, Troy, New York, was published in *The American Literary Magazine*, 2:4 (April 1848), 246–254; quote, 248–249. Willard went on to endorse the male-headed family, represented politically by the husband, but she also introduced the notion of a concurrent and parallel female legislative assembly, along the lines of the Quaker women's meeting, where women's interests – care of the schools, of the poor, of public morality, and of female education – would be fully represented. Intriguingly, a Philadelphia schoolgirl had made a similar proposal in 1793; see Priscilla Mason's salutatory address in *The Rise and Progress of the Young Ladies' Academy of Philadelphia* (Philadelphia, 1794), pp. 94–95. For the contrasting view, based squarely in individual rights, see the July 1848 Seneca Falls "Declaration of Sentiments" and the ensuing controversy, reprinted in *WFF*, vol. 1, docs. 74–76.

remembered – but the women – they are forgotten! Yet, is it not expected that they are to be governed by the fundamental laws which are to be made – laws to which they will have given no assent. And is it not expected that there shall be for them, that, for which America fought her independence, taxation without representation? If it be said, as is truly the case, that men are the natural guardians of women, then we would ask, how is it proposed to convince them that their interests are to be regarded, when they, who alone know them, are to be left wholly unconsulted?

Emma Willard noted that "even in monarchies women have not generally been barred from the succession to the sovereignty," and despite the Salic law in France, she viewed the reigns of queens and empresses in other lands – Isabella, Elizabeth, Maria Theresa and Catherine II – as proof of the fact "that the mind of woman is not necessarily feeble, and unequal to questions of law and policy."[78]

The ultimate response of the men of the Constituent Assembly to the women of *La Voix des Femmes* came in July, following the brutal repression of the insurgent Parisian workingmen. Not only were all women's clubs closed down, as half a century earlier in 1793, but women were explicitly forbidden to participate in political associations of any kind. Their newspaper was shut down as well. The rationalization for this move, as presented by the Assembly's *rapporteur*, the liberal protestant pastor Athanase Coquerel (whose candidacy for the Constituent Assembly *La Voix des Femmes* had earlier supported and whose affiliation, through his aunt Helena Maria Williams, to the now legendary Mary Wollstonecraft was well known), insisted that "the suitable and legitimate place for women is in private life and not in public life" and invoked "historic memories" as sufficient in themselves to exclude women.[79]

One woman continued to defy this exclusion. In August Jeanne Deroin published one issue of a new paper, *La Politique des Femmes*, which she continued as *L'Opinion des Femmes* early in 1849. In April 1849 she publicly announced her candidacy for the upcoming Legislative Assembly as a democratic socialist. The shift in Deroin's arguments is, however, noticeable. From the equal rights arguments based on equal association of the sexes, so predominant in the women's rhetoric in early 1848, Deroin leaned ever more heavily on relational arguments, in this case on the motherhood argument, for full citizenship for women.[80] She succeeded only in

---

[78] Willard, letter to Dupont de l'Eure, 249.
[79] On the closing of the women's clubs, including Coquerel's remarks, see *WFF*, vol. 1, docs. 71, 72, 73.
[80] On the candidacy of Jeanne Deroin, see the documents in *WFF*, vol. 1, docs. 84 and 85; for her "Woman's Mission" text, see doc. 77; quote, p. 262.

provoking Proudhon, Michelet, and a number of other men to issue an ultimatum, objecting to any notion of women in political life and threatening to withdraw from women even the right of petition.[81]

Male authority had trumped female influence. The shutout of all women, single or married, from French political life in the wake of "universal" suffrage was virtually complete. Universal manhood suffrage itself was briefly rescinded in May 1850 (only to be reinstated under the Second Empire by Napoléon III). Later that year Jeanne Deroin and Pauline Roland were arrested and jailed for breaching the sanctions against political associations. In November 1851, Pierre Leroux attempted unsuccessfully to obtain the municipal vote for single or widowed women in the National Assembly, by adding "*et les Françaises majeures*," after "*les Français*" to the electoral law. This effort earned him only a congratulatory note from the distinguished and francophile English political philosopher John Stuart Mill.[82] The capstone was women's exclusion from publishing a "political" periodical, under the 1852 Organic Decree on the Press.[83] Thus were the boundaries of women's "sphere" or "space" in France clearly demarcated. As Deroin and Roland put it in their "Appeal to the Convention of the Women of America," written from prison in the midsummer of 1851, "The darkness of reaction has obscured the sun of 1848, which seemed to rise so radiantly." The right of the strongest had once again triumphed. "No mention was made of the right of woman in a Constitution framed in the name of Liberty, Equality, and Fraternity."[84]

---

[81] "A M. Michelet. Droit politique des femmes," 1 May 1850; in translation in *WFF*, vol. 1, doc. 85.

[82] Leroux published the letter from Mill, dated 28 November 1851, in his collection, *La Grève de Samarez, poème philosophique* (Paris: E. Dentu, 1863), vol. 1, pp. 338–340. With the letter Mill had enclosed a copy of the *Westminster Review* article published in July 1851 under Harriet Taylor Mill's name and "écrit de concert par moi et ma femme ou plutôt par ma femme."

[83] The English translation of Art. 1 of the Organic Decree on the Press underscores its male exclusivity: "newspaper or periodical work treating of political matters or of social economy, and appearing either regularly and at a fixed day or in parts and irregularly, can be produced or published without the prior authorisation of the government. This authorisation can be granted only to a Frenchman who has reached his majority and enjoys all his civil and political rights." In Frank Maloy Anderson, ed., *The Constitutions and other Select Documents Illustrative of the History of France, 1789–1907*, (2nd ed., New York, 1908; republished New York: Russell & Russell, 1967; original publication in 1904), p. 549. This explicit exclusion of women was continued by the new press law of 11 May 1868, which in so many other respects was far more liberal.

[84] Jeanne Deroin & Pauline Roland, "Letter to the Convention of the Women of America," 15 June 1851; read to the National Woman's Rights Convention in Worcester MA, October 1851 by Mr. W. H. Channing, in conjunction with his presentation on women's civil and political rights; republished in the *Proceedings*, pp. 32–35, and in the *History of Woman Suffrage*, ed. Elizabeth Cady Stanton, Susan B. Anthony, & Matilda J. Gage, vol. 1 (Rochester, NY: Susan B. Anthony, 1881), pp. 234–237; reprinted in *WFF*, vol. 1, doc. 87, and now available online.

With property qualifications abolished, the identification of manhood with political authority in France stood starkly revealed. As the English novelist Virginia Woolf later summarized the situation, in another even more hostile context, "There! There can be no doubt of the odour now. The cat is out of the bag, and it is a Tom!"[85] It would take another hundred years to overturn this deliberate exclusion of women from French political life, and fifty more years after that before the principle of parity in women's representation and participation in governmental affairs would become embedded in French constitutional law.

[85] Virginia Woolf, *Three Guineas* (London: The Hogarth Press, 1938), p. 52.

CHAPTER 3

Biomedical Thinking, Population Concerns, and the Politics of Sexual Knowledge

The insistence of French women and men on women's influence and power in their culture coexisted uneasily with ongoing efforts to ensure their formal subordination to male control and their eviction from political authority. Increasingly, justifications of male rule and female subordination seemed to require ever more complex, elaborate, and sexually biased constructions of knowledge – or, as historian Ruth Harris put it, "an unprecedented amount of 'natural knowledge' purporting to give a scientific account of women's innate incapacity."[1] Indeed, within a context of competing claims about gender relations, by the eighteenth century the claims of physicians and secular (or "natural") philosophers had not only challenged but threatened to supersede the "eternal truths" established by theologians and church authorities. Thanks to the tools of scientific inquiry, especially medical investigations, and the development of increasingly elaborate physiological expertise, they promulgated – in print – new visions of sociopolitical structure permeated by biomedical understandings of the so-called natural world.[2]

Feminist literary critics and some theory-driven historians have postulated that male anxieties about social and cultural change were "inscribed" on women's bodies, or to put it another way that the body became a metaphor for discussing sociopolitical issues, a "site for analysis".[3]

---

[1] Ruth Harris, *Murders and Madness: Medicine, Law, and Society in the Fin de Siècle* (Oxford: Clarendon Press; New York: Oxford University Press, 1989), p. 22.

[2] I have adopted the term "biomedical" instead of "biological" at the suggestion of Bob Nye, who rightly points out that this term more accurately describes nineteenth-century thinking about physiological difference. See Robert A. Nye, *Crime, Madness, and Politics in Modern France: The Medical Concept of National Decline* (Princeton, NJ: Princeton University Press, 1984), p. xii. Ludmilla Jordanova also prefers this term. See her article, "Naturalizing the Family: Literature and the Bio-Medical Sciences in the Late Eighteenth Century," in *Languages of Nature: Critical Essays on Science and Literature*, ed. L. J. Jordanova (London & New Brunswick, NJ: Rutgers University Press, 1986), 86–116.

[3] Recent examples include some of the contributions to *The Female Body in Western Culture: Contemporary Perspectives*, ed. Susan Rubin Suleiman (Cambridge, MA: Harvard University Press,

This evocative (and unduly abstract) conceptualization of the issue may have the potential to illuminate many dark corners, but among other things it masks (even erases) the evidence provided by women's daily experience and the sexual politics that have shaped its expression. Women's bodies are not simply metaphoric constructions, mere playgrounds for linguistic acrobats; our bodies grow, they sense, they bleed, they conceive, they give birth, they lactate, they ache, they age, they house the very minds that give rise to language and to the promise of rational thought. What is more, our bodies are subject to physical control and abuse by others who are bigger, stronger, or more ruthless. Indeed, women's bodies, in their physicality, are both magical and troublesome.

My approach to the history of the woman question differs from that of literary critics or historians devoted to the hegemony of "discourse" in constructing social "reality" by insisting on the centrality of sexed physical bodies, and on the cultural politics of male control over female reproductivity. My approach will certainly attend to the elaboration of discourse, but it will do so by focusing on the speakers – men who inhabit bodies of their own and have a particular interest in controlling the bodies (and minds) of women, but also on the women who talk back. I place these representations of women's bodies within the long chronological scope and highly charged historical context of such discussions in France that span many centuries. Where evidence permits, I will introduce the objections and counterarguments made by the increasing numbers of women who challenged, based on their own perceived bodily experiences, the male-centered sexual politics of medical knowledge. These were articulate, literate, and well-informed women who refused to remain the silent objects of male physicians' gazes, discourses, and efforts to justify their control.

The Gender Implications of Biomedical Thinking

Biomedical thinking about the two sexes and their reciprocal relationship in society had become central to European debate on the woman question well before the French Revolution or the nineteenth century.[4]

1986); and Bram Dijkstra, *Idols of Perversity: Fantasies of Feminine Evil in Fin-de-siècle Culture* (New York: Oxford University Press, 1986).

[4] In this debate, speakers were concerned with only two sexes. They would have been quite astounded by the 1993 proposal by Anne Fausto-Sterling, "The Five Sexes: Why Male and Female Are Not Enough," *The Sciences* (March–April 1993), 20–25. See also her book, *Myths of Gender: Biological Theories about Women and Men* (New York: Basic Books, 1985; 2nd ed., 1992). They would have been even more surprised by the post-modern, post-feminist proposal that gender and sex should be

It did not begin with Darwin or Freud (who indeed leaned heavily on prior medical discussion), nor did it originate in Victorian England or the United States, as has sometimes been suggested in recent English-language accounts. In France, such thinking can be traced back at least to the sixteenth century, when small clusters of university-trained physicians drawing on an earlier tradition of biomedical thinking about women in the ancient texts of Aristotle and other now-canonical writers of the Graeco-Roman world (Galen, Hippocrates) set about to reformulate, elaborate, and expand on their ideas.[5] In particular, the corpus of medical writings by Hippocrates, translated into Latin and published in 1525, had quite a bit to say about the diseases of women; these writings had a significant influence on medical writers, even through the fragments that appeared in French translation.[6]

Physicians, like theologians and rhetoricians, held prestigious places among the learned men of early modern Europe. Although, from our perspective, they understood very little about the body's mysteries,

considered irrelevant. For a well-contextualized series of essays on this body of knowledge, see *Feminism and the Body*, ed. Londa Schiebinger (Oxford: Oxford University Press, 2000). For more on current thinking about sexual multiplicity, see Anne Fausto-Sterling, *Sexing the Body: Gender Politics and the Construction of Sexuality* (New York: Basic Books, 2000), and Joan Roughgarden, *Evolution's Rainbow: Diversity, Gender, and Sexuality in Nature and People* (Berkeley & Los Angeles: University of California Press, 2004).

5 Scholarship on biomedical thinking about the woman question in early modern Europe is enormously rich and evocative, beginning with Ian Maclean, *The Renaissance Notion of Woman: A Study in the Fortunes of Scholasticism and Medical Science in European Intellectual Life* (Cambridge, UK: Cambridge University Press, 1980), and Paul Hoffmann, *La Femme dans la pensée des lumières* (Paris: Editions Ophrys, 1978), which discusses many works by physician/philosophers. For feminist interpretations, see Evelyne Berriot-Salvador, "Le Discours de la médecine et de la science," in *Histoire des femmes*, vol. 3, ed. Natalie Zemon Davis & Arlette Farge (Paris: Plon, 1991), and Lindsay B. Wilson, *Women and Medicine in the French Enlightenment: The Debate over "Maladies des Femmes"* (Baltimore: Johns Hopkins University Press, 1993). For Aristotle's influence on all of these writings, see Maryanne Cline Horowitz, "Aristotle and Women," *Journal of the History of Biology*, 9:2 (Fall, 1976), 183–213. Thomas Laqueur's *Making Sex: Body and Gender from the Greeks to Freud* (Cambridge, MA: Harvard University Press, 1990) posits a change from a one-sex to a two-sex model during the eighteenth century. Laqueur's argument – and his chronology – have been contested by Katharine Park & Robert A. Nye, "Destiny is Anatomy," *The New Republic*, 204 (18 February 1991), and by Michael Stolberg, "A Woman Down to her Bones: The Anatomy of Sexual Difference in the Sixteenth and Early Seventeenth Centuries," *Isis*, 94:2 (June 2003), 274–299, to which Laqueur and Londa Schiebinger have both responded in the same issue.

6 See Alison Klairmont Lingo, "Female Diseases and Images of the Womb in the Work of Louise Bourgeois," paper presented to the 38th annual conference of the Western Association of Women Historians, 5–7 May, 2006. Consulted with permission of the author. Louise Bourgeois, royal midwife to Marie de Médici, became the first woman to publish her medical "Observations" on gynecology and obstetrics in 1609, leaning heavily on Hippocratic texts but also providing her own original twist. For a biographical study, see Wendy Perkins, *Midwifery and Medicine in Early Modern France: Louise Bourgeois* (Exeter, UK: University of Exeter Press, 1996).

including that of conception, and could cure very few of the many bodily ailments they encountered, they nevertheless felt utterly self-confident about what they did know and they were eager explorers and exploiters of bodily knowledge. Some of these physicians could not resist the urge to philosophize about the material world more generally, or – especially in the wake of the French Revolution – to prescribe behavioral or sociopolitical remedies for human ills and social disorder. Their particular brand of science addressed the problem of unlocking the secrets of "nature" through a more precise knowledge of human physiology. As their understanding deepened, it became increasingly useful to others in their efforts not only to articulate the differences between women and men but also to rejustify hierarchical relations between the sexes in the interest of maintaining sociopolitical order, in parallel with the political and legal developments discussed earlier.

In Chapter 1, I referenced the linking of women with culture, as opposed to nature, during the eighteenth century. In fact the juxtaposition of "nature" with "culture" appears to have emerged in French discourse in the late seventeenth century. By the late eighteenth century, with the rise of romanticism in literature and a cultural focus on sentiment over reason, accompanied by a nostalgia for nature, biomedical approaches to the woman question had become significant in the efforts of French men of learning to rethink the implications of "Nature" with a capital "N" for their own purposes. Indeed, one could argue that physicians and their allies sought to reincorporate women, and with them their ostensible power and influence, into Nature's realm, with the effect of reclaiming Culture – and its authority – for themselves. However, as feminist historians have recently been reminding anthropologists (who, following the celebrated twentieth-century anthropologist Claude Lévi-Strauss and, before him, the renowned nineteenth-century historian Jules Michelet, have relied so heavily and uncritically on the conceptual juxtaposition of Nature/Culture) the term Nature itself was a cultural construct rife with value judgments.[7]

---

[7] On the historical construction of the Nature/Culture dichotomy, see Maurice Bloch and Jean H. Bloch, "Women and the Dialectics of Nature in Eighteenth-Century French Thought," in *Nature, Culture, and Gender*, ed. Carol MacCormack & Marilyn Strathern (Cambridge, UK, & New York: Cambridge University Press, 1980), pp. 25–41; Ludmilla Jordanova, "Natural Facts: A Historical Perspective on Science and Sexuality," also in *Nature, Culture, and Gender*, ed. MacCormack and Strathern, pp. 42–69; and Penelope Brown and Ludmilla Jordanova, "Oppressive Dichotomies: The Nature/Culture Debate," in *Women in Society: Interdisciplinary Essays*, ed. The Cambridge Women's Studies Group (London: Virago, 1981), pp. 224–241. The contemporary critique by feminist anthropologists began with Nicole-Claude Mathieu, "Homme-culture et femme-nature?" *L'Homme: Revue française d'anthropologie*, 13:3 (July–September 1973), 101–113, and entered the

The same criticism can, of course, be made of the scientific neologism "Biology."[8]

As the contributions of physicians to the elaboration of the medical, behavioral, and sociopolitical discourse increased, their insights became inextricably woven into new articulations of male political and legal thought. Well before the nineteenth century, an "extraordinary valuation" (the phrase is Robert A. Nye's) would be placed on medical knowledge in addressing all sorts of sociopolitical problems.[9] Take, for example, this comment by Voltaire in 1764 (shortly after the conclusion of France's seven-year long war with England): "Physique," he wrote, "always governs ethical behavior. . . . The periodic emissions of blood that inevitably weaken women during this period, the illnesses that result from their suppression, the time of pregnancy, the necessity of nursing infants and watching constantly over them, the delicacy of their appendages, all make them unsuitable for the fatigues of war and the fury of combat."[10] Voltaire, who argued elsewhere that the Salic Law exclusion of women from the French throne was sheer nonsense, nevertheless acceded in other significant respects to the biomedical conventions of his day.

English-language scholarly literature of the 1970s with Sherry B. Ortner, "Is Female to Male as Nature Is to Culture," in *Women, Culture, and Society*, ed. Michelle Zimbalist Rosaldo & Louise Lamphere (Stanford, CA: Stanford University Press, 1974), pp. 67–87; orig. publ. in *Feminist Studies*, 1 (1972), 5–31. Ortner's footnotes do not acknowledge Mathieu or the French discussion, apart from Claude Lévi-Strauss, who invoked this dichotomy in his influential book, *Les Structures élémentaires de la parenté* (Paris: Presses Universitaires de France, 1949).

[8] In the wake of feminist critiques of science (especially the biological sciences) by Evelyn Fox-Keller (1984), Anne Fausto-Sterling (1985), Sandra Harding (1986), and Ruth Hubbard (1990), historian Gisela Bock has called on sister historians to take a critical look at the term "biology" itself as a social construct; see her essays, "Women's History and Gender History: Aspects of an International Debate," *Gender and History*, 1:1 (Spring 1989), esp. 11–15, and "Challenging Dichotomies," in *Writing Women's History: International Perspectives*, ed. Karen Offen, Ruth Roach Pierson, & Jane Rendall (London: Macmillan, and Bloomington: Indiana University Press, 1991), pp. 1–23.

[9] Nye, *Crime, Madness, and Politics*, p. xii. In addition to Nye and Harris, analyses of the ways in which biomedical thinking was deployed by Third Republic psychiatric and forensic physicians to refine the case for female incapacity can be found in Jan Goldstein, "The Hysteria Diagnosis and the Politics of Anticlericalism in Late Nineteenth-Century France," *Journal of Modern History*, 54:2 (June 1982), 209–239; for one specific application of this thinking, see Patricia O'Brien, "The Kleptomania Diagnosis: Bourgeois Women and Theft in Late Nineteenth-Century France," *Journal of Social History*, 17:1 (Fall 1983), 65–77.

[10] Voltaire, Art. "Femme," *Dictionnaire philosophique* (1764); reprinted in *Oeuvres complètes de Voltaire*, vol. 14 [vol. 7, pt. 2] (Paris:, 1817), 989. Here Voltaire was probably contesting the claims put forth earlier on behalf of women's participation in war and combat by Poullain de la Barre and the anonymous "Sophia" (1739; in French 1750, attributed to "Miladi P."). Or he could have been responding to the controversy that swirled (in the early 1760s) around the sex of the Chevalier d'Éon, a French military officer and diplomat who often dressed as a woman; see Gary Kates, *Monsieur d'Éon is a Woman: A Tale of Political Intrigue and Sexual Masquerade* (New York: Basic Books, 1995).

Doctors were by no means the sole participants in the debate, however, as this example suggests. Other secular critics, and in particular Denis Diderot, founder of the *Encyclopédie*, drew on the language of biomedical thinking to counter the arguments of materialist environmentalists such as Helvétius.[11] As the Paris-based *philosophes* attempted to reformulate the ideological bases of social order to counter Catholic theology, they too turned to the close observation of "nature"; in short order, moralizing physicians and their allies, the men of science, were challenging theologians for domination of learned reflection on the construction of the sociopolitical order. In so doing, these men developed what I will call here a "biotheology" in which ideas about the unknown and causality were displaced from God to Nature. Dismissing Church authority as a hotbed of superstition, the *philosophes* attempted to ground what they called positive or social law in "natural law," thereby locking the "nature/culture" dichotomy firmly into Western secular thought.[12] As concerned the sexes, this meant that they attempted, both in learned treatises and through more popular discussion, to explain not only the nature of man but the essence

---

[11] See Denis Diderot, "Refutation suivie de l'ouvrage d'Helvétius intitulé l'Homme" (1773–1775, published posthumously) in *Oeuvres complètes de Diderot*, vol. 2 (Paris, 1875), pp. 275–456, esp. 319. Diderot's use of medical knowledge in discussing "woman" is extensively analyzed in a number of works; see Part IV, chapter 7 in Hoffmann, *Femme dans la pensée* (cited earlier, n. 5), and Laura W. Fleder, "Female Physiology and Psychology in the Works of Diderot and the Medical Writers of his Day" (Ph.D. dissertation, Columbia University, 1978). Fleder, like others, underscores the centrality of the womb and reproduction to Diderot's analysis. See also Elizabeth J. Gardner, "The Philosophes and Women: Sensationalism and Sentiment," in Woman and Society in 18th Century France, ed. Eva Jacobs et al. (London: Athlone, 1979), pp. 19–27, and Letizia Gianformaggio, "The 'Physical Organisation', Education and Inferiority of Women in Denis Diderot's Refutation of Helvétius," in *Women's Rights and the Rights of Man* (Aberdeen: Aberdeen University Press, 1990), pp. 52–61.

For analyses of the treatment of women in the *Encyclopédie* by earlier women scholars, see Mme P. Charbonnel, "Repères pour une étude du statut de la femme dans quelques écrits théoriques des *philosophes*," *Études sur le XVIII siècle*, ed. Roland Mortier & Hervé Hasquin, 3 (Brussels: Éditions de l'Université de Bruxelles, 1976), pp. 93–100. Terry Smiley Dock, *Woman in the Encyclopédie: A Compendium* (Madrid: Ediciones José Porrúa Turanzas, 1983; originally a Ph.D. diss., Vanderbilt University, 1979) is particularly helpful; the earlier version of Dock's study is drawn on by Sara Ellen Procious Malueg, "Women and the *Encyclopédie*," in *French Women and the Age of Enlightenment*, ed. Samia Spencer (Bloomington: Indiana University Press, 1984), pp. 259–271.

[12] For manifestations of "biotheology" in the late eighteenth and early nineteenth centuries, see especially Yvonne Knibiehler, "Les Médecins et la 'nature féminine' au temps du Code Civil," *Annales: Economies, Sociétés, Civilisations*, 31:4 (July–August 1976), 824–845; Jean-Pierre Peter, "Entre femmes et médecins à la fin du XVIIIe siècle," *Ethnologie française*, 6:3–4 (1976), 341–348; and Yvonne Knibiehler & Catherine Fouquet, *La Femme et les médecins: analyse historique* (Paris: Hachette, 1983). See also Barbara Haines, "The Interrelations Between Social, Biological, and Medical Thought, 1750–1850: Saint-Simon and Comte," *British Journal for the History of Science*, 11, pt. 1, n° 37 (March, 1978), 19–35; and Erna Olafson Hellerstein, "Women, Social Order, and the City: Rules for French Ladies, 1830–1870" (Ph.D. dissertation, University of California, Berkeley, 1980).

of woman. Explorations of women's physiological and sexual specificity became increasingly prevalent; for most physicians, fascinated as they were by human physiology, this meant, in practice, reducing women to their reproductive organs and discussing them exclusively in terms of their generative capacity.[13] As historian of science Londa Schiebinger has demonstrated, even depictions of female skeletons began to emphasize sexual difference.[14] What historian Thomas Laqueur has termed "a biology of incommensurability" came to grip the imaginations of these learned and influential men.[15]

In eighteenth-century France, following the four articles on "Femme" in the fourth volume of the *Encyclopédie* (1756), Jean-Jacques Rousseau's treatise on education, *Émile* (1762), which grounded differing education for each sex on physiological difference, Voltaire's *Philosophical Dictionary* (quoted earlier), which underscored it, and Dr. Pierre Roussel's *Système physique et morale de la femme* (1775), a decisive emphasis on "natural" sexual difference and its sociopolitical consequences came to permeate the thinking of a broader range of educated men.[16] Then, as revolutionary France led Europe in casting aside orders of rank and caste determined by birth, as well as identification by religious affiliation, in the name of "equality," post-revolutionary French thinkers increasingly invoked so-called natural or biological differences as a basis for separating categories of persons, and for attempting to redistribute the spaces (public versus domestic) in which each category would carry out its respective

---

[13] Gynecology had already become an increasingly important medical specialization; see, for example, the six-volume treatise on women's diseases by Jean Astruc, *Traité des maladies des femmes* (Paris: chez P. Guillaume Cavelier, 1761–1765). In France, however, contrasting with England, royal authorities continued to emphasize providing good training for midwives, and in the later nineteenth century, training women doctors to treat (exclusively) women patients. Midwives, meanwhile, came under the authority of the male medical establishment. See Jacques Gélis, *La Sage-femme ou le médecin: Une nouvelle conception de la vie* (Paris: Fayard, 1988), and especially Nina Rattner Gelbart, *The King's Midwife: A History and Mystery of Madame du Coudray* (Berkeley & Los Angeles: University of California Press, 1998).

[14] See Londa Schiebinger, "Skeletons in the Closet: The First Illustrations of the Female Skeleton in Nineteenth-Century Anatomy," *Representations*, n° 14 (Spring 1986), 42–82, for the development of increasingly differentiated anatomical representations of the skeleton on the European continent. This article is reprinted in *Feminism and the Body*, ed. Schiebinger, pp. 25–57. See also Schiebinger's book, *The Mind Has No Sex? Women in the Origins of Modern Science* (Cambridge, MA: Harvard University Press, 1989) and her article, "Why Mammals are called Mammals: Gender Politics in Eighteenth-Century Natural History," *American Historical Review*, 98:2 (April 1993), 382–411.

[15] Thomas Laqueur, "Orgasm, Generation, and the Politics of Reproductive Biology," *Representations*, n° 14 (Spring 1986), 1–41.

[16] Pierre Roussel, *Système physique et morale de la femme* (Paris: chez Vincent, 1775). The treatise of Dr. Roussel, which was inspired by Rousseau and very influential among the *philosophes*, went through at least seven editions by 1820.

contributions.[17] We have seen the concrete effects of this redistribution in the Jacobin's exclusion of women from political life. Following the Revolution, philosopher-physicians such as the misogynistic J.-J. Virey insisted that the differences between women and men (and, thus, their sociopolitical roles) were irrevocably grounded in physiology (with an emphasis on childbearing for women), not simply a consequence of their differing educations as many reformers, both women and men, had been claiming. "*Femme vient de* foemina *qui vient de* foetare, foetus, *parce que sa destination naturelle est d'engendrer.*"[18]

Legal theoreticians seemed especially impressed with the significance of such biomedical arguments for the elaboration of "positive" law. In the aftermath of the revolutionary upheavals, this resulted in the effective collapsing of male/female categories with the political/legal categories of public/private; as we have seen, nowhere is an arbitrary public/private prescription more clearly embedded in law than in the French Civil Code.[19] Subsequent opponents of women's emancipation during the nineteenth and early twentieth centuries would relentlessly deduce social roles – and "prove" the necessity of women's subordination by insisting on female and male physiological traits. Thus were male muscular strength and relative female "weakness" constantly reinvested with political significance. Positive law, in the perception of such opponents, could not avoid taking such "natural" differences, construed as physiological differences

---

[17] Several scholars insist on the politicization of medicine during the revolutionary years. See Jacques Léonard, *La Médecine entre les pouvoirs et les savoirs* (Paris: Aubier-Montaigne, 1981), pp. 110–126, and Elizabeth A. Williams, *The Physical and the Moral: Anthropology, Physiology, and Philosophical Medicine in France, 1750–1850* (Cambridge, UK: Cambridge University Press, 1994), p. 17.

[18] See in particular Virey's encyclopedia articles: "Femme," *Dictionnaire des sciences médicales* (53 vols., 1812–1822), vol. 14 (1815), pp. 503–572; and "Femelle," "Femme," "Féminin," *Nouveau Dictionnaire d'Histoire naturelle* (36 vols. 1816–1819), vol. 11 (1817), pp. 332–339. For a discussion of Virey's views, see Knibiehler, n. 12, and Geneviève Fraisse, "Le Genre humaine et la femme chez J.-J. Virey, ou Une certaine harmonie d'inégalités correspondantes," in *Julien-Joseph Virey, naturaliste et anthropologue*, ed. Claude Bénichou & Claude Blanckaert (Paris: J. Vrin, 1988), pp. 183–206.

[19] See Chapter 2 in this volume. The revived public/private distinction was central to the sociopolitical arguments of Jean Bodin, in his influential *Six Books of the Republic* (1576) and, subsequently, to the political theorizing of Jean-Jacques Rousseau. For the latter, see Joel Schwartz, *The Sexual Politics of Jean-Jacques Rousseau* (Chicago: University of Chicago Press, 1984) and Carol Blum, *Rousseau and the Republic of Virtue: The Language of Politics in the French Revolution* (Ithaca, NY: Cornell University Press, 1986). On the significance of Roussel and other French doctors for sociopolitical thought in the pre-revolutionary period, see Bloch & Bloch, "Women and the Dialectics of Nature"; Jordanova, "Natural Facts"; and Brown & Jordanova, "Oppressive Dichotomies." For the immediate post-revolutionary period, see Knibiehler, "Médecins et 'nature féminine'," and Knibiehler & Fouquet, *Femme et médecins*, cited in n.12. See also Geneviève Fraisse, "Le Genre humaine et la femme . . .", and her book *Muse de la Raison: La Démocratie exclusive et la différence des sexes* (Paris: Alinea, 1989), esp. chapter 3. Fraisse's study has been translated as *Reason's Muse: Sexual Difference and the Birth of Democracy* (Chicago: University of Chicago Press, 1994).

centered in reproduction and its consequences, into account. That some educated women were not unaware of the potential for reinforcing sexual hierarchy inherent in this post-revolutionary repositioning of women as the "weaker sex" is attested by the self-anointed "*femme philosophe*," the playwright and poet Constance Pipelet in a bittersweet verse published in 1797:[20]

> Let the anatomist, blinded by his science,
> Artfully calculate the power of a muscle,
> Infer, without appeal, 'twixt the more and the less,
> That his wife owes him eternal respect.

And indeed, well into the nineteenth century, there was virtually no appeal. Inasmuch as biomedical discourse remained effectively a male discourse, its objects – the bodies of women – were continually subjected to male constructions and reconstructions. Virey's counterrevolutionary analyses were joined by a series of other books, including the *Histoire naturelle de la femme* (1803) by Jacques-Louis Moreau (de la Sarthe), Gabriel Jouard's *Nouvel Essai sur la femme considerée comparativement à l'homme* (1804), and Charles-François Menville's *Histoire philosophique et médicale de la femme* (1845; 2nd ed., 1858).[21] Other lengthy treatises by male doctors focused on specific aspects of women's "limiting" physical

[20] Constance Pipelet, *Épître aux femmes* (Paris: Firmin Didot, 1797), as republished in *Oeuvres complètes de Madame la princesse Constance de Salm*, 4 vols., vol. 1 (Paris, 1842), p. 13. Translated in *The Defiant Muse: French Feminist Poems from the Middle Ages to the Present: A Bilingual Anthology*, ed. Domna C. Stanton (New York: The Feminist Press, 1986), p. 115. This brief excerpt is part of a much longer poem. On Constance de Salm, see Christine Planté, "Constance Pipelet: La Muse de la Raison et les despotes du Parnasse," in *Les Femmes et la Révolution française*, ed. Marie-France Brive (Toulouse: Presses Universitaires du Mirail, 1989), vol. 1, pp. 285–294, and Elizabeth Colwill, "Laws of Nature / Rights of Genius: The *Drame* of Constance de Salm," in *Going Public: Women and Publishing in Early Modern France*, ed. Elizabeth C. Goldsmith & Dena Goodman (Ithaca, NY: Cornell University Press, 1995), pp. 224–242. The names of this author are confusing: she was born Constance-Marie deThéis in 1767, but published under her married name, Pipelet; following her divorce from Pipelet de Leury, she married again in 1803 to the Prince de Salm-Reifferschied-Dyck, and published as the Princesse de Salm until her death in 1845.

[21] Jacques-Louis Moreau (de la Sarthe), *Histoire naturelle de la femme, suivie d'un traité d'hygiène, appliquée à son régime physique et moral aux différentes époques de la vie*, 2 vols. in 3 (Paris: Duprat, 1803); Gabriel Jouard, *Nouvel Essai sur la femme considerée comparativement à l'homme, principalement sous les rapports moral, physique, philosophique*, etc., *avec des applications nouvelles à sa pathologie* (Paris: chez l'auteur, 1804); and Charles-François Menville de Ponsan, *Histoire médicale et philosophique de la femme considerée dans toutes les époques principales de sa vie*, 3 vols. (Paris: Amyot, 1845). The title of the second edition (1858) was reversed to read *Histoire philosophique et médicale* . . .. Additional works of this type have been recovered by Sean M. Quinlan: see his article, "Physical and Moral Regeneration after the Terror: Medical Culture, Sensibility and Family Politics in France, 1794–1804, *Social History*, 29:2 (May 2004), 139–164; and Sean Quinlan, *The Great Nation in Decline; Sex, Modernity and Health Crises in Revolutionary France c. 1750–1850* (Aldershot, Hamps., UK: Ashgate, 2007). See as well June Burton, *Napoléon and the Woman Question:*

conditions, including menstruation, childbirth, and eventually the "climacteric," as they baptized the cessation of menstruation early in the nineteenth century.[22]

Women's Fight to Obtain Medical Knowledge

Women without professional credentials had a hard time making themselves heard over these authoritative male voices. Indeed, as medical practice in France became professionalized, women found themselves increasingly marginalized.[23] In Paris, academic medical practitioners took systematic steps to regulate and control midwives, and, for a time, to sidestep women's demands for training as physicians in the faculty of medicine. Eventually the tables would turn, but not without a struggle.

A long-standing demand of some Frenchwomen, particularly among trained midwives and their allies, concerned access to professional medical training (and thereby authoritative medical knowledge) on equal terms with men. In contrast to England, where male doctors had made heavy inroads into obstetrics, midwifery in France had taken a different path. In the mid-eighteenth century, the "King's Midwife," Madame du Coudray, accompanied by her obstetrical mannequin, had toured the countryside for over twenty years, training country midwives in proper techniques for bringing women safely through childbirth.[24] Even so, Queen Marie-Antoinette called on the services of a male obstetrician to attend the births of her children.[25] Under Napoléon I, medical authorities institutionalized

Discourses of the Other Sex in French Education, Medicine, and Medical Law, 1799–1815 (Lubbock: Texas Tech University Press, 2007).

[22] E.g., Adam Raciborski, *De la puberté et de l'âge critique chez la femme, au point de vue physiologique, hygiénique et médical* ... (Paris: J.-B. Baillière, 1844); *Traité de la menstruation: ses rapports avec l'ovulation* (Paris: J.-B. Baillière, 1868). In *Woman in the Encyclopédie* (p. 57), Terry Dock remarks that the *Encyclopédie* does not provide a major discussion of menopause. On the naming of menopause by male doctors, see Joel Wilbush, "La Menespausie – The Birth of a Syndrome," *Maturitas*, vol. 1 (1979), 145–151. For this reference and many others that follow the story into the early twentieth century, I am indebted to the work of Mary Lynn Stewart, especially her book, *For Health and Beauty: Physical Culture for Frenchwomen 1880s–1930s* (Baltimore: Johns Hopkins University Press, 2001).

[23] See Alison Klairmont Lingo, "Empirics and Charlatans in Early Modern France: The Genesis of the Classification of the 'Other' in Medical Practice," *Journal of Social History*, 19:4 (June 1986), 585–603, and Lingo, "Print's Role in the Politics of Women's Health Care in Early Modern France," in *Culture and Identity in Early Modern France*, ed. Barbara Diefendorf & Carla Hesse (Ann Arbor: University of Michigan Press, 1993), pp. 203–221.

[24] On Madame du Coudray's astonishing career, see Gelbart, *The King's Midwife*. One of Coudray's obstetrical models can still be viewed in a museum in Rouen.

[25] On Jacques-Andre Millot, Marie-Antoinette's personal obstetrician, who turned to writing self-help sex advice manuals during the post-revolutionary period, see Sean M. Quinlan, "Sex and the

the training of midwives, placing it under the direct supervision of the male-dominated medical faculties.[26] Celebrated midwife-superintendents of the midwifery training programs in Paris, such as Marie-Anne-Victoire Boivin (who directed the Paris Maternity Hospital), contested the incessant intervention of male obstetricians in the birth process.[27]

In the early 1830s a report trickled back to Paris from Egypt about an experimental program designed to train young black slave women as doctors or *hakimas*.[28] Some French women thought they should be able to become physicians as well, including Suzanne Voilquin, who trained with the *hakimas* in Egypt and subsequently practiced as a midwife in Russia as well as in France. In the 1840s several male reformers, notably P. Rozier, Étienne Cabet, and Ernest Legouvé, came out in support of these women's demands.[29] During the 1848 revolution, a group of Parisian midwives led by Suzanne Voilquin petitioned the Luxemburg Commission to be constituted as a state service (*corps d'état*) in order to alleviate the difficulties they were experiencing in making a living in competition with

Citizen: Reproductive Manuals and Fashionable Readers in Napoleonic France, 1799–1808, in *View from the Margins: Creating Identities in Modern France*, ed. Kevin J. Callahan & Sarah A. Curtis (Lincoln: University of Nebraska Press, 2008), pp. 189–217.

[26] For a general overview of the history of midwifery, see A. Lutaud, "Sages-Femmes," *Dictionnaire encyclopédique des sciences médicales*, 3e sér., vol. 6 (SAA-SAR) (Paris, 1878), pp. 110–130, and Paul Delaunay, *La Maternité de Paris, 1625–1907* (Paris: Jules Rousset, 1909). For the pre-revolutionary period, see Richard L. Petrelli, "The Regulation of French Midwifery in the Ancien Regime," *Journal of the History of Medicine and Allied Sciences*, 26:3 (July 1971), 276–292, and, for the critical period of the Empire, June Burton, "The Organization of a National System of Midwifery Education in France under Napoléon I," paper presented to the Southern Historical Association, St. Louis, 1978. A revised and updated version of this material appears in Burton's book, *Napoléon and the Woman Question.*

[27] Marie-Ann[e]-Victoire Gillain Boivin, *Mémorial de l'art des accouchemens, ou Principes fondés sur la pratique de l'Hospice de la Maternité de Paris et sur celle des plus célèbres praticiens nationaux et étranger*, 3rd ed. (Paris: chez Méquignon aîné, 1824).

[28] "Fatme-Effendi" (lettre de Caire de M. de Ségur-Dupeyron), *Journal des Débats*, 22 April 1839. These women doctors, or *hakimas*, were trained at a school founded in 1827 by a young French physician, Dr. Antoine B. Clot; see Laverne Kuhnke, "The 'Doctoress' on a Donkey: Women Health Officers in Nineteenth-Century Egypt," *Clio Medica*, 9:3 (September 1974), 193–205; also Kuhnke's book, *Lives at Risk: Public Health in Nineteenth-Century Egypt* (Berkeley & Los Angeles: University of California Press, 1990). Suzanne Voilquin encountered the *hakimas* during her sojourn in Egypt with the Saint-Simonians and probably trained at the same school, which was attached to a military hospital. See John David Ragan, "A Fascination for the Exotic: Suzanne Voilquin, Ismayl Urbain, Jehan d'Ivray and the Saint Simonians, French Travelers in Egypt on the Margins" (Ph.D. Dissertation, New York University, 2000).

[29] Demands for women doctors during the 1840s included: P.-M. Rozier, *De la Condition sociale des femmes, du taux de leurs salaires, et de la recherche de la paternité à l'occasion des enfants trouvés, suivis de considérations sur les établissements de secours et l'aptitude des femmes à l'exercice de la médécine, avec une notice sur la régence des femmes, et lettres diverses*, 2nd ed. (Paris: Impr. J. Juteau, 1842), pp. 97–102. See also Etienne Cabet, *Voyage en Icarie*, 2nd ed. (Paris: J. Mallet, 1842), and Ernest Legouvé, *Histoire morale des femmes* (Paris: G. Sandré, 1849), pp. 412–413.

credentialed male birth-facilitators. Another women, who signed herself "Henriette (artiste)," countered this demand by asserting that the only real solution to the midwives' dilemma was to obtain the doctorate in medicine, so they could compete directly with the doctors in treating women's maladies as well as in delivering babies. The 20th April issue of *La Voix des Femmes* announced the opening of a private *Collège Médical des Dames* by a Dr. Malatier (61 rue de Provence, Paris).[30] At least one Frenchwoman, Jenny P. d'Héricourt, completed her professional training in midwifery at the Paris Faculty of Medicine. She also trained as a certified homeopathic physician during this period; in the 1850s and early 1860s she would directly challenge the male physicians' discourse (and that of their followers, such as Jules Michelet) on the purported weakness of women's bodies and minds.[31]

Meanwhile the women continued their quest for professional medical education.[32] By the 1860s, state action would be forthcoming. French women can thank the Empress Eugénie and the minister of education, Victor Duruy, for making possible their access to professional medical education. The decision to admit properly qualified women to the medical faculties was made in 1868 at a meeting of the Council of Ministers presided by Eugénie (acting as regent while Napoléon III was out of town, though presumably with his consent), and apparently over the objections of some ministers. The Empress and Duruy would subsequently formulate plans to open a medical school expressly for women in November 1870, but these plans would be thwarted by the outbreak of war with Germany and France's defeat.[33] Thanks to the 1868 decision, the authorities of the

[30] See the petition of the Paris midwives in *La Voix des Femmes*, n° 28 (20 April 1848); reprinted in *Le Grief des femmes*, ed. Maïté Albistur & Daniel Armogathe, vol. 1 (Paris, 1978), pp. 289–291, and the counterargument by "Henriette, artiste," in *La Voix des Femmes*, n° 31 (22 April 1848).

[31] See Karen Offen, "Qui est Jenny d'Héricourt: Une Identité rétrouvée," *1848: Révolutions et mutations au XIXe siècle*, no. 3 (1987), 87–100; the original English text of Héricourt's "autobiography" is published in Offen, "A Nineteenth-Century French Feminist Rediscovered: Jenny P. d'Héricourt, 1809–1875," *Signs: Journal of Women in Culture and Society*, 13:1 (Fall 1987), 144–158. Héricourt's pioneering analysis will be discussed further in the next two chapters.

[32] In the 1860s, other demands for opening medicine to women came from Mme A. Gael (pseud. Augustine [Lesourd] Girault), *La Femme médicin, sa raison d'être au point de vue de droit* (Paris: E. Dentu, 1868), and Charles Fauvéty, "Les Femmes-médicins," *La Solidarité* (1 April 1868). See also Suzanne Voilquin, *Souvenirs d'une fille du peuple* (Paris: Maspero, 1978; orig. publ. 1866), p. 68.

[33] According to Edmée Charrier, *L'Évolution intellectuelle féminine* (Paris: Éditions Albert Mechlinck, 1931), pp. 289–290, it was the Empress, presiding that day over the Council of Ministers, who swung the vote. The ensuing controversy about Eugénie's political role in *L'Opinion nationale* (20 August and 2 September 1868) is most illuminating of contemporary prejudices about women's role in political life. For Duruy's account of the medical school project for women and copies of his correspondence with the Empress, see his *Notes et souvenirs, 1811–1894*, vol. 2 (Paris: Hachette, 1902), pp. 196–211.

Paris Faculty of Medicine admitted four women to prepare the examinations for medical degrees.[34] But decades would pass before the medical establishment would permit women to compete for hospital internships and longer still before they were able to develop sufficient expertise to successfully challenge the hegemonic discourse of male physicians on women's bodies. It took even longer before women, whether learned or not, could begin to speak more openly and forcefully about their own physical, emotional, and sexual needs and desires, and about what treatments women really might need. Ordinary women doubtless spoke to the midwives, and even to their physicians, about their concerns, but, for the most part, their observations have not come down to us.

Medical Discourse and Population Politics

Biomedical thinking about women in France was, for centuries, mostly a male monopoly. It developed not only with reference to the debate about women's power and influence, along with deliberate intent to exclude them from political authority (as well as medical knowledge), but also in tandem with a growing concern about national population growth. This peculiarly problematic issue of population provoked a series of attempted interventions by French savants, physicians, and governmental officials to regulate aspects of personal behavior, including sexual behavior and its consequences, which had earlier been the prerogative of the Catholic Church. In the early years of the reign of Louis XIV, his finance minister (from 1665 to 1683) Jean-Baptiste Colbert and his associates concerned themselves not only with the fate of children already born but also with prospects for stimulating the birth rate and various aspects of sexual commerce. Their goal, embodied in the 1666 Edict on Marriage, was to foster population growth as a central aspect of the new "mercantilist" economic policy, mainly through offering financial incentives to French men. As historian Leslie Tuttle has observed, "treatises on marriage and children were in fact more numerous than works devoted to commerce, currency, colonies, or the grain trade."[35]

---

[34] The four women were Mary Putnam (later Jacobi) of the United States (who evidently had come to study in 1866), Elizabeth Garrett (later Anderson) from England, Catherine Gontcharoff from Russia, and Madeleine Brès from France.

[35] Leslie Tuttle, "Gender and Mercantilism: The Example of Natalist Policy," *Proceedings of the Western Society for French History, 2002*, vol. 30 (2004), 145–154; quote, 146. For additional information on these policies, see Tuttle, "Sacred and Politic Unions: Natalism, the Family and the State in Old Regime France, 1666–1789" (Ph.D. dissertation, Princeton University, 2000), and

Interventions by the male-dominated French state would ultimately encompass not only the systemic encouragement of marriage (viewed as a civil contract, not a sacrament) but also insistence on men's obligation to father children, discouragement of fertility control (whether through contraceptive practices or abortion), efforts to reduce illegitimate births, to prohibit infanticide and promote breastfeeding of infants by their mothers, to regulate midwifery, commercial wet-nursing, women's employment (including prostitution), and even to provide limited forms of day care for working mothers. By the early twentieth century, these efforts would encompass projects designed to combat infant mortality, to establish paid maternity leave and family allowances, and to honor mothers of large families (though without financial incentives until the mid-twentieth century).

As this list suggests, such efforts at social control on behalf of population growth increasingly asserted direct authority over women's bodies; the beginnings of these efforts antedated the Revolution by several centuries but would intensify in the nineteenth and twentieth centuries. If *paternité* was the image that embodied male kingship, and *fraternité* that of male citizenship in the new republican nation, *maternité* offered a powerful counterpoint to both.[36] In early modern France, population worries had effectively become an affair of state; this emphasis would continue under the republics of the nineteenth and twentieth centuries. The politics of population would inflect the theory and practice of physician-philosophers, of state officials, and of French feminists. It would shape the political response of monarchists and republicans alike to feminist demands for emancipation in ways that historians cannot afford to underestimate.[37] Indeed, I am arguing here (as I have previously) that the

---

her book, *Conceiving the Old Regime: Pronatalism and the Politics of Reproduction in Early Modern France* (New York: Oxford University Press, 2010).

[36] See Lynn Hunt's provocative psychoanalytic interpretation, *The Family Romance of the French Revolution* (Berkeley & Los Angeles: University of California Press, 1982).

[37] I first elaborated this argument in my article, "Depopulation, Nationalism, and Feminism in Fin-de-Siècle France," *American Historical Review*, 89:3 (June 1984), 648–676. It incorporates an extensive bibliographical critique of the gender-blind character of French demographic literature prior to that date. See also Louise A. Tilly, "Demographic History Faces the Family: Europe since 1500," *Trends in History*, 3:3–4 (Spring/Summer 1985), 45–68. For a subsequent chapter in gender-blind demographic history, see Richard Tomlinson, "The 'Disappearance' of France, 1896–1949," *The Historical Journal*, 28:2 (June 1985), 405–415. More recently, see Joshua Cole, "'There Are Only Good Mothers': The Ideological Work of Women's Fertility in France before World War I," *French Historical Studies*, 19:3 (Spring 1996), 639–672.

My thinking about the links between depopulation, nationalism, and feminism was initially stimulated by the studies of Joseph John Spengler, *France Faces Depopulation* (Durham, NC: Duke University Press, 1938: reprinted with a new postscript, 1979); Wesley Douglass Camp,

population issue was central to the elaboration of both nationalist and feminist thought and action during these years; it would continue to shape the theory and practice of the French women's rights movement as well as the republic's political response to the women's demands even into the Fourth and Fifth Republics. For many decades, it remained a feature specific to French society.

Under the monarchy France had become the most populous and powerful state in Europe, its kings preoccupied since the sixteenth century by the politics of population. The Roman Catholic Church had already set a precedent, treating abortion and infanticide as acts that could trigger excommunication, and such a sanction did produce a considerable moral effect among believers. But secular rulers (even those sanctified by God) were not content with this. An early state measure, dating from Henri II in 1556, had already called on civil authorities to obtain "declarations of pregnancy" from unmarried mothers-to-be, with the intent of damping down clandestine abortion and infanticide by making these crimes punishable by death.[38] Colbert instituted measures, in addition to those mentioned earlier, to combat ecclesiastical celibacy in the pursuit of population growth.[39] Such measures notwithstanding (whether they were effective is another question), commentators continually bemoaned depopulation; the historian Jacques Gélis depicts a "great demographic fear" during the eighteenth century.[40] These concerns were reflected by Rousseau who, in his *Social Contract* (1762), argued that the rate of

Marriage and the Family in France Since the Revolution: An Essay in the History of Population (New York: Bookman, 1961), and Etienne Van de Walle, *The Female Population of France in the Nineteenth Century: A Reconstitution of 82 Departments* (Princeton, NJ: Princeton University Press, 1974). Subsequently, two important and complementary works have appeared: Joshua Cole, *The Power of Large Numbers: Population, Politics, and Gender in Nineteenth-Century France* (Ithaca, NY: Cornell University Press, 2000), and Carol Blum, *Strength in Numbers: Population, Reproduction, and Power in Eighteenth-Century France* (Baltimore: The Johns Hopkins University Press, 2002).

[38] On these declarations of pregnancy, see Marie-Claude Phan, "Les Déclarations de grossesse en France, XVIe – XVIIIe siècles: Essai institutionnel," *Revue d'Histoire Moderne et Contemporaine*, 22:1 (January–March 1975), 61–88. See also Cissie Fairchild, "Female Sexual Attitudes and the Rise of Illegitimacy: A Case Study," *Journal of Interdisciplinary History*, 8:4 (Spring 1978), 627–667; and the subsequent exchange between J.-L. Flandrin and Fairchild in *JID*, 9:2 (Autumn 1976), 309–321.

[39] See Joseph J. Spengler, *French Predecessors of Malthus* (Durham, NC: Duke University Press, 1942; republished, New York: Octagon Books, 1965); *Économie et population; Les Doctrines françaises avant 1800. Bibliographie générale commentée*, Institut National des Etudes Démographiques; travaux et documents, n° 28 (Paris: INED, 1956); and Philippe Ariès, *Histoire des populations françaises et de leurs attitudes devant la vie depuis le XVIIIe siècle* (Paris: Seuil, 1971; orig. publ., 1948). See also the unpublished study by Roderick Phillips, "Family and Population Policies under the Old Regime and the Revolution," paper presented to the Western Society for French History, November 1987, Las Cruces, NM.

[40] Gélis, *La Sage-femme ou le médecin*, p. 72.

reproduction (i.e., population increase) must be considered the principal criterion by which good government could be judged.[41] His inference was that the current situation, under Louis XV, was far from satisfactory; city women in particular were not bearing children. Rousseau was by no means alone in his concern. Thirty years later, French revolutionary leaders (all male) would become adamant about easing restrictions on marriage in order to facilitate family formation and promote childbearing. And, in response to Rousseau's *Julie* and ensuing cultural fashion, breastfeeding became not only fashionable among elite women but, during the Revolution, a hallmark of political correctness.[42] Indeed, the revolutionary Convention decreed on 28 June 1793 that neither mother nor child would be eligible for state financial support in case of indigence unless the mother (including the unmarried) nursed her infant with her own breast milk.[43]

Despite such vigorous interventions, France became the first European nation to experience an absolute decline in the birth rate. Demographic historian Jacques Dupâquier insists that the actual statistical drop in the French birth rate dates only from 1800, in the aftermath of the revolution (and at the outset of Napoléon's military campaigns).[44] Even so, in

---

[41] Jean-Jacques Rousseau, *The Social Contract*, transl. Maurice Cranston (Penguin ed., 1968), Book III, chapter IX, pp. 129–130.

[42] See Phillips, "Family and Population Policies," cited in n. 39. See also Marie-France Morel, "Théories et pratiques de l'allaitement en France au XVIIIe siècle," *Annales de Démographie Historique 1976*, 393–426, and Mary Jacobus, "Incorruptible Milk: Breast-Feeding and the French Revolution," in *Rebel Daughters: Women and the French Revolution*, ed. Sara E. Melzer & Leslie W. Rabine (New York: Oxford University Press, 1992), pp. 54–75. Rousseau is often credited with stimulating the return to breastfeeding by elite women; see Barbara Corrado Pope, "The Influence of Rousseau's Ideology of Domesticity," in *Connecting Spheres: Women in the Western World, 1500 to the Present*, ed. Marilyn J. Boxer & Jean H. Quataert (New York: Oxford University Press, 1987), pp. 136–145.

[43] I thank Marilyn Yalom for this reference; see her book, *A History of the Breast* (New York: Knopf, 1997), esp. chapter 4 – "The Political Breast," p. 115. This document can be consulted in the *Archives parlementaires de 1787 à 1860*, 1st ser., vol. LXVII (1905), p. 614.

[44] See Jacques Dupâquier, *La Population française aux XVIIe et XVIIIe siècles* (Paris: Presses Universitaires de France, 1979), and his earlier articles, "Sur la Population française aux XVIIe et XVIIIe siècles," *Revue Historique*, 239 (January–March 1968), 43–79; in English as "French Population in the 17th and 18th Centuries," in *Essays in French Economic History*, ed. Rondo Cameron (Homewood, IL: published for the American Economics Association by R. D. Irwin, 1970), pp. 150–169; (with M. Lachiver), "Sur les Débuts de la contraception en France ou les deux malthusianismes," *Annales: Économies, Sociétés, Civilisations*, 24:6 (November–December 1969), 1391–1406 (in response to Antoinette Fauve-Chamoux & Cécile Dauphin, "La Contraception avant la Révolution française: l'exemple de Châtillon-sur-Seine," *Annales: E. S. C.*, 24:3 [May–June 1969], 662–684); "Les Caractères originaux de l'histoire démographique française au XVIIIe siècle," *Revue d'Histoire Moderne et Contemporaine*, 23:2 (April–June 1976), 182–202. See also the articles by Dupâquier and others in "Dénatalité; l'antériorité française, 1800–1914," a special issue of *Communications*, n° 44 (1986), and Jacques Dupâquier, *Histoire de la population française*, 4 vols. (Paris: Presses Universitaires de France, 1988), esp. vols. 3 & 4.

1791 the revolutionary government had authorized an edict that prescribed severe punishment for abortionists, though not for aborting women.

Napoléon, like his predecessors, worried about population issues and began to take precautions against loss. His celebrated riposte to Madame de Staël in late 1797, when she asked him who he considered to be the greatest woman in the world, living or dead – "the woman who has [borne] the most children" – should be read in this context, as should his subsequent interest in fostering the Maternal Societies throughout France.[45] His attitude concerning women was purely instrumental, and even (in his Orientalist mode) anticipated multiple wives as a necessity, as this quotation from June 1816 (addressed to a group of women) clearly reveals:[46]

> Woman is given to man to bring forth children. A single wife cannot suffice a man for that purpose. She cannot be his wife when she is pregnant; she cannot be his wife when she is nursing; she cannot be his wife when she is ill; she ceases to be his wife when she can no longer give him children. Man, whom nature does not limit either by age or by any of these other inconveniences, should therefore have several wives. . . . You aspire to equality? This is craziness! Woman is our property; we are not hers; for she gives us children and man does not give any to her. She is therefore his property, as the tree is that of the gardener.

In the 1810 Penal Code, Napoléon's legislators defined abortion as a criminal offence, with severe penalties against both the abortionist and the abortee.[47] Imperial officials had already asserted further surveillance over the education and practice of French midwives, who had long been suspected by male authorities of practicing abortion on the side.[48] The government also exerted increasing control, especially at the municipal

---

[45] This interchange is documented by the comte de Las Cases, *Le Mémorial de Sainte-Hélène*, 2 vols. (reprint ed., Paris: Garnier frères, 1895; orig. publ. in Paris: L'Auteur, 1823–1824), vol. 2, pp. 962–965; quote, p. 963. On Napoléon's encouragement of maternal societies, see Christine Adams, "Maternal Societies in France: Private Charity Before the Welfare State," *Journal of Women's History*, 17:1 (Spring 2005), 87–111.

[46] Napoléon at St. Helena, 3 June 1816; as documented by the comte de Las Cases, *Le Mémorial de Sainte-Hélène*, vol. 1, chapter 6 (1895 ed.), p. 682.

[47] Art. 317 of the Penal Code of 1810. See "Dossier: L'histoire de l'avortement," *L'Histoire*, n° 16 (October 1979), with articles by Paul Veyne, J.-L. Flandrin, Jeanne Gaillard, and R.-H. Guerrand. See also Jacques Dupâquier, "Combien d'avortements en France avant 1914?" *Communications*, n° 44 (1986), 87–106, which also includes a useful source bibliography.

[48] See Burton, "The Organization of a National System of Midwifery Education," cited in n. 26. For earlier efforts to regulate and improve midwifery training in France, see Richard L. Petrelli, "The Regulation of French Midwifery in the Ancien Regime," *Journal of the History of Medicine and Allied Sciences*, 26:3 (July 1971), 276–292, and Nina Rattner Gelbart, "Mme du Coudray's Manual for Midwives: the Politics of Enlightenment Obstetrics," *Western Society for French History, Proceedings 1988*, vol. 16 (1989), 389–396, and her book *The King's Midwife*.

level, over what historian George Sussman has baptized the "wet-nursing industry," which, by shipping urban babies off to country wet nurses for a fee, was blamed for inadvertently causing thousands of infant deaths.[49] Nineteenth-century experts in forensic medicine began to construct an entire literature around the problems of abortion and infanticide, while government authorities sought to prosecute and convict abortionists and their clients. Feminist historians have reconstructed and analyzed these sustained and interlinked attempts at control and regulation. Nancy Jaicks has pointed out how the campaigns against abortion and suspect midwives intensified following the publication of Ambroise Tardieu's landmark "medical-legal study of abortion" (1855–1856) in the *Annales d'Hygiène Public*.[50] Rachel Fuchs has documented the practice of abortion and infanticide as they appear in case records of the Paris Assize Courts, while James Donovan has examined trials and the high rate of acquittals.[51]

None of these interventionist measures succeeded in fostering population growth. By the late nineteenth century, France's population in absolute numbers would be overtaken by that of the surrounding monarchies – Germany and England. As the French birth rate continued its downward turn, and infant mortality levels remained high, doctors, moralists, and politicians would fret over the long-range implications of these figures for national economic, political, and military strength. In their eyes, France's very survival as a powerful nation-state seemed to be at stake. Few of them would have appreciated the dispassionate arguments of today's demographic historians, who have concluded that France was in fact leading the way in a phenomenon of societal development now referred to as the "demographic transition."[52]

[49] George Sussman, *Selling Mother's Milk: The Wet-Nursing Business in France, 1715–1914* (Urbana: University of Illinois Press, 1982).

[50] Ambroise Tardieu, "Étude médico-légale sur l'avortement," *Annales d'Hygiène Publique*, vol. 53 (1855), 394–442, & vol. 54 (1856), 113–169. See June K. Burton, "Human Rights Issues Affecting Women in Napoleonic Legal Medicine Textbooks," *History of European Ideas*, 8:4–5 (1987), 427–434. For studies of Tardieu, see Jeanne Gaillard, "Le Médecin et l'avortement au XIXe siècle," *L'Histoire*, n° 16 (October 1979), 35–37, and Nancy Robin Jaicks, "The Crime of Abortion and the Medical-Legal Expert: Female Practice and Male Proscription in Nineteenth-Century France," paper presented at the 8th Berkshire Conference on the History of Women, Douglass College, June 1990. See also Jaicks's dissertation, "Angel-Makers: The Crime of Abortion in Nineteenth-Century Lyon" (Ph.D. dissertation, Columbia University, 1993). For an important overview, see Angus McLaren, "Abortion in France: Women and the Regulation of Family Size, 1800–1914," *French Historical Studies*, 10:3 (Spring 1978), 461–485.

[51] Rachel Ginnis Fuchs, *Poor and Pregnant in Paris: Strategies for Survival in the Nineteenth Century* (New Brunswick, NJ: Rutgers University Press, 1992), chapters 8–9; James M. Donovan, "Abortion, the Law, and the Juries in France, 1825–1923," *Criminal Justice History*, vol. 9 (1988), 157–188.

[52] On the "demographic transition," see the various articles by Dupâquier and others, cited earlier.

France was not the sole country to experience a falling birth rate in the late nineteenth century; indeed, all the major industrializing nations had begun to record similar drops, though they lagged well behind the French. In the aftermath of the German victory over France in 1870–1871 and France's loss of Alsace-Lorraine, leaders of the new French republican government would become painfully aware of the international implications of the birth rate decline and would take additional steps to stop it; the German victory, meanwhile, would underscore the relationship between population growth and national might, as then measured by military (and increasingly economic) strength. Indeed, alarm over the slowness of French population growth, with its important implications for France's international standing, would affect virtually every political issue that arose during the Third Republic, from education and marriage law reform to taxes, military conscription, and rearmament. Most republicans were committed to a defense of the liberal and egalitarian principles of the Revolution, as incarnated in the Declaration of the Rights of Man, and they felt certain that the installation of the new republican regime would return France to its greatness of former times. But none could ignore "depopulation," its causes, and its possible implications for a republic's success. A formidable literature on this subject would emerge during the later years of the nineteenth century, as we will see in my subsequent volume.

Until recently, few works by demographers, or by demographic historians for that matter, had acknowledged the existence of these debates, let alone the fact most startlingly obvious to historians of women and the family and to feminist critics – that fertility is not an abstraction, and the birth rate not a mere statistic. Children are borne by women and aggregate statistics on nuptiality and fertility (whether legitimate or illegitimate) depend to a great extent on discrete acts of consent (and resistance) by individual women as well as on the desires of men. Both sexes act within a concrete legal, socioeconomic, political, and cultural context that structures intercourse – and its consequences – within a framework of drastically unequal power relations. It is impossible, for instance, to comprehend the French alarm over population – and over women's aggregate behavior – in the late nineteenth century by looking only, as Etienne Van de Walle has done, at long-term demographic trends.

A different aspect of the problem is revealed when we note that the primary sources in the population debate are themselves heatedly partisan and, in particular, dismissive of women's agency in questions pertaining to population growth or stagnation. As historians Joan Scott and Joshua Cole have pointed out, the very choice of statistics presented by a writer or published by a government agency could be affected by that writer's or agency's views on the emancipation of women.[53] And it took centuries to overcome the blindness of mercantilist economic theories to "the enormous value of the labor of France's women who carried, gave birth to, and nurtured the soldiers and merchants" needed not only by monarchs but also by republics.[54] Indeed, the sexual politics of knowledge infused this debate, and more generally the entire debate on the woman question from beginning to end.

Investigating and Debating Women's Sexual Behavior

Another significant thread in the fabric of French biomedical discourse was sexuality and, yes, sexual behavior. From the later eighteenth century on, a favorite topic of the male physician-philosophers and savants (well before the Marquis de Sade began to publish his shocking texts in the 1790s) was sex, and particularly the erotic capacity of the female body (which they often linked to the "problem" of women's power and influence) and its psychological consequences. For them, women were "the sex" (*le sexe*) and women connoted sexuality. Women's capacity for sexual expression could be at once fascinating – and fearful – from a male perspective. This had been true for many centuries, as the medieval historian Monica H. Green has documented.[55] And the fear and the fascination would continue throughout the eighteenth century and well beyond. Beginning with Dr. Bienville's treatise on nymphomania, published in 1771, French male physicians were probing the secrets of women's sexual pleasure.[56] They also produced a voyeuristic literature on "unnatural" sexual acts, "infertile pleasures" including carnal relations between women (*tribadisme*) and

---

[53] See Joan W. Scott, "A Statistical Representation of Work: 'Le Statistique de l'industrie à Paris, 1847–1848'," chapter 6 in her *Gender and the Politics of History* (New York: Columbia University Press, 1988), and Cole, *Power of Large Numbers*.

[54] Quote from Tuttle, "Gender and Mercantilism," 151.

[55] See the excellent review essay by Monica H. Green, "Female Sexuality in the Medieval West" *Trends in History*, 4:9 (1990), 127–158.

[56] See Jean-Marie Goulemot's introduction to the reprinted edition of Bienville, *De la Nymphomanie, ou fureur utérine* (Paris, 1980), and G. S. Rousseau, "Nymphomania, Bienville and the Rise of Erotic Sensibility," in *Sexuality in Eighteenth-Century Britain*, ed. Paul-Gabriel Boucé (Manchester, UK, and Totowa, NJ: Barnes & Noble, 1982), pp. 95–119. In addition, see the early nineteenth-century doctors' discussions of hermaphroditism as reconstructed by Michel Foucault through the case of Herculine Barbin, *Herculine Barbin, dite Alexina B., documents présentés par Michel Foucault* (Paris: Gallimard, 1978); these documents were originally published in 1874. See also Thomas Laqueur's article on orgasm (cited in n. 15). and "'Amor Veneris, vel Dulcedo Appeletur,'" on the "scientific discovery" of the clitoris (1989), reprinted in *Feminism & the Body*, ed. Schiebinger, pp. 58–86.

incest, which would, among other things, inform the vicious campaigns against Marie-Antoinette during the early years of the revolution.[57] And, of course, they also launched the investigation of hysteria, or what they called uterine furor, which was deemed a peculiarly feminine ailment until the later nineteenth century, when Dr. Charcot demonstrated, through his research, the existence of hysteria in men. Indeed, the erotic would never disappear from the French discussion, in contrast to the situation in early nineteenth-century England and America.[58]

Conflicts between the Roman Catholic Church and the French state encompassed the patrolling of intimate relationships. Of course, physicians took up some of the related questions. The Church had continually preached the line of unrestricted population growth, which it continues to preach today. Consequent on this was its concern about "unproductive" sexual intercourse and condemnation of human intervention to thwart pregnancy, whether through contraception, abortion, or infanticide. "Since the beginning, the Catholic Church's hostility to abortion follows from its condemnation of infertile pleasures," historian Jean-Louis Flandrin once observed.[59] The same could be said of the Church's hostility to a variety of other cultural practices that concerned sexual activity, especially outside marriage but also within, contraception being the most notable.[60] Yet, by the eighteenth century, despite the nominal Catholicism of the French population, the separation in practice of human sexual activity and pleasure from reproduction was manifest, despite the best

---

[57] See especially Lynn Hunt, ed., *Eroticism and the Body Politic* (Baltimore: Johns Hopkins University Press, 1991), including Hunt's essay, "The Many Bodies of Marie Antoinette: Political Pornography and the Problem of the Feminine in the French Revolution," pp. 108–130.

[58] See the remarks of the British physician, William Acton, on this subject: "I am ready to maintain that there are many females who never feel any sexual excitement whatever." *The Functions and Disorders of the Reproductive Organs*, 8th American ed. (Philadelphia: P. Blakiston, 1894); the critical passages are reprinted as document 37(ii) in *Victorian Women: A Documentary Account of Women's Lives in Nineteenth-Century England, France, and the United States*, ed. Erna Olafson Hellerstein, Leslie Parker Hume, & Karen M. Offen (Stanford, CA: Stanford University Press, 1981), p. 178. Yet Acton's views had a French precedent: on the determined efforts of earlier (around 1800) French physicians engaged with elaborating the "science of man" to characterize women's sexuality as passive, in order to bolster the image of men's own sexual prowess and self-sovereignty, see Elizabeth Colwill, "Women's Empire and the Sovereignty of Man in *La Décade philosophique*, 1794–1807," *Eighteenth-Century Studies*, 29:3 (Spring 1996), 265–289; esp. 274–276.

[59] Jean-Louis Flandrin, "L'avortement dans l'ancienne France (XVIe-XVIIIe siècles)," *L'Histoire*, n° 16 (October 1979), 34.

[60] Still the best study on contraception in Catholic thinking is John T. Noonan, Jr., *Contraception, a History of its Treatment by the Catholic Theologians and Canonists* (Cambridge, MA: Harvard University Press, 1966). But see also the important critique by P.P.A. Biller, "Birth-Control in the West in the Thirteenth and Early Fourteenth Centuries," *Past and Present*, n° 94 (February 1982), 3–26.

efforts of church and lay authorities to criticize, then attempt to reassert control over sexual behavior. Even though no one, even medical scientists, yet understood the process of conception (though there were many theories, including the theory that the male seed was the sole active ingredient), both churchmen and laymen did understand that sexual intercourse between a man and a woman could – and should – engender offspring. They became suspicious when it did not inevitably do so.

In light of the populationist concerns discussed earlier, the modes and consequences of "immoral behavior" also came to encompass virtually all sexual activity outside marriage – adultery, prostitution, concubinage, even masturbation. Such topics also attracted the combined attention of secular male philosophers, physicians, and police authorities. These practices, along with the efforts of authorities to intervene and regulate them, have also elicited the attention of many historians. The analyses of the philosopher Michel Foucault and the historians influenced by his insights have revealed the extraordinarily abundant and obsessively controlling character of French (male) discourse on sexual behavior from the eighteenth century on.[61] These concerns were even more richly expressed in the period following the French Revolution, offering historians unprecedented insights into the gendered character of sociopolitical problems throughout the nineteenth century. We may not know so much about the private behavior of particular individuals, but we do know a great deal about what was being said or speculated about it.[62]

The topics of contraception, abortion, and infanticide – all central to populationist concerns – first underwent historians' scrutiny, followed by the currently fashionable topics of homosexuality and pornography, stimulated by late twentieth-century interests in sexual liberation. Scholars at first showed less interest in the power relationships of sex within or outside marriage, taking male hegemony almost for granted. These power relationships were glossed over by speaking of "the family," "the couple," or "parents," as Flandrin himself so often did.[63] We have since learned how important it is to distinguish whose sexuality and whose interests are being

---

[61] On these matters, see Angus McLaren, "Some Secular Attitudes toward Sexual Behavior in France, 1760–1860," *French Historical Studies*, 8:4 (Fall 1974), 604–625, esp. pp. 617ff., and McLaren's book, *Sexuality and Social Order: The Debate over the Fertility of Women and Workers in France, 1770–1920* (New York: Holmes & Meier, 1983). See also the essays in Hunt, ed., *Eroticism and the Body Politic*.

[62] Historian Anne Marie Sohn has combed French archives looking for first-hand testimonies on this subject. See Sohn, *Chrysalides: Femmes dans la vie privée (XIXe-XXe siècles)*, 2 vols. (Paris: Publications de la Sorbonne, 1996).

[63] See Jean-Louis Flandrin, *Families in Former Times: Kinship, Household and Sexuality* (Cambridge, UK: Cambridge University Press, 1979; orig. publ. in French, 1976).

discussed and who is doing the talking.[64] As Monica Green has indicated, looking only at "the authoritative structures in society" will not produce the evidence necessary to assess intimate behavior.[65]

A more critical reading of Roman Catholic prescriptive literature reveals that one of the principal features of Christian marriage, as constructed by church theologians and apologists over the centuries, was to advocate (in contrast to the perspective of Napoléon Bonaparte, quoted earlier) the containment of a man's sexual activity (reprehensible as it might be considered) to one woman, his wife. One means of doing this was to insist that she be accessible to him at all times. Asking a man to curb his inclinations, once he had gotten into the habit of sexual gratification, seemed out of the question to (ostensibly celibate) male church authorities. This throws a new light on Madame de Sévigné's much-quoted advice to her married daughter in early 1672, following the birth of a son and heir (after several failed attempts), not to succumb to the temptation of sleeping with her husband again, if she wanted to avoid another immediate pregnancy. Sévigné's words are worth quoting: "I also want to warn you about one thing that I maintain to the face of you and your husband. That is, if, after being purified [i.e., churched], you even have the idea . . . of sleeping with M. de Grignan, be assured that you will get pregnant. And if one of your matrons says the contrary, she will be corrupted by your spouse. Following this advice, I have nothing more to say."[66] Not only the church but also Colbert and his minions would have strongly disapproved of such motherly advice, had they gotten wind of it.

---

[64] See Green, "Female Sexuality in the Medieval West." Monica Green provides a salutary look at changing views and debates within the Catholic Church on issues such as contraception, abortion, infanticide, and sex as a solely procreative act. She also criticizes scholarship that embraces (uncritically) the views of the "authoritative structures in society" (p. 129) and insists on the importance of scientific as well as theological debate: "The sheer amount of medieval scientific and medical discussions on sexuality might have challenged Foucault to rethink his belief that the creation of a scientific 'sexual discourse' was a characteristic of the modern period" (p. 141).

[65] Green, " Female Sexuality," 129.

[66] See Marie de Rabutin-Chantal, marquise de Sévigné, *Correspondance*, ed. Roger Duchêne, 3 vols. (Paris: Gallimard/La Pléiade, 1972–1978) vol. 1, letters 232 (5 January 1672) & 233 (8 January 1672), pp. 410–413; quote, p. 413. My translation. Mme de Grignan, Sévigné's beloved daughter married the older M. de Grignan in 1671; he had gone through two previous wives, producing several daughters but no son to inherit his very considerable estate. With him (who was syphletic) she experienced six pregnancies in eight years, becoming increasingly worn down and producing increasingly unhealthy babies. Her mother obsessed about her daughter losing her much-vaunted beauty in the process and more than once cautioned her not to sleep with her husband. Of their four children, one son was stillborn, another, the heir, survived to adulthood; two daughters completed the family.

In light of my earlier arguments about the perceived importance of women's power and influence in France, it seems useful to explore the balance of power in intimate heterosexual relationships, particularly in marriage. The analysis of changing attitudes toward intercourse taboos offers a particularly fruitful avenue for investigating the historical dynamics of the marriage relationship. Although (as I have suggested earlier) it continues to be difficult to obtain firsthand evidence about the actual sexual behavior of couples, a great deal can be inferred by reading against the grain the examples and prescriptions found in Catholic – and secular – advice literature (and, as Anne-Marie Sohn has demonstrated, in the realm of court records).[67]

Textual evidence suggests that the Church's view of marriage had been designed, first and foremost, to accommodate men's sexual urges, even as theologians condemned lust and endorsed celibacy as a superior state for the church elite. Marriage, deemed a sacrament once entered into, had no escape clause for either party, except through annulment.[68] Within the late medieval Church's construction of the marital institution, husbands were clearly privileged, even as their relationship to their wives was moralized.[69] Recreational sex was not viewed kindly; Antoine Hotman argued in a late sixteenth-century treatise that one important aspect of Oxford theologian John Wycliffe's earlier teachings (for which he was posthumously condemned for heresy in 1415 by the Council of Constance) was his call for a ban on all heterosexual intercourse that did not lead to offspring.[70] Yet, if we credit the evidence provided by later Catholic confessional manuals (studied by Flandrin), wives were supposed to be at the complete disposition of their husbands; there were, theoretically speaking, no circumstances (except perhaps during holy days) under which a confessor could absolve a Catholic wife for refusing her husband's embrace – not during her menstrual periods, not during pregnancy, not during nursing, not during illness. A wife's acquiescence to a husband's desire was perhaps a

---

[67] See Sohn, *Chrysalides: Femmes dans la vie privée (XIXe-XXe siècles),* cited in n. 62.

[68] Annulment proceedings took a very bizarre form in seventeenth-century France, notably in trials of husbands for impotence. See Pierre Darmon, *Le Tribunal de l'impuissance: Virilité et défaillances conjugales dans l'ancienne France* (Paris: Seuil, 1979), also in English, *Trial by Impotence: Virility and Marriage in Pre-Revolutionary France* (London: Chatto & Windus, 1985).

[69] Flandrin, *Families in Former Times.* For the development of penances for sexual sins in the confession manuals of the early church prior to codification of canon law, see Pierre J. Payer, *Sex and the Penitentials: The Development of a Sexual Code, 550–1150* (Toronto: University of Toronto Press, 1984).

[70] Antoine Hotman, *Traicté* [sic] *de la dissolution du mariage par l'impuissance et froideur de l'homme ou de la femme* (Paris, 1610; orig. publ. 1581), p. 8.

sin, but a lesser sin than her refusal. A woman's "I do" in the marriage ceremony constituted a "yes" for all time and, seemingly, under all circumstances. As one cleric put it, in 1782, "Women should remind themselves that by entering the Married State, they have subjected themselves to all these tribulations; they must remind themselves that they are Christians; that they must love their husbands in and for God; they must better love and suffer these trials, than to expose their husbands to incontinence and mortal sin."[71] Intercourse taboos, in other words, were not integral to the French Catholic notion of adult sexuality in marriage, as they apparently continued to be in other cultural contexts. The existence of such taboos elsewhere, or earlier, was much discussed.[72]

Intercourse during pregnancy was one issue; intercourse during lactation was another, more problematic practice, one that directly illuminates the sexual dynamics of Catholic marriage prescriptions. The conflict created for a woman by the nutritional needs of her infant and the sexual desires (dare we call it lust?) of her husband (and herself) was most often resolved – at least among the French upper classes (but also among the working classes) – by hiring surrogates, either in-house, or putting the babies out to wet nurses in the rural countryside. A significant number of these outsourced babies never returned alive to their parents, and this sad fact had serious implications for population growth. Husbands took or rather demanded priority, with the sanction of the Church, and wives, though conflicted, acquiesced, in order to stave off philandering. Wet nurses, on the other hand, were strictly forbidden carnal relations, for fear it would spoil their milk.[73] The case quoted from Fromageau's *Dictionnaire des cas de conscience* (1733) by Flandrin epitomizes the concerns and the Church's resolution:

> Jeanne, having had a first child by her husband, wishes to feed it herself; but, since her husband wishes to demand of her his conjugal rights, she asks whether she is obliged to satisfy him during all the time that she is nursing her child, or whether she can refuse him without sinning?

[71] Père Féline, *Catéchisme des gens mariés* (Caen, 1782; republished in Brussels, 1881), p. 30.
[72] See, for comparative purposes, the controversy concerning the Norwegian Law of Bogarthing, which regulated sexual abstinence during breastfeeding. Ole J. Benedictow, "The Milky Way in History: Breast Feeding, Antagonism between the Sexes and Infant Mortality in Medieval Norway," *Scandinavian Journal of History*, vol. 10 (1985),19–53, and the rejoinder by Sølvi Sogner, "Allaitement au sein et abstinence sexuelle au moyen âge," *Annales de Démographie Historique 1986* (1987), 353–359.
[73] On this issue, see the insightful article by Antoinette Fauve-Chamoux, "La Femme devant l'allaitement," *Annales de Démographie Historique 1983* (1984), 7–22.

Fromageau concluded that "The wife should, if she can, put her child out to nurse, in order to provide for the frailty of her husband by paying the conjugal due, for fear that he may lapse into some sin against conjugal purity."[74]

It is in this context, where women's fertility would soon resume and new pregnancies ensue, Flandrin believes, that French married couples began to experiment with creative forms of birth control. He argues, further, that it was at women's insistence that French husbands increasingly adopted "courtly" approaches, wooing their wives rather than forcing them, and agreeing to practice *coitus interruptus*, or withdrawal prior to ejaculation.[75]

As population-conscious physicians intervened in the debate, consideration of intercourse taboos found its place in the medical literature. These discussions seem to accompany directly medical interest in saving children and in restricting male concupiscence and the "problem" of onanism, or seed-spilling, by which was more usually meant masturbation (but sometimes also *coitus interruptus*).[76] Physicians were less keen than the Catholic moralists to sanction intercourse under every and all circumstances. For instance, Dr. Roussel, in his *Systeme physique et morale* made a strong argument for sexual continence during nursing, on behalf of the baby.[77]

From the early nineteenth century on, these secular French physicians changed tack. They advised married women against intercourse during pregnancy, but they also acknowledged (like the confessors) the impracticability of an absolute prohibition. Rather, they recommended caution and moderation on the woman's part, on behalf of the child. From Moreau (de la Sarthe), writing in 1803, to Menville de Ponsan (1845, 1858) who plagiarized Moreau, the doctors' emphasis turned insistently (from the needs of the husband) to the well-being of the growing child. "Can one reasonably believe that the *foetus*, whose existence is so frail, can support without danger the disorder often produced by the entire ecstatic economy of voluptuousness?" Menville de Ponsan wrote in 1845.[78] But the problem

---

[74] Fromageau, as quoted in Flandrin, *Families*, p. 206. A similar view (with comparable examples), also cited by Flandrin, p. 207, can be found in the Latin treatise of Thomas Sanchez, *Disputationum de sancto matrimonii sacramento*, 3 vols. (Antwerp, 1607), vol. 3, book IX, on the conjugal "debt."

[75] Flandrin, *Families*, pp. 220–225.

[76] On "onanism," see McLaren, "Some Secular Attitudes . . . " More recently, see Claude Langlois, *Le crime d'Onan: le discours Catholique sur la limitation des naissances, 1816–1930* (Paris: Belles lettres, 2005).

[77] See Roussel, *Système physique et morale de la femme* (1775), p. 361. In the 7th ed. of 1820, see pp. 215–216.

[78] See Moreau (de la Sarthe), *Histoire naturelle de la femme*, vol. 2, pp. 299–301; also Menville de Ponsan, *Histoire philosophique et médicale de la femme*, pp. 191–194, 260–262. Hellerstein, "Women,

of containing and satisfying male desire remained, as would be vividly suggested in 1872 by Alexandre Dumas *fils*, when he articulated for a mostly male audience not only the psychological complexity of becoming a father but also of coping with a wife's decision to nurse the child and to distance the husband from her bed.[79] This account from 1872 bears quoting at length:

> Nurse! But to nurse is a matter of ten or twelve months! You go to find the doctor. He must make your wife understand reason. (You already need another to make her understand reason). She is not strong enough! It will wear her out! It will wear her down! For the child, a nurse, a good stout country woman is certainly preferable. The health of the child must come first. You do not give the doctor all the reasons there are: but he understands the rest. "Doctor, put yourself in my place, etc., etc."
>
> The woman persists; she wants to nurse; she would reproach herself for eternity not to have done her duty, and in the case that something happened to the baby, she would never pardon herself. Nothing is as good for a baby as the mother's milk. It is not enough to give birth, one must also give life, etc.
>
> What can you say to that? And so it goes for a year. After which, if you have been very good, you will again be admitted . . . to become a father? No, to make her a mother.
>
> You bow your head; there you are, vanquished, in your turn by the feminine, the eternal feminine. It has used you for the work it has to do. It attracts you, seduces you, utilizes you, sends you away. It retakes you and eliminates you, according to the needs of destiny and function. And know well, in passing, that it is ever the same, whatever the plane on which you encounter woman. She never takes you for yourself, she never takes you but for herself.

As this text suggests, sexual politics in the French context was not a simple matter. According to historian Mary Lynn Stewart, the most outspoken male physician of the later nineteenth century, Adolphe Pinard, posted a notice in his prenatal clinic, "All pregnant women must refuse sexual relations for their entire pregnancy."[80] Pinard, not surprisingly, was a

---

Social Order, and the City", p. 195, indicates that two dissenting French medical men writing during the July Monarchy – the homeopath Léon-François-Adolphe Simon (1830) and the physician Joseph-Antoine-Hector Chomet (1846) – both supported intercourse during pregnancy, and the physician Jules Hatin (1832) advocated it during nursing as well. Chomet's book was directed specifically to women.

[79] From Alexandre Dumas *fils*, *L'Homme-femme* (1872), reprinted in *Le Dossier Tué-là! constitué, édité, et plaidé par André Lebois* (Avignon: E. Aubanel, 1969), pp. 62–63.

[80] See Stewart, *For Health and Beauty*, p. 126.

leading pronatalist campaigner for bringing babies to term and lowering infant mortality. Like his predecessors, he would insist that the survival of the future child must take precedence over the carnal desires of either parent.

Returning to the issue of contraceptive practices, French physicians seemed more concerned with counseling patients against them than in assisting patients to explore their options. They considered sexual intercourse healthy – albeit in moderation. One doctor, L.-F.-E. Bergeret, published a book in 1868 concerning conjugal "fraud," warning his readers of the harmful effects of thwarting Nature; the book, full of case studies and attesting to the passionate nature of many of the good doctor's patients, was quickly translated into English as well as going through eight editions in French.[81] Publishing physicians, in any case, remained wary of providing contraceptive advice well into the twentieth century.

French physicians also developed a great interest in decoding sexual difference, focusing on the sexual organs of the female body and their functioning; as the historian Jean-Pierre Peter rather melodramatically characterizes their attitude, "the woman's body is (and should be) possessed by medical discourse." [82] The clitoris, the uterus, the ovaries, the breasts, ultimately sex hormones, would become subjects of the utmost fascination to male physicians and anatomists, and female bodily processes such as menstruation, parturition, and lactation, even orgasm, in conjunction with various "feminine ailments" from leucorrhea to "hysteria" attracted their scientific and sometimes voyeuristic attention.[83] Medical writers from the early eighteenth century on obsessed over the puzzle of

---

[81] Louis-François-Étienne Bergeret, *Des Fraudes dans l'accomplissement des fonctions génératrices, dangers et inconvénients pour les individus, la famille et la société* (Paris: J. B. Baillière et fils, 1868); in English, *The Preventive Obstacle, or Conjugal Onanism: The Dangers and Inconveniences to the Individual, to the Family, and to Society, of Frauds in the Accomplishment of the Generative Functions*, transl. P. de Marmon (New York: Turner & Mignard, 1870). See *Victorian Women*, doc. 40(ii) for excerpts.

[82] See Jean-Pierre Peter, "Entre femmes et médecins: Violence et singularités dans les discours du corps et sur le corps d'après les manuscrits médicaux de la fin du XVIIIe siècle," *Éthnologie Française*, 6:3–4 (1976), 341–348; quote, 344. Peter's analysis is based on a corpus of sixty late eighteenth-century works from the *Société royale de médecine* in Paris.

[83] For the debates about female pleasure, particularly whether or not female orgasm was required for conception, see Lynn Salkin Sbiroli, "Generation and Regeneration: Reflections on the Biological and Ideological Role of Women in France (1786–96)" in *Literature and Medicine during the Eighteenth Century*, ed. M. M. Roberts & Roy Porter (London: Routledge, 1993), pp. 266–285, and the two articles by Thomas Laqueur, cited in n. 5 and 15.

It seems significant that menopause was not discussed in French male medical literature until the later eighteenth century, but took up a great deal of space after the French Revolution. See Wilbush, "Menespausie – The Birth of a Syndrome," cited in n. 22. Wilbush discounts the explanation by the common but misguided belief that women rarely lived till menopause, suggesting instead that it was only after upper-class women abandoned women healers and began to consult with male physicians,

how to produce boy or girl babies on demand.[84] One French physician, P. Brouardel, published an article in 1900 responding to the question of whether a woman might be capable of sexual relations while she was asleep.[85]

As I mentioned earlier, it was in mid-eighteenth century France that the first drawings of a specifically female skeleton appeared in print. These illustrations (drawn by a woman anatomist) connoted sexual difference by emphasizing pelvic width and smaller cranium, relative to the male skeleton. This was one more indication of the search for the material underpinnings of sexual difference. At the same time, however, feminist critics had already begun to challenge women's ostensible "inferiority" to men by pointing to their disadvantaged education and socialization.[86] Londa Schiebinger asks pertinently, "Why does the search for sex differences become a priority of scientific research at particular times, and what political consequences have been drawn from the fact of difference?" She finds answers to these two questions within the context of scientific sexual politics, and the effort to "distance science from the feminine, and to identify it with the masculine."[87] I would argue that it had even more significance with regard to the formation of masculine identity itself, via the differentiation of the "manly" from the "feminine," as sheer physical strength was becoming less important for survival. For a very long time, especially in the post-revolutionary nineteenth century, physicians and scientists would succeed in perpetrating their notions of radical "biological" difference and turning arguments about women's "otherness" into disqualifying sanctions that would undergird debates over women's intellect, their "genius," and plans for suitable education. When women began to talk back, however, they would have a great deal to say, and not only would they reclaim their "difference" as a positive advantage but also call for female-centered knowledge. "As long as science remains exclusively in

---

that the physicians in gynecology developed a literature on the subject. I owe this reference to Mary Lynn Stewart.

[84] See Jean-Claude Bénard, "Fille ou garçon à volonté: un aspect du discours médical au XIXe siècle," *Ethnologie Française*, 11:1 (1981), 63–76, and Quinlan, "Sex and the Citizen" (cited in n. 25).

[85] P. Brouardel, "Une Femme peut-elle avoir des rapports inconscients pendant le sommeil?," *Annales d'Hygiène Publique et de Médecine Légale*, ser. 3, 43 (1900), 43–82. I owe this reference to Ruth Harris.

[86] See Karen Offen, "Reclaiming the European Enlightenment for Feminism; or Prologomena to Any Future History of Eighteenth-Century Europe," in *Perspectives on Feminist Political Thought in European History: From the Middle Ages to the Present*, ed. Tjitske Akkerman & Siep Stuurman (London & New York: Routledge, 1998), pp. 85–103. A slightly revised version of this article appears in Offen, *European Feminisms*, chapter 2.

[87] See Schiebinger, "Skeletons in the Closet," quote, 72.

the hands of men," explained the self-educated *savante* Clémence Royer in 1859, "it will never go down into the depths of the family and society. . . . Why . . . should [women] be excluded from the hunt for truth?"[88]

[88] Clémence Royer, *Introduction à la philosophie des femmes, cours donné à Lausanne par Mlle A.C.R.: Leçon d'ouverture* (1859), transl. by Sara Miles, in appendix to her Ph.D. dissertation, "Evolution and Natural Law in the Synthetic Science of Clémence Royer" (University of Chicago, 1988). Used with permission.

CHAPTER 4

Education, Intellect, and the Politics of Knowledge

Does the mind really have no sex, as the ex-Catholic cleric and Cartesian philosopher François Poullain de la Barre insisted in 1673? The most important sex organ, the one that was deemed to lay at the base of women's ostensible inferiority in French society, was the brain, the much-venerated seat of Reason. In fact, controversies about the relative capabilities of women's and men's brains, their respective intellectual capacities and potential for "genius," and about gender socialization were very old features of the centuries-old French debate over the equality of the sexes, particularly among savants and physicians. Partisans on either side of this debate elaborated their perspectives in considerable detail – and their arguments epitomized what we now call sexual politics. For women, whose minds were the objects of these controversies, the stakes were enormous, because the conclusions bore not only on evaluations of their everyday behavior but also on their opportunities for schooling and their prospects for self-expression.

To have a "female brain" should not imply either superiority or inferiority.[1] Difference, and even then a wide spectrum of differences, should not and must not justify male domination of women. Yet, the continuing fascination with women's brains (as well as their bodies) and the denigration of women's intellect by some male writers had become a staple of European history both before and after the Revolution and long acted to undergird claims to masculine domination. France has bequeathed us a particularly full record of debates on this subject.

Early Debates on Women's Intellect and Education

In the late fourteenth century, well before the invention of the printing press, such denigration flared up during a public exchange over the

---

[1] See Louann Brizendine, *The Female Brain* (New York: Morgan Road Books, 2006).

celebrated medieval epic poem, *Le Roman de la Rose* (The Romance of the Rose). This time a literate woman writer spoke up to dispute the ugly things that men were saying about the intellectual capacities of her sex. "If women, though, had written all those books," the court-based writer Christine de Pizan asserted in 1399, "I know that they would read quite differently. For well do women know the blame is wrong. The parts are not apportioned equally, because the strongest take the largest cut and he who slices it can keep the best."[2] De Pizan's loaf-slicing metaphor makes it clear that she (and thus her readers) clearly understood that knowledge, both its formation and access to it, was not "neutral"; sexual politics lay at its base.

In her subsequent *Book of the City of Ladies* (1405), Christine de Pizan appealed to the authority of "Lady Reason" to right the wrongs of women. "Just the sight of this book [by Mathéolus] ... made me wonder how it happened that so many different men – and learned men among them – have been and are so inclined to express both in speaking and in their treatises and writings so many wicked insults about women and their behavior."[3] Christine's brave rejoinders made such an impact that they traveled throughout the leading courts of Europe. By the early sixteenth century learned courtiers such as Henri Corneille Agrippa de Nettesheim could flatter women rulers by composing texts such as *Sur la noblesse et l'excellence du sexe féminin* ... (1529 in Latin, 1537 in French), in which he proposed that "If we had permitted our women to make the laws and to write History, what tragic and hideous narratives women would have been able to write about the unmentionable wickedness of their unworthy males."[4]

By the mid-sixteenth century, the climate of opinion had changed dramatically – queens ruled in many European states. Certain royal sovereigns – and those who sought to please them – commissioned a total of six sets of massive tapestries based on the lessons in Pizan's *City of Ladies*; they adorned halls in every major court in Europe, spreading

---

[2] Christine de Pizan, "The Letter of the God of Love," lines 417–422, as translated from the Harley Ms. 4431, British Library, by Thelma S. Fenster, in *The Writings of Christine de Pizan*, sel. & ed. Charity Cannon Willard (New York: Persea Books, 1994), p. 149. My thanks to Susan Groag Bell for helping me locate this verse.

[3] Christine de Pizan, *The Book of the City of Ladies*, transl. Earl Jeffrey Richards (New York: Persea Books, 1982), pp. 3–4.

[4] Henri Corneille Agrippa de Nettesheim, *Sur la noblesse et l'excellence du sexe féminin, de sa prééminence sur l'autre sexe, 1537*, preface by Marie-Josephe Dhavernas (Paris: côté-femmes éditions, 1990). An earlier reprint is *De l'excellence et de la superiorité de la femme; ouvrage traduit du Latin de C. Agrippa, avec les commentaires de Roetig* (Paris: Louis, 1801).

pictoral vindication of female intelligence and authority in royal, aristocratic, and intellectual circles.[5] That all six sets of these massive tapestries have since disappeared might be due strictly to rats and the ravages of time, but I am tempted to speculate that it might also be the result of deliberate censorship of such subversive ideas. Many other, more seemingly innocuous tapestries from those royal courts, portraying men's hunting and military scenes, have survived intact.

Climates of opinion rarely seem to stabilize, especially as concerns the "woman question." Following the rehabilitation of the so-called Salic Law by French jurists in the 1590s, anti-woman prejudice raised its ugly head once again, as we have seen in Chapter 2. Women's rule was controversial, but so was women's intellectual prowess. Controversy flared up again in the first half of the seventeenth century around a pair of "learned ladies" – Marie Le Jars de Gournay (1566–1645), the French author of a strongly worded treatise on the equality of the sexes, and the younger Dutch Anna-Maria Van Schurman (1607–1678), known as the "star of Utrecht," who was an enthusiastic admirer of Mlle de Gournay. In her treatise *Grief des dames* [Ladies' Complaint] (1626), Gournay vociferously defended her sex from the stream of attacks: "Happy you are, Reader, if you do not belong to this sex, which has been deprived of liberty and kept from all benefits; which has also been excluded from all virtues and barred from obligations, offices, and public functions: in a word, deprived of power."[6]

As for Anna-Maria Van Schurman, her Latin treatise on whether or not Christian women should be learned (1638) appeared in French translation in 1646, accompanied by the correspondence with her long-standing advisor, the Leiden professor André Rivet (who would become tutor to the future prince of Orange; Rivet's French family name suggests that he may have been a Huguenot in exile).[7] Rivet countered Van Schurman's cautiously argued claims by insisting that although humanistic learning might be suitable for a very few maidens, it should never be generalized to

---

[5] See Susan Groag Bell, *The Lost Tapestries of the City of Ladies: Christine de Pizan's Renaissance Legacy* (Berkeley & Los Angeles: University of California Press, 2004).

[6] See Marie Le Jars de Gournay, *De l'Égalité des hommes et des femmes* (1622); reprinted as *Égalité des Hommes et des Femmes, 1622*, preface by Milagros Palma (Paris: côté-femmes, 1989). A recent study of Mlle de Gournay is Michèle Fogel, *Marie de Gournay: Itinéraires d'une femme savante* (Paris: Fayard, 2004).

[7] Anna Maria Van Schurman, *Question célèbre s'il est nécessaire ou non que les filles soient sçavantes* (Paris: Rolet le Duc, 1646); an English translation can be consulted in Anna Maria Van Schurman, *Whether a Christian Woman Should be Educated and Other Writings from her Intellectual Circle*, ed. & transl. by Joyce L. Irwin (Chicago: University of Chicago Press, 1998), pp. 48–54; quotes, pp. 49, 50. See also the Dutch anthology, *Anna Maria Van Schurman 1607–1678: Een Uitzonderlijk geleerde vrouw* (Zutphen: Walburg Pers, 1992).

all women for whom it would be "neither useful nor appropriate," given their responsibility for domestic matters. "If conduct and studies follow the makeup of the body, it is certain that the author of nature so formed the sexes differently in order to signify that He had destined men to one set of things and women to another." Rivet preferred and indeed recommended the approach of the widely known and highly influential sixteenth-century Spanish writer Juan-Luis Vivès, who emphasized household arts over learning and argued that having too many learned women would not be "in the public interest."[8] To applaud an exception was one thing; to turn it into a rule was another.[9] The customary sexual division of labor, so favorable to men, must be upheld! When even a few women begin to step into territories that men think should be exclusively occupied by them, the latter often seize on the notion of separate spheres, with domesticity for women, as a convenient counterstrategy; this was hardly a nineteenth-century development. Similar efforts to consign women to domesticity erupted in the seventeenth century, following the period of civil unrest historians call *La Fronde*, when noble women actually took to the battle-field and the king's own cousin, known as the Grande Mademoiselle, led an army into battle against the young Louis XIV.

Meanwhile, a few articulate, well-placed, and well-educated French women began publishing novels and holding conversations in which women talked back to their menfolk. By the 1660s, these novels contained a serious dose of social criticism; French debate over women's intellect and claims to learning culminated in the quarrels over "learned women" and the iconoclastic critique of institutionalized marriage that was filtering out in novels and from the salons of the "Prétieuses" (memorialized, albeit in an extremely unfriendly manner, in Molière's celebrated plays, *L'École des femmes* (The School for Wives, 1662–1663) and *Les Femmes savantes* (The Learned Ladies, 1672).[10] Every French schoolchild knows the famous lines of Arnolphe from *L'École des femmes*: "Yours is the weaker sex, please

[8] Rivet's letter of 6 November 1637 is analyzed in Elsa Dorlin, *L'Évidence de l'égalité des sexes: Une philosophie oubliée du XVIIe siècle* (Paris: L'Harmattan, 2000), pp. 65–70.
[9] For further discussion of the works by Gournay and Van Schurman and their respective impact, see Dorlin, *Évidence*.
[10] Joan DeJean, *Tender Geographies: Women and the Origins of the Novel in France* (New York: Columbia University Press, 1991), and "Notorious Women: Marriage and the Novel in Crisis in France, 1690–1715," *The Yale Journal of Criticism*, 4:2 (1991), 67–85; also Karen Offen, "How (and Why) the Analogy of Marriage with Slavery Provided the Springboard for Women's Rights Demands in France, 1640–1848," in *Women's Rights and Transatlantic Antislavery in the Era of Emancipation*, ed. Kathryn Kish Sklar & James Brewer Stewart (New Haven: Yale University Press, 2007), pp. 57–81.

realize; It is the beard in which all power lies." Molière's Arnolphe is the spokesman for the patriarchal order:

> And though there are two portions of mankind,
> Those portions are not equal, you will find,
> One half commands, the other must obey;
> The second serves the first in every way.

Those lines, coupled with the subsequent proclamations of Clitandre and Chrysale from *Les Femmes savantes* (performed ten years later), would for centuries thereafter be flung in the face of any woman who coupled ambition with intellectual or literary talent. Here is young Clitandre (the suitor of Henriette) speaking (Act 1, scene 3):[11]

> . . . female sages aren't my cup of tea.
> A woman should know something, I agree,
> Of every subject, but this proud desire
> To pose as erudite I can't admire.
> I like a woman who, though she may know
> The answers, does not always let it show;
> Who keeps her studies secret and, in fine,
> Though she's enlightened, feels no need to shine
> By means of pompous word and rare quotation
> And brilliance on the slightest provocation.

And then (in Act 2, scene 7) we encounter Chrysale (the father of Henriette, the prospective bride of Clitander) responding to his sister Bélise (who is herself a "learned lady" with a passion for astronomy) by invoking the topsy-turvy world argument against women acquiring too much knowledge at the expense of their household duties:[12]

> Stop trying to see what's happening in the moon
> And look what's happening in your household here,
> Where everything is upside-down and queer.
> For a hundred reasons, it's neither meet nor right
> That a woman study and be erudite.
> To teach her children manners, overlook

---

[11] Molière, *Les Femmes savantes* (1672); I draw on the Flammarion soft cover edition of Molière's *Oeuvres complètes*, vol. 4 (1979), pp. 304 & 321. For the English, I quote the Richard Wilbur translations: Jean Baptiste Poquelin de Molière, *The School for Wives and The Learned Ladies, translated into English verse and introduced by Richard Wilbur*. Harvest Edition 1991 (Orlando, FL & San Diego, CA: Harcourt, Inc., 1991). For Arnolphe, p. 72; for Clitandre, p. 180; for Chrysale, p. 214.

[12] In English, *pourpoint* is a doublet; while *haut-de-chausse* signifies breeches. In modern translation: a woman must only know the difference between the jacket (Wilbur says "vest") and the pants. In fact, a doublet is a close-fitting man's jacket, which may or may not have sleeves.

> The household, train the servants and the cook,
> And keep a thrifty budget – these should be
> Her only study and philosophy.
> Our fathers had a saying which made good sense:
> A woman's polished her intelligence
> Enough, they say, if she can pass the test
> Of telling a pair of breeches from a vest.

In short, renounce your learning, oh, women – stick to your domestic duties, carry them out to your husband's satisfaction, and raise his children – without his help.

It seemed clear that Molière's characters were speaking to a contemporary obsession with regard to women's heads, the capacity of their brains for learning, and their aspirations to acquire (and, Heaven forbid, even to shape) knowledge. Indeed, "good women" were sometimes depicted in mid-seventeenth century French prints as headless. Laure Beaumont-Maillet has catalogued a considerable number of such prints, including a series concerning Lustucru, the "*forgeron des têtes [de femmes]*," circa 1660.[13] It seems highly doubtful that the artists who drew these demeaning images of beheaded women were female, or that the artists were not themselves deeply implicated in the woman question debates.

Against these insulting images and prescriptions, François Poullain de la Barre (1647–1723) would dramatically assert (rebuking the Arnolphes, Clitandres, Chrysales, and others skeptical about or upset by the utility of higher learning for women) that, on the basis of reason, "the mind has no sex" (even though the body does) and that, given equal educational opportunity, women could do absolutely anything that men could do. In his provocative *Traité de l'égalité des deux sexes* [Treatise on the Equality of Both Sexes] (1673), a benchmark for claims on behalf of women's equality, he would propose a series of "scientific" objections, critiquing the so-called education that was then offered to women:[14]

> In all that which is taught to Women, do we see any thing that tends to solid instruction? It seems on the contrary, that men have agreed on this

---

[13] See Laure Beaumont-Maillet, *La Guerre des sexes, XVe-XIXe siècles: Les Albums du Cabinet des Estampes de la Bibliothèque Nationale* (Paris: Albin Michel, 1984), esp. p. 9 and p. 24.

[14] François Poullain de la Barre, *Traité de l'égalité des deux sexes* (Paris, 1673). The quotation provided here is from the English translation of 1677 by A. L., *The Woman as Good as the Man; Or, the Equality of Both Sexes*, ed. with an Introduction by Gerald M. MacLean (Detroit: Wayne State University Press, 1988), p. 139. On Poullain's formative role in stimulating the Enlightenment, see the groundbreaking study by Siep Stuurman, *François Poulain de la Barre and the Invention of Modern Equality* (Cambridge, MA: Harvard University Press, 2004). Poulain and Poullain are alternative spellings.

sort of education, on purpose to abase their courage, darken their mind, and to fill it only with vanity, and fopperies; there to stifle all the seeds of Vertue, and Knowledge, to render useless all the dispositions which they might have to great things, and to take from them the desire of perfecting themselves, as well as we by depriving them of the means.

For the next two hundred years, opponents of such claims as Poullain's (most of whom were physicians and natural philosophers) determined to prove him wrong, arguing that the mind was just as sexed as the body, and, moreover, that women's brains and intellects were not only different but worse – inherently *inferior* to those of men. They appealed to the findings of Nature in the areas of anatomy and physiology to justify such arguments, and as historian Londa Schiebinger has so convincingly demonstrated, they thereby planted gendered power relations squarely at the heart of modern "science."[15]

In addition to constructing theoretical and pseudo-scientific arguments based in alleged sexual difference, opponents of Poullain's theses focused on what women *should* do (à la Chrysale), not what they *could* do. In fact, the later functionalist (or social utility) arguments for training women to be mother-educators on behalf of the nation – which would become so prominent during and after the French Revolution – had a long, and not so glorious, past. This concept had been rearticulated in extremely conservative terms during the later seventeenth century (in the wake of women's participation in the Fronde, the debates on "learned women" and "the mind has no sex") by the eminent bishop Fénelon as part of his political vision for reforming the aristocracy and the court of Louis XIV. Fénelon's utilitarian (and in the context of the strong reaction against learned women, counterrevolutionary) instructional formula was designed to inculcate the necessary blend of general culture, domestic arts (including, importantly, a knowledge of estate management), and Catholic piety necessary to produce gracious and skillful wives and mothers (or, in case of dire economic necessity, teachers).[16] It was a solid program in its way, but hardly one

---

[15] See Londa Schiebinger, *Nature's Body: Gender in the Making of Modern Science* (Boston: Beacon Press, 1993).

[16] François de Salignac de la Mothe-Fénelon, *Traité sur l'éducation des filles* (1687). A classic English edition is H.C. Barnard, ed. *Fénelon on Education* (Cambridge, UK: Cambridge University Press, 1966). Fénelon's treatise continued to influence educational thought on the woman question throughout the nineteenth century. It would be republished in three different editions in the late nineteenth century alone, including one version intended specifically for republican educators; thus it would become required reading in many of the Third Republic's normal schools for women. On Fénelon's outsize influence, see Paul Rousselot, *Histoire de l'éducation des femmes en France* (Paris: Didier, 1883), vol. 2, p. 437.

calculated to foster either critical thinking or personal autonomy among its intended pupils. In all events, "learned women" – particularly those who displayed their learning publicly or pedantically – would remain objects of scorn. What was more, at St. Cyr, the girls' school founded by Madame de Maintenon (the morganatic wife of Louis XIV) to train daughters of the so-called impoverished nobility, even public theater performances by the pupils drew criticism as immodest and thus inappropriate.

Catholics and secularists alike had long insisted on the importance of channeling female influence to bolster their respective visions of society. Fénelon's reform program for educating daughters of the less affluent nobility was taken up with enthusiasm throughout Europe during the eighteenth century. In France, secular Enlightenment writers published many tracts and treatises on the education of girls, debating and detailing appropriate curriculum, and invariably channeling girls toward domestic activities.[17] Distinguished academicians, such as Bernard le Bovier de Fontenelle of the Paris Academy of Sciences, encouraged women's consumption of scientific knowledge but at the same time dissuaded them from dabbling in its production.[18] Ancient languages (then the backbone of the classical humanities) presented a particularly controversial subject of discussion; in 1726, the influential educator Charles Rollin raised the question in his *Traité des études* as to whether the study of Latin (still the academic European *lingua franca*, though French had by then made serious inroads as the language of courts and diplomacy) was appropriate for girls. He finally concluded against it as inappropriate, making an exception (for religious reasons) in the case of nuns. His reasoning, too, was wholly utilitarian: "Everything that is related to the internal management of a household: that is the science of women; that is the occupation

---

The historical importance of Fénelon's program, coupled with Mme de Maintenon's founding of St-Cyr, was to offer girls of the high (albeit "impoverished") aristocracy an education for rural family life instead of for the convent or for life at court. See Carolyn C. Lougee, "Noblesse, Domesticity, and Social Reform: The Education of Girls by Fénelon and Saint-Cyr," *History of Education Quarterly*, 14:1 (Spring 1974), 87–113. In addition to its influence in France, this program had an enormous influence throughout Europe in the eighteenth century, especially in the German states and in Russia. For other aspects of seventeenth-century girls' education, see Elfrieda T. Dubois, "The Education of Women in Seventeenth-Century France," *French Studies*, 32:1 (January 1978), 1–19, and the publications of Elizabeth Rapley.

[17] In her book *L'Éducation des filles au temps des Lumières* (Paris: Éditions du Cerf, 1987), Martine Sonnet insists on just how very conservative and Christian the education of girls in Paris had become in the eighteenth century.

[18] See Fontenelle's *Conversations on the Plurality of Worlds*, transl. H. A Hargreaves, intro. Nina Rattner Gelbart (Berkeley & Los Angeles: University of California Press, 1990), and Mary Terrall, "Gendered Spaces, Gendered Audiences: Inside and Outside the Paris Academy of Sciences," *Configurations*, 3:2 (1995), 207–232.

that they've been assigned by Providence and for which they have more talent than men."[19]

Important eighteenth-century political theorists such as Montesquieu (Charles de Secondat, baron de la Brède et de Montesquieu, 1689–1755), in his anonymously published *Lettres Persanes* [Persian Letters] (1721), would, however, revive Poullain's challenging suggestion that giving young women an education equivalent to that given young men might provide cause to doubt the imputed inferiority of women in matters of the mind.[20] The French academician Abbé de Saint-Pierre, writing in 1730, concurred. He insisted that the education of women should be given just as much attention as the education of men, and posited that well-ordered states should assure its effective organization; several years later he proposed a plan for a network of girls' colleges, or secondary schools, based on the model of St. Cyr.[21]

Others would probe the causes that lay behind the antifeminists' claims, looking for political answers. A certain M. Daube, writing in the *Journal des Scavantes* (1743), claimed that the very authority of husbands derived solely from their position as *chef de famille*, not from any purported "excellence" of their sex. Daube insisted that education was responsible for the difference in the sexes, and – that in order to assure dominance – men had deliberately warped women's education.[22] In the sixth volume of the *Encyclopédie* (1756), the Chevalier de Jaucourt startled many readers by positing that the very authority of husbands was arbitrary, running "contrary to natural human equality."[23] It is clear from these examples that not all men in the first half of the eighteenth century were hostile to the notion of women's equality, educationally or in other respects.

---

[19] Charles Rollin, *Traité des études* (1726); see his *Oeuvres complètes* (1817–1818), vols. 16–17.

[20] The two-volume *Lettres persanes* appeared anonymously (Cologne: chez Pierre Marteau; Amsterdam: chez Pierre Brunel, 1721), and became an immediate best seller. Only later was it revealed to be the work of Montesquieu. On the woman question, see in particular Letter 38.

[21] Charles-Irénée Castel, abbé de Saint-Pierre, "Projet pour la perfection de l'éducation des filles," in *Oeuvres diverses de M. L'abbé de Saint-Pierre* (Paris: Briasson, 1730, vol. 2, pp. 128–129; and "Projet pour multiplier les colleges de filles," in *Ouvrages de morale et de politique*, 14 vols. (Rotterdam: chez Jean David Beman; Paris: Briasson, 1733), vol. 4, pp. 247–260.

[22] See M. Daube, "De l'autorité des maris sur leurs femmes," *Journal des Scavantes* (1743), 429ff.

[23] Louis, chevalier de Jaucourt, "Femme (Droit Nat.)," in *L'Encyclopédie*, 6 (Paris, 1756), 471–472; transl. Karen Offen in Susan Groag Bell & Karen Offen, *Women, the Family, and Freedom: The Debate in Documents, 1750–1950* (Stanford, CA: Stanford University Press, 1983), hereafter *WFF*, vol. 1, doc. 6. Jaucourt's essay takes a radically different turn than the other essays concerning "woman" in the *Encyclopédie*. See Terry Smiley Dock, *Woman in the 'Encyclopédie': A Compendium* (Madrid, 1983). For other articles in English translation, see "The Encyclopedia of Diderot and D'Alembert Collaborative Translation Project" directed by Dena Goodman at www.hti.umich.edu/d/did.

Building on a rising tide of pro-woman thinking, Pierre-Joseph Boudier de Villemert, author of an extremely influential and much translated treatise, *L'Ami des femmes* (first published anonymously in 1758), promoted women's role as a civilizing force – the complements to – and the tamers of men. He argued in favor of cultivating their intelligence to that end – but solely to that end. Nicholas Baudeau, writing in 1762, strengthened the argument by proposing a plan for secular *national* education that would fully include female citizens: "We must pose as a fundamental maxim that the Daughters of the Nation are destined each to become within their class, *Citoyennes*, Wives, and Mothers."[24]

The debate about women's brains, intelligence, suitable education, and civilizing mission continued to reverberate throughout the entire eighteenth century, in tandem with complaints about repressive marriage laws and constraining role expectations for women.[25] Women would begin to speak out forcefully on these subjects, and particularly on the question of mental capacity. In Paris, Madame de Beaumur, editor of the *Journal des Dames*, asserted in 1761 that "we women think under our coiffures as well as you do under your wigs. We are as capable of reasoning as you are," and in a subsequent issue (early 1762) she sharply criticized men's attitudes toward women's education: "If we have not been raised up in the sciences as you have, it is you who are the guilty ones." She blamed men for using their physical superiority to "annihilate" women's natural gifts.[26]

The topic of appropriate education for girls was, of course, central to Jean-Jacques Rousseau's very influential novel/tracts of the early 1760s – *Julie, ou la nouvelle Héloise,* and *Émile, ou De l'éducation* (particularly Book V, on the education of Sophie, Emile's companion-to-be) – and provoked a voluminous response from his female readers.[27] At the core of his argument

---

[24] See Charles-Irénée Castel, abbé de Saint-Pierre, "Project for perfectionner l'éducation des filles," in *Oeuvres diverses de Monsieur l'abbé de Saint-Pierre* (Paris, 1730), p. 96; Pierre-Joseph Boudier de Villemert, *L'Ami des femmes* (1750; this work also appeared in English, American, and Italian editions); Nicolas Baudeau, "De l'Éducation nationale," *Ephémérides du Citoyen, ou Chronique de l'esprit national,* 4:4 (12 May 1766), 49–64.

[25] Londa Schiebinger, *The Mind Has No Sex? Women in the Origins of Modern Science* (Cambridge, MA: Harvard University Press, 1989). Schiebinger has documented this debate on a pan-European scale.

[26] Mme de Beaumer, *Journal des Femmes,* issues of November 1761 and March 1762; see Nina Rattner Gelbart, *Feminine and Opposition Journalism in Old Regime France* (Berkeley & Los Angeles: University of California Press, 1987), p. 107, and esp. chapter 3.

[27] There is a huge literature on Rousseau, some of which is referenced in Chapter 2, n. 33. For useful summaries of his views on the woman question, see Phyllis Stock, "The Theory and Practice of Women's Education in Eighteenth-Century France," *Eighteenth-Century Life,* 2:4 (1975–1976), 79–82; and Samia I. Spencer, "Women and Education," in *French Women and the Age of Enlightenment,* ed. Samia I. Spencer (Bloomington: Indiana University Press, 1984), pp. 83–96.

lay the stark proposition that girls should be educated to serve men, even as he insisted on women's powerful (indeed, even fearful) influence. Although many women found inspiration in some of Rousseau's writings (notably *Julie*, which popularized the mother-educator model), it is difficult to imagine that they were thrilled to read Book V of *Émile*, or, for that matter Rousseau's earlier pronouncements on women's lack of genius.[28] In fact, in dialogue with Rousseau several years prior to publication of *Julie* and *Émile*, the leading *Encyclopédiste* Jean le Rond d'Alembert (1717–1783) retorted that, given their abysmal education, women never had a chance:[29]

> The slavery and the kind of degradation in which we have placed women; the fetters we place about their minds and souls; the futile jargon, as humiliating for them as for us, to which we have reduced our dealings with them, as if they had no reason to cultivate, or were unworthy of cultivating it; finally the pernicious, I would say almost murderous education we prescribe for them, without permitting them to have any other; an education in which they learn almost uniquely to contradict themselves unceasingly, to have no sentiments that they are not forced to suppress, no opinion they don't have to hide, no single thought they don't have to disguise. We treat the natural in them like we treat it in our gardens; we seek to ornament it by suffocating it. If most nations have acted like ours with respect to women, it is because everywhere the men have been the strongest, and that everywhere the strongest have been the oppressors of the weakest.

For the responses of three of Rousseau's women readers – Catharine Macaulay, Mary Wollstonecraft, and Germaine de Staël – see *WFF*, vol. 1, docs. 11–14. For an excellent in-depth feminist analysis of responses by Rousseau's women readers, see Mary Seidman Trouille, *Sexual Politics in the Enlightenment: Women Writers Read Rousseau* (Albany: SUNY Press, 1997), and for a provocative reassessment of Rousseau's impact, see Jennifer J. Popiel, *Rousseau's Daughters: Domesticity, Education, and Autonomy in Modern France* (Hanover & London: University Press of New England, for the University of New Hampshire Press, 2008).

For a sketch of the important and continuing French influence on girls' education in other parts of Europe, see Karen Offen, "Liberty, Equality, and Justice for Women: The Theory and Practice of Feminism in Nineteenth-Century Europe," in *Becoming Visible: Women in European History*, ed. Renate Bridenthal, Claudia Koonz, & Susan Stuard, 2nd ed. (Boston: Houghton Mifflin, 1987), esp. pp. 346–347. Further documentation for the earlier centuries can be accessed in the articles in *L'Éducation des jeunes filles nobles en Europe XVIIe-XVIIIe siècles*, ed. Chantal Grell & Arnaud Ramière de Fortanier (Paris: Presses de l'Université Paris-Sorbonne, 2004), which document French educational influence in Italy, Russia, Poland, and Hesse.

[28] In his "Lettre à Mr. D'Alembert sur les Spectacles," (1758), Rousseau asserts that women possess no genius. "Les femmes, en général, n'aiment aucun art, ne se connoissent à aucun, et n'ont aucun génie." See J.-J. Rousseau, *Lettre à Mr. D'Alembert sur les Spectacles*. Édition critique par M. Fuchs (Lille: Librairie Giard; Genève: Librairie Droz, 1948); quotation pp. 138–139, n. 2.

[29] "Lettre de M. D'Alembert à M. J. J. Rousseau sur l'article 'Genève,' tiré du VIIe volume de *l'Encyclopédie* ... (1759)," in Jean Le Rond d'Alembert, *Oeuvres philosophiques, historiques, et littéraires*, vol. 5 (Paris: Jean-François Bastien, 1805), 349–356. Transl. KO.

D'Alembert dotted the "I"'s and crossed the "T"'s, acknowledging openly that sexual politics were in play. On the subject of girls' education and potential, it was clear where his sympathies lay.

The post-Rousseauean 1770s and 1780s saw further publications. The great naturalist Buffon echoed Daube, d'Alembert, Beaumer, and others, arguing (1771) that, because men were physically stronger than women, "the most frequent use – and the greatest abuse – that man has made of his strength is to have subjugated and treated, often in a tyrannical manner, this half of the human race created to share with him the joys and hardships of life."[30] Two members of the Académie Française, Antoine-Léonard Thomas and Denis Diderot (renowned for coediting the *Encyclopédie* with d'Alembert), weighed in on these educational debates. Thomas critiqued (in passing) the current state of women's knowledge as superficial rather than solid, preferring what he believed to be a more solid knowledge base among sixteenth-century elite women.[31] Diderot's stylish retort underscored women's physiological and mental difference from men, their wild uterus and uterine furors, the mental instability caused by their menstrual periods, and yet, in fact, he indicated that women's reading of the world served them better, perhaps, than all men's books – for, "when women do have genius, its imprint is more original than in us."[32]

Neither Thomas nor Diderot proposed specific improvements to be made in women's education. That was left to Louise d'Épinay (1726–1783), who in her private letter to the Abbé Galiani, and in her published works, *Conversations d'Emilie* (1774, 1776, 2nd ed., 1782), and her fictionalized autobiography, *Histoire de Madame de Montbrillant* (1783), not only criticized the pitiful learning opportunities offered to elite girls, but (in her educational agenda for her granddaughter, in the *Conversations*) laid out a solid plan for strengthening those offerings.[33] The French philosopher

---

[30] Georges-Louis Leclerc, comte de Buffon, *Histoire naturelle, générale et particulière, avec la description du Cabinet du Roi*, vol. 2 (Paris: Imprimerie Royale, 1771), p. 553.

[31] Antoine-Léonard Thomas, *Essai sur le caractère, les moeurs, et l'esprit des femmes dans les différens siècles* (Amsterdam: chez E. van Harrevelt, 1772), in *Oeuvres de Thomas*, vol. 1, part 2 (Paris: A. Belin, 1819), p. 615.

[32] Denis Diderot, *Sur les femmes* (1772). Originally published in Grimm's *Correspondance littéraire*; reprinted in *Oeuvres complètes de Diderot*, vol. 2 (Paris, 1875), 251–262; quote, p. 262. On the responses to Thomas, see Mary Seidman Trouille, "Sexual/Textual Politics in the Enlightenment: Diderot and d'Épinay Respond to Thomas's Essay on Women," *Romanic Review*, 85:2 (March 1994), 98–116.

[33] Louise-Florence-Petronille de Tardieu d'Esclavelles, marquise d'Épinay. Letter from Mme d'Épinay to the abbé Galiani, 14 March 1772. First published by Benedetto Croce, "Una lettera inedita della signora d'Épinay e il 'Dialogue sur les femmes' dell'abate Galiani," in *Mélanges d'histoire littéraire*

Elisabeth Badinter describes Madame d'Épinay as having been in her youth "entirely a prisoner of the pedagogy of submission."[34] By the 1770s, however, she had by all accounts overcome the defects of her upbringing. She became the proponent of education of children by their own mothers, their best guide in the process of becoming an adult, even though she had been unable to carry out this program in the education of her own two children. Her greatest published contribution to the debates on the woman question, the *Conversations*, resulted from her taking charge of her 2-year-old granddaughter, Emilie, in 1769. In 1784 this work was crowned by the Académie Française (which refused to admit women but did allow them to win prizes) as the most useful book of the year.

Challenging Jean-Jacques Rousseau (whose patron she once was) on many fronts (though not on women's primarily domestic and maternal vocation), Louise d'Épinay argued that she would "refuse to place limits on knowledge for persons of my sex." Science itself was not the problem, she insisted, but rather the way in which women often maladroitly displayed their knowledge.[35] The substance of the education she proposed was solid, and most importantly (as Badinter and others have pointed out), it was based on the author's own life experiences, both as a mother and as a friend of the *philosophes*. D'Épinay had found her own voice; she spoke directly to other women and she published the book under her own name. In particular, she counseled her granddaughter that it was essential to cultivate and embellish her reasoning faculties, above all else, because knowledge would provide "new sources of pleasure and satisfaction," "resources against boredom," "consolation in times of adversity," and that these were "benefits that nobody could take away from you, that would free you from dependence upon others," and that would enhance a woman's personal "liberty" and "strength." In short, women so educated would not have to

---

générale et comparée, offerts à Fernand Baldensperger, 2 vols. (Paris: Honoré Champion, 1930), vol. 1, pp. 178–180. Also her *Les Conversations d'Emilie* (Leipzig: chez S. Lebrecht Crusius, 1774; Paris, 1776; 2nd ed., 2 vols. Paris: Belin, 1782), and *Histoire de Madame de Montbrillant* (1783; republished by Gallimard in a critical edition, 3 vols., 1951) On d'Épinay see especially Elisabeth Badinter, *Emilie, Emilie: L'ambition féminine au XVIIIème siècle* (Paris: Flammarion, 1983), and Ruth Plaut Weinreb, *Eagle in a Gauze Cage: Louise d'Épinay, femme de lettres* (New York: AMS Press, 1993). The 1782 Belin edition of the *Conversations d'Emilie* has been republished as vol. 342, *Studies on Voltaire and the Eighteenth Century* (Oxford: Voltaire Foundation, 1996), with a long introduction in French by the editor, Rosena Davison.

[34] Badinter, *Emilie, Emilie*, p. 354.

[35] "Je ne me permets point de fixer les bornes du savoir aux personnes de notre sexe … ," *Les Conversations d'Emilie*, 12e conversation, vol. 2 (1822 ed.), pp. 200–201 – as quoted by Badinter in *Emilie, Emilie*, p. 403.

depend on or subordinate themselves to men. This was, in Badinter's judgement, Louise d'Épinay's ultimate revenge against Rousseau.[36]

In these years, other male writers submitted their observations to a series of public essay competitions devoted to the subject of girls' education, its aims and goals. In 1777, for example, the Academy of Besançon put forward the question, "In what way might the education of women contribute to the moral improvement of men?"[37] Several other regional academies – Châlons-sur-Marne and Rouen – also sponsored contests on the improvement of women's education in the early 1780s.[38] Women educators began to intervene in these debates.[39] A number of women authors began publishing literature targeted at children, especially girls.[40] In her widely acclaimed novel cum educational treatise *Adèle et Théodore* (1782), the *femme de lettres*, Catholic educator, and *"governeur"* to the children of the Duc d'Orléans, Stéphanie-Félicité de Genlis (1746–1830) proposed a model of private education and instruction by mothers to directly counter the laissez-faire, experiential model projected by Rousseau. In her quasi-authoritarian approach, Genlis's mother-educator becomes the arch-surveillante of the child who guides her charge carefully through a sequence of moral exercises and observations, bolstered by an extensive and targeted reading list, designed to produce, simultaneously, an exemplary moral wife and mother and a learned though not pedantic woman.[41] Between 1786 and 1789, the writer and journalist Louise Kéralio (later Madame Robert) would assemble and publish a six-volume *Collection des*

[36] 12e conversation, vol. 2, pp. 222–223, as quoted by Badinter, plus Badinter's conclusions, all p. 404.

[37] See Jean Bloch, "The Eighteenth Century: Women Writing, Women Learning," in *A History of Women's Writing in France*, ed. Sonya Stephens (Cambridge, UK: Cambridge University Press, 2000), p. 95.

[38] See Dena Goodman's chapter, "Designing an Education for Young Ladies," in her book, *Becoming a Woman in the Age of Letters* (Ithaca, NY: Cornell University Press, 2009), p. 64.

[39] See Anne d'Aubourg de La Bove, comtesse de Miremont, *Traité de l'éducation des femmes, et cours complèt d'instruction*, 7 vols. (Paris: Pierres, 1779–1789). See especially the articles in *Femmes éducatrices au Siècle des Lumières*, eds. Isabelle Brouard-Arends & Marie-Emmanuelle Plagnol-Diéval (Rennes: Presses Universitaires de Rennes, 2007).

[40] On eighteenth-century children's literature for girls, see Patricia A. Clancy, "Mme Le Prince de Beaumont: A Founder of Children's Literature in France," *Australian Journal of French Studies*, 16, parts 1–2 (January–April 1979), 281–287. Also Penny Brown, "'Girls Aloud': Dialogue as a Pedagogical Tool in Eighteenth-Century French Children's Literature," *The Lion and the Unicorn*, 33:2 (April 2009), 202–218.

[41] Stéphanie-Félicité Ducrest de Saint-Aubin, comtesse de Genlis, *Adèle et Théodore, ou lettres sur l'éducation*, 3 vols. (Paris: Lambert & Baudouin, 1782) – the "Bibliothèque scolaire" indicated for Adèle at age 7 included d'Épinay's *Les Conversations d'Emilie*. Genlis objected strenuously to the "atheism" of Enlightenment thought. On the resurgence of scholarly interest in Genlis, see the pathbreaking essays in *Madame de Genlis: Littérature et éducation*, ed. François Bessire & Martine Reid (Rouen: Publications des Universités de Rouen et du Havre, 2008).

meilleurs ouvrages françois composés par des femmes, dédiée aux femmes françoises for the edification of women readers.[42] This was the harbinger of an extensive literature of anthologized women's texts that would be produced in the nineteenth century, which is under study by literary historian Vicki Mistacco.[43]

The French Revolution and the "Problem" of Educating Girls

The outbreak of Revolution in 1789 propelled the subject of national public education for girls – and boys – to center stage, its content and goals tightly entangled with debates about according (or not) political rights and active citizenship.[44] When the marquis de Condorcet filed his report on public instruction in 1791, he argued that the Convention should legislate that "Instruction should be the same for women and men," and that boys and girls should be instructed together.[45] However, by late 1791, Talleyrand's arguments for public utility would trump Condorcet's claims for women's right to equal education. "It is impossible here to separate questions relative to women's education from an examination of their political rights," Talleyrand asserted:[46]

---

[42] Louise Félicité (Guinement de Kéralio) Robert, *Collection des meilleurs ouvrages françois, composés par des femmes, dédiée aux femmes françoises*, 6 vols. (Paris: chez l'auteur, 1786–1789). The qualifier françois (not française) is correct in this title, which drives copy editors mad. On Kéralio, see See Carla Hesse, "Revolutionary Histories: The Literary Politics of Louise de Kéralio (1758–1822)," in *Culture and Identity in Early Modern Europe*, ed. Barbara Diefendorf & Carla Hesse (Ann Arbor: University of Michigan Press, 1993), pp. 237–259.

[43] See Vicki Mistacco, ed. *Les Femmes et la tradition littéraire: Anthologie du Moyen Age à nos jours*, 2 vols. (New Haven: Yale University Press, 2005–2006). Mistacco's current project, "The Impulse to Anthologize," studies anthologies, biographical dictionaries, and other compendia of women's writing published by women between 1750 and 1970. It is sketched out in "Genlis à contre-courant: De l'influence des femmes," in *Madame de Genlis: littérature et éducation*, ed. François Bessire & Martine Reid (Rouen: Publications des Universites de Rouen et du Havre, 2008), pp. 97–115.

[44] On the Revolutionary debates concerning women's education, see especially Françoise Mayeur, *L'Éducation des filles en France au XIXe siècle* (Paris: Hachette, 1979), pp. 26–33.

[45] Marie-Jean-Nicolas Caritat, marquis de Condorcet, "Sur l'Instruction publique: Première mémoire: Nature et objet de l'instruction publique," in *Oeuvres de Condorcet*, ed. Arthur Condorcet O'Connor & François Arago, 12 vols. (Paris, 1847–1849), vol. 9, pp. 214–224. Originally published in the *Bibliothèque de l'homme public, ou analyse raisonnée des principaux ouvrages françois et étrangers*, etc., ed. M. Condorcet et al., seconde année, 1 (Paris, 1791), pp. 64–77. Partially translated in *WFF*, vol. 1, doc. 19.

[46] Charles-Maurice de Talleyrand-Périgord, *Rapport sur l'instruction publique, fait au nom du comité de constitution, à l'Assemblée nationale, les 10, 11 et 19 septembre 1791 (Projet de décrets sur l'instruction publique* (Paris, 1791). For Mary Wollstonecraft's tempered objections, see Karen Offen, "Was Mary Wollstonecraft a Feminist? A Contextual Re-reading of *A Vindication of the Rights of Woman*, 1792–1992," in *Quilting a New Canon: Stitching Women's Words*, ed. Uma Parameswaran (Toronto,

> When raising [daughters], one must thoroughly understand their destination. If we acknowledge that [women] have the same rights as men, they must be given the same means to make use of them. If we think that their share should be uniquely domestic happiness and the duties of the household [*la vie intérieure*], they should be formed early on to fill this destiny.

Thus, because the new Constitution disallowed women's political participation, women's education should not prepare them for active citizenship. Subsequently, the men in power would find unacceptable Constance Pipelet's fervent claims on behalf of the "rights of genius" for women.[47] The counsels of Madame de Genlis's friend Madame Legroing La Maisonneuve (1764–1837), in her *Essai sur le genre d'instruction le plus analogue à la destination des femmes* (1799), seemed more to their liking.[48]

Such narrowly utilitarian (and decidedly antifeminist) perspectives survived the Revolution, undergirding Napoléon's plans for the founding of girls' boarding schools (for the daughters of his decorated military officers, and for orphaned girls from military families under the auspices of the Légion d'Honneur). Napoléon intended that religion, not intellectual development, become the dominant focus: "Make believers of them, not reasoners."[49] Madame Campan, who in 1794 had organized the first secular *pension* (boarding school) to provide a thorough education for elite young women (it was attended by Napoléon's sisters), took charge of the first of these schools at Écouen, envisioning a more rigorously academic curriculum than the emperor had anticipated. Her ambition (like that of Madame Genlis) was to offer elite girls a substantive intellectual experience, though she also kept her eye on the prospect of their future limited opportunities, marriage and, of course, motherhood – and, possibly,

---

Ont.: Sister Vision, 1996), pp. 3–24; revised version in *Globalizing Feminisms 1789–1945*, ed. Karen Offen (London: Routledge, 2010), pp. 5–17.

[47] Constance-Marie de Théis Pipelet de Leury, later the princesse de Salm, was a key player in these debates; see her verse, quoted in Chapter 3. See also Elizabeth Colwill, "Laws of Nature / Rights of Genius: The *Drame* of Constance de Salm," in *Going Public: Women and Publishing in Early Modern France*, ed. Elizabeth C. Goldsmith & Dena Goodman (Ithaca, NY: Cornell University Press, 1995), pp. 224–242, esp. p. 234. In 1794 Pipelet staged her opera *Sapho*, in Paris. See Jacqueline Letzer & Robert Adelson, "French Women Opera Composers and the Aesthetics of Rousseau," *Feminist Studies*, 26:1 (Spring 2000), 69–100.

[48] See Françoise-Thérèse-Antoinette Legroing La Maisonneuve, comtesse de. *Essai sur le genre d'instruction le plus analogue à la destination des femmes* (Paris: Impr. De Dufart, 1799 3rd edition, 1844).

[49] Napoléon, "Notes sur l'établissement d'Écouen," addressed to the comte de Lacépède, grand chancellor of the Legion of Honor, 15 May 1807, as reprinted in Gabrielle Reval, *Madame Campan, assistante de Napoléon* (Paris: Albin Michel, 1931); English translation in *WFF*, vol. 1, doc. 23. Quote, p. 95.

employment if needed to sustain themselves.[50] This latter idea constituted a dramatic change in thinking about the futures of elite women. These debates did not, however, address the minimal schooling opportunities available for lower-class girls much before the 1830s.

Controversies over Educating Girls in the Early Nineteenth Century

In the post-revolutionary period, experimental scientists began to explore the question of sexing "genius" by measuring the size of women's brains; in 1817, following her death, the scientists even dissected the brain of the great writer Germaine de Staël, who in her novel *Corinne* had claimed genius for women (and was considered by many to be the greatest genius of her time). According to her friend and admirer Charles Lacretelle (who was a partisan of women's higher education and tried unsuccessfully to open the Sorbonne to young women), her brain weighed "1 livre, 3 onces" less than the brain of an ordinary man.[51] Such evaluations did not, of course, take into account the relatively smaller body mass of women that would later complicate nineteenth-century debates about sexual difference in the study of brain and skull volumetrics.

At stake in these debates about women's intellect, genius, and their need to learn were women's claims to equality, emancipation, and unobstructed participation in the world of knowledge, production, and public affairs. At risk were the equally assertive counterclaims to confine women (especially those of the leisured classes) to the so-called private or domestic sphere, under the supervision of husbands or other male authorities. Debates over the education of upper-class girls were in fact riddled with sexual politics.[52]

---

[50] On Madame de Campan's initiatives, see Reval, *Madame Campan*; Barbara Scott, "Madame Campan, 1752–1822," *History Today*, 23:10 (October 1973), 683–690; and especially the pioneering study of Rebecca Rogers, *Les Demoiselles de la Légion d'Honneur: Les maisons d'éducation de la Légion d'honneur au XIXe siècle* (Paris: Plon, 1992), chapters 1 & 3.

[51] Charles de Lacretelle, *Testament philosophique et littéraire*, 2 vols. (Paris: P. Dufart, 1840), vol. 2, p. 173. On his efforts to open his courses to young women in 1810, see Claude Perroud, "Les femmes aux cours de la Sorbonne en 1810," *Revue Pédagogique* (July 1918), 24–28. The Council of the Faculty of Letters quickly called a halt to Lacretelle's initiative.

[52] The history of education has been one of the great growth areas in late twentieth-century French historiography. When I first began working on French women's history, I found that extant scholarly studies in the history of French education since the Revolution (and before) focused almost exclusively on the expansion of formal instruction for boys. See, for example, Antoine Prost, *Histoire de l'Enseignement en France, 1800–1967* (Paris: A. Colin, 1968); R. D. Anderson, *Education in France, 1848–1870* (Oxford: Clarendon Press, 1975); and Joseph N. Moody, *French Education Since Napoléon* (Syracuse, NY: Syracuse University Press, 1978). The pioneering 1980 issue of *Historical Reflections*, entitled *The Making of Frenchmen: Current Directions in the History of Education in*

They were about nothing less than the sociopolitical construction of sex, of masculinity and femininity, which we call "gender," and about the power relationships that ensued from it.[53]

By the early nineteenth century the mother-educator, descended from Fénelon, popularized by Rousseau (as an alternative to "emancipation"), and promoted (with a more or less emancipatory twist) by Louise d'Épinay and Madame Campan (more) and Stéphanie de Genlis (less) had become the focus of male and female educational reformers alike, both progressive and neo-traditional. During the Revolution, a few publications had explicitly touted republican motherhood, as for example, the *Avis aux mères républicaines, ou Mes Refléxions sur l'éducation des jeunes citoyennes* (n.p., n.d.) by Citoyenne Guerin-Albert.[54] Under the Empire the mother-educator theme continued its

France, 1679–1979, ed. Donald N. Baker & Patrick J. Harrigan (Waterloo, Ont., Canada: Historical Reflections Press, 1980), was among the first efforts to redress the balance, with a number of articles on girls' education by French and North American scholars. Harrigan's excellent review article, "Women Teachers and the Schooling of Girls in France: Recent Historiographical Trends," *French Historical Studies*, 21:4 (Fall 1998), 593–610, summarizes the state of the field as of the late 1990s, providing many more valuable references. See the excellent review essay by Rebecca Rogers, "L'Éducation des filles: Un siècle et demi d'historiographie," *Histoire de l'Éducation*, n° 115–116 (September 2007), 37–79.

For the period under discussion here, see the excellent study by Mayeur, *L'Éducation des filles en France au XIXe siècle* (cited in n. 44), which deals with Catholic as well as secular schools, and the state-of-the-art synthesis by Rebecca Rogers, *From the Salon to the Schoolroom: Educating Bourgeois Girls in Nineteenth-Century France* (University Park: Penn State University Press, 2005). Summary survey articles by these two authors include Mayeur, "The Secular Model of Girls' Education," in vol. 4 of the widely translated *History of Women in the West*, ed. George Duby & Michelle Perrot (Cambridge, MA: Harvard University Press, 1993), pp. 228–245, and Rogers, "Learning to be Good Girls and Women: Education, Training and Schools," in *The Routledge History of Women in Europe since 1700*, ed. Deborah Simonton (London: Routledge, 2006), pp. 93–133. See also, for a specifically comparative view, Christina de Bellaigue, *Educating Women: Schooling and Identity in England and France, 1800–1867* (Oxford & New York: Oxford University Press, 2007). The website www.inrp.fr/she/femmes/ attests to a renewed interest in incorporating women into research on the history of instruction (*enseignement*).

Other earlier but still valuable works on the early and mid-nineteenth century include: Laura S. Strumingher, *What Were Little Girls and Boys Made Of? Primary Education in Rural France, 1830–1880* (Albany: SUNY Press, 1983), which focuses on socialization elements in the curriculum; Isabelle Bricard, *Saintes ou pouliches: L'éducation des jeunes filles au XIXe siècle* (Paris: A. Michel, 1985), which covers a broader spectrum of privileged young women's experiences; Sharif Gemie, *Women and Schooling in France, 1815–1914: Gender, Authority and Identity in the Female Schooling Sector* (Keele, UK: Keele University Press, 1995) looks at teachers. Catholic girls' schooling is treated below. For bibliographical notes concerning the post-1880 period, see the subsequent volume.

53 See Joan W. Scott, "Gender: A Useful Category of Analysis," *American Historical Review*, 91:5 (December 1986), 1053–1075.

54 *Avis aux mères républicaines, ou Mes Refléxions sur l'éducation des jeunes citoyennes* (n.p., n.d.) by Citoyenne Guerin-Albert. This undated work is referenced by Carla Hesse and Jennifer Popiel; the online catalogue at the Bibliothèque Nationale de France lists two copies. Another reference to republican motherhood is in a play, *Barra, ou la mère républicaine: drame historique, par la citoyenne femme Villiers* (Dijon: Impr. de P. Causse, An 2); reproduced in Elke Harten & Hans-Christian Harten, *Femmes, culture et révolution* (Paris: FNSP & des femmes, 1989), doc. 24, pp. 372–429.

development in the quasi-official *Annales de l'Éducation* edited by Pauline de Meulan (later Guizot) and François Guizot from 1811 to 1814, particularly in a series of articles by Pauline de Guizot from 1812 which, in the guise of a series of diary entries by a mother concerning the education of her daughters, advocated serious learning for elite women to soak up their excess energy.[55]

Historian Carla Hesse remarks that "proponents of the new biology advocated a very limited education for women, tailored narrowly to their maternal role."[56] What Hesse does not acknowledge is that astute middle-class women would find that they could subvert this seemingly narrow, utilitarian formula by demanding more extensive and higher quality education for themselves – ostensibly so they could do their job as mothers better, but also so they could expand their sociopolitical influence into the public realm. Historian Barbara Corrado Pope, who has analyzed the publications of early nineteenth-century women educators including Mesdames Campan, de Rémusat, Albertine Necker de Saussure (Madame de Staël's cousin from Geneva), Pauline Guizot, and Le Groing La Maisonneuve, has highlighted the extent of women's agency in shaping the role of maternal educator to suit their own purposes.[57]

Male educators also drummed on this theme. The former revolutionary Marc-Antoine Jullien proposed a course of historical readings for girls based in women's history, arguing that well-chosen readings of this sort

---

Harten & Harten discuss the Guerin-Albert text (pp. 131–132) but do not reproduce it. This book is bursting with women's petitions to the revolutionary legislative bodies.

[55] See June K. Burton, *Napoléon and the Woman Question: Discourses of the Other Sex in French Education, Medicine, and Medical Law, 1799–1815* (Lubbock, TX: Texas Tech University Press, 2007), pp. 48–51, concerning Guizot's & Meulan's *Annales de l'Education.* Cf. also Robin Bates, "Madame Guizot and Monsieur Guizot: Domestic Pedagogy and the Post-Revolutionary Order in France, 1807–1830," *Modern Intellectual History,* 8:1 (April 2011), 31–59.

[56] Carla Hesse, *The Other Enlightenment: How French Women Became Modern* (Princeton, NJ: Princeton University Press, 2001), p. 132.

[57] For the post-revolutionary period, see in particular the work of Barbara Corrado Pope, "Maternal Education in France, 1815–1848," *Proceedings of the Western Society for French History, 1975,* vol. 3 (1976), 368–377; "Revolution and Retreat: Upper-Class French Women after 1789," in *Women, War, and Revolution,* ed. Carol R. Berkin & Clara M. Lovett (New York: Holmes & Meier, 1980), pp. 215–236; and "Mothers and Daughters in Early Nineteenth-Century Paris" (Ph.D. dissertation, Columbia University, 1981). See also Geneviève Fraisse, "La Petite fille, sa mère et son institutrice (Les femmes et l'école au XIXe siècle)," *Les Temps modernes,* n° 358 (May 1976), 1959–1988, on educators' notions about the public primary schooling of girls and the training of their lay *institutrices* to be surrogate mothers. The point is further underscored by Yvonne Knibiehler et al., *De la Pucelle à la minette: les jeunes filles de l'âge classique à nos jours* (Paris: Temps actuels, 1983), and Marie-Françoise Lévy assesses the Catholic prescriptive educational writings of the mid-nineteenth century in *Des Mères en filles; l'éducation des françaises 1850–1880* (Paris: Calmann-Lévy, 1984). This emphasis continued well into the Third Republic, as we will see subsequently. See also Bricard, *Saintes et pouliches;* Popiel, *Rousseau's Daughters;* and especially Rogers, *Salon to the Schoolroom,* chapter 1.

could help women channel their influence in salutory ways. "It is through the well-directed influence of women," Jullien argued, "that one can regenerate men, reform education and legislation, improve individual and public morals, calm hateful passions, prevent deadly disagreements, and possibly one day put a stop to the abominable plague of war."[58] In 1834 Louis Aimé-Martin subtitled his widely read handbook on the education of mothers, "the civilization of mankind by women," and in 1848 Ernest Legouvé touted the moral mother as the antidote to the controversial Saint-Simonian *femme libre*.[59] The *mère-éducatrice* offered a capacious and multidimensional image that would appeal to men and women alike, though often for entirely different reasons. All these reformers believed that in post-revolutionary France friendly persuasion and good role models must ultimately triumph over force; however, most were exceedingly cautious in framing their claims for women's advancement.

Post-Rousseauean French authors of manuals on domestic economy, moralists, and religious reformers all advocated substantially identical programs for a woman's educative role in society: she was charged with the socialization of sons until they reached school age, and of daughters until they married. For this role (one that should, not incidently, keep her in her "place") women had to be well prepared. Particularly in the republican vision of France's future, the mother-educator must serve as the moral center of family as well as the engine for the social regeneration of the nation. Educators even encouraged women school teachers to think of themselves as surrogate mothers; Paul Rousselet would underscore the retrospective importance of this vision for the Third Republic in 1882: "The figure of the mother, the born teacher, dominates all feminine pedagogy of the nineteenth century."[60]

By the 1860s, however, a number of reformers – both Catholics and secularists – would argue publicly that some upgrading in the intellectual

---

[58] Marc-Antoine Jullien, *Esquisse d'un plan de lectures historiques rapporté spécialement à l'influence des femmes* (Paris: au Bureau central de la *Revue encyclopédique*, 1821); articles with this same title appeared in the *Journal des Femmes* in October 1832. Quote from the issue of 20 October 1832, p. 209.

[59] Louis Aimé-Martin, *De l'Éducation des mères de famille, ou De la civilisation du genre humain par les femmes* (Paris: Garnier, 1834). In its English translation by Edwin Lee (London: Whittaker, 1842; Philadelphia: Lea & Blanchard, 1843), this book also exerted a considerable influence in the English-speaking world. Aimé-Martin also edited the collected works of Fénelon and Bernardin de Saint-Pierre. See also Ernest Legouvé, *Histoire morale des femmes* (Paris: Gustave Sandré, 1849), esp. Book 4.

[60] Rousselot, *Histoire de l'éducation*, vol. 2, p. 428. In her introduction to *L'Éducation des filles au temps de George Sand* (Arras: Artois Presses université, 1998), p. 11, Michèle Hecquet confirms this view: "La mère éducatrice est une image maîtresse de cette époque."

content of female schooling beyond the primary level (reading, writing, and arithmetic, with a heavy dose of religion and some needlework) was not only desirable but necessary. Formal approaches to domestic economy would also gain ground. A few would claim (echoing Louise d'Épinay, and including Ernest Legouvé) that women should be educated for their own self-development. But the more common argument remained based on social utility, alternatively in the service of the Christian faith or for the good of the nation.[61] The historian Jules Michelet worried that women were too much in the hands of the priests, and advocated a wholly secular education for girls.[62] Others insisted that women's schooling should be beefed up in terms of content so that wives could converse with their more-educated husbands. This fell far short of endorsing the compatibility of women and science, argued for in the 1860s by the Italian progressive Salvatore Morelli, whose work on this subject was published in French,[63] but it was nevertheless a step in a progressive direction.

Despite the severe setbacks delivered to women's aspirations to participate in French political life during the revolutionary and post-revolutionary years, it is nevertheless clear that all participants in the debates about women's overall situation in French society increasingly acknowledged their societal importance, their influence, and potential capabilities, even as some denigrated their abilities in comparison to those attributed to men. In fact, the development of additional formal schooling for French girls had made considerable strides and public pressure was mounting to obtain for them equal opportunities at the primary, and eventually, the secondary level. By mid-century most thinking persons

---

[61] Of the mid-nineteenth-century writers, both Legouvé (in his *Histoire morale*) and Eugène Pelletan (in "La Femme au XIXe siècle," *Revue des cours littéraires*, 13 March 1869 [reprinted in-extenso as a brochure, Paris, 1869]) argue that women should also be educated for the sake of their own self-development, though they make the case primarily on functional grounds.

[62] See Jules Michelet, *Le Prêtre, la femme, et la famille* (1845), in *Oeuvres complètes de Jules Michelet*, vol. 9 (Paris: E. Flammarion, 1895); excerpts transl. KO in *WFF*, vol. 1, doc. 46.

[63] Salvatore Morelli, *La Femme et la science; ou la solution du problème humain*, transl. from the Italian by G. Cipri (Paris: E. Dentu, 1862). Morelli pinned his hopes for social regeneration on the education of women in science (as opposed to superstition), especially as mothers. See Angélique Arnaud's positive appraisal of Morelli's free-thinking ideas in "La Femme et la science, d'après le livre de Salvatore Morelli," *Le Droit des Femmes*, n° 55 (15 May 1870). See also the earlier exchange of letters between Morelli and John Stuart Mill on the subject of girls' education in *Le Droit des Femmes*, n° 50 (10 April 1870). In characteristic liberal fashion, Mill opposed instituting a single top-down governmental program, preferring competing approaches to schooling (including the Catholic program) while Morelli advocated a uniform (secular) curriculum based on "the truth, and nothing but the truth." Morelli's contributions have been documented in *Salvatore Morelli (1824–1880): Emancipazionismo e democrazia nell'ottocento Europeo*, ed. Ginevra Conti Odorisio (Naples: Edizioni Scientifiche Italiane, 1992).

agreed that girls as well as boys should be offered some sort of organized instruction at the advanced level. The societal necessity of basic literacy and skills was, by then, too well established. No one in the mid-nineteenth century would propose, as did Molière's character Alceste, in his *École des femmes*, but also Restif de la Bretonne in *Les gynographes* (1777)[64] and Sylvain Maréchal in 1800 (albeit purportedly tongue-in-cheek), that women should never be taught to read or write because it would distract them from their domestic duties.[65] Even their domestic duties seemed to require these skills, especially reading and writing and many more besides, as the pioneering domestic economy manuals of Madame Gacon-Dufour, and later Elisabeth Celnart, underscored.[66] But some women would claim

---

[64] Nicolas-Edmé Restif de la Bretonne, *Les Gynographes; ou Idées de deux honnêtes femmes sur un projet de règlement proposé à toute l'Europe pour mettre les femmes à leur place, & opérer le bonheur des deux sexes . . .* 2 vols. in 1. (La Haie: Gosse & Pinet, 1777).

[65] Pierre-Sylvain Maréchal, *Projet d'une loi portant défense d'apprendre à lire aux femmes* (Paris: Massé, 1801). Maréchal's project did not pass unnoticed. In the same year two women published vigorous protests against his "sottise": see Mme [Albertine] Clément-Hémery, *Les Femmes vengées de la sottise d'un philosophe du jour, ou réponse au projet de loi de M. S...M... portant défense d'apprendre à lire aux femmes* (Paris: Mme Benoist, 1801), and Mme [Marie-Armande-Jeanne d'Humières] Gacon-Dufour, *Contre le projet de loi de S...M..., portant défense d'apprendre à lire aux femmes, par une femme qui ne se pique pas d'être femme de lettres* (Paris: Chez Ouvrier et Barba, 1801). Clément-Hémery's rebuttal is reprinted (along with an earlier piece by Gacon-Dufour, and a number of others) in *Opinions de femmes: de la veille au lendemain de la Révolution française* / préface de Geneviève Fraisse (Paris: côté-femmes, 1989). All three works are now available in one volume: *Projet d'une loi portant défense d'apprendre à lire aux femmes; 1801/Sylvain Marechal; texte présenté par Bernard Jolibert; suivi des réponses de Marie-Armande Gacon-Dufour et Albertine Clément-Hémery* (Paris: L'Harmattan, 2007).

    For analysis of this discussion, see Françoise Aubert, "Les Femmes, doivent-elles apprendre à lire? Une polémique en 1801," *Studi sull'uguaglianza, contributi alla storia*, ed. Corrado Rosso (Pisa: Golliardica, 1973), vol. 1, 76–97; Michel Delon, "Combats philosophiques, préjugés masculins, et fiction romanesque sous le Consulat," *Raison Présente*, n° 67 (1983), 67–76; and subsequently Geneviève Fraisse, *Muse de la raison: La Démocratie exclusive et la différence des sexes* (Aix-en-Provence: Alinea, 1989); in English as *Reason's Muse: Sexual Difference and the Birth of Democracy* (Chicago: University of Chicago Press, 1996), chapter 1.

[66] See the following works by Madame Gacon-Dufour: *Recueil pratique d'économie rurale et domestique* (Paris: Roret, 1802); *Manuel de la ménagère à la ville et à la campagne, et de la femme du basse-cour*, 2 vols. (Paris: Roret, 1805); her didactic novels, including one entitled *De la nécessité de l'instruction pour les femmes* (Paris: Roret, 1805), and her penultimate work, *Manuel complèt de la maîtresse de maison et de la parfaite ménagère, ou guide pratique pour la gestion d'une maison à la ville et à la campagne* (Paris: Roret, 1826), which was continually updated and reissued throughout the nineteenth century by Madame Celnart. On these innovative guidebooks to the new domestic economy, see Elizabeth Fox-Genovese, "The Ideological Bases of Domestic Economy: The Representation of Women and the Family in the Age of Expansion," in Elizabeth Fox-Genovese & Eugene Genovese, *Fruits of Merchant Capital* (New York: Oxford University Press, 1983), pp. 229–336, notes pp. 442–447, and Burton, *Napoléon and the Woman Question*, pp. 74–77. Fox-Genovese insists that Gacon-Dufour appropriated the entire domestic sphere for women, with marriage as a full conjugal partnership based in a sexual division of labor. In fact, in the female-administered households envisaged by Gacon-Dufour, men were for all practical purposes absent. Women were counseled to appropriate and govern the entire sphere of the household, whether rural

even more. The question was just how extensive a formal education might this entail. Would the "white goose" become an endangered species?

Organizing Girls' Schools: Religious or Secular?

Under the restored monarchies, politicians balked at institutionalizing girls' schooling on a par with that for boys. The Guizot law of 1833 had established a mandate for boys' public primary education only; decisions about girls' schooling remained in the hands of male-headed families, with widely varying results.[67] Only in 1838 would the French government embark on an effort to create separate women's normal schools to train teachers of girls.[68] Activist women in Paris expressed extreme frustration at the government's unwillingness to equalize girls' education.[69] One particularly outspoken schoolmistress, Josephine Bachellery, a frequent contributor to the *Tribune de l'Enseignement,* called for the establishment of national public secondary – and vocational – education for girls and the female equivalent of the men's École Polytechnique to train the young women who would lead the charge. Women educators such as Bachellery envisioned the realization of these projects in 1848 when Hippolyte Carnot took over as the Second Republic's minister of public instruction. Bachellery's published "Letters on the Education of Women" (1840, 1848) insisted not only that women's minds needed to develop in directions that rendered them socially useful (rather than oriented to otherworldly

or urban. For comparison, see the domestic economy manuals of Madame Pariset, *Manuel de la maîtresse de la maison, ou, Lettres sur l'économie domestique* (Paris: Audot, 1821; new ed. 1852); and Cora Millet-Robinet, *Maison rustique des dames* (1st ed., 1844–1845; 9th ed., 1873, published by the Librairie agricole de la maison rustique). I have not yet encountered a systematic comparative analysis of these French household management manuals.

67 Note the remarks of Robert Dale Owen, "Situation of Women and Progress of Popular Instruction in France," *The Crisis,* 1:43 (29 December 1832), 171; (orig. pub. in *New York Free Enquirer*). Owen complimented the French for their civility and for the efforts then underway through popular education to instruct "those who live by their daily labour" as well as the middle classes. "Were there but a political revolution in France," he observed, "this would be the finest country – the very first, perhaps, in the race of moral and intellectual improvement in the world."

68 See Anne T. Quartararo, *Women Teachers and Popular Education in Nineteenth-Century France: Social Values and Corporate Identity at the Normal School Institution* (Newark: University of Delaware Press, 1995), and Rebecca Rogers, "La Sous-maîtresse française au XIXe siècle: Domestique ou enseignante stagiaire?" in *Les Enseignantes: Formations, identités, représentations XIX-XX siècles,* ed. Mineke van Essen & Rebecca Rogers (special issue of *Histoire de l'Éducation,* n° 98 [May 2003], 37–60); and Christina de Bellaigue, "The Development of Teaching as a Profession for Women before 1870," *The Historical Journal,* 44:4 (2001), 963–988.

69 In *La Démocratie à l'épreuve des femmes* (Paris: Albin Michel, 1994), Michèle Riot-Sarcey sheds an entirely new light on the centrality of the education issue for French women's rights advocates during the 1830s and 1840s.

religious models) but reminded her readers that, increasingly, everyone needed to work for a living, and that paid work was henceforth "a source of prosperity for all" – including women. She argued that "only public education has the power to develop the intelligence of women on a grand scale," both by improving their general knowledge and also developing their special aptitudes. Only by this means could women really become men's partners – their "confidants," "counselors," and "collaborators." Well-educated women were vital, she insisted, to forming a nation, to getting people of every social class to pull together behind it.[70] The Comtesse d'Agoult, writing as "Daniel Stern," put it even more strongly in 1847: "Equal possibility for intellectual development: this is the fundamental equality, the only one to which it is useful to pretend, because it implies all the others; the only one it is an iniquity to withhold, today just as yesterday."[71]

With passage of the Falloux Law in 1850, following the defeat of the 1848 revolution, the friends of progressive educational reform found themselves out of power. This law reinstated Catholic educators as teachers and authorized the establishment of independent (Catholic) schools and it obligated each municipality in France with eight hundred inhabitants or more to provide a primary school for girls as well as for boys. The Catholic laymen who framed this law certainly considered a rudimentary primary education for girls necessary, but an even more important factor in this decision was their unconditional disapproval of coeducational settings for schooling girls.[72] Schooling was not as yet compulsory for children of either sex; this was a goal the republicans would achieve only in 1882. But as historians Raymond Grew and Patrick J. Harrigan have amply demonstrated, already many French girls did attend school, if only for a few years, and if not all women could write, a significant proportion could read.[73] This is not to discount the fact that in some rural areas of France, the

---

[70] Josephine Bachellery, *Lettres sur l'éducation des femmes* (Paris: chez les libraires Lemoine et Mansut, 1848), 237 pages. See also the earlier version, *Lettres sur l'éducation des femmes* (Paris: rue Basse du Rempart, 20, 1840). The quotations are from the 1848 edition, pp. 211, 213, and 214.

[71] Daniel Stern, "Esquisses morales: Pensées sur les femmes," *La Revue indépendante*, n.s., vol. 9 (25 September/10 October 1847), 109.

[72] Objections to coeducation had a long history in France. As early as 1640, Louis XIII wrote to the bishop of Poitiers, calling for the suppression of *écoles mixtes*. Cited by Christine Fauré, *Democratie sans les femmes* (Paris: Presses Universitaires de France, 1985), chapter 3, p. 107 (in the English edition, p. 59). See also the articles in *CLIO: Histoire, Femmes et Sociétés*, n° 18 (2003): "Coéducation et mixité," ed. Françoise Thébaud & Michelle Zancarini-Fournel.

[73] Initial statistical results were presented by Raymond F. Grew & Patrick J. Harrigan, "Girls' Schooling in Nineteenth-Century France," paper given at the Western Society for French History, Albuquerque, NM, October 1984. See, further, Grew and Harrigan, *School, State, and*

possibilities for primary instruction for both boys and girls remained minimal. The historian Eugen Weber has brought to our attention an official 1863 estimate that revealed some 20 percent of the French population neither spoke nor understood the French language. For these rural inhabitants, especially in the South and West of France, "The mother tongue was not the tongue of their mothers."[74] The children from these rural areas had first to learn French at school as a second language.

Most discussions of school curriculum for girls, both at the primary and secondary levels, remained fixated on utilitarian prescriptions concerning woman's domestic role, especially (as has been mentioned earlier) their potential significance as early educators of children. These were, as has already been suggested, politically motivated prescriptions. Certainly, most people considered the elementary skills of reading, writing, and arithmetic as useful for women of all classes as for men, but educators still considered addition of needlework and other domestic arts to the curriculum as *de rigueur* for all girls.[75] The French made a conscious effort to train upper-class girls (*les démoiselles*) for the domestic role that was insistently being prescribed for them in life. However, this did not mean strictly housekeeping; the intent was not to turn out housemaids but rather household managers (the parameters of Fénelon's objective of training noble girls as estate managers had shrunk considerably). Progressive prescriptions for women's education focused more on creating a moral environment and forming character than on dusting or sewing – not to mention critical thinking. Indeed, most arguments for educating women to domesticity in France went well beyond housekeeping; given the continuing attention paid to women's influence, their role as wife and mother could not be easily dismissed. All the more reason why it had to be channeled, sculpted, and hemmed in by prescription and curricular constraints.

The growth of educational opportunities for girls in nineteenth-century France was (as many historians have pointed out) greatly stimulated by the

    Society: The Growth of Elementary Schooling in Nineteenth-Century France (Ann Arbor: University of Michigan Press, 1991).

[74] Eugen Weber, *Peasants into Frenchmen: The Modernization of Rural France 1870–1914* (Stanford, CA: Stanford University Press, 1976), chapters 18–20 discusses schooling, the Church's role in the countryside, and the slow and painful process of exterminating superstition, magic, old cults, and bad hygiene. Quote, p. 334.

[75] The comte de Falloux, author of the 1850 education law, commented indignantly in the National Assembly on women's domestic inaptitude, noting that only 17 out of 100 Parisian women knew how to sew; he said he had seen women of 40 and 50 still trying to acquire this skill. In the National Assembly, 11 April 1849; cited by Julie-Victoire Daubié, *Des Progrès de l'instruction primaire: Justice et liberté!* (Paris: Librairie de Mme Claye, 1862), p. 96.

ongoing rivalry between Church and State for control of women's influence, which both factions acknowledged as a significant social force. The
historian Jules Michelet had made this rivalry a public issue in the 1840s
and Bachellery's publications spoke to this point as well. As one conservative writer, L.-C Michel, put it in 1868, the Christians and the secularists
(this writer used the term "anti-christians") both "aspire to exercise a
diametrically opposed influence on the governance of minds and affairs;
both are aware of the considerable role that the education of girls can play
in [establishing] that influence." In an age of mass politics, Michel pointed
out, the instruction of *le peuple* counted: thus, men in government had
suddenly discovered "that even if women did not elect or vote, they were
the ones who raised those who do vote and elect, and that in order to
dominate the minds of men with the aid of education, it was first necessary
to master that of women."[76]

By the early 1860s the greater proportion of teachers in girls' primary
education, even in the municipal schools, were uncertified nuns.[77] In
response to a competition sponsored by the ministry of public instruction
in late 1860 concerning the primary education needs in rural communes, a
middle-aged teacher Julie-Victoire Daubié (1824–1874) submitted a study,
Du Progrès dans l'enseignement primaire, in which she criticized the male
monopolies that existed in public education. She particularly objected to
the lesser qualifications required for nuns who taught than for secular
schoolmistresses; in fact, she qualified the 1850 law as "a disaster" for
women teachers who were not nuns. Unlike women religious, she argued,
secular female teachers must be adequately paid. She remarked that before
any new laws were made, the existing laws should be enforced. She called
on the minister of education to study developments in public education in
the United States and in Germany.[78] Her critique was not welcomed at the
ministry. But ministers could and did change.

---

[76] L.-C Michel, "De l'Éducation des filles: Ce qu'elle doit être, ce qu'elle est, ce qu'elle deviendrait
sous le régime de la circulaire ministerielle du 30 Octobre 1867," *Le Correspondant* (10 April 1868),
51–73; quotes, 51, 52. This author endorsed Dupanloup's opposition to the secular *cours*.

[77] See Claude Langlois, *Le Catholicisme au féminin: les congrégations françaises à supérieure générale au
XIXe siècle* (Paris: Cerf, 1984). See also Rebecca Rogers, "Reconsidering the Role of Religious Orders
in Modern French Women's Education," *Vitae Scholasticae*, 10:1–2 (1991), 43–51, and Rebecca
Rogers, "Retrograde or Modern? Unveiling the Teaching Nun in Nineteenth-Century France,
Social History, 23:2 (May 1998), 147–164. Lévy, *Mères en filles*. See also Sarah A. Curtis, *Educating the
Faithful: Religion, Schooling, and Society in Nineteenth-Century France* (DeKalb: Northern Illinois
University Press, 2000), whose work illuminates the development of Catholic primary education in
the diocese of Lyon.

[78] Daubié, *Des Progrès dans l'instruction primaire*.

In 1864, the philosopher and writer Jules Simon (1814–1896) published his celebrated critique of the inadequacy of girls' primary education in the schools run by the Catholic women's orders, which he claimed was due to the insufficient intellectual credentials required of the teaching religious. It first appeared in the *Revue des Deux Mondes* in August 1864 and touched off a firestorm in the press.[79] His book followed in 1865. Some of the points he made echoed those made previously by Daubié in her 1859 essay. Although Simon professed to be a liberal republican, like Michelet, he was in many ways still a social conservative. He was interested far more in liberating women from the influence of the Church than in effecting any real change in their assigned destinies. In a subsequent report (1879) on the secondary education of girls, Simon would argue that the primary education girls received was still not adequate to form mothers of families, which remained the ultimate goal.[80]

The critiques launched by Daubié and Simon foreshadowed the beginning of an aggressive effort during the last years of the Second Empire (continued during the first decades of the Third Republic) by anticlerical republicans, including a significant number of women, to wrest control of female instruction at the primary level from the Catholic religious orders by professionalizing teacher training, by substituting lay teachers trained and certified by the state, and by establishing public institutions for the education of women at the secondary level.[81]

The arguments of both factions were constrained in two areas, however. First, as has been mentioned, coeducation was anathema to most nineteenth-century French educators; whenever possible, they argued, the sexes must be schooled separately, especially after the age of 10.[82] Rules to that

[79] Jules Simon, "L'Enseignement primaire des filles en 1864," *Revue des Deux Mondes*, 15 August 1864; later reprinted in his *L'École* (Paris: Lacroix, 1865). The only study of Simon in English ignores his ongoing interest in the woman question as well as his wife's activity in women's rights groups in the 1860s and 1870s; see Philip A. Bertocci, *Jules Simon: Republican Anticlericalism and Cultural Politics in France, 1848–1886* (Columbia, MO: University of Missouri Press, 1978).

[80] See the report on Simon's presentation ("L'enseignement secondaire des jeunes filles") at a meeting of the Académie des Sciences Morales et Politiques, in *Journal des Économistes*, 4th ser., 6:17 (May 1879), 232. Simon framed his insistence on better secondary schooling for French girls in comparison to foreign examples, notably the United States, Switzerland, and Germany, but also Russia and Greece.

[81] For a study of the state normal schools established during the nineteenth century to train women primary school teachers, see Quartararo, *Women Teachers and Popular Education in Nineteenth-Century France*. Such schools were few and far between prior to the Second Empire, and only during the Third Republic did the government undertake a systematic effort to establish them. Quartararo's book follows the story up to 1914.

[82] Objections to coeducation in earlier times did not inevitably lead to the physical separation of boys and girls in the *petites écoles* founded throughout rural France. See Karen E. Carter, "'Les garçons et

effect had been enacted in Year III of the Revolution and again by the royal ordinance of 29 February 1816.[83] Most agreed that boys must have male teachers, and girls must have female teachers (the women educators such as Bachellery were especially insistent on developing more opportunities for female teachers). In particular, single male teachers must not be let near adolescent girls. In his 1864 speech in the Corps Législatif, Hippolyte Carnot spoke in support of a six million franc allotment to fund the establishment of more girls' schools as a "good investment that would reap excellent interest" (*argent bien placé et qui donnerait de beaux intérêts*); he argued that even if male teachers had to be appointed, they should be married and their wives should also be teachers.[84] As the American medical student Mary Putnam wrote home to her mother from Paris in 1867, "The French . . . social system is constructed . . . entirely on the principle of keeping young men and women as far apart as flame and gunpowder."[85] It would take decades for progressive reformers to erode the deep-seated prejudice against coeducation, despite the attempts of a few later reformers – notably the notoriously anarchist educator Paul Robin – to convince their countrymen that schooling boys and girls together could work perfectly well in France, and that (as the more pragmatic Americans had recognized) it was far more economical.[86] But the controversial Robin would stand alone.

Second, the "domesticating" focus in the curriculum for girls' schools was extremely difficult to dislodge, despite concerted efforts by progressive feminist women. In early 1871 a committee of Parisian women produced a report on the reform of primary education in which they advocated not

les filles sont pêle-mêle dans l'école': Gender and Primary Education in Early Modern France," *French Historical Studies* 31:3 (Summer 2008), 417–443.

[83] See the decree of 27 Brumaire, an III, article 7, which divided primary schools into two separate sections, with a male teacher and a female teacher. Under the Restoration, Article 22 of the royal ordinance of 29 February 1816 prohibited mixed schools altogether (at least in theory): "Les garçons et les filles ne pourront jamais être réunis pour recevoir l'enseignement."

[84] Hippolyte Carnot, *Discours sur l'enseignement des filles, prononcé au Corps Législatif, dans la séance du 19 mai 1864* (Paris: Pagnerre, 1864), 14-page offprint; quotes, pp. 7, 12.

[85] *Life and Letters of Mary Putnam Jacobi*, ed. Ruth Putnam (New York: G. P. Putnam Sons, 1925), p. 121.

[86] French educators had long been intrigued with (though wary of) the American example. See in particular, Célestin Hippeau, "L'Éducation des femmes et des affranchis en Amérique depuis la guerre de sécession," *Revue des Deux Mondes*, 15 September 1869. On Robin, see Angus McLaren, "Revolution and Education in Late Nineteenth-Century France: The Early Career of Paul Robin," *History of Education Quarterly*, 21:3 (1981), 317–335. French resistance to coeducation lasted well into the twentieth century. See Edouard Breuse, *La Coéducation dans les écoles mixtes* (Paris, 1970). See especially Rebecca Rogers's comparative essay, "Mixité et coéducation: état des lieux d'une historiographie européenne," *CLIO: Histoire, Femmes et Sociétés*, n° 18 (2003), 177–202 (special issue cited in n. 72).

only coeducation but also full parity in educational opportunity for girls and boys.[87] This forward-looking program clearly contradicted the prevailing wisdom concerning utilitarian education designed to keep each sex in its separate space. Literacy, domestic training, and some literary and scientific instruction were not the only elements of schooling advocated for French girls. Vocational training for girls of the poorer classes figured on the educational agenda as well. But these latter efforts, which were part of a pan-European initiative, will be discussed in Chapter 6, on economics and employment.

Controversies Surrounding Secondary Education for Girls

After getting off to a rocky start, secondary education for girls developed privately and at the local level. In 1837, the July Monarchy's Council of Public Instruction laid out curricular requirements for private educational establishments in the department of the Seine. But in 1853, the imperial government effectively suppressed girls' secondary education.[88] In the 1860s, the debate on the woman question once again focused on the subject of secondary schooling for girls. Before 1880, when the passage of the Sée law would inaugurate public secondary education for young women of the upper classes, there were, apart from private tutoring (and the quasi-public schools for select girls established by Napoléon and administered by the *Légion d'Honneur*), only two avenues open for them to acquire advanced instruction: the boarding schools run by Catholic religious orders and private secular *pensions* located in the larger cities. In

---

[87] See *Rapport présenté au nom de la Commission des dames chargée d'examiner les questions rélatives à la réforme de l'instruction primaire par Mme Coignet, rapporteur, suivi d'un appendice par Mme Fanny Ch. Delon* (Paris: Imprimerie administrative de Paul Dupont, 1871). Clarisse-Josephine Gauthier Coignet was active in women's rights and progressive lay educational circles. She and her *consoeurs* made excellent political use of the Hippeau report (cited in n. 86), on the education and capabilities of girls in the United States, as well as the publications of André Léo and John Stuart Mill's *On the Subjection of Women* (1869), which had quickly appeared in French translation the same year as *L'Assujetissement des femmes*, trad. de l'anglais par M. E. Cazelles (Paris: Guillaumin, 1869; 2nd ed., 1876).

    This report has been analyzed by Barry H. Bergen, in his article, "Education, Equality, and Feminism: The 1870 Women's Commission on Education Reform," *Proceedings of the Western Society for French History, 1992*, ed. Norman Ravitch (Riverside, CA: WSFH, 1993), pp. 293–302. Bergen has remarked (p. 293) that "embedded in the commission's considerations of educational questions, lies a sophisticated argument for equal rights in the larger society. Moreover, this argument, in its clear formulation of women's rights as a function of individual liberties rather than women's special role in the family, departs from the standard accounts of the origins of liberal feminism in nineteenth-century France."

[88] See Rogers, "Mixité et coéducation," pp. 48–49.

either setting, the quality of instruction could vary from quite good to woefully inadequate. Many of these schools were still inspired, directly or indirectly, as we have said, by the educational philosophy of Fénelon. It goes without saying, therefore, that these institutions did not prepare their female pupils in Latin and Greek for the *baccalauréat* examination, an obligatory rite of passage for young men who wished to enter the faculties of the French university system, and from there, the prestigious liberal professions. This was as yet virtually unthinkable. Here educated Frenchmen fully revealed their biases as they endlessly reiterated their conviction that woman's vocation was to be found in the *foyer*, not in the forum. Well into the Third Republic, the liberal professions – as well as political life – were designated as, and defended as, men's territory, while the role of the *femme au foyer* was celebrated, elaborated, and urged upon girls as their particular destiny.

It is worth remarking, however, that (unlike political rights) the classical *baccalauréat* had never been legally closed to women. Since its establishment as the first university degree during the early nineteenth century, the *baccalauréat* had become a male prerogative by sheer force of custom.[89] The first woman to succeed in challenging masculine privilege on this point was none other than Julie-Victoire Daubié, whom we met earlier in this chapter. The granddaughter of a *maître-des-forges* (another source says her father was an accountant) from Fontenoy-le-Château in the Vosges, she had studied at home with her eldest brother (a priest) and mastered the required Greek and Latin. Subsequently, she went abroad to study German and then became a tutor in Lyon.[90] In 1859 she submitted the winning entry, *La Femme pauvre*, in an essay contest sponsored by the Academy of Lyon, of which more will be said in Chapter 6. In 1861, at the age of 37, and with the backing of François Arlès-Dufour, a prominent Lyon textile merchant and Saint-Simonian, she presented herself as a candidate for the *baccalauréat* in the Academy of Lyon and passed with honors. Despite her success, the then minister of public instruction refused

[89] This is not to say that other prohibitions had not been put in place. In 1810, the historian and publicist Charles de Lacretelle (later a member of the Académie Française) had tried to open the Sorbonne to young women, beginning a series of public lectures on their behalf. In response, the Council of the newly formed Faculty of Letters handed down a formal decision prohibiting their attendance; no such prohibition of attendance by women seems to have been in place at the faculty in Lyon or other faculties in the provinces. See the brief account by Lacretelle in his *Testament philosophique et littéraire*, vol. 2, note on pp. 324–325 (cf. n. 51); and Cl[aude] Perroud, "Les Femmes aux cours de la Sorbonne," *L'Enseignement public: Revue Pédagogique*, n.s. 73:7 (July 1918), 24–28.

[90] The sources I have consulted do not reveal whether Daubié went to Freiburg in southern Germany, or Freiburg (Fribourg) in Switzerland.

to issue her a diploma, on the grounds (so the story goes), that to do so would "disgrace" his ministry. The minister's refusal generated considerable coverage in the press and he ultimately capitulated in 1862. As was true of educational pioneers in many countries during the nineteenth century, Daubié would become an important contributor to the campaign for women's rights, focusing on educational and economic issues, and especially the vote, during the Second Empire and early Third Republic.[91]

During the 1860s another man on the liberal Left would lead the political campaign for public secondary education of French girls. Victor Duruy served as Napoléon III's reforming minister of public instruction from 1864 to 1870. His effort in late 1867 to establish secondary courses for girls in French urban centers under governmental sponsorship ignited the wrath of the Catholic hierarchy and provoked a celebrated polemic with the bishop of Orléans, Félix Dupanloup. This Catholic educator was himself a great champion of educating women (at least up to a certain point), but he believed that the circumstances had to be right. He was particularly distressed by two central features of Duruy's program: first, that the girls would be taught by male professors from the boys' lycees (many of whom were considered to hold "advanced" anticlerical opinions and also might be potential sexual predators) and, secondly, that the courses would meet in the town halls, that is, in "public places."[92] For Dupanloup and his supporters, this combination was anathema. In

---

[91] Daubié was also one of the first women in France to earn the *licence ès lettres* (1871); when she died in 1874, she was preparing a doctorate. On her remarkable career, see *Revue de l'Instruction publique*, 29 August 1861; *Le Temps*, 16 January 1862; and Léon Richer, "Une Nouvelle victoire," *L'Avenir des Femmes*, n° 76 (12 November 1871).

Retrospective accounts include: "Georges Bath" [Léon Richer], in *L'Avenir des Femmes*, 1 November 1874; E. Levasseur, "Mlle Julie-Victoire Daubié," *Journal des Économistes*, 3e ser., 37 (1875), 154–156; Comtesse de Magallon, "Le Féminisme: Victoire Daubié," *La Nouvelle Revue* (15 August 1898), 677–695; Claude Pasteur, *Les Pionnières de l'histoire* (Paris: Éditions du Sud, 1963), pp. 229–232; and P[aulette] Bascou-Bance, "La Première Femme bachelière: Julie Daubié," *Bulletin de l'Association Guillaume Budé*, 4th ser., n° 1 (March 1972), 107–113. See also *Lettres à Julie Victoire Daubié (1824–1874): La première bachelière de France et son temps*, compiled and presented by Raymonde Bulger (New York: Peter Lang, 1992).

[92] There are now three scholarly studies of Duruy's ministry: see Jean Rohr, *Victor Duruy, Ministre de Napoléon III, essai sur la politique de l'instruction publique au temps de l'Empire libéral* (Paris: Librairie générale de droit et de jurisprudence, 1967); Sandra Horvath-Peterson, *Victor Duruy and French Education: Liberal Reform in the Second Empire* (Baton Rouge: Louisiana State University Press, 1984), based on her Ph.D. dissertation, Catholic University of America, 1971; and Jean-Charles Gesiot, *Victor Duruy: historien et ministre (1811–1894)* (Villeneuve-d'Ascq: Presses Universitaires de Septentrion, 2009). On the controversy over girls' secondary education, see Sandra Horvath [-Peterson], "Victor Duruy and the Controversy over Secondary Education for Girls," *French Historical Studies*, 9:1 (Spring 1975), 83–104; Françoise Mayeur, "Les Évêques français et Victor Duruy: Les Cours sécondaires de jeunes filles," *Revue d'Histoire de l'Église de France*, 57, n° 159 (July–December 1971), 267–304, and Mayeur, *Éducation des filles*, chapter 5.

Dupanloup's own archdiocese of Orléans, he threatened parishioners who dared to send their daughters to these courses with excommunication.[93] It was therefore highly significant that the Empress Eugénie, who had championed Duruy's effort (and earlier had stepped in to assist Julie-Victoire Daubié in taking possession of her diploma), chose deliberately to enroll her motherless nieces (the daughters of the Spanish grandee, the Duke d'Alba and his late wife, Eugénie's sister).[94] These public courses were a temporary, controversial experiment, and most did not survive the fall of the Second Empire.

Young Women, Higher Education, and the Professions

Julie-Victoire Daubié's 1861 triumph in the *baccalauréat* examination paved the way for other women who aspired to higher education, crowned by university degrees and potential access to careers in the liberal professions. Nor were their aspirations exactly a secret. In early 1862, Daubié and Clémence Royer, the translator of Darwin's *Origin of Species*, entered into a heated exchange in the Parisian press on the subject of women and professions with August Nefftzer, editor of *Le Temps*.[95] Other young women soon followed in Daubié's footsteps, making news as they went. In November 1867, for instance, *Le Temps* announced that Marie-Thérèse Gaillard, 16 years of age, had just obtained her "*bac*" in the Paris Faculty of Letters, with brilliant

---

93   See Félix Dupanloup, "Femmes savantes et femmes studieuses," in *Le Correspondant*, 25 April 1867; *M. Duruy et l'éducation des filles; lettre à un de ses collègues (16 Novembre 1867)* (Paris: C. Douniol, 1867); *Seconde lettre sur M. Duruy et l'éducation des femmes, (Décembre 1867)* (Paris: C. Douniol, 1867); *La Femme Chrétienne et française; dernière réponse à M. Duruy et à ses défenseurs (Janvier 1868)* (Paris: C. Douniol, 1868). Catholic girls' education was nevertheless reinvigorated by Dupanloup's important philosophical statement, *La Femme studieuse* (Paris: C. Douniol, 1869; also published in English as *Studious Women; from the French of Monseigneur Dupanloup, bishop of Orleans*, transl. R. M. Phillimore [Boston: P. Donahoe, 1869]) which appeared in the wake of his controversy with Duruy. In this work he took issue with Catholic neo-traditionalist thought as incarnated by Maistre, and argued for an educational program that transcended purely household-related matters to include the classics. This work was followed by his *Lettres sur l'éducation des filles et sur les études qui conviennent aux femmes dans le monde* (Paris: J. Gervais, 1879). Reassessments of Dupanloup's long-range impact include Mayeur, *Éducation des filles,* and *Éducation et images de la femme chrétienne en France au début du XXème siècle*, ed. Françoise Mayeur & Jacques Gadille (Lyon: L'Hermès, 1980).
94   Henri Rollet, "Le féminisme de l'impératrice Eugénie," *Souvenir napoléonien,* n° 358 (April 1988), 49–56. Rollet underscored the empress's admiration for women of achievement, whose company she cultivated and whom she publicly recognized whenever possible.
95   See the exchange between Julie Daubié, Clémence Royer, and Aug. Nefftzer on the subject of women's aspirations to enter the liberal professions and sciences, in *Le Temps*, 6 December and 16 December 1862. The paper's editor, Nefftzer, favored their studying and even embarking on liberal careers but strongly disapproved of their aspiration to play a role in political life.

marks.[96] The matter of preparing girls for the same baccalaureate examinations the boys took would, however, remain unresolved until 1924.

The next big breakthrough in women's education came in the schools of medicine. As was discussed in Chapter 3, entry to professional medical training on a par with the physicians was a long-standing demand of some French women. Already, in 1849, the British-born American physician Elizabeth Blackwell had come to France to acquire hands-on experience at La Maternité; she quickly became known to the French feminists of that time.[97] In 1865, a German woman, Mathilde Theyessen, passed the French examinations to become an "*officier de santé et de pharmacie*," and claimed to be the first state-certified women physician in Europe.[98] Elizabeth Garrett from England and Mary Putnam from the United States soon tried their luck in Paris.

In 1868, having previously obtained the authorization of the Council of Ministers during Empress Eugénie's brief regency, the Paris Faculty of Medicine admitted four women (three from other countries) to follow courses and prepare their examinations in medicine.[99] The first

---

[96] *Le Temps*, 20 November 1867.

[97] See Elizabeth Blackwell, *Pioneer Work in Opening the Medical Profession to Women* (London & New York: Longmans, Green, & Co., 1895); reissued, with an introduction by Mary Roth Walsh (New York: Schocken Books, 1977). See esp. chapter 4: "Study in Europe, 1849." Articles about Elizabeth Blackwell's medical successes appear in Jeanne Deroin's *Almanach des femmes* for 1852 (Jersey: Imprimerie universelle, 1852) and 1853 (London: J. Watson, 1853). Blackwell had successfully graduated from an all-male medical college in upstate New York in the late 1840s and then came to Paris for practical experience at the Paris women's hospital, La Maternité. In England and the United States, medical colleges exclusively for women opened only in the 1870s.

[98] See clipping, "La Première femme-docteur d'Europe," *Le Siècle médical*, 15 February 1933, in BMD, DOS THE. Theyessen's accomplishment is also acknowledged in Regine Deutsch, *The International Woman Suffrage Alliance: Its History from 1904 to 1929* (London: Board of the Alliance, 1929), p. 27.

[99] This move was bitterly opposed by some French physicians: see, for example, the diatribe by Dr. H. Montanier in *La Gazette des Hôpitaux*, 21 March 1868, which was extensively quoted in E. Beaugrand, "Médecins-femmes," *Dictionnaire encyclopédique des sciences medicales*, 2nd ser., vol. 5 (MAR-MED; 1874), 604–605. Elizabeth Garrett came to Paris to earn a medical degree, after having already obtained an English apothecary's license, which allowed her to practice medicine. Authorities quickly closed this legal loophole, however, and the Scottish University of St. Andrews subsequently refused her request to sit for diploma exams in medicine; it was then that she decided to try in Paris. Both Garrett and Putnam left personal accounts: see Elizabeth Garrett Anderson, "The History of a Movement," *The Fortnightly Review* (March 1893), 404–417; and Putnam's *Life and Letters of Mary Putnam Jacobi*, chapters 4–9, which includes a vivid record of her Paris medical training as documented in her letters home. For comparative purposes, see E. Moberly Bell [Enid Moberly], *Storming the Citadel: The Rise of the Woman Doctor* (London: Constable, 1953); Jean Donnison, *Midwives and Medical Men: A History of Inter-Professional Rivalries and Women's Rights* (New York: Schocken Books, 1977); and Mary Roth Walsh, *"Doctors Wanted: No Women Need Apply": Sexual Barriers in the Medical Profession, 1835–1975* (New Haven: Yale University Press, 1978).

Frenchwoman admitted, Madeleine Brès, was 25 years old, married, and a licensed midwife. She passed the *baccalauréat-ès-sciences* in August 1868; in order to register, as a married woman, to become a doctoral candidate in medicine, she had to present her husband's written authorization, which remains to this day in her dossier as testimony to the legal incapacity of married women.[100] Mlle Marie Verneuil ultimately became the first French woman to earn the doctorate in medicine; she was followed in 1875 by Madame Brès in Paris (whose thesis work had been interrupted by the Franco-Prussian war) and Androline Domergue at Montpellier, and in 1876 by a Madame Ribard, from Nantes.[101] These were the first French women to storm the bastille of higher education in France; women from other countries accompanied them, including several more English women who, following Elizabeth Garrett's counsel, had abandoned medical study at Edinburgh University, during its brief experiment of admitting women, because of the repeated obstacles placed in their path by male opponents.[102] Even this triumph, though, did not permit the women to compete

---

[100] Alexandrine-Magdeleine Brès, née Gébelin (1842–1925), the first French woman doctor, attested to Empress Eugénie's active interest in assuring her medical education; see her account in *Revue Universitaire* (1921): 2, 145–146 (republished in English translation in *Victorian Women*, pp. 428–429). Her success at the *baccalauréat* and her forthcoming registration at the Paris School of Medicine were announced in *L'Opinion nationale*, 1 August 1868, with the comment, "Le meilleur moyen de prouver le mouvement, c'est de marcher"; see also the issue of 7 August 1868. Her husband's notarized authorization for her enrollment, dated 24 October 1868, is preserved in her dossier at the Archives nationales. She received her degree in 1875, after interruptions, and was awarded the *palmes académiques* in 1878. From 1883 to 1895 she edited the periodical, *Hygiène de la Femme et de l'Enfant*. In 1893 admirers founded a *crèche* (childcare center) in her honor. See the dossiers on Brès at the BMD and in the Archives nationales, AJ16 (Académie de Paris) 6837, and especially Caroline Schultze, *La Femme-médecin au XIXe siècle* (Paris: Ollier-Henry 1888), which was based on papers given to the author for her thesis by Mme Brès. See also Mélanie Lipinska, *Histoire des femmes médecins, depuis l'antiquité jusqu'à nos jours* (Paris: Librairie G. Jacques, 1900), pp. 411–413.

[101] See the list of women holding French university degrees in *Le Temps*, 12 April 1879. The list was originally published in *La Gazette des Femmes*; it included five doctors of medicine, three *licencières*, and twenty-eight recipients of the *baccalauréat*. According to Lipinska's *Histoire des femmes médecins*, Mme Ribard from Nantes went on to serve in north Africa and Egypt, and ultimately Vietnam, where she died.

[102] One of these women, Jeanne-E. (Auber) Schmahl, married a Frenchman and remained in Paris, where she would become an important figure in the French women's rights movement during the 1890s and 1900s. See her retrospective account, covered in "Les Premiers vingt ans de l'émancipation des femmes anglaises," *L'Éclair*, 31 October 1892. According to this account, the other three who came to study in Paris were the misses Chaplin, Bovill, and Barkhir. For Jeanne Schmahl's later career, especially her *L'Avant courrière* campaigns for specific changes in French law, see my subsequent volume. Another English woman who came to Paris in 1873 to study medicine was Anna Kingsford. See *Anna Kingsford: Her Life, Letters, Diary, and Work*, ed. Edward Maitland, 2 vols. (London: G. Redway, 1896).

for internships in the Paris hospitals – a battle would have to be fought to break this logjam.

At the Faculty of Letters in Paris, circumstances were more difficult. Although women were already able to enroll for courses and degrees at the University of Zurich (the sole European university open to women in the early 1860s), at the Sorbonne they were barred from attending regular lectures until the 1880s.[103] The Paris Faculty of Law admitted a smattering of women as auditors, but only in 1884–1885 could they register as students and enroll for the examinations. The *École des Beaux Arts* would refuse to admit women until the 1890s, and then did so only after a society of women artists mounted a sustained campaign.[104] The *grandes écoles* remained closed to women. The *École des Chartes* resisted until 1906, the *École Centrale* until 1912, and the *École Polytechnique* until 1972. Lectures at the Collège de France, the Museum, and the Jardin des Plantes, however, remained open to women and some lecturers attracted sizeable crowds. There were many ways for women to obtain informal education but virtually none that conferred formal certification.

Revealing and Debating the Sexual Politics of Knowledge

Not surprisingly, these developments at the levels of secondary and higher education in France accompanied yet another wave of speculation, claims, and counterclaims concerning women's brainpower and creative potential, accompanied by the growth of a more general feminist critique of knowledge. In the mid-1850s several French women writers attempted to seize the high ground, claiming knowledge and the opportunity to formulate it in their own right, thus going beyond the old debate about women's creativity by demonstrating it. Thereby they hoped to mute questions as to whether women could create works of "genius," or should settle for being the mothers of "men of genius," as the British historian Henry Buckle suggested in 1859. Jenny P[oinsard]. d'Héricourt (1809–1875), whom we met earlier in her effort to obtain formal medical training, struck

---

[103] See the important retrospective study by Edmée Charrier, *L'Évolution intellectuelle féminine* (Paris: Éditions Albert Mechlinck, 1931), pp. 148–149, 152–155. See also Lacretelle, *Testament philosophique et littéraire*, cited in n. 51, and Paul Janet, "L'Éducation des femmes," *Revue des Deux Mondes* (1 September 1883), 51.

[104] On the campaign to open Beaux-Arts to women, see Tamar Garb, *Sisters of the Brush: Women's Artistic Culture in Late Nineteenth-Century Paris* (New Haven: Yale University Press, 1994). On one private art academy that did welcome women, see Gabriel P. Weisberg, & Jane R. Becker, eds., *Overcoming All Obstacles: The Women of the Académie Julian* (New York: The Dahesh Museum, & New Brunswick, NJ: Rutgers University Press, 1999).

the first blow in a renewed series of feminist efforts to claim knowledge and "Genius" as Women's Right. "Politics" of the usual sort may have been off-limits for discussion by women in these early years of the Second Empire, but the politics of knowledge were obviously not.

In an 1855 article, "On Woman's Future," published in French in Turin (capital of the Kingdom of Piedmont), d'Héricourt reminded her readers of the Saint-Simonians' earlier call for women to speak out. "Today," she wrote, "several women have disengaged themselves from the secular absorption of their sex and have developed their own individuality. These women, and I am one of them, can now reply to that call . . . and that is what I am going to do."[105]

Challenging established wisdom, Jenny P. d'Héricourt revealed herself as a full-fledged combatant on a par with men in the knowledge wars. Invoking the law of progress, she traced out a theory of gender formation. Organic modifications, she argued, have their seat in the brain, which is "essentially modifiable."[106] There are now women who have had a mascu-line education who are in possession of rational faculties, just as there are men who preponderantly display feelings. "It is *radically false*," she argued, "that nature made men rational and women emotional; it is education and morals that made them thus: feelings and rationality are equally distrib-uted. . . . The brain is the instrument of progress." The mind may have no sex, but the initially genderless brain requires exercise to develop. No more women's nature, women's destiny, women's functions, no more women's sphere. Women, just like men, are en route to "individual independence." Finally, argued d'Héricourt, women must cease asking for their rights and *take them*. They must remain womanly, not emulating masculine habits or airs, and they must ally themselves in solidarity with other women. "Victory," d'Héricourt insisted, "will belong to those who are united by affection and a common goal, who know how to *dare* and to act."[107]

[105] Jenny P. d'Héricourt, "De l'avenir de la femme," *La Ragione* (Turin), n° 54 (27 October 1855), 26–31, and n° 56 (10 November 1855), 59–64. This quote is from the October installment, 31.

On Héricourt, see Karen Offen, "A Nineteenth-Century French Feminist Rediscovered: Jenny P. d'Héricourt, 1809–1875," *Signs: Journal of Women in Culture and Society*, 13:1 (1987), 144–158. See also Alessandra Anteghini, *Socialismo e femminismo nella Francia del XIX secolo: Jenny d'Héricourt*. Quaderni dell'Istituto di Scienza Politica, Università di Genova (Genoa: ECIG, 1988); Caroline Arni & Claudia Honegger, "Jenny P. d'Héricourt (1809–1875): Weibliche Modernität und die Prinzipien von 1789," in *Frauen in der Soziologie: Neun Porträts* (Munich: C. H. Beck, 1998), pp. 60–98; and Caroline Arni, "'La toute-puissance de la barbe': Jenny P. d'Héricourt et les novateurs modernes," *CLIO*, n° 13 (2001), 145–154.

[106] "De l'avenir de la femme" (part 2), *La Ragione*, n° 56 (10 November 1855), 59.

[107] "De l'avenir de la femme," *La Ragione*, n° 54 (27 October 1855), 60–64 *passim*.

Intellectually unleashed, Jenny P. d'Héricourt also challenged biblical authority, insisting that claims for the equality of the sexes based on Christian belief (much discussed in recent years) were in fact not true. Citing multiple examples from the Old and New Testament alike, she demonstrated that "both proclaim the inferiority of woman, imposing on her the most absolute submission to her father and her husband, refusing her every right, as daughter, spouse, mother, alienating her from the priesthood, from science, from instruction, denying her intelligence, outraging her modesty, torturing her feelings, permitting the sale and exploitation of her beauty, preventing her from inheriting or owning property."[108] Catholicism, in her view, was a particular obstacle: a falling away from blind faith would be a good thing for women.

It was on the crest of these attacks that Jenny P. d'Héricourt confronted the antifeminism of her countryman from the Franche-Comté, the printer Pierre-Joseph Proudhon (1809–1865), an economic thinker and secular philosopher who had become a leading spokesman for the workers' mutualist movement; he was also known as the staunch adversary of Jeanne Deroin in her 1849 electoral campaign. In a heated exchange, published in the *Revue Philosophique et Religieuse*, d'Héricourt challenged Proudhon's published views on the woman question, which dated back to 1841. She also published his response to her, in which Proudhon argued that women's cause must not be separated from that of men, that justice could never make woman man's equal, and that the "inferiority of the feminine sex did not constitute either serfdom or humiliation, or a lessened dignity," but rather the opposite. He considered the agitation of women on behalf of women's rights as "a madness due precisely to the infirmity of the sex, and to its incapacity to know itself and to govern itself alone."[109]

Jenny P. d'Héricourt quickly counterattacked in print, claiming that Proudhon was effectively applying a double standard for justice as concerns women. In reply, Proudhon sketched the outline of what would become his infamous "calculus" of the inferiority of women to men. The discussion terminated abruptly in March 1857, when Jenny declared Proudhon's failure to respond to her rebuttal to be his admission of defeat.

Proudhon's response to d'Héricourt was forthcoming with the publication in 1858 of his major work, *De la Justice dans la Révolution et dans*

---

[108] See her series of four articles: "La Bible et la question des femmes," in *La Ragione* (September–October 1857). Quote: issue of 24 October 1857, 38–39. A slightly different version had appeared the previous August as a single article in the *Revue Philosophique et Religieuse* (Paris).

[109] Proudhon's letter, quoted in "M. Proudhon et la question des femmes," *Revue Philosophique et Religieuse*, 6:21 (December 1856), 7.

l'Église (On Justice in the Revolution and in the Church), notoriously in the section on "Love and Marriage." Singling out the would-be emancipators of woman, Proudhon let loose: "Feminine indiscretion has caught fire; a half-dozen inky-fingered insurgents obstinately try to make woman into something we do not want, reclaim their *rights* with insults, and defy us to bring the question out into the light of day."[110] Emancipation, Proudhon insisted, maintaining his earlier formula "housewife or harlot" [*ménagère ou courtesan*] amounted to prostitution. He then laid out the details of his calculus of women's "physical, intellectual, and moral inferiority" to men, based on the Aristotelian premises of what G. J. Barker Benfield aptly named "the spermatic economy," and what we might now call the testosterone imprint. "The complete human being," Proudhon proclaimed, "is the male." With regard to intellect, he claimed: [111]

> Genius is . . . virility of spirit and its accompanying powers of abstraction, generalization, invention, conceptualization, which are lacking in equal measure in children, eunuchs, and women. . . . To the generation of ideas as to the generation [of children] woman brings nothing of her own; she is a passive, enervating being, whose conversation exhausts you as much as her embraces. He who wishes to conserve in its entirety the strength of his body and his mind will flee her; she is a murderer.

In short, women cannot produce "seed," i.e., "ideas," but serve as passive receptacles for the seed and ideas of men, even as they drain away manly energy. Few statements published by French men have been more blatantly antifeminist than this! So much for the ostensible and often-vaunted "liberalism" of the socialist Proudhon.[112]

In her book *La Femme affranchie* (1860), Jenny P. d'Héricourt returned to the charge: "We demand our right, because we are persuaded that woman has to set her stamp on Science, Philosophy, Justice and Politics."[113] She was joined by the young Juliette Lamber (later the celebrated

---

[110] P.-J. Proudhon, *De la Justice dans la Révolution et dans l'Église* (1858), in *Oeuvres complètes de P.-J. Proudhon*, new ed., ed. Célestin Bouglé & Henri Moysset, vol. 12 (Paris: M. Rivière, 1935); critical passages transl. by KO in *WFF*, vol. 1, doc. 95, pp. 325–330. All quotes from this translation.

[111] *WFF*, vol. 1, p. 329.

[112] See the essay by Monique Canto-Sperber, "Proudhon, the First Liberal Socialist," in *A Vast and Useful Art: The Gustave Gimon Collection on French Political Economy*, ed. Mary Jane Parrine (Stanford, CA: Stanford University Libraries, 2004), pp. 84–97. In assessing Proudhon's "liberalism" against his "socialism," this author seems surprisingly oblivious to his deeply entrenched (and well-documented) male chauvinism and how that fundamentally compromised his commitment to freedom of the "individual." Proudhon's "individual" was unquestionably gendered masculine.

[113] Jenny P. d'Héricourt, *La Femme affranchie* (Brussels: A. Lacroix, Van Meenen et Cie, 1860); in English translation as *A Woman's Philosophy of Woman, or Woman Affranchised; An Answer to*

salonnière and journalist Juliette Adam), who published a book-length refutation of Proudhon's ideas.[114] "M. Proudhon," Lamber argued,[115]

> has tried to establish that the subordination of woman is based on nature, and he has attempted to construct an *order* that would maintain this subordination and a justice that would sanction it. He wanted to perpetuate the reign of force by legitimizing it; that is his crime. This crime is unpardonable . . . in the eyes of any woman who is conscious of her own *moral value, her personality, her natural autonomy*. God willing – and woman too – it will soon be equally unpardonable in the eyes of thinking human beings of both sexes.

In Lausanne, another French woman had already begun to set her stamp on science and philosophy. In the late 1850s Clémence Royer opened a course for ladies on "woman's philosophy," defending the position that women had a special sort of genius. "What I must find," she explained in her introductory lecture, "is a form, a feminine expression of science." "It is . . . a new art which I have to create," an art that could give life to the cold and virile character of science, an art that could engage women fully in scientific endeavors. "As long as science remains exclusively in the hands of men," Royer explained, "it will never go down into the depths of the family and society. . . . Why . . . should [women] be excluded from the hunt for truth?"[116]

Royer went on to publish (in 1862) her French translation of Charles Darwin's *Origin of Species*, which she prefaced with a long and iconoclastic commentary. In the 1870s, following her return to France from Switzerland, Royer would become a controversial participant in the Anthropological Society of Paris, objecting vociferously to the work of a team of

Michelet, Proudhon, Girardin, Legouvé, Comte, and Other Modern Innovators (New York: Carleton, 1864; reprinted by Westport, CT: Hyperion Press, 1981), and excerpted in *WFF*, vol. 1, doc. 98. Quote, *WFF*, vol. 1, p. 346.

[114] Juliette Lamber (pseud. Juliette Lambert Lamessine [Adam]), *Idées anti-proudhoniennes sur l'amour, la femme et le mariage* (Paris: A. Taride, 1858; 2nd ed., 1861; new ed., Dentu, 1868). Translated excerpts in *WFF*, vol. 1, doc. 96, pp. 331–335.

[115] As translated in *WFF*, vol. 1, doc. 96, p. 331.

[116] Clémence Royer, *Introduction à la philosophie des femmes, cours donné à Lausanne par Mlle A.C.R.: Leçon d'ouverture* (1859), as translated by Sara Miles, in appendix to "Evolution and Natural Law in the Synthetic Science of Clémence Royer" (Ph.D. dissertation, University of Chicago, 1988). Quoted with permission from Miles, pp. 397, 405, 407.
  On Royer, see Geneviève Fraisse, *Clémence Royer, philosophe et femme de sciences* (Paris: Éditions la Découverte, 1985); Joy Harvey, "'Strangers to Each Other': Male and Female Relationships in the Life and Work of Clémence Royer," in *Uneasy Careers and Intimate Lives: Women in Science, 1789–1979*, ed. Pnina G. Abir-Am & Dorinda Outram (New Brunswick, NJ: Rutgers University Press, 1987), and Joy Harvey, *Almost a Man of Genius: Clémence Royer, Feminism, and Nineteenth-Century Science* (New Brunswick, NJ: Rutgers University Press, 1997). See also Aline Demars, *Clémence Royer, l'intrépide: la plus savante des savantes; autobiographie et commentaires* (Paris: L'Harmattan, 2005).

male physicians who had begun to measure skulls and weigh brains, some in an effort to assert masculine superiority. In the 1890s, Royer would be feted as a feminist heroine.

Measuring Brains, Skulls, Heights, and Weights

Such interventions as these stimulated a new wave of "scientific" research on sexual differences (as did similar developments in England, Germany, and the United States). Women's skulls, women's brains, women's intellectual capabilities all became the subjects, not only of discussion, speculation, and criticism, but also of "scientific" measurement that subsequently became intricately interwoven with questions of racial ranking.[117] By the 1860s, the hunt for sexual difference as translated by brain and skull measurements had become a full-fledged research field for anatomists, physiologists, physicians, and budding anthropologists, some of whom translated the relative volume of the skull and the weight of the brain into indices of masculine superiority and female inferiority. A certain doctor C. Sappey responded to both these questions in 1861, in a paper presented to the Biological Society, noting that the sixteen male skulls he had studied were larger than the sixteen female skulls, but that the difference within the sexes seemed to be greater than the differences between the sexes.[118] But what could such information ultimately reveal about women's intellect and educational potential, their talent, indeed, their propensity for genius? Even Darwin, Herbert Spencer, and other evolutionary thinkers outside France would enter this discussion, which would become truly transnational.

In the midst of this developing scientific interest and disputes about women's brains and intelligence, a new phase of an older debate about whether women writers could or should be elected to the Académie

---

[117] See Robert A. Nye, *Crime, Madness, & Politics in Modern France: The Medical Concept of National Decline* (Princeton, NJ: Princeton University Press, 1984); Lynn Salkin Sbiroli, "Generation and Regeneration: Reflections on the Biological and Ideological Role of Women in France (1786–96)" in *Literature and Medicine during the Eighteeenth Century*, ed. M. M. Roberts & Roy Porter (London: Routledge, 1993), pp. 266–285; on Cuvier's contribution, Anne Fausto-Sterling, "Gender, Race, and Nation: The Comparative Anatomy of 'Hottentot Woman in Europe'," *Deviant Bodies*, ed. Jennifer Terry & Jacqueline Urla (Bloomington: Indiana University Press, 1995); reprinted in *Feminism and the Body*, ed. Londa Schiebinger (New York: Oxford University Press, 2000), pp. 203–233.

[118] M. le docteur C. Sappey, "Recherches sur le volume et la capacité du crâne, sur le volume et le poids de l'encéphale, comparés chez l'homme et chez la femme," lues à la Société de Biologie, dans sa séance du 18 mai 1861, *Comptes-rendus des Séances et Mémoires de la Société de Biologie, 1861*, 3rd ser., vol. 3 (Paris, 1862), Section "Mémoires," pp. 109–120.

Française erupted in 1862.[119] Partisans of women's election repeatedly invoked "genius" as a commodity that some women did possess; they put forth the name of the prolific and internationally known novelist George Sand (who many had acclaimed a genius since the 1830s, following on the claims made in the name of Sand's famous predecessor, Germaine de Staël) as being the most eminently qualified candidate for a seat in the Academy.[120] These debates ran on into 1865, when the Empress Eugénie came down on the side of women's "genius." As the last act of her second regency in early June 1865, she publicly affirmed her conviction by awarding the cross of the *Légion d'Honneur* to the renowned French painter Rosa Bonheur. "It was my desire," she proclaimed, "that the last act of my regency be consecrated to showing that in my eyes genius has no sex."[121]

But the question of relative brain size as a differentiating sexual characteristic would not go away. The eminent French physician and anthropologist Paul Broca, a champion of women's education, also engaged in analyses concerning women's brain size, postulating in 1873 that according to the data he had seen, it was clear that there was a historical, evolutionary, that is, cultural explanation for women's smaller brains; in his view, civilization increasingly provided women with male protection, and thus, compared to women and men among savage peoples, the physical and mental differences between the sexes grew wider in proportion to the degree of civilization.[122] In other words, women's "inferiority" could be considered an artifact of "progress," but also potentially remediable.

[119] See *Les Femmes et l'Académie française* (Paris: Éditions de l'Opale, 1980), which reprints (out of chronological order) the following texts: J . . . S . . . 1863. "Les Femmes à l'Académie" [Discours de reception de Madame * * *. Réponse de M. * * *], pp. 37–80; George Sand, *Pourquoi les femmes à l'Académie?* (Paris: Michel-Lévy, 1863), pp. 81–100 ; and Louis Lacour (de La Pijardière), *La Question des femmes à l'Académie* (Paris: Impr. de D. Jouaust, 1865), pp. 13–35. For a scintillating presentation of three centuries of debate about women and the academies, see Christian Gury, *Les Académiciennes* (Paris: Éditions Kimé, 1966).

[120] See Patricia Thomson, "George Sand and English Reviewers: The First Twenty Years," *Modern Language Review*, 67:3 (July 1972), 501–516. Despite serious reservations about Sand's scathing critique of the institution of marriage, the reviewer in England's *The Athenaeum* proclaimed her "a Woman of genius" (issue of December 1834, cited by Thomson, p. 502).

[121] The Empress's remarks of 10 June 1865 are recorded in Rosa Bonheur's account, in *Rosa Bonheur, sa vie, son oeuvre*, by Anna Elizabeth Klumpke (Paris: E. Flammarion, 1909), p. 264. This work is now available in English: see Anna Klumpke, *Rosa Bonheur: The Artist's (Auto)biography*, translated by Gretchen Van Slyke (Ann Arbor: The University of Michigan Press, 1997, 2001). Only rarely does the empress get credit in Second Empire scholarship for her attraction to and encouragement of female talent and achievement, or her efforts on behalf of girls' education; the sole exception I have found is a short article by Henri Rollet, "Le Féminisme de l'impératrice Eugénie," *Souvenir napoléonien*, n° 358 (April 1988), 49–56.

[122] See Paul Broca, "Sur les Crânes de la caverne de l'Homme-Mort," *Revue d'Anthropologie*, 2:1 (Paris, 1873), 45–46 (English translation in *WFF*, vol. 1, doc. 111). The vast literature on this subject

Women Writers Talk Back

Great women artists like Rosa Bonheur were still relatively few and far between, but in the 1860s, women writers with their "inky fingers" were multiplying fast. World-renowned French women writers such as Madame de Staël and, particularly, George Sand (whose prolific works had become widely known throughout the Atlantic world and in Russia) had emerged as targets of choice for antifeminist invective, including that of Proudhon. But by 1867, when the journalist Jules Barbey d'Aurevilly, seeking what he thought was an easy target, sought to belabor the bluestocking, inky-fingered insurgent theme once again, he met with vigorous rejoinders from two women intellectuals, the prolific writer Olympe Audouard (1830–1890), whose consciousness of women's issues had been thoroughly aroused by the difficulties she had encountered trying to make a living as a writer, and Maria Deraismes (1828–1894), who had just launched her midlife career as a charismatic public speaker for women's rights.[123]

In fact, for several centuries, despite the repeated condemnations of "*femmes savantes*" (learned women) and "*bas bleus*" (bluestockings), women intellectuals in France had been actively writing and publishing their works, and not infrequently they had used novels as a forum for critiquing women's lot. In the mid-seventeenth century, the novels of Madeleine de Scudéry denounced marriage in its current form as analogous to slavery. In the eighteenth century, as increasing numbers of French women learned to read and write, women's publishing had, in fact, increased dramatically, as the range of articles in the collection *Going Public* attest.[124] Whole industries grew up to furnish women who wrote (in particular, letters, which often remained unpublished, but also books for publication) with appropriately scaled-down writing desks and feminine writing equipment, as Dena Goodman has shown.[125] Historian Carla Hesse has challenged the

---

includes a fascinating study by Carl Sagan, *Broca's Brain: Reflections on the Romance of Science* (New York: Random House, 1979).

[123] A choice sample of Barbey d'Aurevilly's vicious (though not particularly original) polemic: "La femme bas-bleu est une virago de l'intelligence, chez laquelle l'hypertrophie cérébrale déforme le sexe et produit la monstruosité." Quoted by Olympe Audouard, *M. Barbey d'Aurevilly. Réponse à ses requisitoires contre les bas-bleus. Conférence du 11 avril* (1870), p. 13. Barbey's attacks on women writers have been reprinted in various volumes of his *Les Oeuvres et les hommes, XIXe siècle*. See especially *Les Bas-bleus* (1878), sér 1, vol. 5.

[124] See *Going Public: Women and Publishing in Early Modern France*, ed. Elizabeth C. Goldsmith & Dena Goodman (Ithaca, NY: Cornell University Press, 1995), and Nina Gelbart's study of the *Journal des Femmes* (cited in n. 26).

[125] See Dena Goodman, *Becoming a Woman in the Age of Letters* (Ithaca, NY: Cornell University Press, 2009).

notion that the Revolution barred women from participation in the "public sphere" (though admittedly the Jacobins did bar women specifically from political association and participation, a prohibition that remained in place throughout the entire nineteenth century). Hesse has inventoried the women authors in print between 1750 and 1800, remarking that "the number of French women in print exploded dramatically (more than trebling) in the decade after 1789."[126] And, indeed, the pace of publication by women continued to accelerate dramatically in the nineteenth century and into the twentieth. Only rarely, though, were their works deemed worthy of academic study by the men who constructed the literary canon.[127]

Already in the 1780s and 1790s, as we have seen, some women writers and educators were insisting on the importance of publications by women, historically and in their time. In Hesse's view, it was the commercialization and democratization of cultural life that made the careers of these women writers possible.[128] At the same time, however, their very appearance

---

[126] Carla Hesse, "French Women in Print, 1750–1800: An Essay in Historical Bibliography," *Studies on Voltaire and the Eighteenth Century*, n° 359 ["The Darnton Debate," ed. Haydn T. Mason] (Oxford: The Voltaire Foundation), pp. 65–82; quote, p. 69. See also Hesse, *The Other Enlightenment*, and Béatrice Slama, "'Un chantier est ouvert . . .': Notes sur un inventaire des textes des femmes du XIX siècle," *Romantisme*, n° 77 (1992), 87–94. Raymond Trousson, *Romans de femmes du XVIIIe siècle* (Paris: Robert Laffont, 1996) has counted 261 novels by 105 women published between 1735 and 1825; as reported by Jean-Yves Mollier, "Les Femmes auteurs et leurs éditeurs au XIXe siècle: Un long combat pour la reconnaissance de leurs droits d'écrivains," *Revue Historique*, n° 638 (2006 [2]), 313–333; reference 321.

[127] Other recent studies in English of French women writers include: Eva Martin Sartori & Dorothy Wynne Zimmerman, eds., *French Women Writers: A Bio-Bibliographical Source Book* (Lincoln: University of Nebraska Press, 1991); Diana Holmes, *French Women's Writing, 1848–1994* (London & Atlantic Highlands: Athlone Press, 1996); and Sonya Stephens, ed., *A History of Women's Writing in France* (Cambridge, UK: Cambridge University Press, 2000). See also the annual volumes published by Women in French (WIF), and the website of SIEFAR (Société Internationale pour l'Étude des Femmes de l'Ancien Régime) which features women writers from the pre-revolutionary period and their texts on its website www.siefar.org. See also Katharina M. Wilson, ed., *An Encyclopedia of Continental Women Writers*, 2 vols. (New York: Garland, 1991), which contains many French entries. The inventory would be substantially greater if it included the many women who published in genres other than imaginative fiction, plays, and poetry.

Today, the publications of French women writers, ranging from fiction, poetry, and theatre plays to essays, histories, and journalism, are enjoying more attention and analysis than ever before, thanks to the efforts of Francophone and Anglophone women scholars in both literary and historical studies. Even those women writers who dedicated themselves to the production of children's literature are attracting academic attention. See, for example, Elisabeth-Christine Muelsch, "Creativity, Childhood, and Children's Literature, or How to Become a Woman Writer: The Case of Eugénie Foa," *Romance Languages Annual*, 8 (1997), 66–73; see also Muelsch, "Eugénie Foa and the Institut des Femmes," in *Women Seeking Expression: France 1789–1914*, ed. Rosemary Lloyd & Brian Nelson. Monash Romance Studies 6 (Melbourne: Monash University, 2000), pp. 86–101.

[128] Hesse, "French Women in Print," p. 82.

provoked the development of the new biological theories (see Chapter 3) that attempted to contain women; as Hesse argues that the "full-blown assault" was directed "not on women in general, but specifically on *women writers* after the French Revolution." "This new mode of argumentation," she asserts, "went right to the heart of cultural life itself, questioning the capacity of women for moral self-regulation and their suitability for the production of knowledge through reading and writing."[129] As Hesse has indicated, and as we have documented earlier in this chapter, a number of women writers of every point on the political spectrum, from Constance Pipelet (de Salm) and Germaine de Staël to Stéphanie-Félicité de Genlis, retaliated in kind, defending women's right to speak their minds in print.[130]

In the 1830s and 1840s, male critics such as Jules Janin continued to denigrate as *bas-bleus*, these women writers who ostensibly renounced "beauty, grace, youth, the happiness of marriage, the chaste cares of maternity, everything represented by the home [*foyer domestique*], the family, etc., trying to live by the strengths of their minds . . ." and their "terrible ink-stained fingers."[131] In other words, such male critics saw them as unlovely, unloveable, and unfortunately independent. Janin made fun of them as "*femmes hommes de lettres*," practitioners of the "sickness of feminine literature," and called out to find a remedy for such abominations, "declassed beings that have no equivalent among any other people in antiquity or in modern times." Moreover, he insisted, "The *femme de lettres* has suddenly sprouted in literature, like a mushroom from the manure pile."[132] There seemed to be no limits on how low such critics could sink.

Janin's problem was, in part, that some French women writers had begun to dispute male privilege as well as male pronouncements in print. They were doing so not only in novels, in the tradition of Madeleine de Scudéry, Germaine de Staël, and George Sand, but also in the Parisian

[129] Hesse, *The Other Enlightenment*, pp. 131–132.

[130] In addition to the work by Pipelet cited in Chapter 3, n. 20, these included Mme de Staël's *De la littérature* (1800); and Mme de Genlis's *De l'influence des femmes sur la littérature* (1811). See Hesse, *The Other Enlightenment*, pp. 134–142.

[131] Jules Janin, "Le Bas-Bleu," in *Les Français peints par eux-mêmes*, vol. 5 (Paris: L. Curmer, 1842), pp. 201–231; quotes, pp. 201–202, and 204.

[132] Janin's outburst of French invective foreshadows the celebrated – and comparable – bashing of women writers by the American author, Nathaniel Hawthorne, who in 1855 denounced the "d—d mob of scribbling women." Hawthorne had recently returned from a stay in Paris when he wrote this; see Ann Douglas Wood, "The 'Scribbling Women' and Fanny Fern: Why Women Wrote," *American Quarterly*, 23:1 (Spring 1971), 3–24.

periodical press, with the publication in the 1830s of the *Journal des Femmes, La Femme Nouvelle / Tribune des Femmes*, the *Gazette des Femmes* (which was subtitled: *Journal des Droits Politiques et Civils des Françaises*), and others, notably in Lyon.[133] A sprinkling of French women, of whom the best known is Flora Tristan, pioneered investigative journalism and campaigned for the reestablishment of civil divorce, while Hortense Allart engaged the theme of "Woman and the Democracy of our Time" in 1836.[134] Others, including Sand and Allart, were, through their novels, daring to rewrite republican political theory to include women, as historian Whitney Walton has so engagingly demonstrated.[135] This was clearly viewed as an affront by men like Janin.

Feminist scholars have chronicled the world of French women writers during the 1830s and 1840s and have also catalogued the unfriendly artistic responses to the "woman of ideas" during that period.[136] Their findings reveal that male hostility seemed to mount in proportion to the increase in the number of women who attempted to live by their pens and, more especially, to their commercial success.[137] It was less the case that Rousseau's prediction was coming true – that "when the time comes that women are no longer concerned with men's well-being, men will no longer be good for anything at all"[138] – but more the case that many (though by

[133] See, for the period before 1850, Evelyne Sullerot, *Histoire de la presse féminine en France, des origines à 1848* (Paris: A. Colin, 1966); Laura S. Strumingher, "Mythes et réalités de la condition féminine à travers la presse féministe lyonnaise des années 1830," *Cahiers d'Histoire*, 21:4 (1976), 409–424; Laure Adler, *A l'aube du féminisme: Les premières journalistes, 1830–1850* (Paris: Payot, 1979); Claire Goldberg Moses, "Saint-Simonian Men/Saint-Simonian Women: The Transformation of Feminist Thought in 1830s France," *Journal of Modern History*, 54:2 (June 1982), 240–267; Claire G. Moses & Leslie Rabine, *Feminism, Socialism, and French Romanticism* (Bloomington: Indiana University Press, 1993); and Cheryl A. Morgan, "Unfashionable Feminism? Designing Women Writers in the *Journal des Femmes* (1832–1836)," in *Making the News: Modernity and the Mass Press in Nineteenth-Century France*, ed. Dean de la Motte & Jeannene M. Przyblyski (Amherst: University of Massachusetts Press, 1998). pp. 207–232.

[134] See, among other works, Hortense Allart, *La Femme et la démocratie de notre temps* (Paris: Delaunay, 1836); Flora Tristan, *Pétition pour le rétablissement du divorce à Messieurs les députés, le 20 décembre 1837* (Paris: Impr. de Mme Huzzard, 1838); and *Promenades dans Londres* (2nd ed., Paris: H.-L. DeLoye, 1840); and the documentary volume *Paroles oubliées: Les femmes et la construction de l'État-nation en France et en Italie (1789–1860)*, by Christiane Veauvy & Laura Pisano (Paris: A. Colin, 1997).

[135] Whitney Walton, *Eve's Proud Descendants: Four Women Writers and Republican Politics in Nineteenth-Century France* (Stanford, CA: Stanford University Press, 2000).

[136] See Christine Planté, *La Petite Soeur de Balzac: Essai sur la femme auteur* (Paris: Seuil, 1989), and Janis Bergman-Carton, *The Woman of Ideas in French Art, 1830–1848* (New Haven: Yale University Press, 1995).

[137] Not all would experience commercial success; see the case of Clotilde de Vaux, discussed by Mary Pickering in "Clotilde de Vaux and the Search for Identity," in *The New Biography*, ed. Jo Burr Margadant (Berkeley & Los Angeles: University of California Press, 2000), pp. 137–170.

[138] See Jean-Jacques Rousseau, *Émile*, Book 5; retranslation in *WFF*, vol. 1, doc. 10, p. 45.

no means all) of these women writers had begun to explore and criticize the foundations of men's well-being at women's expense – unjust marriage laws upholding the patriarchal family, educational deprivation, financial dependence, etc. These women writers were, first of all, concerned with improving their own well-being, especially in terms of legal and economic independence, but in so doing they necessarily addressed the dramatic imbalance in the relations between the sexes and attacked the very foundations of male privilege, culminating in the mid-century publications of Jenny P. d'Héricourt and Juliette Lamber(t) Adam, whose strongly worded contributions have been discussed earlier.

It is worth considering the fact that in French the word "writer" [*écrivain*] was gendered masculine – that in order for men to talk about women who were authors, they labeled them as "*femmes auteurs*" or "*femmes écrivains*."[139] In France, both then and now, the sex of the author seems to matter a great deal. Even today, in the early twenty-first century, the issue of what to call a woman who writes, and in particular what she chooses to call herself, remains subject to contestation, as a recent exchange in the French press over the neologism *écrivaine* indicates.[140] Why, we ask, should the sex of the writer still matter so much? Why should such words continue to be marked by gender? Why, indeed, should the French language continue to favor the masculine "gender" over the feminine "gender," as it has done since the rules of French grammar were set out in the early seventeenth century?

As so many women (and men) began to express their thoughts and creativity, the expanse of literary genres in which they published grew. Who, irrespective of sex, can be considered as writers – novelists? poets? playwrights? historians? essayists? journalists? letter writers? memoir writers? writers of educational treatises? translators? Indeed, what constitutes "literature"? This problem has proved vexing to scholars who have attempted to inventory the published texts produced by French women during the nineteenth century (and since). Women wrote and published in every genre imaginable. Which writers, asks historian Béatrice Slama,

---

[139] See Christine Planté, "La Désignation des femmes écrivains," in *Langages de la Révolution (1770–1815). Actes du 4ème colloque international de léxicologie politique* (Paris: INALF/Klincksieck, 1995), pp. 409–416.

[140] That what to call women who write is still an issue is attested by a 2005 exchange in the French press between Frédéric Beigbeder, "Mon premier article réac," *Lire* (February 2005), in which he objects vehemently to the word "*écrivaine*," and the response in *Le Monde* (16 February 2005), "Écrivaines et fières de l'être!" by Florence Montreynaud, Benoîte Groult, Annie Ernaux, & Maryse Wolinski, on behalf of the association *Encore Féministes*.

should be considered "woman authors"?[141] Looking back over the objections that women who write have had to overcome in France, this seems a good problem to have. The "genius" of French women had manifested itself in myriad forms, and the upcoming generations could look forward to better schooling and more opportunities, thanks to those who fought on their behalf. Spearheaded by the leadership of a new generation of men, those who would found the Third Republic, opportunities for girls to learn would expand dramatically in the early 1880s. Progressive men such as Jules Ferry would demand – and be in a position to enact – educational equality for both sexes as well as all classes at the primary level and Camille Sée would spearhead the campaign for public secondary education for bourgeois girls. We will discuss the debates that occurred during these later campaigns in our subsequent volume; here we will investigate a case study in the sexual politics of knowledge – the emergence and development of women's history.

---

[141] See Slama, "Un chantier est ouvert..." (cited in n. 126).

CHAPTER 5

The Politics of Women's History in Nineteenth-Century France

For centuries, the writing of history served as the handmaiden of political affairs and a celebration of masculine power and ideas, nowhere more so than in France, where the politics of knowledge was thoroughly permeated by gender. Nevertheless, in the context of debates over the woman question, a lively countercurrent of women's history developed which, especially in the nineteenth century, closely paralleled – and mutually interacted with – the expansion of the diametrically opposed movements for subordinating and liberating them. Such interaction has been characteristic of much of political and intellectual history, even that of a more "established" nature. In fact, in France the academic, or "scientific," study of women's history derived from – and responded to – precisely the same concerns about freedom (and its converse, authority and order imposed from above) that informed the early development of other historical genres in the Western tradition, and can be viewed in much the same way. This is so because the development of women's history in Western nations has always been tightly intertwined with campaigns for human rights. The acknowledgement of women's contributions and achievements is intrinsic to that discussion. Interest in reconstructing the history of women manifested itself in tandem with agitation to assert, on the one hand, the timelessness and necessity of the patriarchal family and to justify male rule, and on the other hand, to reconfigure women's political, legal, and educational status in an emancipatory direction, as is clear from the previous chapters.[1]

---

[1] Portions of this chapter have appeared in Karen Offen, "The Beginnings of 'Scientific' Women's History in France, 1830–1848," *Proceedings of the Western Society for French History, 1983*, vol. 11, ed. John Sweets (Lawrence, KS, 1984), pp. 255–264; and Karen Offen, "Women's Memory, Women's History, Women's Political Action: The French Revolution in Retrospect, 1789–1889–1989," *Journal of Women's History*, 1:3 (Winter 1990), 211–230. An earlier version appeared in German as "Die Geschlechterpolitik in der französischen Frauengeschichte des 19. Jahrhunderts," in *Geschichtsdiskurs*,

It is, then, not surprising to discover that French thinkers were among the earliest to posit gender as a central category for historical analysis; already in 1803 the Vicomte de Ségur, in a book entitled *Women: Their Condition and Influence in Society*, argued that "the proper study of mankind . . . includes the study of both sexes," and insisted that "we must write their [i.e. women's] history."[2] That is to say that "we" men must write the history of women. Ultimately, women would also enter the ranks of women's historians.

There had, of course, been a long and persistent historical tradition of writing about "women worthies," dating back to manuscript books such as Boccaccio's *De Claris Mulieribus* (Famous Women, 1374) and Christine de Pizan's *Book of the City of Ladies* (1405). Practitioners of this form of women's history were often motivated to provide role models for new generations of women, celebrating not only aspects of women's public renown but probing their personal lives, and often their morality as well. Some examples since rediscovered may provide helpful reminders of the magnitude of these earlier projects. In addition to the collective and individual biographies of women worthies singled out by Natalie Zemon Davis, novels by seventeenth-century French women began to offer lightly disguised accounts of women's participation in the Fronde.[3]

In the mid-eighteenth century, Louise-Marie-Madeleine de Fontaine Dupin (c. 1707–1799), the second wife to a very wealthy *fermier-général* (tax farmer) and thereby *chatelaine* of the spectacular chateau of Chenonceau, saw the need for a comprehensive history of women. In 1746 she hired the young Jean-Jacques Rousseau as her secretary and research assistant. Unfortunately, her encyclopedic project never saw publication (though extensive manuscripts from it are now scattered across several

---

vol. 3: *Die Epoche der Historisierung*, ed. Wolfgang Küttler, Jörn Rüsen, & Ernst Schulin (Frankfurt-am-Main: Fischer Verlag, 1997), pp. 100–117.

[2] Alexandre-Joseph-Pierre, vicomte de Ségur, *Women: Their Condition and Influence in Society*, 3 vols. (London: Longman & Reese, 1803), vol. i, iii, iv. Originally published as *Les Femmes; leur condition et leur influence dans l'ordre social chez différents peuples anciens et modernes* (Paris: Treuttel & Wurtz, 1803).

[3] On the "women worthies" tradition in European historiography, see Natalie Zemon Davis, "'Women's History' in Transition: The European Case," *Feminist Studies*, 3:3–4 (Spring–Summer 1976), 83–103, and Bonnie G. Smith, "Comment on Session: The History of Women's History in Nineteenth-Century France," *Proceedings of the Western Society for French History, 1983*, vol. ii, ed. John Sweets (Lawrence, KS, 1984), esp. pp. 267–271. The historiography of women's history in France, as elsewhere, deserves more sustained scholarly attention than it has heretofore received, but see the comparative analyses of Bonnie G. Smith, "The Contribution of Women to Modern Historiography in Great Britain, France, and the United States, 1750–1940," *American Historical Review*, 89:3 (June 1984), 709–732, and Bonnie G. Smith, *The Gender of History: Men, Women, and Historical Practice* (Cambridge, MA: Harvard University Press, 1998).

important literary archives, including Yale and the University of Texas).[4] Nevertheless, following this formative experience, Rousseau (the lover of many women) could not get the woman question off his mind; as we have seen, he ultimately developed into a pronounced antifeminist, a perspective he would demonstrate to the world in the fifth book of *Émile* (1762), his treatise on education.

Several successfully published multivolume compendia about famous and noteworthy women dotted the French literary landscape from the 1760s on, indeed, well into the nineteenth century, as Bonnie G. Smith and Brita Rang have conclusively shown.[5] These included a six-volume work on illustrious women of France by Jean Zorobabel Aublet de Maubuy, published between 1762 and 1768, a two-volume work on the intellect of famous women from the century of Louis XIV to the present, by Pons-Augustin Alletz, and in 1769 two compendia, the two-volume *Portable Historic Dictionary of Famous Women*, by Jean-François de La Croix (de Compiègne), and the more expansive five-volume *Literary History of French Women, or Historical and Critical Letters containing a Summary of the Life and an Analysis of the Works by Women that have Distinguished Themselves in French Literature, by A Society of Men of Letters*, by Joseph de La Porte, Jean-François de La Croix, and Jean Maineau.[6] Supplementing these very substantial works was the 1772 tract by the poet Antoine-Léonard Thomas of the Académie Française, entitled *Essay on the*

---

[4] On Madame Dupin's never-completed venture in women's history, see René-Gaston Vallet, comte de Villeneuve-Guibert, *Le Portefeuille de Madame Dupin, dame de Chenonceaux* (Paris: Calmann-Lévy, 1884), pp. 15–17. Rousseau is uncharacteristically discreet about this assignment in his *Confessions*. But see Anicet Sénéchal, "Jean-Jacques Rousseau, secrétaire de Madame Dupin, d'après de documents inédits, avec un inventaire des papiers Dupin dispersés en 1957 et 1958," *Annales de la Société Jean-Jacques Rousseau*, 36 (1963–1965), 173–290, and Robert Shackleton, "Montesquieu, Dupin, and the early Writings of Rousseau," in *Reappraisals of Rousseau: Studies in Honour of R. A. Leigh*, ed. S. Harvey et al. (Totowa: Barnes & Noble, 1980), pp. 234–250. More recently, see Angela Hunter, "The Unfinished Work on Louise Marie-Madeleine Dupin's Unfinished *Ouvrage sur les femmes*," *Eighteenth-Century Studies*, 43:1 (Fall 2009), 95–111, and Jean Buon's biographical study, *Madame Dupin: Une féministe à Chenonceau au siècle des lumières, biographie* (Paris: Éditions La Simarre, 2013).

[5] See Smith, n. 3, and Brita Rang, "'A Learned Wave': Women of Letters and Science from the Renaissance to the Enlightenment," in *Perspectives on Feminist Political Thought in European History*, ed. Tjitske Akkerman & Siep Stuurman (London: Routledge, 1998), pp. 50–66. Most of Rang's findings are published in German.

[6] See Jean Zorobabel Aublet de Maubuy, *Les Vies des femmes illustres de la France*, 6 vols. (Paris: Duchesne, 1762–1768); Joseph de La Porte, Jean-François de La Croix, & Jean Maineau, *Histoire littéraire des dames françoises, ou Lettres historiques et critiques contenant un précis de la vie et une analyse raisonnée des ouvrages des femmes qui se sont distinguées dans la littérature françoise, par un société des gens de lettres* (Paris: Lacombe, 1769); and Jean-François de La Croix (de Compiègne), *Dictionnaire historique portatif des femmes célèbres*, 2 vols. (Paris: L. Cellot, 1769).

Character, Manners, and Genius of Women in Different Ages, which was quickly translated into English and published in Philadelphia in 1774.[7] The stories included in these biographical dictionaries provided evidence not only of women's intelligence and achievements through the centuries, particularly in letters and in the sciences, but also their prowess as contemporary heads of state (notably Catherine II of Russia and Maria-Theresa of Austria); such evidence became essential in subsequent campaigns for women's rights, especially during the French Revolution and thereafter.

In light of Napoléon's insistence on subordinating women in the Civil Code, it is ironic that in 1804, the same year the Code was promulgated (and a year after Ségur issued his call for writing women's history), a certain dame Briquet dedicated her own biographical dictionary of "Frenchwomen and naturalized foreign women in France, known by their writings," to the emperor.[8] This genre of women worthies' historical literature would receive another boost in the late 1820s and 1830s, with the publication of several more important biographical compendia on women writers, including another woman-authored work by Fanny de Mongellaz on the influence of women on the morals and destinies of nations.[9] The genre would continue to flourish throughout the century.

In the early nineteenth century, several other women writers would argue that the telling of their history should not be left to men. In late 1832 an article signed by a certain "Marie de G***" appeared in the *Revue*

---

[7] Antoine-Léonard Thomas, *Essai sur le caractère, les moeurs, et l'esprit des femmes dans les différens siècles* (Amsterdam: chez E. van Harrevelt, 1772). In English as 2 vols.: *Essay on the Character, Manners, and Genius of Women in Different Ages* (Philadelphia, 1774). Thomas's work can also be consulted in his collected works, *Oeuvres de Thomas* (1819), and online in the Gerritsen Collection of Women's History.

[8] Marguerite-Ursule-Fortunée Bernier, dame Briquet, *Dictionnaire biographique des Françaises et des Etrangères naturalisées en France, connues par leurs écrits* (Paris: Treuttel & Wurtz, 1804). On the dedication, see Smith, "Comment," (cited n. 3), p. 268.

[9] Mme F. Mongellaz [Fanny Burnier Mongellaz], *De l'Influence des femmes sur les moeurs et les destinées des nations, sur leurs familles et la société*, 2 vols. (Paris: L.-C. Michaud, 1828; 2nd enlgd. ed., 1831); this work had aspirations to provide a "global history of women."

  Works published in Paris (by male authors) on the "women worthies" tradition between 1830 and 1848 included: Adolphe de Chesnel (de la Charbouclais) [pseud. Alfred de Montferrand], *Biographie des Femmes auteurs contemporaines françaises* (Paris: n.p., 1836); E. Lairtullier, *Les Femmes célèbres de 1789 à 1795 et leur influence dans la révolution* (Paris: n.p., 1840); C.-A. Sainte-Beuve, *Portraits de femmes* (Paris: Didier, 1844; new ed., 1855); A.-J.-V. Leroux de Lincy, *Les Femmes célèbres de l'ancienne France* (Paris: Leroi, 1848). By comparison, in the United States, the first published book on women's history (also in the tradition of the "women worthies") was Elizabeth Fries Lummis Ellet's two-volume work, *The Women of the American Revolution* (New York: Baker & Scribner, 1848). On this latter work, see Carol Ruth Berkin & Mary Beth Norton, *Women of America: A History* (Boston: Houghton-Mifflin, 1979), pp. 4–5.

encyclopédique.[10] In it the author called out for the writing of a substantive history of women, which did more than discourse on the merits or faults of women and which would include "an historic resumé of the condition of women in past centuries that might serve to exhibit the gradual improvement [*perfectionnement*] that has taken place in their condition." "The study of the improvements made in the past," the author added optimistically, "would allow one to conjecture improvements to come." In her view, such a work should be capped by a portrayal of the current condition of women, according to which one could specify the successive improvements to be accomplished, taking into account "the general views of Providence."[11]

Marie de G*** was clearly interested in tying the history of women to the more general discussion of progress, a connection that had been explicitly, if occasionally, acknowledged by earlier social critics as diverse as Charles Fourier and Louis de Bonald.[12] A second, more assertive aspect, however, should also be mentioned. The article's context, coupled with its author's explicit expression of admiration for the upright Madame Roland (guillotined in 1793 for "mixing in politics," make it evident that Marie de G*** meant to clear herself of all association with the innuendos of sexual emancipation connected with the recently discredited Saint-Simonian notion (at least the version promulgated by Prosper Enfantin, leader of the group) of *la femme libre*. Like many others of her generation who rejected Enfantin's emphasis on sexual liberty, her perspective was informed by dedication to the key constructs of nineteenth-century "morality": a commitment to monogamous marriage, a distinct division of sexual roles, and in particular an abiding belief in a positive concept of womanly nature. All these features – a strong belief in progress, an emphasis on linking morality to monogamy, and insistence on a separation of spheres – would recur in the works produced on the history of women's condition during the next decade.

---

[10] Marie de G***, "De la Condition sociale des femmes au dix-neuvième siècle: Lettre aux directeurs de la *Revue encyclopédique*," *La Revue encyclopédique*, 56:168 (December 1832), 598–622. Janet L. Polasky has identified "Marie de G***" as the francophone Belgian women's rights activist Zoé Gatti de Gamond. See Polasky, "Utopia and Domesticity: Zoé Gatti de Gamond," *Proceedings of the Western Society for French History, 1983*, vol. 11, ed. John Sweets (Lawrence, KS, 1984), pp. 273–281.

[11] Marie de G***, "Condition sociale," p. 599.

[12] Compare Louis de Bonald, *Théorie du pouvoir* (1796) in *Oeuvres complètes de M. de Bonald*, ed. l'abbé Migne, 3 vols. (Paris: J. P. Migne, 1859), vol. 1, p. 244, and Charles Fourier, *Théorie des quatre mouvements et des destinées générales* (1808), in *Oeuvres complètes de Ch. Fourier*, 2nd ed., 6 vols. (Paris: Bureaux de la Phalange, 1841–1845), vol. 1, p. 195.

In the intervening ten years, several other women tried their hand at constructing a history of women. One of these was the former Saint-Simonian enthusiast Pauline Roland (who should not be confused with Madame Roland of the French revolution), who in the later 1840s published several derivative articles on the history of women in Gaul and on women's convents during the Middle Ages.[13] Had Roland, a single mother, not been obligated to support her children by writing hack articles, she might well have made an original contribution to women's history; her deep personal commitment to the liberation of women was complemented by an inquisitive and penetrating mind as well as by a talent for writing.[14] Yet Pauline Roland had neither the leisure nor access to libraries and archives, and indeed few Frenchwomen had the education or leisure, much less society's permission to engage in such scholarly pursuits.[15]

Women's consciousness of the political importance of their history, however, remained high. "History must be completely rewritten," asserted one of the principal writers in *La Voix des Femmes* during the 1848 Revolution, Henriette Wild (who signed as "Henriette, artiste"). "Like man, woman is called to explore the domain of history ... For women, history is a lie ... the truth will only appear once feminine observation and intelligence enter into it and, in particular, couple it to feminine interests."[16]

Henriette Wild's critique alludes to the fact that by the 1840s, male scholars associated with the French academies had embarked on a systematic analysis of the past condition and status of women and the family. It is true, however, that they came to the subject with varied political agendas. In contrast to the more amateurish work of their predecessors, their findings and generalizations proceeded from the particular to the general and attempted to shape the contours of future inquiry by looking at

---

[13] Pauline Roland, "Études sur l'histoire des femmes en France," *La Revue indépendante*, n.s. 4 (25 July 1846), 210–231, and n.s. 7 (25 January 1847), 185–206.

[14] See Edith Thomas, *Pauline Roland: Socialisme et féminisme au XIXe siècle* (Paris: M. Rivière, 1956), chapters 11–14.

[15] On the women's demand in 1848 for a women's reading room at the Bibliothèque Nationale, see "Éducation des femmes," *La Voix des Femmes*, n° 1 (20 March 1848). Within the next few months, the women set up a library of their own, announcing occasional contributions of books in their newspaper.

[16] Henriette, artiste, "Les Sages femmes d'Athènes," *La Voix des Femmes*, n° 28 (20 April 1848); reprinted in *Le Grief des femmes*, ed. Maïté Albistur & Daniel Armogathe, 2 vols. (Paris: Éditions Hier & Demain, 1978), vol. 1, pp. 286–289. English translation by Karen Offen in "Getting to the Source: 'What! Such Things Have Happened and No Women were Taught about Them': A Nineteenth-Century French Woman's View of the Importance of Women's History," *Journal of Women's History*, 9:2 (Summer 1997), 147–153.

societal organization and institutional evolution in terms of gender, that is, the social relation of the sexes.[17] The later investigations of the history of the family by French scholars such as Paul Janet and Jules Michelet are all indebted (as is the subsequent work of internationally influential scholars such as Bachofen, Spencer, and Maine, and reformers such as Le Play and Engels) to the more "scientifically sound" scholarship on the history of women published by the pioneering French male scholars of the 1840s.

In the early 1840s the historical "section" of the Académie des Sciences Morales et Politiques initiated a prize competition. The charge laid out by the Académie was: "To trace the history of women's right of succession in the civil and political order of the various peoples of Europe during the Middle Ages."[18] The competition topic was drafted by the historian François Mignet, founder of the study of diplomatic history in France and perpetual secretary of the Académie; it was his aspiration to make philosophical history the queen of the human sciences, and it was he who promoted investigation by historians of contemporary social issues – women, slaves, and the dispossessed.[19] In May 1842 the Académie awarded prizes to three *mémoires* by male scholars: Edouard Laboulaye, *Recherches sur la condition civile et politique des femmes, depuis les Romains jusqu'à nos jours* (Paris: A. Durand, 1843); Edmé-Jacques-Benoît Rathery, "Recherches sur l'histoire du droit de succession des femmes," only a fragment of which was subsequently published; and Louis-Jean Koenigswarter, *Essai sur la législation des peuples anciens et modernes relative aux enfants nés hors mariage.*[20]

Of the three men who shared the Académie's prize, it was the 32-year-old Laboulaye (1811–1883) who became best known and was later

[17] Of particular importance was the recently reconstituted Académie des Sciences Morales et Politiques. The academicians would hardly have described their mission in such language. Nor did their historian; see Ernest Seillière, *Une Académie à l'époque romantique* (Paris: E. Leroux, 1926). Cf. also Dudley Channing Barksdale, "Liberal Politics and Nascent Social Science in France: The Academy of Moral and Political Sciences, 1802–1852," Ph.D. dissertation, University of North Carolina, Chapel Hill, 1986; and, more recently, Sophie-Anne Leterrier, *L'Institution des sciences morales: L'Académie des sciences morales et politiques 1795–1850* (Paris: L'Harmattan, 1995).

[18] Quoted by Edouard Laboulaye in the preface to his *Recherches sur la condition civile et politique des femmes, depuis les Romains jusqu'à nos jours* (Paris: Durand, 1843), vii. At some later point in time, Laboulaye became "de Laboulaye."

[19] On Mignet, see G. P. Gooch, *History and Historians in the Nineteenth Century* (New ed., Boston: Beacon Press, 1959; orig. pub. 1913), pp. 184–189, and, more expansively, Yvonne Knibiehler, *Naissance des sciences humaines: Mignet et l'histoire philosophique au XIXe siècle* (Paris: Flammarion, 1973).

[20] Rathery's 94-page fragment, "Histoire du droit de succession des femmes," appeared in the *Revue de Législation et de Jurisprudence*, nouv. sér., vol. 2 (1843), 61–91; 385–411; 641–672. Koenigswarter's work was published serially in the *Revue de Législation et de Jurisprudence*, vols. 14, 16, 17. His book on the history of the family would appear in 1851 (see n. 57).

considered an important friend of the women's movement. In 1849 Laboulaye was appointed to the chair in comparative law at the Collège de France. He became an enthusiastic student of American history and culture, publishing a history of the United States and translating into French works by Channing, Franklin, and others. After the fall of the Second Empire, Laboulaye would cap a distinguished career in legal scholarship by entering French political life. In the National Assembly of 1871–1875 he would preside over the Center Left group and would subsequently be elected senator-for-life of the new republic.[21] It was his idea that France should honor the United States of America with a gift: that gift was Bartholdi's statue of Liberty, which still graces the New York harbor.[22]

Laboulaye was supremely conscious of the debate on the woman question that had blossomed during the 1830s; the controversies over the Saint-Simonian doctrine of *la femme libre*, the novels of George Sand, the theatrical works by Victor Hugo and the Ancelots, the mid-1830s demands for reform in women's status in marriage law (especially Article 231 of the Civil Code, which demanded obedience from wives) and for the reinstitution of civil divorce, as well as the controversy over women's right to work had made a deep (if not invariably favorable) impression on the educated public. It was doubtless this awareness that provoked Mignet and the Académie to sponsor this competition in the first place. But few addressed the issues as forthrightly as Laboulaye.

Laboulaye dedicated this work to his wife, who had died the previous year. Like the vicomte de Ségur before him, he insisted on the importance of studying the position of women as well as that of men, yet he also noted the novelty of doing so. Historically speaking, he argued, in family law, "the civil and political capacity of women has always and everywhere been dictated by their domestic condition, and whosoever is unfamiliar with the organization of the family in a given epoch will never be able to understand the spirit of the laws that regulated the successorial rights of women."[23] He developed his argument along very broad lines. By focusing on women,

---

[21] On Laboulaye's career, see especially Jean de Soto, "Edouard de Laboulaye," *Revue Internationale d'Histoire Politique et Constitutionnelle*, 5 (1955), 114–150. Laboulaye was highly regarded by Léon Richer, who, along with Maria Deraismes, spearheaded the organized movement for women's rights in the early Third Republic. See his exchange with Richer in *L'Avenir des Femmes*, n° 76 (12 November 1871) and n° 77 (19 November 1871); also, Richer's subsequent quotes from Laboulaye in Léon Richer, *Le Livre des femmes* (Paris: Librairie de la Bibliothèque démocratique, 1872), pp. 60–61. I will say more about Laboulaye's role during the Third Republic in my subsequent volume.

[22] On Laboulaye's involvement, see *The Statue of Liberty: A Transatlantic Story*, by Edward Berenson (New Haven & London: Yale University Press, 2012).

[23] Laboulaye, "Introduction," *Recherches*, p. 11.

he intended to study the organizational evolution of the family with respect to the development of gendered property law and inheritance practices, and in relation to the growth of nation-states.

Laboulaye was no newcomer to the study of the law of property; his first book had treated the organization of real (landed) property in the Western world. He greatly admired the work of German historians of law, whose work, Laboulaye could not resist pointing out, derived from and was worthy of comparison with the work of the French historical school of the sixteenth and seventeenth centuries.[24] In *Recherches*, therefore, Laboulaye refocused his attention on the condition of women in inheritance law, where (as he noted in his introduction) civil and political law came together. The novelty of the subject, he argued, was quite apparent.[25] Against those who would stake claims for national particularism, he argued that throughout Europe the legal condition of women in the family and in property law had gone through similar ameliorative changes at approximately the same time; the study of women's situation would therefore demonstrate, he believed, nothing less than the common evolution of the laws of Europe – the merger of Roman law with German customary law, the importance of the reintroduction of Justinian's Code and the influence of canon law, and finally, the reformation of customary law that had begun in the early sixteenth century and the beginning of codification of the laws that was ongoing. Laboulaye clearly believed in the utility and predictive value of historical knowledge, and he criticized the German historical school's reticence to put their findings to use in hinting at future developments.[26]

Laboulaye's consideration of gender was thus articulated not merely as an analytical tool for understanding historical changes in the socioeconomic organization of the family, but for illuminating what he considered to be a more general and compelling problem: the evolution of a transnational European civilization. By placing the condition of women, as embodied in family legislation and jurisprudence, at the analytical center he believed that he could reveal a common movement toward a unity of ideas throughout Europe.[27]

> If I succeed in convincing the reader that the condition of women, which hitherto has seemed an interior matter scarcely noticed by the laws and

---

[24] Laboulaye, *Recherches*, pp. 2–3. On the contributions of the early modern French historians, see the pathbreaking work by Donald R. Kelley, beginning with *Foundations of Modern Historical Scholarship: Language, Law, and History in the French Renaissance* (New York: Columbia University Press, 1970).

[25] Laboulaye, *Recherches*, p. 4.   [26] Laboulaye, *Recherches*, p. 2.

[27] Laboulaye, "Préface," *Recherches*, xi-xii.

scarcely exceeding the limits of the domestic hearth, has nevertheless experienced throughout Europe and almost simultaneously, the same changes, the same improvements, the same legislative favor, can it be doubted that Europe marches under the empire of common principles, leading to the same results despite differences in language, government, and climate?

Indeed, Laboulaye claimed that such a way of looking at history could lead to the regeneration both of legal science and political science alike.[28] These were broad claims indeed on behalf of the utility of a gendered analysis of legal history, even as an instrumental tool.

As the above summary suggests, and his book underscores, Laboulaye was, in fact, a great believer in the doctrine of progress and in the social mission of history. Of Protestant descent, he brought a liberal Christian perspective to his study of women's situation in inheritance law. He envisaged the progress of the several peoples of Europe toward a common destiny, "the realization ever more complete of the idea Christ brought to earth, the fraternity of all nations, the equality of all individuals, because as individuals and as nations we are all equally the children of the same father, who is God, brother of the same brother who is Jesus Christ."[29]

At first glance, Laboulaye's interpretation of progress in women's condition seemed astonishingly progressive. Wherever the family was a *political* institution, he argued, the situation of women was rigorously inferior and they were kept in strict dependency; in contrast, wherever the state was strongly organized and the family had no political role (and where family ties were thus based primarily on affection), women attained nearly the same legal level as men, and in some cases were even favored by the law.[30]

The rise of the state implied, in other words, a decline in the relative power of the patriarchal family. This was, in Laboulaye's estimation, the direction in which all legislation had been heading since the Middle Ages. The greatest advance had been encapsulated, Laboulaye claimed, in the French Civil Code, which had abolished both primogeniture (sole inheritance of an estate by the eldest son) and even the right of masculinity in questions of succession. This meant that daughters could inherit on an equal footing with sons. Civil equality of the sexes, Laboulaye optimistically insisted in his conclusion to Book IV, was henceforth guaranteed.[31]

Today's scholars of French women's history are all too acutely aware that the reform Laboulaye spoke of in the French laws of succession was

---

[28] Laboulaye, *Recherches*, xii.   [29] Laboulaye, *Recherches*, xi.
[30] Laboulaye, "Introduction," *Recherches*, pp. 11–12; see also Book II, pp. 173–174.
[31] Laboulaye, *Recherches*, Book IV, pp. 437–439.

virtually the sole improvement for women embodied in the Code. In light of the developments sketched in his chapter I concerning the Code's legal subordination of wives, we would qualify with a "well, hardly ... " his smug assertion that the Civil Code provided the capstone to French-women's civil equality. And, indeed, most nineteenth-century critics of the Code still considered the legal condition of married women to be highly prejudicible. The famous Article 213, which stipulated that the husband must command and the wife obey was only the most notorious provision; equally objectionable was the Code's revision in 1816 to outlaw civil divorce and the prohibition against paternity suits by women who found themselves pregnant outside marriage.

These are, of course, criticisms based on our rejection of women's subordination in marriage. Laboulaye, writing in 1842–1843, was a progressively minded man, but he was not interested in rejecting such subordination outright. Indeed, the social mission of history was, as conceived by Laboulaye, to inform his contemporaries of the *necessary limits* on women's emancipation. Here the doctrine of Progress postulated caution. Laboulaye's exposition of history here addressed directly the claims then being made by democrats in France and Chartists in England about the relationship between property and suffrage, arguments designed by men for men's purposes, but which could be (and were being) all too easily turned to the advantage of women of property, not to mention women as individual subjects.[32]

These considerations, and others, point to the limits of Laboulaye's vision. Like so many men and women of his generation, he was thoroughly imbued with a concept of women's "nature"; like them, he spoke of the "weakness of the sex" as well as of its "goodness."[33] If he thought nine-teenth-century women capable of holding and managing real property, it did not follow that he endorsed claims made on their behalf for a governmental role. He was no radical democrat. Like his colleague, Alexis

---

[32] For an overview, see Susan Groag Bell & Karen M. Offen, *Women, the Family, and Freedom: The Debate in Documents, 1750–1950*, 2 vols. (Stanford, CA: Stanford University Press, 1983), vol.1, pp. 227–238; and Karen Offen, "Liberty, Equality, and Justice for Women: The Theory and Practice of Feminism in Nineteenth-Century Europe," in *Becoming Visible: Women in European History*, ed. Renate Bridenthal, Claudia Koonz, & Susan Mosher Stuart (2nd ed., Boston: Houghton Mifflin, 1987), pp. 335–373. For particulars, see Claire G. Moses, *French Feminism in the Nineteenth Century* (Albany, NY: SUNY Press, 1984); Barbara Taylor, *Eve and the New Jerusalem: Socialism and Feminism in the Nineteenth Century* (London & New York: Pantheon, 1983); and Jane Rendall, *The Origins of Modern Feminism: Women in Britain, France, and the United States, 1780–1860* (New York: Schocken, 1984).

[33] Laboulaye, "Introduction," *Recherches*, p. 13.

de Tocqueville, he believed firmly that women's place was in the domestic sphere. In a chapter central to his argument, Laboulaye took an unequivocal stand, based on his interpretation of history, *against* women's participation in public life – the world of the *forum*:[34]

> The conjugal house, such is the peaceable domain in which the woman ought to reign supreme; it is there that happiness lies for her, her children, and her spouse, not in those agitations of public life in which the man himself loses the serenity of his soul and is soon no longer master of his heart.

He elaborated on this theme at even greater length in the final section of his *mémoire* entitled – "What should one think of the government of women?" Laboulaye's conclusion ended with a thoroughly Knoxian blast against the women monarchs of the sixteenth century:[35]

> ... for one Elizabeth how many Mary Stuarts! ... [Women's] kingdom is elsewhere; it is in the domestic foyer, in the family sanctuary that they are truly sovereigns; a sweet sovereignty that does not trouble the tranquility of their hearts, that no ambition renders jealous, that no revolt disrupts, and that – rare thing in an empire – creates the happiness and joy of all who live under this vigilant protection!

Thus did one of the first "scientific" historians of women interpret women's history. Laboulaye, like so many other nineteenth-century French liberals, here revealed his true colors as an advocate of women's subordination in marriage, of a hierarchy of separate spheres for men and women; he deployed history to justify a political stand, not in favor of unlimited change for women, but to oppose the participation of women in government. He also utilized women's history to demonstrate the superiority of the French Civil Code as concerned female property rights and to suggest that other European nations might be well-advised to fall in line. Laboulaye's book represents an instance in which the history of women (at least with respect to property rights, or civil liberty) was invoked to build an historical case for the inevitability of a particular concept of gender relations that did not incorporate political rights (or even further civil rights) for women.

There were other important male contributors to the writing of women's history following Laboulaye. Ernest Legouvé (1807–1903), dramatist, essayist, and (later) member of the Académie Française, offered a far more liberal interpretation of women's past – and particularly, of their

---

[34] Laboulaye, *Recherches*, Book IV, p. 447.   [35] Laboulaye, *Recherches*, p. 528.

future – than Laboulaye. Legouvé's important *Histoire morale des femmes* [Moral History of Women], first offered to the public as a series of lectures at the Collège de France in the spring of 1848 and published as a book in 1849, went through ten editions between its initial printing and the final edition of 1896. This author argued for a broad extension of women's rights and of their participation in society, and for an end to hierarchy in the relationship of the sexes. His extensive program of reforms in the civil and educational situation of women, predicated on the notion of "equality in difference," offered a concrete and influential program for radically restructuring the institutional arrangements for marriage and women's roles within the existing order of family centeredness and private property.[36] Yet even Legouvé would balk at giving women the vote. "In my thinking," he argued in a letter to the editor of *La Commune* in April 1848, "women should have a place in the State, but *a place different than that of men.... .* They should become the Republic's commissioners for the national contribution."[37] In other words, they could go door to door, soliciting contributions from every household member, as women had done in England to collect signatures for petitions to abolish slavery.

Legouvé put women's history to political use in order to support every aspect of his case for reform. Indeed, the historical portions of the *Histoire morale* reveal its author's optimism and faith in progress, but in contrast to Laboulaye, he thought that even in the law, women's status should be further remediated. Legouvé believed passionately in the march toward equality and he attempted to ground his program for reform on his understanding of the past. Comparing women's plight in ancient and medieval history with their situation in more recent times, Legouvé saw many signs that to him suggested women's situation was improving. He continually documented this progress with examples from the past.[38] In contrast to the Saint-Simonians and other anticlerical men, he argued, following Abbé Grégoire, that Christianity had played a powerful historic role in advancing the status of women.[39] Though critical of particular aspects of the Catholic Church's position on the woman question, the

---

[36] Karen Offen, "Ernest Legouvé and the Doctrine of 'Equality in Difference' for Women: A Case Study of Male Feminism in Nineteenth-Century French Thought," *Journal of Modern History*, 58:2 (June 1986), 452–484.

[37] Ernest Legouvé, "Au citoyen directeur-gérant de La Commune," *La Commune de Paris: Moniteur des Clubs*, n° 30 (Friday, 7 April 1848), 1; transl. KO.

[38] *Histoire morale*, p. 132. See Book V, 349–364, on the role of women in history.

[39] See Legouvé's arguments concerning the historic importance of Christianity for women in Book III, chapter 4, esp. 200–202, and in Book V, chapter 1, 355–364. Cf. also Abbé Henri Grégoire, *De l'influence du Christianisme sur la condition des femmes* (1821); reprinted in *Oeuvres de l'abbé Grégoire*,

Histoire morale leaves no doubt that Legouvé shared many of the Christian humanist motives that permeated reform politics in 1840s France.

Based on his appreciation of history, Legouvé articulated a wide-ranging program of reforms in law, education, and economics. First, he laid out a series of reforms that would benefit young unmarried women, for he was well aware that these reforms might be more easily granted than those he would subsequently suggest. As he astutely observed, "When you speak of improving the situation of girls, all the fathers are on your side, but when you propose increasing women's rights, all the husbands are against you."[40] Thus, to appeal to fathers he insisted on: 1) the establishment of a system of public education for girls; 2) a law on seduction that would give young women recourse to legal action, namely, the right to file suit for breach of promise; 3) a higher minimum age for marriage (the legal age was then fifteen, though the customary age was in the early twenties); and 4) the right of young engaged women to participate in the drafting of their marriage contracts.

For married women, Legouvé advocated major changes in the Civil Code: 1) an end to their legal subjection in marriage; 2) their right to administer and to dispose of part of their personal property (under the dowry regime certain properties, which did not constitute part of the dowry and were therefore not inalienable, could be designated as *biens paraphernaux* and could then be administered separately); 3) their right to appear in court without a husband's formal permission; 4) limitation of a husband's power over the person of his wife; and 5) creation of a family council that would regulate this latter power. For mothers, he urged a series of reforms that would give them: 1) legal power over their own children equivalent to that granted to fathers; 2) a law to enable unwed mothers to file paternity suits; and 3) the creation of a family council that could judge serious disagreements between fathers and mothers. He also championed the restoration of civil divorce. For women considered as members of the community, Legouvé advocated their admission as legal guardians and to family councils, their admittance to the so-called private professions (letters, teaching), and admission within certain limits to the "public and social professions" (those of notary or lawyer).[41]

Apart from the Fourierists, no one in France – male or female – had articulated a more comprehensive program for change in the status of

---

vol. 13 (Nendeln, Liechtenstein, 1977). Alain Decaux, *Histoire des françaises*, 2 vols. (Paris: Perrin, 1972), offers a restatement of this view.

[40] *Histoire morale*, p. 154.   [41] *Histoire morale*, pp. 446–448.

women. Jenny P. d'Héricourt, author of *La Femme affranchie* (1860), and a woman who (as we have seen) was notoriously hard to please when it came to men's opinions on the woman question, praised Legouvé's contribution a decade later: "Legouvé . . . does not demand all that he believes just, but all that seems to him mature and possible. We should thank him for his prudence; he has brought over many men to our cause, and has prepared them to hear the voice of woman, speaking loudly and firmly by her right as a wife and a human being, as a worker and a member of the social body."[42]

Another historian of overriding importance for our appreciation of the debate over the woman question in French historiography during the 1850s and 1860s was Jules Michelet (1798–1874). Not coincidentally, he, like Laboulaye, was also an active member of the Académie des Sciences Morales et Politiques. Much has been written about the outsized influence of Jules Michelet in shaping republican views on the woman question. Indeed, it was Michelet who most eloquently raised the specter of clerical influence over women in the 1840s, who subsequently etched into the minds of many otherwise progressive men the new medicalized vision of woman as invalid, "ceaselessly suffer[ing] from love's eternal wound," but who also insisted (like Auguste Comte) that woman must become a secular goddess, under male control, with her mission "to renew the heart of man," with "love as her true sphere of labor."[43] His lyric romanticization of women, coupled with the latest knowledge in medical physiology, made for unforgettable (and to many women, intolerable) reading. Like Rousseau (who also had lost his mother when he was very young), Michelet was clearly obsessed by the "otherness" and the power of womanhood. And like the arguments of Rousseau, Comte, and Legouvé, those of Michelet cast a long shadow in the French debates on the woman question.

Michelet's concern with the woman question became far more explicit, indeed, almost obsessive, following the failure of republican revolution of 1848. In 1850 he would offer a series of lectures on "The Foyer" at the Collège de France.[44] These sketched the direction that he would develop

---

[42] Jenny P. d'Héricourt, *A Woman's Philosophy of Woman, or Woman Affranchised* (New York: Carleton 1864), p. 154; originally published as *La Femme affranchie* (2 vols., Brussels: A. Lacroix, 1860).

[43] See Jules Michelet, *De Prêtre, la femme et la famille* (Paris: E. Flammarion, lst ed., 1844); *L'Amour* (Paris: Hachette, 1859); and *La Femme* (Paris: Hachette, 1860). All are available in the 40–volume *Oeuvres complètes de J. Michelet*, ed. Gabriel Monod (Paris: Flammarion, 1893–1898), as well as in later editions. Michelet's works were quickly translated into English. For pertinent excerpts in English, see *WFF*, vol. I, docs. 46, 97.

[44] See Anthony P. Pisano, "*La Nouvelle Beatrice*: The Role of Woman in the Life and Writings of Jules Michelet, 1848–1860" (Ph.D. dissertation, University of Notre Dame, 1974). Pisano drew on the

in several widely read and very influential works, combining his enormous historical erudition with political purpose: *Les Femmes de la Révolution* (1854), *L'Amour* (1859), *La Femme* (1860), and *La Sorcière* (1862).

The publication of Michelet's diaries in the 1960s, coupled with the centenary of his death in 1974, precipitated an abundant secondary literature (mostly by literary deconstructionists) concerning his views on the woman question.[45] The focus in this literature has not routinely been on Michelet's view of the history of France, which remains his greatest achievement, but on the psychopathology of his relationship to his young second wife as revealed in the diaries and its impact on his later writings, especially *L'Amour* and *La Femme*. This scholarship shortchanged the impact on his interpretation of womanhood of women's political participation in the revolution of 1848.

Of special interest here is Michelet's *Les Femmes de la Révolution* (Women of the Revolution), published in 1854.[46] Much of the material in this widely read book had already appeared in the first two volumes of Michelet's *History of the French Revolution* (c. 1847).[47] What is interesting about its republication in this form, at this time, is Michelet's political purpose: like Laboulaye before him, he clearly intended to justify with historical evidence the claim that women's place was in the family, not in political life.[48] Translations into German (1854) and English (1855) appeared almost immediately.

---

unpublished manuscript of Michelet's course at the Collège de France, which is preserved in the archives of the Bibliothèque de la Ville de Paris.

[45] See Jules Michelet, *Journal; texte intégral, établi sur les manuscrits autographes et publié pour la première fois, avec une introduction, des notes et de nombreux documents inédits par Paul Viallaneix (et Claude Digeon)*, 4 vols. (Paris: Gallimard, 1959–1976). The explosion of literary analyses of Michelet's views on women in the 1970s and early 1980s include: Jeanne Calo, *La Création de la femme chez Michelet* (Paris: Nizet,1975); Linda Orr, *Jules Michelet: Nature, History, and Language* (Ithaca, NY: Cornell University Press, 1976); Edward K. Kaplan, *Michelet's Poetic Vision, A Romantic Theory of Nature, Men, and Women* (Amherst: University of Massachusetts Press, 1977); José Cabanis, *Michelet, le prêtre et la femme* (Paris: Gallimard, 1978); and Thérèse Moreau, *Le Sang de l'histoire: Michelet, l'histoire et l'idée de la femme au XIXe siècle* (Paris: Flammarion, 1982). See also the biography of Michelet by Stephen A. Kippur, *Jules Michelet: A Study of Mind and Sensibility* (Albany: SUNY Press, 1981), and Arthur Mitzman, "Michelet and the Republican Mission, 1868–70: The Policing of Eros," *Journal of the History of Sexuality*, 3:1 (1992), 1–32.

[46] *Les Femmes de la Révolution* was originally published in 1854. Five editions appeared between 1854 and 1877; see also vol. 16 of Michelet's *Oeuvres complètes* and the 1988 reprint (Paris: Carrère) in conjunction with the bicentennial of the French Revolution. The first English translation was published by Meta Roberts Pennington (Philadelphia: H. C. Baird, 1855). Also significant from the standpoint of a male agenda for writing women's history are Michelet's subsequent interpretations of *Jeanne d'Arc* and *La Sorcière*, published slightly later. Neither will be discussed here.

[47] Pisano, *"La Nouvelle Beatrice."*   [48] Pisano, *"La Nouvelle Beatrice,"* p. 55.

Prior to Michelet's study, the history of women's role in the great revolution had been detailed in an anecdotal fashion by Louis DuBroca, published within a decade after the revolution. A far more important account was that by E. Lairtullier in *Femmes célèbres de 1789 à 1795 et leur influence dans la Révolution*, published in 1840 "to serve as a follow-on and complement to all the histories of the French Revolution."[49] In the instance, he was referring to the multivolume works published in the 1820s and 1830s by Adolphe Thiers and Mignet.[50] Lairtullier's book, with its myriad portraits (including Théroigne de Méricourt, Olympe de Gouges, Charlotte Corday), informed a number of later writers, including Ernest Legouvé and Theodore Stanton (compiler of *The Woman Question in Europe* [1884]), and may have very well have stimulated Michelet himself to ponder the connections between women and revolution.[51]

Michelet's study of women's activism in the French revolution constructed a sort of "*femme-mémoire*"; he dedicated his study "to wives, mothers, and daughters" and in quintessential Micheletian fashion, he waxed lyrical about the "superhuman" maternal influence of women on the male generation of 1760. What may be more surprising to modern audiences is that Michelet also gave women an unprecedented amount of credit for effective political action; he insisted on their important role in the October days of 1789. The 6th of October, he said, was the women's counterpart of the 14th of July: "The men conquered the Bastille, and the women captured the King!"[52] Although Michelet accorded only passing reference to the Dutch women's rights activist Etta Palm, he did specifically mention Condorcet's 1790 "Plea for the Citizenship of Women," even though he did not go on to discuss it. He found more fascinating the story of the exotic Théroigne de Méricourt, who seemed to appear at every major revolutionary event clothed in her red jacket and riding pants; the brilliant though more domesticated Madame Roland (to whom he devoted

---

[49] Louis DuBroca, *Les Femmes célèbres de la Révolution* (Paris: l'auteur, 1802); in English as *Interesting Anecdotes of the Heroic Conduct of Women, Previous to and During the French Revolution. Transl. from the French of M. Du Broca, and other writers of authenticity* (1st American ed., Baltimore: Fryer & Clark, 1804); and subsequently, *Heroic Women of France* (Cincinnati, 1846); E. Lairtullier, *Les Femmes célèbres de 1789 à 1795* (see n. 9).

[50] L. A. Thiers, *Histoire de la Révolution française*, 1st ed., 10 vols. (Paris, 1823–1827); F. A. Mignet, *Histoire de la Révolution française depuis 1789 jusqu'en 1814*, 1st ed. (Paris, 1824). On this early historiography, see Paul Farmer, *France Reviews its Revolutionary Origins* (New York: Octagon, 1948).

[51] Ernest Legouvé, *Histoire morale des femmes* (1st ed., Paris: Gustave Sandré, 1849); Theodore Stanton, "France," in Stanton, *The Woman Question in Europe* (New York: G. P. Putnam's Sons, 1884). pp. 234–238.

[52] Michelet, *Femmes de la Révolution*, p. 92.

two chapters); and the Society for Revolutionary Republican Women, founded in 1793 by Pauline Léon and Claire Lacombe (whom both he and Lairtullier referred to as "Rose" Lacombe), demanding to form military brigades, to march, and to bear arms like the men. But in the end Michelet's history rescinded the credit he had given to the revolutionary women by delivering a powerful cautionary message – to women. In fact, he insisted that every political faction during the revolution had been destroyed by women! Michelet's revolutionary *femme-mémoire* was a dangerous creature, one that republican men must subject to male control.[53] Not surprisingly, Michelet's interpretation was anathema to women's rights activists!

But Michelet did not let matters rest there. During the 1850s he continued his contemplation of women, their roles, and responsibilities. In *L'Amour* and *La Femme*, he established a rationale and method for instituting a secular patriarchy.[54] Steeped in the important contributions of French medical researchers in reproductive physiology during the 1840s, Michelet established himself as one of the first historians to take up what we would now call a sociobiological or biomedical approach; he cast his view of women in terms of an unrelenting physiological reductionism, an absolute and unbridgeable physical difference between the sexes that effectively *required* woman's subordination to man. "Woman," argued Michelet, must necessarily remain under man's authority within his household, her mind as well as her body fertilized by his superior attributes; he even advocated cutting woman off from her family of birth, thereby rendering her totally dependent upon her husband. And yet, he couched this materialism in a language of mystical idealism: "Oh, woman, fragile globe of incomparable alabaster, wherein burns the lamp of God."[55]

[53] On Michelet's obsession with controlling women, see the analysis by Moreau, *Sang de l'histoire* (cited n. 45). See also Helga Grubitzsch, "A Paradigm of Androcentric Historiography: Michelet's *Les Femmes de la Révolution*," in *Current Issues in Women's History*, ed. Arina Angerman, et al., (London: Routledge, 1989), pp. 271–288.

[54] Michelet's prescriptions should be compared with the practices of patriarchal control within the household achieved by the English Puritans more than a century and a half earlier, as well as with those of German evangelical protestants. See Sheila Rowbotham, *Hidden from History: Rediscovering Women in History from the 17th Century to the Present* (New York: Vintage/Random House, 1976; orig. publ. London: Pluto Press, 1973), p. 9. Materials for further comparison can be found in Lawrence Stone, *The Family, Sex, and Marriage in England, 1500–1800* abridged ed. (New York: Harper & Row, 1977); and Steven Ozment, *When Fathers Ruled: Family Life in Reformation Europe* (Cambridge, MA: Harvard University Press, 1983).

[55] *La Femme* (1860), as quoted in *WFF*, vol. 1, p. 342. See also the analyses of the ideas Michelet expressed in these two works by Erna Olafson Hellerstein, "Women, Social Order, and the City: Rules for French Ladies" (Ph.D. dissertation, University of California, Berkeley, 1980); Moses, *French Feminism*, pp. 158–161. See also James Smith Allen, "'A Distant Echo': Reading Jules

The literary critic Jules Lemaître later observed rightly that the fact that Michelet so adored women excluded him from the feminist camp (to say the least). Remarking some years later on Michelet's extensive working-class readership, Léopold Lacour (who would publish his own, well-documented history of women in the French Revolution in 1896) concluded that, "all in all, the great lyric moralist had done more harm than good to women."[56]

Michelet was not alone in this respect. It is a significant fact that in the backlash against the revolutions of 1848, neo-conservative male writers such as Louis Koenigswarter, Paul Bernard, and Frédéric Le Play even produced justificatory historical defenses of "patriarchy."[57] This is important because the very appearance of these works testifies to the fact that male rule could no longer be taken for granted; this phenomenon could also be found in the German-speaking world, particularly in the writings of Le Play's counterpart, Wilhelm Heinrich Riehl, who in his quest to discover the historic "natural" German family finally fell back on biblical authority to show that women's emancipation must not be allowed.[58] To top off the list, we find the arch-Catholic Louis Veuillot publishing *Le Droit de seigneur au Moyen Age* (1854), which went into many subsequent editions.[59] The history of the family had itself become a battleground, and the status of women vis à vis the male-headed authoritarian family was the key issue. These sorts of publications, and there were a number of others, fuelled the "knowledge wars" of the 1850s and 1860s. The 1861 publications of J.- J. Bachofen in Basel and Henry Sumner Maine in England set off a new, better-known round of debate on these questions – a debate with international ramifications. Maine argued (based on evidence of ancient laws) that since time immemorial society had been organized around patriarchal families, while Bachofen (drawing on evidence grounded in

Michelet's L'Amour and La Femme in 1859–60," *Nineteenth-Century French Studies*, 16:1–2 (1987), 30–46.

[56] See Lemaître, "L'Amour selon Michelet," (1896) in his *Les Contemporains: Études et portraits littéraires*, 8 vols. (Paris: H. Lecène & H. Oudin, 1886 ff.), vol. 7, pp. 47–66; quote, p. 52; Léopold Lacour, *Humanisme intégral; le Duel des sexes; la Cité future* (Paris: P. Stock, 1897), p. 180.

[57] As, for example, Louis-Jean Koenigswarter, *Histoire de l'organisation de la famille en France depuis les temps les plus reculés jusqu'à nos jours* (Paris: A. Durand, 1851); Paul Bernard's prize-winning study, *Histoire de l'autorité paternelle en France* (Montdidier: Radenez, 1863), and Frédéric Le Play's *La Réforme sociale en France*, 2 vols. (Paris: Plon, 1864).

[58] On Riehl (and the German philosopher Arthur Schopenhauer, who thought along the same lines), see Offen, *European Feminisms*, pp. 130–131.

[59] See Louis Veuillot, *Le Droit de seigneur au Moyen Age* (Paris: L. Vivès, 1854; 2nd ed., 1871; 3rd ed. 1878). Veuillot developed a (dubious) reputation for being more Catholic than the Pope.

myth and religion) argued that although early societies had undoubtedly been matriarchal (we would now say matrilinear), these societies had been superseded by what he considered the "superior" form of patriarchy.[60]

But not all the publications pertaining to women's history supported this authoritarian version of the past. Another thread began to spin out with the publication in 1863 of Amédée Lefaure's *Le Socialisme pendant la révolution française (1789–1798)*, with a chapter on "Les Droits de la femme" that included precious documents from the revolutionary period.[61] Not only that, but two veteran women's rights activists from the 1830s and 1840s, Eugénie Niboyet and Suzanne Voilquin, both of whom had been deeply engaged with the Saint-Simonians and the women dissidents, and had become activists again in 1848, published memoirs – possibly the first memoirs written by earlier pro-woman activists for the benefit of a new generation.[62]

Perhaps because of these complicated and controversial beginnings and the wide range of opinions expressed and evidence cited, writing the history of women (and implicitly, a gender-centered historical analysis) would exert a continuing fascination for those engaged in the campaigns for women's rights. It would also stimulate continuing inquiry among male investigators in the academies and the universities of Third Republic France. In the hundred-plus years between the 1842 competition sponsored by the Academy of Moral and Political Sciences and the end of the Second World War, when French women obtained the vote, hundreds of doctoral theses on woman-related topics would be written by scholars (mostly men) in the faculties of economics and law, in history faculties, and in medical schools, both in Paris and the provinces. Sociologists and anthropologists would pour over these questions too. Many of these academic theses – which deserve analysis as a discrete body of

---

[60] Much has been written about the later aspects of the debate that swirled around the findings of Bachofen, Maine, and other contributors, though usually as a run-up to discussing Frederich Engels, *Origins of the Family, Private Property and the State*. Some of the documents (and earlier bibliography) are available in *WFF*, vol. 1. For another perspective, see the scintillating article by Ann Taylor Allen, "Feminism, Social Science, and the Meanings of Modernity: The Debate on the Origin of the Family in Europe and the United States, 1860–1914," *American Historical Review*, 104:4 (October 1999), 1085–1113, and her book, *Feminism and Motherhood in Western Europe, 1890–1970: The Maternal Dilemma* (New York: Palgrave Macmillan, 2005). French feminists would rediscover Bachofen's writings on matriarchy in the early twentieth century.

[61] Amédée Lefaure, *Le Socialisme pendant la Révolution française (1789–1798)* (Paris: E. Dentu, 1863). See especially chapter III – "Les Droits de la femme."

[62] See Eugénie Niboyet, *Le Vrai livre des femmes* (Paris: E. Dentu, 1863), and Suzanne Voilquin, *Souvenirs d'une fille du peuple* (1866); republished with an introduction by Lydia Elhadad (Paris: F. Maspero, 1978).

scholarship – were clearly intended to establish a secular, neo-traditionalist rationale for the subjection of women in a secularized patriarchal family. It is sobering to contemplate such reasons for establishing the respectability of women's topics in history.[63]

Even so, there were several promising developments on the side of the women's rights activists. By the end of the century, the first women to earn doctorates in the faculties of the University of Paris would also choose (or would be assigned) thesis topics that considered such matters as the history of women in medicine and in the professions.[64] And some of them, like their predecessors Jenny P. d'Héricourt and Clémence Royer, also began to challenge the prevailing androcentric knowledge base and to question why women's views had been ignored or suppressed.

This review of French contributions to the developing history of women prior to 1870 underscores the difficulties, in opinion and belief, that early and mid-nineteenth century French feminists faced as they made their claims, and why they so badly needed not only access to libraries and archives that would allow them to write their own histories but also more formal university training in and admission to the scholarly professions. It will surprise no reader, then, to discover that a call for a history of women written from women's perspective would be one of the major discussion items on the agenda at the First International Women's Rights Congress, convened in Paris in 1878, and would rank *first* on the agenda at the Second International Women's Rights congress of 1889, which marked the centennial of the French Revolution.

Looking ahead, we find that in 1900 the painter and lecturer Marguerite Souley-Darqué would launch (and later publish) her classes in *féminologie* (what we would now call women's studies) at the Collège Libre des Sciences Sociales.[65] By the end of the second decade of the twentieth century, some of the most often cited reference works in women's history

---

[63] See Michele Longino Farrell, *Performing Motherhood: The Sévigné Correspondence* (Hanover & London: University of New England Press, 1991). This author thinks that Madame de Sévigné's letters were acceptable to those who compiled the French literary canon – not merely because the letters were beautifully written, but also their author did not challenge the status quo.

[64] Among the first, Caroline Schultze, *La Femme-médécin au XIXe siècle* (Paris: Thèse de doctorat, Faculté de Médecine, 1888); Sarmisa D. Bilcesco, *De la Condition légale de la mère en droit romain et en droit français* (Paris: Thèse de doctorat, Faculté de Droit, 1890); Jeanne-Marie-Marguerite Chauvin, *Des Professions accessibles aux femmes en droit romain et en droit français, et l'évolution historique de la position économique de la femme dans la société* (Paris: Thèse de doctorat, Faculté de Droit, 1892).

[65] See Edmond Char, "Un cours de féminologie," in the newly launched women's magazine *Femina*, n° 30 (Avril 1902), 125. See Marilyn J. Boxer, "Women's Studies in France circa 1902: A Course on Feminology," *International Supplement to the Women's Studies Quarterly*, vol. 1 (January 1982),

would have their origins in French academic doctoral dissertations: these included the remarkable studies by Léon Abensour, Marguerite Thibert, and others who, because they worked with sympathetic mentors, would lay the foundations for the scholarly history of French feminism.[66] More will be said about the significance of these and other historical works in my subsequent volume. Now we turn to consider the debates on the woman questions as concerns women's gainful employment and its contestation.

26–27. Marguerite Souley-Darqué would subsequently publish two volumes, *L'Éducation féministe. La Femme et le Code. Le servage de l'épouse* (Lyon: Société d'Éducation et d'Action féministe, 1907, 24 pp.), and the book-length *L'Évolution de la Femme* (Ghent: Société Cooperative "Volksdrukkerij", 1908). She also published a series of articles on Nietzsche in *La Fronde*.

[66] Léon Abensour, *La Femme et le féminisme avant la Révolution*, thèse de doctorat, Faculté des lettres, Université de Paris (Paris: E. Leroux, 1923; reprinted 1977); Marguerite Thibert, *Le Féminisme dans le socialisme français de 1830 à 1850*. Thèse de doctorat, Faculté des Lettres, Université de Paris (Paris: M. Giard, 1926).

CHAPTER 6

The Politics of Women's Work in France before 1870

Since time immemorial women have worked. They have not always worked outside the household, nor always in industrial production or service industries, nor invariably for pay – much less for pay equal to that of men. The findings of many historians of women confirm this fact.[1] But most women workers had difficulty to support or sustain themselves through their labor, other than that which was done in the household. In Michelle Perrot's words, "the history of women's work is inseparable from that of the family, of the relationship of the sexes and their social roles," a perspective developed at greater length for the nineteenth century by Louise Tilly and Joan Scott in *Women, Work, and Family*.[2] Mostly the women under discussion were wives and mothers. To many contemporaries, and then to historians, young single women appeared primarily as potential wives and mothers, who might be employed only temporarily prior to marriage. The problems emerged when there were not enough men to "take care" of all the women. In France this problem would be exacerbated by demographics: in the Napoleonic wars alone, historians estimate that well over a million French men died and hundreds of

---

[1] See Madeleine Guilbert, "L'Évolution du travail des femmes dans l'industrie," in Madeleine Guilbert, *Les Fonctions des femmes dans l'industrie* (Paris: Mouton, 1966) and Michelle Perrot's collected essays, *Les Femmes, ou les silences de l'Histoire* (Paris: Flammarion, 1998). See also the theme issues Perrot has edited: "Travaux de femmes dans la France du XIXe siècle," *Le Mouvement social*, n° 105 (October–December 1978), 3–10; and "Métiers de femmes," *Le Mouvement social*, n° 140 (July–September 1987). More recently see Sylvie Schweitzer, *Les Femmes ont toujours travaillé: Une histoire de leurs métiers du XIXe et XXe siècles* (Paris: Odile Jacob, 2002). A particularly well-conceptualized comparative overview of women's work can be consulted in chapter 7, "Working for a Living," in Lynn Abrams' *The Making of Modern Woman* (London: Longman, 2002).

[2] Michelle Perrot, "De la Nourrice à l'employée," introduction to "Travaux de femmes" (1978), quote, 5; also Louise A. Tilly and Joan W. Scott, *Women, Work, and Family* (New York: Holt, Rinehard & Winston, 1978; rept., New York: Routledge, 1989), pp. 5–8. See also Elizabeth Fox-Genovese, "Women and Work," in *French Women and the Age of Enlightenment*, ed. Samia I. Spencer (Bloomington: Indiana University Press, 1984), pp. 111–127.

thousands more were severely incapacitated.[3] And many other, earlier wars had preceded the unprecedented bloodletting that occurred in European lands between 1792 and 1815.

Historical perspectives on women and paid work have greatly broadened, thanks to insights from recent research. Looking at the Western world retrospectively, feminist historians now insist that the singular combination of a late marriage age for both sexes and opportunities for paid labor by young unmarried women, in combination with the unpaid labor of wives and mothers in the household, may have played a determinant role in the rise of capitalism.[4] This broader approach proposes a fundamental paradigm shift, but it would be misleading to interpret it as evidence that these young working women, even those who worked for meager pay, viewed themselves as agents of social change.[5] Only in more recent times have women, whether single or married, aspired to sustain themselves through paid labor outside the family setting, to spend their pay upon themselves, and to demand the "right" to work and pay equal to that accorded to men. Indeed, it could be argued that the advent of women's campaign for economic independence is a primary signifier of a modernity based on a vision of the individual as autonomous that, even in the nineteenth century, would remain highly controversial.

Olwen Hufton has written eloquently of the economy of makeshifts that prevailed during the later eighteenth century, in which the great majority of French women and men struggled to make ends meet. For most, survival remained primary; hopes for attaining prosperity or reshaping the sexual order were secondary. Hufton's findings underscore the necessity of contributions by both sexes and all ages to sustaining life itself

---

[3] Statistics on the demographics of war vary greatly; overall, the numbers of casualties are huge. One estimate is that a total of 5 million died in the Napoleonic Wars; see David Gates, *The Napoleonic Wars, 1803–1815* (London & New York: Arnold, 1997). Another estimate gives 1.8 million French and allies dead in action, disease or missing. See Wikipedia, entry: Napoleonic Wars casualties, http://en .wikipedia.org/wiki/Napoleonic_Wars_casualties.

[4] See the brilliant analyses by Mary S. Hartman, *The Household and the Making of History: A Subversive View of the Western Past* (Cambridge, UK: Cambridge University Press, 2004), and Mary Jo Maynes, Birgitte Søland, and Christina Benninghaus, eds., *Secret Gardens, Satanic Mills: Placing Girls in European History, 1750–1960* (Bloomington: Indiana University Press, 2005). For comparative purposes, these two works should be read in tandem with Amy Erickson's provocative findings on the impact of *couverture* of English wives in marriage (in which the property of women who married was effectively confiscated by husbands and added to their own) on the early formation of capital. See Amy Erickson, "Coverture and Capitalism" *History Workshop Journal*, no. 59 (Spring 2005), 1–16, and Maria Ågren & Amy Louise Erickson, *The Marital Economy in Scandinavia and Britain 1400–1800* (Abington: Ashgate, 2005).

[5] See my review essay discussing these works: "Surveying European Women's History since the Millenium: A Comparative Review," *Journal of Women's History*, 22:1 (Spring 2010), 154–177.

in economic circumstances that were far from bountiful for most and, of necessity, family-based, not individual in character.[6] Even though kings, courtiers, administrators, and merchants lived luxuriously, poverty was rampant even in the kingdom of France, the country many contemporaries considered as possibly the most prosperous in all of Europe.

Taking the Long View on Women's Work

In France, women's work developed some special characteristics – controversial characteristics. What was the reality of "women's work," especially women's employment, in France in the centuries that preceded the revolution and up to the Third Republic? What were these women doing when they "worked"? What conditions governed their labor? How were those conditions changing? And how did women – and men – think about remunerative work in particular? Can we consider disputes over women's paid labor to be a new phenomenon?

Contemporary on-the-ground observers had much to say about women's paid labor in France in this critical period. Foreign visitors (especially the English and Americans) had long denounced the unsuitability to their sex of many French women's tasks. Just prior to the French Revolution, the American observers Abigail Adams and Thomas Jefferson (then living in France) both commented scathingly on the types of heavy physical labor they observed French women doing. In a letter to her aunt, Adams wrote in 1785:[7]

> In Europe all the lower class women perform the most servile labour and work as hard without door as the men . . . In France you see them making hay, sowing, plowing, and driving their carts along. It would astonish you to see how laborious they are and that all their gain is coarse bread and a little ordinary wine, not half so good as our cider. The land is all owned by marquises, counts and dukes for whom these poor wretches toil and sweat.

Jefferson was even more scathing: during his 1787 tour of France he observed, in the Champagne region, "women and children carrying heavy burthens [sic], and labouring with the hough. This is an unequivocal indication of extreme poverty." And, he added pointedly, "Men, in a

---

[6] Olwen H. Hufton, *The Poor of Eighteenth-Century France, 1750–1789* (Oxford: Clarendon Press, 1974); and Hufton, "Women and the Family Economy in Eighteenth-Century France," *French Historical Studies*, 9:1 (Spring 1975), 1–22.

[7] Abigail Adams to her aunt, Mrs. Cotton Tufts, 3 September 1785, Adams Papers, Reel 365; I am indebted to Edith B. Gelles for this reference.

civilised country, never expose their wives and children to labour above their force or sex, as long as their own labour can protect them from it."[8] Comments such as these continued into the nineteenth century, when in 1855 an unidentified American woman, having recently traveled in France, reported that:[9]

> We find women occupying positions and exercising many functions in Europe, especially in France and Switzerland, which are generally with us considered exclusively masculine. I have seen women digging, hoeing, mowing and reaping in the fields, carrying trunks like porters, harnessed into carts, sometimes alone, sometimes in company with a man, to draw water about the streets, acting as guides over the glaciers, and in short performing every species of manual labor.

As these observations (and others like them) suggest, and as the French writer Evelyne Sullerot once astutely remarked: "Public opinion only becomes concerned about the question of women's work when such work presents itself in forms and conditions approximating those agreed upon for men . . . Public opinion gets upset over women working when certain norms, which . . . carefully limit the man-woman cleavage in the tasks and styles of life, are violated."[10] Women engaged in heavy physical labor violated these norms; critics deemed such strenuous work, when done by women, as "uncivilized." Such observations confirm that notions about an appropriate sexual division of labor, a hierarchy of labor, and pay scales were deeply entrenched well before the nineteenth century. Studies of women's work in early modern Europe confirm that (with the exception of certain mixed-sex corporations) even when such work took place in the same location as that of men, the tasks women performed had (for the most part) been rigorously distinct, household-oriented, generally subordinate to those of men, and almost always more poorly paid.[11]

---

[8] *The Papers of Thomas Jefferson*, ed. Julian P. Boyd, vol. 11 (Princeton, NJ: Princeton University Press, 1955); earlier published in Jefferson's *Memoirs* (1829), vol. 2.

[9] "E", "Letters from Paris," *The Una*, 3:1 (January 1855), 11. Comparable remarks are cited by G. de Bertier de Sauvigny, *La France et les français vus par les voyageurs Américains, 1814–1848*, vol. 2 (Paris: Flammarion, 1985), chapter 28, pp. 35–47.

[10] Evelyne Sullerot, *Histoire et sociologie du travail féminin: Essai* (Paris: Garnier, 1968), p. 11. Sullerot offers a stimulating and well-informed summary of the changes in patterns of women's work, based largely on the meticulous research of Madeleine Guilbert (cited in n. 1, n. 90). On pp. 31–34 she analyzes the "dedans/dehors" dichotomy, tracing it directly to its sources in Xenophon's *Economics*, and observing how it quickly became translated into "dedans/dessous" (inside/underneath) in the discourse of classical Athens.

[11] For synthetic overviews of women's work in early modern Europe, see Merry E. Wiesner, "Spinning Out Capital: Women's Work in the Early Modern Economy," in *Becoming Visible: Women in European History*, ed. Renate Bridenthal, Claudia Koonz, & Susan Stuard, 2nd ed. (Boston:

What these particular Anglophone observers did not comment on were issues about the sexual division of labor and pay scales among urban women workers who performed other kinds of lighter and more skilled labor as members of woman-only guilds. Already in 1675 Louis XIV had intervened to protect the dressmakers [*couturières*] of Paris against the master-tailors by organizing them as a protected community with its own statutes and officers; this development was replicated in Rouen and Le Havre (1721). In eighteenth-century Paris, there were at least five all-female guilds.[12] In consequence, from the later seventeenth century on,

Houghton Mifflin, 1987), pp. 221–249; and a revised version, "Spinning Out Capital: Women's Work in Preindustrial Europe, 1350–1750," in *Becoming Visible* (3rd ed., 1997), pp. 203–231, and Barbara A. Hanawalt, "Introduction" to *Women and Work in Preindustrial Europe*, ed. Barbara A. Hanawalt (Bloomington: Indiana University Press, 1986), vii–xviii. See also the important review essays by Judith M. Bennett, "'History That Stands Still': Women's Work in the European Past," *Feminist Studies*, 14:2 (Summer 1988), 269–283, and Olwen Hufton's review essay on the history of [European] women and work in *Signs: Journal of Women in Culture and Society*, 14:1 (Autumn 1988), 223–228, which reassesses the thesis of Alice Clark about the pre-capitalist "good old days" for women's work in light of recent scholarship that shows those "good old days" are in fact mythic.

On women's employment in *ancien régime* France, the classic studies remain those of Henri Hauser, "Le Travail des femmes aux XVe et XVIe siècles," *Revue Internationale de Sociologie*, 5:5 (May 1897), 337–351, and Guilbert, "L'Évolution du travail des femmes dans l'industrie"(cited in n. 1), esp. pp. 21–43. Subsequent studies that examine women's work in various French-speaking cities include: Maurice Garden, *Lyon et les lyonnais au XVIIIe siècle* (Paris: les Belles Lettres, 1970); Natalie Zemon Davis, "Women in Crafts in Sixteenth-Century Lyons," *Feminist Studies*, 8:1 (Spring, 1982), 47–80 [reprinted in *Women and Work in Preindustrial Europe*, ed. Hanawalt, cited in n. 11]; for Francophone Geneva, E. William Monter, "Women in Calvinist Geneva (1550–1800)," *Signs: Journal of Women in Culture and Society*, 6:2 (Winter, 1980), 189–209. For a seventeenth century overview, see James B. Collins, "The Economic Role of Women in Seventeenth-Century France," *French Historical Studies*, 16:2 (Fall 1989), 436–470; Collins argues (p. 468) that the panoply of efforts made by men to constrain women were in fact recognition of the economic and social power they had achieved. "The independent and . . . equal female was an enormous threat to patriarchal society, because women *were* society. A man needed a wife to become a real (lay) member of adult society." Studies of women's work in other European cities, which confirm the overall pattern of sexual separation, appear in the Hanawalt volume, also cited in n. 11, and in Martha C. Howell, *Women, Production, and Patriarchy in Late Medieval Cities* (Chicago: University of Chicago Press, 1986), whose arguments concerning women's economic power inspired the revisionist interpretation of Collins.

For Paris, Angela Groppi, "Le Travail des femmes à Paris à l'époque de la Révolution française," *Bulletin d'Histoire économique et sociale de la Révolution française, 1979* (Paris, 1980), 27–46, and Raymonde Monnier, "L'Évolution de l'industrie et le travail des femmes à Paris sous l'Empire," also in the 1979 *Bulletin d'Histoire économique et sociale*, 47–60. Also, for the revolutionary era, see Dominique Godineau, *The Women of Paris and Their French Revolution* (Berkeley & Los Angeles: University of California Press, 1998), and Lisa DiCaprio, *The Origins of the Welfare State: Women, Work, and the French Revolution* (Urbana: University of Illinois Press, 2007).

[12]   On women in the guilds and corporations before 1774, see the survey by Léon Abensour, *La Femme et le féminisme avant la Révolution* (Paris: E. Leroux, 1923), pp. 184–196, and more recently, Carol. L. Loats, "Gender, Guilds, and Work Identity: Perspectives from Sixteenth-Century Paris," *French Historical Studies*, 20:1 (Winter 1997), 15–30. See also the brief note on 1675 in Paul Gemaehling, *Travailleurs au rabais; la lutte syndicale contre les sous-concurrences ouvrières* (Paris: Bloud & cie, 1910), p. 130. See especially Clare Haru Crowston, "Engendering the Guilds: Seamstresses, Tailors, and the

some of these guild-affiliated women workers insisted on upholding a sexual division of labor in the trades when it worked to their advantage. We know, for example, that some city-based French women working in the elite trades registered complaints about various forms of male intrusion into "their" occupations. Other evidence uncovered by women's historians suggests that groups of male workers were deliberately attempting (and sometimes succeeding) to nudge women out of the more lucrative positions in the trades and crafts that the latter had held (sometimes even monopolized) in preindustrial times and were refusing them entry into newer types of work. For example, Cynthia Truant's investigation of the merchant-mistress linen drapers in Paris reveals that in 1737 the male dry-goods merchants guild was attempting to undercut the women's monopoly of the cloth hall, and Daryl Hafter has shown how increasing tax demands on the guilds by the king's officials in Paris eroded women's control of the mixed-sex spinners' guild in Rouen.[13] Clare Crowston observes that, in contrast to the tailors, who "saw their status as guild masters as imbricated with their role as male heads of household" (which offered certain privileges to master's wives, daughters, and widows), ... "the seamstresses viewed guild membership as a mark of independence from the patriarchal family."[14] These conflicts, and the issues they raise about the changing family economy and the possibility of female autonomy, lie at the heart of French debates, especially the economic aspects, on the woman question.

In consequence of the increasing specialization of tasks due to ever more complex modes of production, and the jockeying for economic advantage that increasing wealth brought with it, the boundaries between women's and men's work became increasingly fluid and subject to shift – and to

Clash of Corporate Identities in Old Regime France," *French Historical Studies*, 23:2 (Spring 2000), 339–371, and *Fabricating Women: The Seamstresses of Old Regime France, 1675–1791* (Durham: Duke University Press, 2001). See also Judith G. Coffin, *The Politics of Women's Work: The Paris Garment Trades, 1750–1915* (Princeton, NJ: Princeton University Press, 1996); and her earlier article "Gender and the Guild Order: The Garment Trades in Eighteenth-Century Paris," *Journal of Economic History*, 54:4 (December 1994), 768–793, and the publications of Cynthia M. Truant and Daryl Hafter, cited in n. 13 and n. 17.

[13] See Cynthia M. Truant, "The Guildswomen of Paris: Gender, Power, and Sociability in the Old Regime," *Proceedings of the Western Society for French History, Las Cruces, N. M., 1987*, ed. William Roosen, vol. 15 (Flagstaff, AZ, 1988), 130–138; and Daryl M. Hafter, "Power vs. Privilege: A Case Study of the Spinner's Guild in Eighteenth-Century Rouen," paper presented to the Social Science History Association, Bloomington, IN, 1982. See also the five essays concerning France in *European Women and Preindustrial Craft*, ed. Daryl M. Hafter (Bloomington: Indiana University Press, 1995), and especially Daryl Hafter, *Women at Work in Pre-Industrial France* (University Park, PA: Penn State University Press, 2007).

[14] See Crowston, "Engendering the Guilds," p. 341.

contestation. In the later eighteenth century, as textile production itself, long a bastion of women's work in spinning and weaving, became the first industry to undergo mechanization and centralization, some women sought to stave off threats to newly acquired possibilities for their remunerative work in domestic industry by catering to the luxury goods trade; other women began to seek employment in the emerging workshops or small factories, where they could earn a decent wage and thereby harness industrialization for their own benefit.[15] Indeed, dramatic changes in women's opportunities for paid labor lay at the core of the Industrial Revolution.[16]

In 1776 the king's liberalizing prime minister Turgot, reacting to a century of highly centralized economic practices and regulations, attempted to abolish the French guild system, arguing (among other reasons) that it was inequitable to women. He insisted that the individual's "right to work" should not be hindered by the guilds. The Paris guildswomen (linen drapers and seamstresses) also effectively defended their guild privileges by invoking the language of "rights"; as Truant has pointed out, both guilds "openly defend women's rights to a degree of economic independence and self-sufficiency."[17] Turgot's initiative did not succeed and when his successor reestablished the corporations in August of that year, he prohibited the exclusion of women from the men's guilds – and conversely, prohibited the exclusion of men from the women's guilds.[18]

[15] See, among other important studies, Gay L. Gullickson, *Spinners and Weavers of Auffay: Rural Industry and the Sexual Division of Labor in a French Village, 1750–1850* (Cambridge, UK: Cambridge University Press, 1986) and Tessie P. Liu, *The Weaver's Knot: The Contradictions of Class Struggle and Family Solidarity in Western France, 1750–1914* (Ithaca, NY: Cornell University Press, 1994).

[16] See the gendered reinterpretation of the British Industrial Revolution by Maxine Berg, *The Age of Manufactures 1700–1820: Industry, Innovation, and Work in Britain*, 2nd ed. (London: Routledge, 1994); also her article, "What Difference did Women's Work Make to the Industrial Revolution?" in *Women's Work: The English Experience, 1650–1914*, ed. Pamela Sharp (London: Arnold, 1998; originally published in *History Workshop Journal*). See also Deborah Valenze, *The First Industrial Woman* (New York: Oxford University Press, 1995). For further comparisons with England, see especially the publications of Sonya O. Rose, Barbara Taylor, & Jane Lewis.

[17] See Cynthia Marie Truant, "Parisian Guildswomen and the (Sexual) Politics of Privilege: Defending Their Patrimonies in Print," in *Going Public: Women and Publishing in Early Modern France*, ed. Elizabeth C. Goldsmith & Dena Goodman (Ithaca, NY: Cornell University Press, 1995), 46–61; quote, 56. See also Truant, "La Maîtrise d'une identité? Corporations féminines à Paris aux XVIIe et XVIIIe siècles," *Clio: Histoire, Femmes et Sociétés*, n° 3 (1996), 55–69, and Coffin, "Gender and the Guild Order," cited in n. 12.

[18] On Turgot's reforms, see Abensour, *La Femme et le féminisme*, pp. 196–198. See also the text of the edict of 11 August 1776, which reestablished the corporations, admitted women into the male corporations, and vice versa, in F. A. Isambert, ed. *Recueil général des anciennes lois françaises . . .* , 29 vols. (Paris, 1821–1833), 22: 74–89.

In this new situation, the end of gendered exclusion produced unantici-pated consequences; Parisian working women protested with increasing vehemence that they were being squeezed out of many trades and occupa-tions that had previously been theirs. Such complaints found an echo in Beaumarchais's celebrated comedy, *The Marriage of Figaro* (1784) and resurfaced in the cahiers of 1789, when one group of women petitioned the king to keep men out of women's *métiers*, particularly in the needle-work trades and sales, and another, the flower vendors, called for the reestablishment of their corporation. "Instruction and work" – such were the joint demands of Parisian working women on the eve of the French Revolution.[19] Work, they insisted, was necessary to keep women from the alternative – unemployment and, consequently, prostitution. However, during the Revolution and especially following the abolition of the guilds and the deteriorating economic situation (according to historian Lisa DiCaprio), the language of "rights of subsistence" ultimately trumped that of the "right to work" among such women workers.[20] It took decades for "right to work" claims to reappear.

Twenty-first century readers may need reminding that the triumphant attribution of high social value to manual labor, remunerative or not – and to the accompanying work ethic – is a remarkably recent development in European history.[21] The fact that women (like most men) have worked throughout history does not suggest (*pace* Mary Beard)[22] that those who worked for a living were held in esteem by cultural elites; to ignore this fact is to forget the high value long attributed (since Plato and Aristotle) to the cultivation of leisure and the contemplative life, and to the ascetic, other-worldly trend that overtook organized Christianity between the fall of the Roman Empire and the Renaissance, as it became a state religion and was

---

[19] See, among others, "Petition des femmes du Tiers-État au Roi, 1er Janvier 1789," and "Cahier des doléances et réclamations des femmes," both transl. in Darline Gay Levy, Harriet B. Applewhite, and Mary D. Johnson, eds. *Women in Revolutionary Paris* (Urbana, IL: University of Illinois Press, 1979), pp. 18–21 and 22–26. For additional references, see Jane Abray, "Feminism in the French Revolution," *American Historical Review*, 80:1 (February 1975), 46–47.

[20] See Lisa DiCaprio, "Women Workers, State-Sponsored Work, and the Right to Subsistence during the French Revolution," *Journal of Modern History*, 71:3 (September 1999), 519–551, and DiCaprio, *Origins of the Welfare State* (cited in n. 11).

[21] See Sullerot, *Histoire et sociologie*, pp. 44–83. See also the excellent and still valuable study by Pierre Jaccard, *Histoire sociale du travail de l'antiquité à nos jours* (Paris: Payot, 1960).

[22] See Mary Beard, *Woman as Force in History* (New York: Collier Books, 1971 paperback ed.; orig. publ. 1946), especially chapter 10. Like the theses of Alice Clark, Beard's historical optimism about medieval women's work has been contradicted by the historical studies surveyed by Judith M. Bennett, "'History That Stands Still': Women's Work in the European Past," and Olwen Hufton's review essay in *Signs*, both cited in n. 11.

annexed by the ruling warrior cultures of medieval Europe.[23] The aristocratic male elite in Western societies, including France, considered paid manual labor degrading; as long as it was degrading, it could be left to lower-class men, to women, domestic servants of both sexes, and, most importantly (though only in France's colonies, not the mainland), to slaves.[24]

Secular Enlightenment thinkers (especially the Protestants among them) helped to rehabilitate work and the work ethic in France, as well as to celebrate the "natural" and the family.[25] This change was already evident in the thinking of Denis Diderot in the *Encyclopédie*, in the writings of the Physiocrats, and notably in Turgot's "Preamble" to the 1776 edicts referred to earlier that liberalized trade and abolished the guild system, where he wrote that God "in giving man needs, in making the resource of work necessary for him, made the *right to work* the property of all men, and this property is the first, most sacred and the most imprescriptable right of all."[26] This was a powerful message – for men – and it was promulgated from the top down. Some elite men absorbed the message and applied it to their daughters: for instance, the marquis de Condorcet, the first great champion of women's participation in political life, in a 1794 letter to his daughter Constance, advised her to "learn the habit of work, not only so that you can support yourself without serving a stranger, but also so that your work can satisfy your needs, so that you can be reduced to poverty without being reduced to dependence."[27] He had in mind skilled, reputable labor that occupied both the hands and the mind. The same glorification of work appears in the works of the visionary sociopolitical thinker Charles Fourier, who insisted that (in Jonathan Beecher's words) "full human self-realization was only possible within the world of work."[28]

---

[23] See Jaccard, *Histoire sociale du travail*, pt. I, chapter 4 and pt. II, chapter 2.

[24] See Sue Peabody, *"There Are No Slaves in France": The Political Culture of Race and Slavery in the Ancien Régime* (New York: Oxford University Press, 1996).

[25] See Dianne Lynn Alstad, "The Ideology of the Family in 18th Century France" (Ph.D. dissertation, Yale University, 1971). Alstad contrasted "aristocratic" and "bourgeois" family ideals, and gave heavy emphasis to Rousseau.

[26] Turgot, February 1776, as translated by Clare Crowston in "Engendering the Guilds," pp. 362–363.

[27] Condorcet, "Conseils de Condorcet à sa fille" (1794), For the French text of the "Conseils" and the "Testament," see Condorcet's *Oeuvres*, ed. Arthur Condorcet O'Connor & François Arago, 12 vols. (Paris: F. Didot, 1847–1849), vol. 1, pp. 611–623; quotes, p. 611. As translated by Jane Marie Todd, in Fraisse, *Reason's Muse*, p. 67.

[28] See Jonathan Beecher, *Charles Fourier: The Visionary and His World* (Berkeley & Los Angeles: University of California Press, 1986), chapter 14: "Work in Harmony." Quote, p. 274. In French, see especially the work of Simone Debout-Oleszkiewicz, summarized in "Utopie et contre-utopie: les femmes dans l'oeuvre de Fourier," in *Encyclopedie politique et historique des femmes*, ed. Christine Fauré (Paris: Presses Universitaires de France, 1997), pp. 317–340.

It took some time, however, for such views to sink in among the French upper classes. Well into the nineteenth century, the quintessential French bourgeois male, aping his aristocratic betters, was still in hot pursuit of social promotion and landed leisure through a dowried marriage rather than through his own labor; to this the advertisements in the press for dowries and legal *causes célèbres* attest.[29] For Stendhal's *arriviste* hero, Julien Sorel, in his novel *Le Rouge et le noir* [The Red and the Black, 1830], breadwinning certainly did not feature as a fundamental component of his masculine identity. The ascendance of the work ethic (and family-centered values) on the scale of social values in Western European society corresponds with the rise of the city dwellers – particularly the articulate vanguard of skilled artisans and tradesmen – on the ladder of political and economic power; it parallels the displacement of otherworldly spiritual goals by secular goals, notably the pursuit of and accumulation of wealth. In Pierre Jaccard's view, work has gained in social value as increasing numbers of *free men* (his emphasis) abandoned warfare for production and subsequently sanctified their choice by defending it in print against the derision of élites nourished on a diet of humanistic antipathy for manual labor.[30]

Other factors complicated the growing debates about women's work for pay. First, by the early nineteenth century, as industrialization and the mechanization of industry began to transform economic life in France as throughout much of Western Europe and the Atlantic world, men attempted to redraw and solidify the lines drawn between household and industry, and between men's and women's labor. Their arguments surrounding women's work, its content and its location, became more frequent and more intense, in particular when mechanization threatened the supremacy and privileges associated with masculine muscular power. Secondly, the definition of "work" (*le travail*) itself shifted; it became associated strictly with paid "employment," employment by a firm or workshop located outside the household. This change in terminology was fostered in no small part by the arguments of a new breed of theorists known as political economists, who elaborated a new vision of society and economic life for the post-revolutionary world. In so doing, they succeeded in erasing much of the "work" that women do – the unpaid labor that was henceforth never included in calculations of what we now call the "gross national product." The French group that successfully theorized the

[29] See for a notorious nineteenth-century example, Christina Vella, *Intimate Enemies: The Two Worlds of the Baroness de Pontalba* (Baton Rouge: Louisiana State University Press, 1997).
[30] Jaccard, *Histoire sociale du travail*, esp. p. 157.

exclusion of women from paid work were known as the *Idéologues*, who published an important periodical called the *Décade philosophique*. Although the arguments of the men in the group concerning economics have been well studied, until recently few scholars paid attention to the gender presuppositions of their political and economic arguments.

One of the earliest and certainly one of the most influential advocates of the new politico/economic theory in the 1790s was Pierre-Louis Roederer (1754–1835), a lawyer and political figure from a noble family in Metz who, in a 1793 lecture at the Lyceum (as part of his course on social organization), argued explicitly against Condorcet's views on the equality of the sexes. In asserting that the male-headed family is the basis of civil society, Roederer remarked that "domestic society would no longer be guaranteed" if women were treated as [rights-bearing] individuals. "It would be a strange contradiction to charge wives [*femmes*] with the infinite works of society after having instituted this society to assure them more rest [*repos*], or rather to reserve their strength and their time to the physical work that Nature has imposed upon them."[31] Obviously, he had maternity in mind. Men like Roederer (and his physician-colleague Cabanis) thought they were doing women a favor by excluding wives, who would inevitably become mothers, both from civil society and from the labor market – and also from bothering themselves about government. "Women create men," he said, thus "it is up to the men to work on behalf of the women." Moreover, "maternity is a duty that nothing should distract from; it is also a solitary pleasure which demands social withdrawal; one must concentrate this power of loving in order to conserve it completely and purely." In the meantime the men who constituted civil society, and had political rights, would form a defensive ring that would protect the women and children. Later in his presentation, in speaking of what guarantees women would have against the men, the benevolent Roederer let slip his deeper belief (or perhaps we could call it a sentimental, or chivalrous, conviction) – that "men are born to serve women . . . to protect them, like soldiers who protect the country that provides their happiness." In fact, he argued, women have all the rights – and exert all the influence they need to exert – in their own domestic sphere.

Perhaps the best known of these post-revolutionary political economists, also a member of the *Idéologues*, was Roederer's younger colleague Jean-Baptiste Say (1767–1832). Say belonged to a prominent Lyon Huguenot

---

[31] Paul-Louis Roederer, [Third lecture, 10 February 1793], *Cours d'organisation sociale* (1793), in *Oeuvres du comte P.-L. Roederer*, vol. 8 (Paris: Didot, 1859); quotes, p. 160, 161.

textile merchant family, becoming a member of the circle of thinkers known as the *Idéologues* and editor of the influential post-revolutionary revue, *La Décade philosophique*. He was a member of Napoléon's Council of 100 before he fell out of favor with Napoléon and reinvented himself as the owner-operator of a cotton spinning mill. Above all else, he was a partisan of free trade in the tradition of the Scottish economic philosopher Adam Smith. Say's ideas about women's place (or lack thereof) in the economy, however, developed in the 1790s, in direct response to the economic and political chaos of the French Revolution.

Prior to the publication in 1803 of Say's highly influential *Traité d'économie politique; ou, Simple exposition de la manière dont se forment, se distribuent, et se consomment les richesses* [Treatise on Political Economy], he spelled out his vision of the good society in *Olbie, ou Essai sur les moyens de réformer les mœurs d'une nation* (1800), a utopian treatise he wrote for an essay competition sponsored by the Institut National.[32] The competition addressed the search for ways and means of "transforming" the morals of a nation, and Say's approach was to construct a utopia "describing," in economic historian Evelyn Forget's words, "the ideal future of a republican society."[33] That ideal society's foundation was, according to Say, a male-headed (conjugal) family in which a married man could support all his family members by his earnings, and a married woman could dedicate her energies exclusively to fulfilling the obligations of motherhood and household upkeep, while providing a chaste and orderly moral environment and retaining her sweetness (*douceur*) and femininity. This was, Forget correctly insists, an effort to "purchase social and economic stability at the cost of denying women an independent existence as economic and social beings."[34] This idealized sexual division of labor has come to be known as the "male breadwinner model" (in French, *l'homme pourvoyeur*). And one of its chief characteristics would be a powerful argument against women, especially married women with young children, taking any sort

[32] Jean-Baptiste Say, *Olbie, ou Essai sur les moyens de réformer les mœurs d'une nation* (Paris: Déterville, 1800), in J.-B. Say, *Oeuvres complètes*, ed. Emmanuel Blanc & André Tiran, vol. 5 (Paris: Économica, 2003), pp. 183–236; and Say, *Traité d'économie politique; ou, Simple exposition de la manière dont se forment, se distribuent, et se consomment les richesses*, first published in 1803 in Paris (4th ed., 1819). The 5th ed. (1826) is the basis for the English translation. The 6th edition (1841) is the edition most frequently cited by labor historians.

[33] On *Olbie*, see Evelyn L. Forget, "The Market for Virtue: Jean-Baptiste Say on Women in the Economy and Society" in *The Status of Women in Classical Economic Thought*, ed. Robert Dimand & Chris Nyland (Aldershot, UK: Edward Elgar, 2003), pp. 206–223; quote, p. 211.

[34] Forget, "The Market for Virtue," p. 210. An earlier version of this article is Evelyn L. Forget, "The Market for Virtue: Jean-Baptiste Say on Women in the Economy and Society," *Feminist Economics*, 3:1 (Spring 1997), 95–111.

of employment outside the household, especially in industrial produc-tion.[35] Some of Say's successors issued more extreme prescriptions, arguing not only that women should not perform demanding physical labor, but for an outright ban on women's paid nondomestic labor.[36]

This way of thinking about women's labor (especially that of wives and mothers) bolstered the preconceptions of those who wished to found a new, stable (and as some would say "bourgeois") social order that no longer depended on the separation of the three estates (nobility, clergy, Third Estate). It was in these changing circumstances that so many prominent and learned male social reformers began to argue that French society's best interests would be served when a "public/private" (or separate spheres) division of labor (complementing that they had advocated in political life) be implemented and strictly enforced. This was not an assumption, but an assertion, a prescription, and it was not restricted to "bourgeois" commentators.[37] Such an arrangement would certainly have been more to the liking of those earlier Anglo-American visitors, Adams and Jefferson.

Here, though, the debates on the woman question take a new turn. The new prescriptive wall erected between the worlds of men and women found eager supporters not only among men of the middle classes but also among male artisans and skilled workers. It likewise informed the proliferation of manuals on domestic economy written by women, dis-cussed in Chapter 4. It encouraged the thinking of visionaries like Fourier about how to organize a "New Industrial World," and it also permeated

---

[35] See Book 2, chapter 7 of Jean-Baptiste Say's *Traité d'économie politique* (6th ed., 1841), pp. 371–372. For a feminist analysis of Say's overall position, see Evelyn L. Forget, *The Social Economics of Jean-Baptist[e] Say: Markets and Virtue* (London & New York: Routledge, 1999). A recent study by Elizabeth Marie Sage, *A Dubious Science: Political Economy and the Social Question in 19th Century France* (New York: Peter Lang, 2009), does not reference Forget's work and says nothing about these issues.

[36] Writers who argued against the industrial employment of women (as well as children) from the 1830s on included Jean-Charles-Léonard Simonde de Sismondi, *Études sur l'économie politique*, 2 vols. (Paris: Treuttel & Würtz, 1837–1838); Louis-René Villermé, *Tableau de l'état physique et moral des ouvriers employés dans les manufactures de coton, de laine, et de soie*, 2 vols. (Paris: J. Renouard & Cie., 1840; repr. 1979), and Adolphe Blanqui (following Sismondi), *Des Classes ouvrières en France, pendant l'année 1848* (Paris: Pagnerre, 1849). See also Louis Reybaud, *Études sur le régime de manufactures; condition des ouvriers en soie* (Paris: Michel Lévy frères, 1859), a study of working conditions for silk workers in the Rhineland, Switzerland, and southern France. On the general question, see Jules Tixerant, *Le Féminisme à l'époque de 1848 dans l'ordre politique et dans l'ordre économique* (Paris: Giard & Brière, 1908).

[37] See, for a discussion of other contributors ranging from political, social, and moral economists to Social Catholics and socialists of the 1830s and early 1840s, focused on the relationship between poverty and immorality, see chapter 2 in Rachel Fuchs, *Poor and Pregnant in Paris* (New Brunswick, NJ: Rutgers University Press, 1983).

the workingmen's press. The editors of *L'Atelier*, a monthly publication in Paris, advocated, on the one hand, improvements in the abject situation of women workers in industry (to counter the many problems – abysmal pay, bad working conditions, industrial accidents, sexual harassment in the workplace, price undercutting thanks to competition from production by prisoners, and rampant prostitution during periods of unemployment), but they strongly preferred increasing men's pay, coupled with the complete removal of women (wives) from the labor force. "If the salary of the male worker were generally sufficient for the keep of his family – as it should be – his wife would not be obliged to frequent the workshops. She would be able, while doing a bit of work in her home, to raise the children, send them to school, care for them, and thereby avoid turning out bad subjects later on." Moreover, argued the editors of *L'Atelier*, "The mother of the family . . . would understand her dignity and her duties; and she would raise her daughters with the same feelings, so that they could someday also be good mothers."[38] Such newly beefed-up requirements for motherhood, including the assignment of total responsibility for child-raising to mothers, provided an especially powerful argument against women's work for pay, as well as a stimulus to further the production of mother-educators through appropriate maternal education.[39]

By the mid-1840s, Pierre-Joseph Proudhon (whom we already met in Chapter 4) would present women's "choices" rather crudely in his *Système des contradictions économiques, ou Philosophie de la misère* [The System of Economic Contradictions, or, The Philosophy of Misery, 1844] as "*menagère ou courtesan*" – "housewife or harlot."[40] Here and in his subsequent work *De la Justice* [On Justice, 1858], in which he presented his antifeminist calculus of women's inferiority, Proudhon revealed himself as an unrelenting male chauvinist (despite the fact he was raising three daughters, a life circumstance that would inspire other Frenchmen, such as Ernest Legouvé, to become champions of women's rights); he fiercely

---

[38] "Enquête – De la condition des femmes," *L'Atelier*, 3:4 (30 December 1842), 31–32. Quote, as translated by KO in *WFF*, vol. 1, doc. 57, p. 206.

[39] Even the poet-politician Alphonse de Lamartine endorsed the mother-educator and a normal school to produce trained teachers who could educate mothers such that they could properly educate their own children, especially their daughters. See Lamartine's intervention in the Chamber of Deputies, 30 May 1835, in the *Archives parlementaires*, Ch.D., 30 May 1835, 2e serie, vol. 96, p. 669.

[40] Pierre-Joseph Proudhon, *Système des contradictions économiques, ou Philosophie de la misère* (2 vols., Paris: Guillaumin, 1846), vol. 2, chapter 11, p. 197. He elaborated the alternatives of "*menagère ou courtisane*" for women in his magnum opus, *De la Justice dans la Révolution et dans l'Église*, 3 vols. (Paris: Garnier, 1858). An English translation of the pertinent sections can be consulted in *WFF*, vol. 1, docs. 52 & 95.

opposed women's employment and passionately advocated subordination, domesticity, and maternity as women's lot.[41] Proudhon's harsh statement of this principle found reinforcement at the hands of Auguste Comte, the "father" of sociology, who considered equality of the sexes an impossibility. "Man should provide for Woman," Comte trumpeted in 1848. "It is a natural law of the human race, a law connected with the essentially domestic character of female life."[42] By the time Comte waded into the debate, he could present Rousseau's deliberately calculated rationale for subordinating women, which had also inspired P.-L. Roederer and J.-B. Say, as a "natural law."

Why did these political economists, philosophers, and workers find so objectionable the idea of women bringing income into the household from outside labor? In fact, their objections were neither about income nor its liberating consequences, but about the moral quality and role they assigned to the household, which depended (in their view) on the uninterrupted presence of women's moralizing influence as wives and mothers; their worst-case scenario was that without a woman at the center the "family" as they understood it would disintegrate. Its essential tasks would not be accomplished if women did not stay at home and perform them. Recognizing that "gender" was mutable, they also feared the "masculinization" of women who went out to work.[43] Although these men no doubt thought that their prescriptions would, if realized, be doing many women a

---

[41] Since the initial studies of Proudhon's thought and action by Jules Puech and Célestin Bouglé, few commentators (with the exception of those interested expressly in women's history) have acknowledged Proudhon's elaborate statements on the role of women as central to his political philosophy. For example, the most recent studies in English glance over, treat as embarrassing, or ignore altogether his views on the woman question: see Edward S. Hyams, *Pierre-Joseph Proudhon: His Revolutionary Life, Mind, and Works* (London: J. Murray, 1979); K. Steven Vincent, *Pierre-Joseph Proudhon and the Rise of French Republican Socialism* (New York: Oxford University Press, 1984); and Monique Canto-Sperber, cited in Chapter 4, n. 112.

[42] Auguste Comte, "The Influence of Positivism upon Women" in his *General View of Positivism*, transl. J. H. Bridges (London, 1875; reprint ed., Stanford, CA: Academic Reprints, 1953), p. 276; originally published in the first volume of his *Système de politique positive* (Paris: L. Mathias, 1851). There is also a 1957 "Official Centennial Edition" (New York: R. Speller, 1957). For a recent French reassessment of Comte's views on the woman question, see Sarah Kofman, *Aberrations: le devenir-femme d'Auguste Comte* (Paris: Aubier-Flammarion, 1978), and Mary Pickering's magisterial three-volume opus, *Auguste Comte: An Intellectual Biography* (Cambridge, UK: Cambridge University Press, 1993, 2009).

[43] In the thinking of J.-B. Say, "Women and gentleness [*douceur*] are two ideas I find impossible to separate. The empire of woman is that of weakness over strength; the moment she tries to obtain something by violent means, she is nothing more than a monstrosity." (In his footnote: "They are neither women nor men, these beings in petticoats, with malicious eyes and raucous voices, who amidst the populace of our cities, square off against men, insulting them verbally, their drinks in hand. They are a third sex.") See *Olbie*, in *Oeuvres complètes*, vol. 5, p. 211. Transl. Evelyn Forget, as amended by KO.

favor, by "allowing" them, through the fruits of their husband's labor, to become gracious, sweet, and docile housewives, some articulate working women objected fiercely. These women workers never accepted uncritically the male political economists' notion that marriage to a male breadwinner and domesticity, with the concomitant legal subordination it entailed – and no escape through divorce – was the best solution to *their* needs. Even before the French Revolution, as we have seen, they had begun to speak out publicly in defense of their "right to work." They recognized that earning their own money, becoming self-supporting, was the key to their independence – and that this newfangled "political" economy, with its conventional ideas about marriage and male breadwinners, had the potential to thrust them to the margins of the emerging economic world and lock them into irremediable dependence.

When did nineteenth-century working-class women, who were no longer organized in corporate (or guild) settings, begin to insist on economic independence (from husbands and fathers) and to use the language of rights (and equal pay) with regard to the opportunities opened to them by employment? Sullerot has claimed that "Marie-Pauline's" article, "Que la femme doit travailler," in *La Voix des Femmes*, n° 31 (23 April 1848) marked "the first time in the history of women that work was viewed as an instrument of liberation and no longer as the malediction of the poor."[44] In fact, though, this insight antedated Marie-Pauline, having emerged already during the summer of 1832, when a cluster of young, literate, and mostly single women workers associated with the Saint-Simonians founded the periodical (1832–1834) variously known as *La Femme libre*, *l'Apostolat des Femmes*, and finally the *Tribune des Femmes*. Refusing to use the patronymic, they signed their articles only with their first names, arguing in print – against the theses of the Saint-Simonian men – that economic independence (not the sexual liberation proposed by Prosper Enfantin) was the very foundation for women's moral and legal independence, and (adding a Fourierist element) that cross-class "association" among women held the key to female freedom.

Juxtaposing the very current language of liberty and slavery (the British Parliament having just decreed the emancipation of their colonial slaves),

---

[44] See Sullerot's article, "Journaux féminins et luttes ouvrières, 1848–1849," in *La Presse ouvrière, 1819–1850*, ed. Jacques Godechot (Paris: Société d'histoire de la Révolution de 1848, 1966), p. 109. For further discussion of the issue of women's work in 1848, see especially Jules Tixerant, *Le Féminisme à l'époque de 1848 dans l'ordre politique et dans l'ordre économique* (Paris: Giard & Brière, 1908), Part II, and Claire Goldberg Moses, *French Feminism in the Nineteenth Century* (Albany: SUNY Press, 1984), p. 83.

the writers in the *Tribune* objected to men's insistence that all women must marry to find economic sustenance. To deny women the means to earn an honest living, they argued, only promoted prostitution, not solely outside of marriage but also within it.[45] In describing women of every social class as effectively men's slaves, "Marie-Reine" [Reine Guindorf] called them "*subalternisées*" in relation to education, advanced knowledge (science), the marriage laws that effectively dispossessed wives of property, and – most importantly – the fact that in the economic sector men monopolized all the well-paying jobs. She envisioned women having access to all positions, prepared by a "thorough and serious education," and that then "man would no longer regard his wife as his *property*, his *thing*" (her emphasis). Then the laws would allow women as well as men to dispose of their goods: "we could embrace any profession that suited us, and without being obliged to get a husband's permission." The most immediate goal, however, was "a complete reform in the education of women."[46] "As long as a man provides us our material needs," Marie-Reine continued in a subsequent article, "he can also demand that in exchange we submit to whatever he desires, and it is very difficult to speak freely when a woman does not have the means to live independently."[47] These young working women also demanded the legalization of divorce, a demand that was subsequently reiterated by the flamboyant novelist, travel writer, and social critic Flora Tristan in her 1837 petition to the Assembly.[48] A few even

---

[45] The Saint-Simonian literature abounds with this comparison: see "On Prostitution," by Christine-Sophie, *Apostolat des femmes*, 1:4 (1832), and Claire Démar, *Ma Loi d'Avenir* (1833), published in 1834 by Suzanne Voilquin; republished in Claire Démar, *Textes sur l'affranchissement des femmes (1832–1833)* (Paris: Payot, 1976), pp. 59–94; as translated in Claire G. Moses & Leslie Rabine, *Feminism, Socialism, and French Romanticism* (Bloomington: Indiana University Press, 1993), pp. 288–289, 184, and 203 respectively. The assertion that marriage as a arbitrary means of support for women was simply a legal form of prostitution dates back at least to Daniel Defoe in 1727 and reappears in Mary Wollstonecraft's *Vindication of the Rights of Woman* in 1792. Significantly, George Sand also developed this comparison in her novel *Lélia* (1833); see the English translation of *Lélia* by Marie Espinosa (Bloomington: Indiana University Press, 1978), p. 100.

[46] "Marie-Reine," "Réponse à quelques questions qui nous ont été faites," *Apostolat des Femmes/Tribune des Femmes*, I:111–115; quotes, 113–114.

[47] "Marie-Reine," "Aux femmes," *Tribune des Femmes*, I:201–205, as translated in Moses & Rabine, *Feminism, Socialism, and French Romanticism*, p. 315.

[48] Flora Tristan, *Pétition pour le rétablissement du divorce à Messieurs les députés, le 20 décembre 1837* (Paris: Impr. de Mme Huzzard, 1838); translated in *Early French Feminisms 1830–1940: A Passion for Liberty*, ed. Felicia Gordon & Máire Cross (Cheltenham, UK: Edward Elgar, 1996). pp. 44–46. A petition in favor of divorce also appears in *La Gazette des Femmes*, 1:2 (August 1836). Recent studies of Flora Tristan include Máire Cross & Tim Gray, *The Feminism of Flora Tristan* (Oxford: Berg, 1992), and Susan Grogan, *Flora Tristan: Life Stories* (London & New York: Routledge, 1998).

insisted that women must take full economic responsibility for their own lives and those of their children.[49]

Other women, who may or may not have been associated with the Saint-Simonians, took up this radical line of reasoning. In 1834 a certain Madame E. A. C. [Casaubon] called for a "new social contract" between women and men and in her second published work of that year, *La femme est la famille*, not only opposed women's subordination in marriage but also asserted that a child should bear his or her mother's last name and argued for state subsidies to mothers (a demand that feminists would frequently reiterate during the Third Republic). Dignity and chastity would become women's mark of superiority. In concluding, she appealed to women to demand their full civil and political rights.[50] Zoé Gatti de Gamond, a Belgian francophone feminist who had become a strong supporter of Fourier's system of association and planned community, squarely blamed women's poverty (and, implicitly, the male-dominated sociopolitical order) for all their ills:[51]

> The most direct cause of women's misfortune is poverty; demanding their freedom means above all demanding reform in the economy of society which will eradicate poverty and give everyone education, a minimum standard of living, and the right to work. It is not only that class called "women of the people" for whom the major source of all their misfortunes is poverty, but rather women of all classes.
>
> From that comes the subjection of women, their narrow dependence on men, and their reduction to a negative influence. Men have thus materialized love, perverted the angelic nature of women, and created a being who submits to their caprices, their desires – a domesticated animal shaped to their pleasures and to their needs.

Other writers argued that to constrict women's opportunities for paid labor by laws that did not apply equally to men's labor was to put working women at great disadvantage.

Moreover, the Saint-Simonian women postulated (well before Tristan, much less Marx and Engels) that the fate of women was inextricably linked with that of the proletariat.[52] In fact, one of them, "Jeanne-Désirée"

---

[49] See Moses, *French Feminism*, chapter 4.

[50] Mme E. A. C[asaubon], *Le Nouveau contrat social, ou place à la femme* (Paris: Dupuy, 1834); and E. A. Casaubon, *La Femme est la famille* (Paris: chez Gautier, 1834).

[51] Zoé Gatti de Gamond, *Fourier et son système* (Paris: Capelle, 1841–1842), pp. 247–266; transl. as published in Bonnie G. Smith, *Changing Lives: Women in European History since 1700* (Lexington: D. C. Heath, 1989), p. 174.

[52] Moses, *French Feminism*, chapter 4, and Moses & Rabine, *Feminism, Socialism, and French Romanticism*.

(Désirée Veret), insisted already in 1832 that "only by emancipating women will we emancipate the worker."[53] The right to associate, to band together in collectives, became a key demand of the editors of the *Tribune des Femmes*. In her treatise *L'Union ouvrière* (1844), Flora Tristan reiterated the linked causes of women and the proletariat, advocating an umbrella organization of workers to press for the "right to work and to organize."[54]

Obviously, the term "right to work" not only had various meanings when articulated by men, but right up to 1848 it held significantly different connotations for women, who had to continually reassert their right to work for pay, in addition to contesting the abysmal conditions in which they labored.[55] In fact, the specter of prostitution hung over the heads of many poor single women as well as wives who could not find employment, were abysmally paid, or who lost their jobs or were laid off due to seasonal employment as existed in the garment-making industries.

It is with reference to these debates of the 1830s that we need to reexamine the controversy in the 1840s over the governmental proposal to require that women workers as well as men hold the workers' *livret*, in which a worker's employment record and satisfactory (or unsatisfactory) performance could be logged by employers. The language of the original revolutionary legislation on the *livret* made it perfectly clear that only male workers were covered.[56] In 1841 Baron Charles Dupin put forward a proposal for the regulation of labor in the Chamber of Peers that included a measure to strengthen the laws on the *livret* and apply them to workers of both sexes. Articulate workingmen protested that extension to women was wholly unacceptable and, moreover, that they considered the *livret* an objectionable restraint on their own freedom. Dupin's measure was never enacted at the national level, but in 1844 the mayor of the Croix-Rousse

---

[53] See Jeanne-Désirée [Veret; later Gay]'s article, "Improvement of the Household . . . ," *Tribune des femmes*, I (1832), 36–39; quote, 36, as translated in Moses & Rabine, p. 289.

[54] Flora Tristan, *L'Union ouvrière* (3rd ed., 1844). For an English translation, see *The Workers' Union*, transl. and introd. by Beverly Livingston (Urbana: University of Illinois Press, 1983), p. 54: "For the worker, the right to live is the right to *work*, the only right that can give him the possibility of eating, and thus, of living. . . . This first right has yet to be proclaimed." See Hélène Brion, *Une méconnue, Flora Tristan; la vraie fondatrice de l'Internationale* (Épône: Société d'Édition et de Librairie de l' « Avenir Social », 1919).

[55] See William H. Sewell, Jr., *Work and Revolution in France: The Language of Labor From the Old Regime to 1848* (Cambridge, UK: Cambridge University Press, 1980). Remarkably, "women" and "women's work" do not appear in Sewell's index, nor is there an entry for Flora Tristan. The language of labor analyzed by Sewall is exclusively that of male labor. For a rejoinder, see Coffin, *Politics of Women's Work*.

[56] The text of the regulations can be consulted in Léopold Malepeyre, ed. *Code des ouvriers, ou Recueil méthodique des lois et réglemens concernant les ouvriers, chefs d'atelier, contremaîtres, compagnons et apprentis* (Paris, 1833), Title III, art. 18, on p. 6.

district of Lyon did order that all workers, including women and children, carry the *livret*.[57] This act provoked a surge of discussion of the status of women workers relative to their male colleagues and ultimately resulted in a full-fledged debate on women and work in the Chamber of Peers, just days before the outbreak of the February Revolution in 1848.[58] To require that women workers carry *livrets* was, in effect, to legitimate their status as paid workers, which was exactly what the male labor leaders did not want.

The dispute over *livrets* remained alive and well in the 1850s. As historian Whitney Walton has pointed out, in the Lorraine (in northeastern France), women hand embroiderers (working by the piece at home) resisted officials' efforts to require them to carry the *livret*, as well as merchant manufacturers' efforts to entice them to use embroidery frames; these women appeared to take their right to work for granted and they staunchly defended their right to control the conditions under which they labored.[59] Many facets of this controversy (and others) require further investigation from the standpoint of gender politics.

In the first half of the nineteenth century, though, women's demands for acknowledgment of their right to work did not necessarily imply their

---

[57] On the debate over the *livret* in Lyon, see Laura S. Struminger [Schor], "Les Canutes: Women Workers in the Lyonnais Silk Industry, 1835–48" (Ph.D. dissertation, University of Rochester, 1973), pp. 119–122; but see also Struminger's *Women and the Making of the Working Class, Lyon, 1830–1970* (Toronto & St. Albans, VT: Eden Press, 1979).

[58] A new beginning has been made by Judith DeGroat in her paper, "Representative of Her Class: Images of Working Women in the July Monarchy," paper given to the Society for French Historical Studies, March 17–19, 1988, University of South Carolina. See also DeGroat, "The Public Nature of Women's Work: Definitions and Debates during the Revolution of 1848," *French Historical Studies*, 20:1 (Winter 1997), 31–47. Earlier analyses include Louis Devance, "Femme, famille, travail et morale sexuelle dans l'idéologie de 1848," *Romantisme*, nᵒˢ 13–14 (1976), 79–103; Moses, *French Feminism in the Nineteenth Century*, chapter 6; Joan W. Scott, "'L'Ouvrière! mot impie, sordide . . .': Women Workers in the Discourse of French Political Economy (1840–1860)," in *The Historical Meanings of Work*, ed. Patrick Joyce (Cambridge, UK & New York: Cambridge University Press), pp. 119–142, plus notes, pp. 282–285. Also see S. Joan Moon, "Woman as Agent of Social Change: Woman's Rights during the Second French Republic," in *Views of Women's Lives in Western Tradition*, ed. Frances R. Keller (Lewiston, NY: Edwin Mellen, 1990), pp. 323–359; and esp. Michèle Riot-Sarcey, *La Démocratie à l'épreuve des femmes* (Paris: Albin Michel, 1994); Maïté Bouyssy & Christine Fauré, "En 1848, à Paris," in *Encyclopedie politique et historique des femmes*, ed. Christine Fauré (Paris: Presses Universitaires de France, 1997), pp. 341–360. See also Alice Primi, *Femmes de progrès: Françaises et Allemandes engagées dans leur siècle 1848–1870* (Rennes: Presses Universitaires de Rennes, 2010), chapter 1. Other articles on this period focus more specifically on the women's quest for political rights, as for example, those of Laura Struminger Schor.

[59] See Whitney Walton, "Women Workers 'Lay Down the Law': The Crisis of Embroidery Production in Nineteenth-Century Lorraine," *Proceedings of the Western Society for French History, 1985*, ed. William Roosen, vol. 13 (Flagstaff, AZ, 1986), pp. 196–204. See also Walton, "Working Women, Gender, and Industrialization in Nineteenth-Century France: The Case of Lorraine Embroidery Manufacturing," *Journal of Women's History*, 2:2 (Fall 1990), 42–65; also repr. in Hafter, ed., *European Women and Industrial Craft* (cited in n. 20).

support of the idea that women and men should do the same work, nor that they should occupy the same work spaces. Indeed, French working women and sympathetic male reformers continued to insist on the necessity of restoring a regulated sexual division of labor within the workplace. As in the eighteenth century, women workers enunciated their claims for the right to work in defense of their already extant economic positions against male encroachment. This remarkable fact has been overlooked by many twentieth-century economic and labor historians, due to their overriding preoccupation (until recently) with men's work and their resistance to the notion that, for women, "separate" could ever be equal.[60] In 1848, however, French working men, faced with a huge economic crisis and severe unemployment, shifted their arguments concerning the right to work; instead of independence, they invoked (as in the 1790s) a societal or government obligation either to provide them with jobs or, alternatively, with other means of subsistence.[61] No longer were their arguments about freedom from restraint (in the vein of classical liberalism), but rather for government intervention to provide more favorable restraints on labor conditions as well as entitlements. In response, the new provisional government initially organized national workshops – for unemployed male workers – as though they were the only workers who counted.

Meanwhile, demands for association and the right to organize labor, as well as calls for government intervention on behalf of workers of both sexes featured in the appeals of women during the 1848 Revolution. In their newspaper *La Voix des Femmes* (which published from late March into early June 1848) these women not only demanded full political rights (see Chapter 2) but they also called for "government action to guarantee women's independence through work" (including employment by the state in national workshops for the unemployed and, again, the protection of women's trades against invasion by men). Indeed, their demands went considerably further: they called for the establishment of day-care centers for working-class families, the construction of apartment houses with central kitchens, central heat, central gardens, and reading rooms, mutually funded medical care and midwifery expenses for women, and a vocational school for the daughters of residents.[62] In short, theirs was a

---

[60] See the essays in *Rethinking Labor History: Essays on Discourse and Class Analysis* (Urbana: University of Illinois Press, 1993), ed. Lenard Berlanstein, and *Gender and Class in Modern Europe*, ed. Laura L. Frader & Sonya O. Rose (Ithaca, NY: Cornell University Press, 1996).

[61] See Jaccard, *Histoire social du travail*, chapter 5, "Chômage et droit au travail."

[62] Quote from the introduction to Part III, *WFF*, vol. 1, pp. 233–240. The petition that lays out this broad agenda is "Aux membres de la Commission du Gouvernement, pour l'organisation des

comprehensive economic development program that fully took family and household concerns into account. Not only that, but these women advocated what S. Joan Moon has qualified as the "'domestication' of the public sphere," an argument which was subsequently spun out by Jeanne Deroin in her 1849 articles on "Woman's Mission." Deroin even redefined the state as a "badly managed *'grand ménage'* [large household] requiring women's housewifely skills of order, economy, and administration."[63] Women would thus apply their wifely and motherly skills as well as their domestic skills to the administration of the state. They envisioned a "motherly state," an idea that would be further developed by Hubertine Auclert in the 1880s.

Already on the second of March (just a week following the change of regime) a group of Parisian women workers presented a petition to Louis Blanc, the president of the new revolutionary republic's commission on the organization of labor, calling for women delegates to the commission, the posting of registers where unemployed women could sign up for jobs, national restaurants and other agencies where women could work and begin the process of association.[64] The former Saint-Simonienne Désirée Veret (now known as Désirée Gay) called for civil liberty for women and government guarantees of their independence through work. She confronted the economists: "Until now the economists have only been preoccupied by production and the distribution of wealth, and not at all with the economy of details [domestic economy] whose secrets only woman possesses, and which hold the secret of domestic wellbeing and comfort for many families."[65] In early April, Gay announced a series of meetings on women's work, where women could come to express their views; the findings would be submitted to the Luxembourg Commission.[66] She then became the head of a women's *atelier*, after complaining that women, not men, should administer these government-sponsored national workshops for women, the intent of which was to ease the unemployment crisis. If, as historian Michèle Riot-Sarcey has pointed out, the vote was the keystone in the women's demands of 1848 (discussed in Chapter 2), then "work and

travailleurs," signed by E. Lemonnier, C. Laporte, and Suzanne Voilquin, published in *La Voix des Femmes*, n° 15 (4 April 1848).

[63] Moon, "Woman as Agent of Social Change"in *Views of Women's Lives in Western Tradition*, ed. Keller, pp. 323–359; quote, p. 327. See also S. Joan Moon, "Feminism and Socialism: The Utopian Synthesis of Flora Tristan," in *Socialist Women*, ed. Marilyn J. Boxer & Jean H. Quataert (New York: Elsevier, 1978), pp. 19–50.

[64] This petition appeared in *La Voix des Femmes*, n° 2 (22 March 1848), 2.

[65] Désirée Gay, "Nos principes," *La Voix des Femmes*, n° 10 (30 March 1848), lead article.

[66] Désirée Gay, "Tenir ce qu'on promet," *La Voix des Femmes*, n° 13 (2 April 1848).

instruction were its pillars."[67] The organizers of a Society for the Emancipation of Women, which included Jenny P. d'Héricourt, drew up a petition to the government calling for the establishment of schools for working women as well as a well-capitalized workshop with a *crèche* and two schools nearby so that employed mothers could still be near their children.[68] Other projects emerged, such as Suzanne Voilquin's plea that midwives become government employees so that they could make an honest living, and efforts to organize women teachers and domestic servants as well as women in the garment trades. These women argued more from principle than by embarking on a full-fledged investigation of the terrible working conditions that confronted both women and men in the economic sector – extremely long and taxing working hours, low pay, sexual harassment on the job and enroute to work and back. Much of this misery had already been fully documented by male political and social economists, but the women of *La Voix des Femmes* gave it an entirely different spin – a gendered spin.

In the continuing economic crisis that exacerbated the revolutions of 1848 and the resulting political turbulence, opponents of women's material and moral emancipation branded as wickedly anti-family these eminently practical efforts to solve real problems. To be sure, many of the feminists of that era were socialists, in the sense of seeking social, rather than individual, solutions to these severe problems. But their enemies considered them dangerously socialist, if not indeed communist, and in either case a threat to "private" property, and they would succeed in stirring up public fear that would force the newly elected government to enact repressive measures – which it did in June 1848, with the abrupt closing of the national workshops and dissolution of women's workshops and clubs, accompanied by severe restrictions on the press.

By later 1849 and early 1850 the efforts of Jeanne Deroin and Pauline Roland (along with a number of others) to organize a vast, mixed-sex association of workers' associations offering workers the "right to live" earned them not only the suspicion of the state, but also arrest, trial for political conspiracy, conviction, and six-month prison terms, ostensibly for violating the association laws. Deroin subsequently emigrated to England,

---

[67] Michèle Riot-Sarcey, "Émancipation des femmes, 1848," *Genèses*, n° 7 (March 1992): 194–200; quote 196.

[68] Société pour l'Émancipation des Femmes. *Lettre de pétition. Manifeste. Règles*, signed by Madame Longuevilly, president, and J. P. d'Héricourt, secretary. Archives Nationales, BB^{30} 307, #6802 (Petitions to the Provisional Government, 1848). Reproduced by Riot-Sarcey, in "Émancipation des femmes, 1848," cited in n. 67, 197–200.

while Roland, rearrested and sent to Algeria, died enroute back to France.[69] Désirée Gay left France for neighboring Belgium. Thus did repressive state action decapitate the French women's movement for economic as well as civil and political rights. But the arguments these women put forward did not die with the suppression of their activism, as we will see.

Rethinking the Sexual Division of Labor in the Age of Industrialization

As I have suggested earlier, some nineteenth-century women worker activists in France articulated their firm conviction that women should be entitled not only to employment, but also to monopolize certain positions, in particular the less physically demanding and more detail-conscious positions, even as they called for improved working conditions and a reorganization of production. The range of employments in which women voiced complaints about male encroachment ranged from the postal service and hospital service to hairdressing and ribbon selling. This encroachment by men did not occur, they argued, because such jobs were "public" but because they were relatively lucrative and less strenuous than the more physically demanding "men's work." The women articulated a clear sense of entitlement to such jobs; men, they said, should find employment in "more virile" pursuits. In most areas of employment, as in society at large, all but the most radical critics of French society attempted to maintain a sharp separation of labor along sexual lines, in accordance with the undeniably relative physical strength of women and men.[70] But this separation was not identical with the better-known "public/private" division advocated by some of the liberal political econo-mists, in which women were to occupy a subordinated domestic sphere.

---

[69] See the publications by DeGroat (n. 58), Moon (n. 58, 63), Moses (n. 44), and Riot-Sarcey (n. 58, 67), cited earlier.

[70] A number of nineteenth-century reformers, both male and female, insisted (following J.-B. Say) on the necessity of restoring a regulated sexual division of labor within the workplace itself: see the debates in Constantin Pecqueur, *Économie sociale*, 2 vols. (Paris: Desessart, 1839), vol. 1, pp. 384; Charles Fourier, *Théorie des quatre mouvements*, 2nd ed. (Paris: aux bureaux de « La Phalange », 1841), pp. 220–221. See also Sophie Saint-Amand, *De l'avenir des femmes dans la République* (11 page pamphlet; Paris: Librairie Politique et Litteraire, 1848); the series of editorials on women's work by Désirée Gay in *La Voix des Femmes* (April–June 1848), and in *La Politique des Femmes* (June–August 1848); Ernest Legouvé, *Histoire morale des femmes* (Paris: Gustave Sandré, 1849), p. 429; and Adolphe Guéroult, "Du travail des femmes" (1858) in his *Études de politique et de philosophie religieuse* (Paris: Michel Lévy frères, 1863), pp. 103–104.

It was a far more parallel, complementary construction – separate, complementary, but equivalent spheres of labor in the workplace.

It was also true, though, that as mechanization proceeded, women were beginning to enter a few fields that had historically been dominated by men. The French government had long employed numbers of women in the postal service, for example.[71] Some private employers, led by the publisher Hachette, hired quantities of women to run their railway bookstores.[72] But, a salient characteristic of early trade union activity in France was the effort of some men to consolidate their monopolies of certain skilled occupations – against the intrusion of female competitors.[73] In those rare areas where men and women workers were working in the same sector of production, women's wages ran to roughly half of what a man would get for the same work. In 1843, Flora Tristan quoted a printer who explained to her that it was fair to pay women half as much, "because they go faster than men; they would earn too much if they were paid the same."[74] The results of this line of thinking would begin to bear fruit in the second half of the nineteenth century, as mechanization proceeded and the workers' movement took shape.[75]

Some male craftsmen perceived this wage differential to mean that employers could use the threat of dismissal and replacement by cheaper women workers to undercut any male workers who undertook collective action to defend or better their own position. In a period characterized by cycles of severe unemployment – and French awareness of the much-discussed examples of male displacement from the textile mills in England in the 1840s (chronicled so vividly by Friedrich Engels in his study of the condition of the working class in England, first published in German in 1845, though not in French before 1933) – this threat loomed ominously over male laborers. The fears it evoked would subsequently create a dilemma in attempts to unionize employees of both sexes across a trade; such efforts were constantly hampered by the reality of unequal pay; should the women join, they would have to receive equal pay for equal

---

[71] See Jeanne Bouvier, *Histoire des dames employées dans les postes, télégraphes et téléphones de 1714 à 1929* (Paris: Presses Universitaires de France, 1930), and the book-length study by Susan Bachrach, *Dames Employées: The Feminization of Postal Work in Nineteenth-Century France* (New York: Women in History, no. 8 [Winter 1983]).

[72] See, on women employees at Hachette, Eileen S. DeMarco, *Reading and Riding: Hachette's Railroad Bookstore Network in 19th Century France* (Bethlehem: Lehigh University Press, 2006).

[73] More will be said later on this issue, with reference to the printers' syndicate.

[74] See Flora Tristan, *Union ouvrière* (Paris, 1843); in English as *The Workers' Union*, pp. 92–93.

[75] See Guilbert, *Fonctions des femmes*, pp. 45–49. We now know that in France mechanization and industrialization did not invariably imply large urban "concentrations" of laborers.

work; if they weren't included, the possibility always existed that they might provide scab labor in the event of a strike, rather than standing by the men.[76] To Proudhon's dichotomy between harlot and housewife, economic circumstances added that of "*compagnonne ou concurrente.*" Women's competition for well-paying jobs was a specter that could not be easily erased from working men's brains.

It is also pertinent to inquire as to why the notion of the male as breadwinner, with its accompanying prescription of female domesticity ("public/private," "outside/inside") and the channeling of women's influence and skills into the mother-educator role, appealed to so many people in nineteenth-century France. Why could so many intelligent men – and women as well – so easily endorse August Comte's principle that "Man should provide support for Woman" and that this was "a natural law of the human race"? Why ought women to be "liberated" from all outside work in order to fulfill their moral mission?[77] Why in the eighteenth and nineteenth centuries was there still such receptivity to and reelaboration upon these prescriptive models derived from (and sustained by) the authority of Xenophon, Aristotle, the Old Testament, and the Roman family? Why did such men so vociferously disapprove of the ideas put forward by these pioneering activist women?[78] It seems doubtful that it was entirely attributable to the influence of Rousseau. Nor does it seem sufficient to explain such notions of domesticity for women as simply an epiphenomenon of advancing capitalism, or the product of eighteenth-century liberal bourgeois thinking. It cannot be viewed simply as an imported English notion, confirmed and reinforced in that land by the Poor Laws Amendment Act of 1834.[79]

---

[76] Consequently, unionization in France, once legalized later in the nineteenth century, would progress more smoothly when the women and men in a trade were not in direct competition for the same positions. In the latter case, separate unions for women were far from an uncommon solution. Mixed unions would be organized but never became the norm; when they did exist, it would remain rare to see women in leadership positions. The issue of women in the printers' union would be put to the test in the early twentieth century in a celebrated conflict known to history as the Couriau affair, in which feminists took up the cause of Emma Couriau, a *compositrice* whose husband was thrown out of the Fédération du Livre for allowing his wife to work in printing. This affair will be revisited in my subsequent volume.

[77] The latter notion is put forth by Comte in the preface to his *Catéchisme de la réligion positive* (Paris: l'auteur, 1852), p. 29.

[78] See, for example, the men's objections to women's active participation and especially to their proposing toasts at political banquets in 1848–1849 chronicled by Jacqueline Lalouette, "Les femmes dans les banquets politiques en France (vers 1848)," *Clio: Histoire, Femmes et Sociétés*, n° 14 (2001), 71–91.

[79] See Pat Thane, "Women and the Poor Law in Victorian and Edwardian England," *History Workshop*, n° 6 (Autumn 1978), 29–51. It is indicative of English opinion that in 1867 even the

It seems more likely that such models endured because they appealed to some deeper current in a psychology of masculinity (and femininity) that cut across social classes. Even the renowned press lord Émile de Girardin (who held many otherwise radical ideas and also had a gifted literary wife) supported this vision, as Pauline Roland (herself a single mother) indicated in her 1851 rebuttal, "Has woman the right to Freedom? A simple question." According to Roland, Girardin had stated in print (echoing the political economists) that "the first and supreme function of a mother is to bring into the world healthy, strong and robust children, to nourish and educate them. It is therefore up to men to work, to the woman to look after the household." She retorted with her own question: "Has woman her own life or is her life a mere appendix of man's life?" And she made the point, later reiterated by Juliette Lamber[t] Lamessine (later known as Juliette Adam), that mothering does not "take a whole lifetime," and further, that "many women have no children."[80] Roland then accused the renowned editor of wanting to turn women into baby-making machines. She then claimed that "woman is a citizen by right, if not in fact," and "is entitled to work as is Man, and to have productive, independent employment which will emancipate her from all dependence."[81] We need to understand the psychological appeal to men of the model itself even as we examine rejoinders by women who aspired to economic independence.

Surely it was to this ostensibly bourgeois status as providers, or breadwinners, that the vanguard of working men, mostly artisans, who headed the newly organized urban labor movement in nineteenth-century France clung, as they insisted on the necessity of a family wage for the head of household. In this way, "their" women could stay at home.[82] Such an aspiration incorporated a combination of notions, grounded in strong convictions that a sexual division of labor between home and the world

---

women's rights activist Jessie Boucherett did not question the notion that husbands must support wives; her definition of prosperity for women was when single women could support themselves by working a twelve-hour day and "when the married are not called upon to work at all, beyond their own houses, but are maintained at home by their husbands." See Boucherett, "The Condition of Women in France," *Contemporary Review*, 5:1 (May 1867), 98–113; quote, 99.

[80] Pauline Roland, response to Émile de Girardin, in his publication *Bien-être universel*, sent from Saint-Lazare prison (1850); text 6, pp. 85–91. Quotations as translated in Gordon & Cross (cited in n. 48), pp. 87–88.

[81] Roland, p. 90 in Gordon & Cross.

[82] See Tony Judt, "A Clown in Regal Purple: Social History and the Historians," *History Workshop: A Journal of Socialist Historians*, n° 7 (Spring 1979), 66–94. and my "Response to Tony Judt," in the same journal, n° 10 (Fall 1980), 215. Judt flatly refused to acknowledge that these workers were male chauvinists and patriarchs when it came to considering women's employment.

of productive labor was essential, that "keeping wives" would enhance not only men's comfort and status but that of their wives as well, and would provide a better platform for the upbringing and education of children. In fact, it served as a sign of social promotion – a marker of masculine success, as the workingmen of *L'Atelier* had made clear in 1842.[83]

Historians must not overlook the male-centeredness of the workingmen's vision of this role for women (even as we acknowledge its appeal to many nineteenth-century women, who could thus preserve themselves from what we now refer to as "the double burden"), or the *arrière pensée* that some men saw possibilities for exercising greater control over the women within their households, and might thereby enhance their standing as men among men. Was this aspiration, in fact, becoming a point of male honor in these circles? An affirmation of their manhood? And, for some women, also a point of female honor, or a confirmation of "authentic" womanhood?

Although this vision of domesticity has often been dismissed as "bourgeois" by its critics, a more dispassionate look at its invigoration in French society, in the wake of the Revolution, suggests strongly that its appeal to men may have had as much to do with a redefinition of "manhood" as with social class. Might it be argued that the domestication (and de facto subordination) of women was a primary bonding feature of the newly born "brotherhood" of workingmen? Would such an argument overstate the case? The workingmen of *L'Atelier* would have denied the implication of subordination as they mandated separation of functions (in the context of calls for political rights): "Public functions belong to man; private functions belong to woman – the latter are no less honorable, no less difficult than those functions belonging to man's nature. To refuse woman electoral rights does not make her inferior in any way – it simply submits her to a social necessity that requires a division of functions."[84]

What is certain is that in France the law did not (yet) acknowledge such a mindset. Prior to the nineteenth century it was not a deeply ingrained French tradition (as it had become in England) that husbands should

---

[83] Cf. n. 38. In a penetrating study of the British case, Wally Seccombe likewise pinpoints the skilled artisans as the specific group in which the male breadwinner norm was constructed prior to the Factory Acts; see his article, "Patriarchy Stabilized: The Construction of the Male Breadwinner Wage Norm in Nineteenth Century Britain," *Social History*, 11:1 (January 1986), 53–76. For France, see Laura L. Frader, "Engendering Work and Wages: The French Labor Movement and the Family Wage," in *Gender & Class in Modern Europe*, ed. Laura L. Frader & Sonya O. Rose (Ithaca, NY: Cornell University Press, 1996), pp. 142–164.

[84] *L'Atelier*, "De la souveraineté," 4:5 (February 1844), 67. Transl. KO in *WFF*, vol. 1, doc. 66, pp. 230–231.

provide for wives – or children.[85] French property law as well as custom actually reflected the understanding that both parties would contribute to the expenses of establishing and maintaining a household; hence the pursuit of years of paid work by thousands of young single women to amass capital for a dowry, a factor that Olwen Hufton considers primary in raising the average marriage age for both sexes to the late twenties.[86] Article 212 of the 1804 Civil Code recognized this situation, in providing that "husband and wife owe each other fidelity, support, *and assistance*" (my emphasis). However, this reciprocal proviso was diluted somewhat by Article 214, which stated that the husband was to supply the needs of his wife in accordance with his condition. In contrast to English common law, in which a wife's property became wholly that of her husband, in France community property was established as the dominant marital economic regime. Even so, the Code designated husbands as the sole administrators of marital community property. Yet by retaining as well two alternate systems of marital property, the separation of property regime and the dowry regime, the authors of the Code tacitly acknowledged a wife's economic contribution to the support of the household, and sustained at least a degree of wifely connection to such property.[87] They also preserved the exception for married women who engaged in commerce.[88]

By the 1830s, the experiments of the Saint-Simonians and the consorting of other middle-class intellectuals with skilled artisans and other workers had effectively validated manual labor and the work ethic, as well as the male breadwinner, as essential components of manliness. The men who published *L'Atelier*, and who celebrated the work ethic with such passion, embraced a vision that seemed to be gathering increasing support among the general populace. It was their celebration of the dignity of labor, the

---

[85] Or, as Jessie Boucherett put it in 1867, "In France there is no law to compel a man to maintain his wife." See Boucherett, "The Condition of Women in France," 111. In England, the parish officers could prosecute husbands who did not provide, on the complaint of the wife. In France, "the law affords her no redress, and the infant no protection," 113.

[86] Olwen H. Hufton, "Women, Work, and Marriage in Eighteenth-Century France," in *Marriage and Society: Studies in the Social History of Marriage*, ed. R. B. Outhwaite (London: Europa Publications, 1981; New York: St. Martin's Press, 1982), pp. 186–203; and Hufton, *Poor*, pp. 28–29. See also Hufton's elegant survey, *The Prospect Before Her: A History of Women in Western Europe, 1500–1800* (New York: Alfred A. Knopf, 1996).

[87] Civil Code, Articles 1536 and 1537, and 1540.

[88] Victoria Thompson has underscored the ways in which municipal authorities subsequently succeeded by the later 1860s in disempowering women merchants in the renovated Halles, in an effort to "domesticate" this marketplace and simultaneously discredit the notion of a female breadwinner; see Thompson's article, "Urban Renovation, Moral Regeneration: Domesticating the Halles in Second-Empire Paris," *French Historical Studies*, 20:1 (Winter 1997), 87–109, and her book, The *Virtuous Marketplace* (Baltimore: Johns Hopkins University Press, 2000).

"right" for men to go out to work (and for women to stay at home), that would be embodied in the revolutionary rhetoric of the workers' republic of 1848.[89] Accordingly, the "right" of women to work (and the potential visibility of their unwaged labor in the household) would be rendered problematic, aptly complementing the defeat of their attempts to assert political rights.

How many economically active women were there in mid-nineteenth century France? In the 1850s, following the example of the British, French census takers surveyed for the first time the extent of women's paid labor force participation. But reliable figures were only forthcoming with the censuses of 1866 and thereafter. The 1866 census would reveal that women constituted 30.7 percent of the French labor force. Of 19 million adult women, 24.3 percent were employed; well over half (14 percent of the total) worked in the nonagricultural sector.[90] In fact, it appeared that France had the highest proportion of employed women in the Western world. Some male authorities found this fact deeply troubling. And, despite the loudly trumpeted prescriptions for female domesticity, the rate of women's labor force participation would continue to increase as the century rolled on. According to the authoritative studies by Madeleine Guilbert, between 1870 and 1940, women would fluctuate between 25 and 43 percent of the entire French labor force. The percentage of the female population employed in both agricultural and nonagricultural labor, would rise from 24 percent in 1866 to 38 percent in 1911, peaking at 43 percent in 1921. By

---

[89] See Sewell, Jr., *Work and Revolution in France*, chapter 11. In Sewell's account, the revolution of 1848 is an all-male event; he ignores the gender dimensions of the workers' discourse as well as the campaign for ateliers for women workers. For a corrective, see Joan Wallach Scott, "Men and Women in the Parisian Garment Trades: Discussions of Family and Work in the 1830s and 1840s," in *The Power of the Past: Essays for Eric Hobsbawm*, ed. Pat Thane, Geoffrey Crossick, & Roderick Flood (Cambridge, UK: Cambridge University Press/Maison des Sciences de l'Homme, 1984), 67–93.

[90] Figures from Madeleine Guilbert, "L'Évolution des effectifs du travail féminin en France depuis 1866," *Revue Française du Travail*, 2, n° 18 (September 1947), 754–777; and Guilbert, "Introduction" to her documentary collection, *Les Femmes et l'organisation syndicale avant 1914* (Paris: Éditions du CNRS, 1966). Guilbert has underscored the lack of satisfactory statistics prior to 1866. See also Jean Daric, *L'Activité professionnelle des femmes en France, étude statistique: évolution, comparaisons internationales* (Paris: Presses Universitaires de France, 1947), and Henri Nolleau, "Les Femmes dans la population active de 1856 à 1954," *Économie et Politique: Revue marxiste d'économie*, n° 75 (October 1960), 2–21. These latter two studies are stronger on the twentieth century than on the nineteenth.

A new study by Sylvie Thomas-Buchet, *La Condition juridique des femmes au travail en France au XIXe siècle* (Doctoral thesis, Faculté de Droit et Science Politique, Université de Bourgogne. Lille: Atelier National de Reproduction des Thèses), pp. 10–11, gives the following figures for employed women: 1806, 29.4% of the active population; 1851, 31.5%; 1911, 36.2%. These workers were probably undercounted.

1936, a time of high unemployment, the percentage would only decline to 35 percent, a figure comparable to that for 1906.[91] Clearly, in France, the male breadwinner utopia was just that — a utopia.

In 1855, the French mining engineer turned social investigator, Frédéric Le Play, reacting to the theories of the Saint-Simonians, published the results of an ambitious twenty-year-long study of worker and peasant households all over Europe, hoping to discover the key to social reform that would keep women in their place as men's auxiliaries. He first condemned the principle of equal inheritance for daughters and sons established during the French Revolution. Taking the as yet unreformed English marriage laws as his model, he argued in his treatise, *La Réforme sociale* (1864), that wives should have nothing to do with manufacture, commerce, property, or the professions. He, like Say, Proudhon, Comte and many others, fervently championed separation of spheres and male breadwinners.[92] Le Play did, however, make an effort to calculate the value that women's labor provided to the family economy, but he framed his analysis in terms of two categories of families, those that were "stable" and those that were "disorganized," that is, families "led astray by novelty, scornful of tradition, in revolt against the Ten Commandments and paternal authority."[93]

In fact, few French women could become economically independent individuals or even contribute an equal or proportionate cash share to family sustenance. In France as elsewhere, pay scales for women workers had long been notoriously lower than those for men; capitalized industry

---

[91] Guilbert, "Évolution des effectifs," passim. For comparative figures, see the adjusted statistics in Paul Bairoch, ed., *The Working Population and its Structure*, vol. 1 of *International Historical Statistics*, ed. T. Deldycke, H. Gelders, J.-M. Limbor et al. (Brussels: Université libre de Bruxelles, 1968).

[92] See Frédéric Le Play, *Les Ouvriers européens*, 1st ed. (Paris: Imprimerie Impériale, 1855; 2nd ed., 1879, in 6 vols.); *La Réforme sociale en France, déduite de l'observation comparée des peuples européens*. 2 vols. (Paris: Plon, 1864; 8th ed., 1901); *L'Organisation du travail, selon la coutume des ateliers et la loi du Décalogue* (Tours: Mame; Paris: Dentu, 1870); and *L'Organisation de la famille, selon le vrai modèle signalé par l'histoire de toutes les races et de tous les temps* (Paris: Tequi, 1871). See also the periodical *Ouvriers des Deux Mondes* (published irregularly, 1857–1862; 1875; 1883–1885, 1887–1899, 1900–1913) and the review *La Réforme sociale: Bulletin de la Société d'économie sociale et des Unions de la Paix sociales fondées par P.-F Le Play* (1881–1906) founded by Le Play's followers. An extensive contemporary review of Le Play's books on the family and work is Henri Baudrillart, "La Famille et la loi de succession en France," *Revue des Deux Mondes* (15 April 1872), 827–855.

[93] See the introduction to doc. 67, in *Victorian Women*, transl. from Le Play's *Les Ouvriers européens*, 6: *Les ouvriers de l'occident, populations désorganisées* (2nd ed., 1878). The *Organization of Labor* appeared in English in 1872 in Philadelphia. For other translations from Le Play's work, see *Frederic Le Play: On Family, Work, and Social Change*, transl. & ed. by Catherine Bodard Silver (Chicago: University of Chicago Press, 1982). A recent interpretation is Alan Pitt, "Frédéric Le Play and the Family: Paternalism and Freedom in the French Debates of the 1870s," *French History*, 12:1 (March 1998), 67–89.

simply built on long-standing precedents. As Tilly and Scott have reminded us, most women who would seek employment during the Second Empire and Third Republic did so in the interests of sustaining a family economy, working in traditionally female, poorly paid and often strenuous jobs as agricultural laborers and domestic servants in what by all accounts remained a highly segregated labor force.[94] Domestic service in the households of others, in fact, represented a significant percentage of employed women, and it also contributed to a disproportionate number of unmarried pregnant women, and consequently to high rates of abortion and infanticide.[95]

As was the case in most industrializing countries of Europe, by far the greater proportion of these employed women were young and single, or older and widowed. Even so, France had a greater percentage of women in the labor force who were married with children than comparable countries.[96] It was particularly this category of urban, mostly married female workers who, by farming out their infants in order to work for low pay, contributed to the spectacular growth of the French wet-nursing industry and to the alarming infant mortality rates among newborns in urban industrial centers.[97] These social facts, which male reformers concerned about population growth began to view as national calamities, amplified still further the shrillness of those who opposed the employment of women. In his immensely successful *La Femme* (1860), Michelet condemned outright that most visible of all women workers – the female factory operative.[98]

In 1860, however, an important counterstatement and extension of the argument for women's right to work came from Jenny P. d'Héricourt,

---

[94] Tilly and Scott, *Women, Work, and Family*, Part II.

[95] Theresa M. McBride, *The Domestic Revolution: The Modernisation of Household Service in England and France, 1820–1920* (New York: Holmes & Meier, 1976); for the late nineteenth century and beyond, see Geneviève Fraisse, *Femmes toutes mains: Essai sur le service domestique* (Paris: Seuil, 1979). See also Rachel Ginnis Fuchs & Leslie Page Moch, "Pregnant, Single, and Far From Home: Migrant Women in Nineteenth-Century Paris," *American Historical Review*, 95:4 (October 1990), 1007–1031.

[96] For an early comparative analysis that took into account the higher proportion of working married women in France, see Patricia Branca, "A New Perspective on Women's Work: A Comparative Typology," *Journal of Social History*, 9:2 (Winter 1975), 129–153.

[97] See George Sussman, *Selling Mothers' Milk: The Wet-Nursing Business in France, 1715–1914* (Urbana-Champaign: University of Illinois Press, 1982) and Rachel G. Fuchs, *Abandoned Children: Foundlings and Child Welfare in Nineteenth-Century France* (Albany: SUNY Press, 1984).

[98] Jules Michelet, *La Femme* (Paris: Hachette, 1860), chapter 2, on the *ouvrière*. One should note, however, Joan Scott's critique of the implicit reification of the term *ouvrière* in writing the history of women's work: "Deconstructing Equality-vs-Difference," *Feminist Studies*, 14:1 (Spring 1988), 47. See also her still valuable article, "'L'Ouvrière! mot impie, sordide . . . ': Women Workers in the Discourse of French Political Economy (1840–1860)," in *The Historical Meanings of Work*, ed. Patrick Joyce (Cambridge, UK: Cambridge University Press, 1987).

whom (like Michelet) we met in an earlier chapter. In *La Femme affranchie*, she directly addressed the arguments of Proudhon and Michelet (and indirectly, the liberal political economists). Her rebuttal was forthright and to the point: "To exclude woman from active occupations in order to confine her to the cares of the household," she declared forcefully, "is to attempt an impossibility, to close the way to progress, and to replace woman beneath the yoke of man."[99] Concurrently, Juliette Lamber[t] argued that "work alone has emancipated men; work alone can emancipate women." This young mother countered the ongoing obsession with women in the home: "I maintain that family life does not suffice for the physical, moral, and intellectual activity of woman. The role of broody hen is, no doubt, most respectable, but it is not suited to everyone; nor is it so absorbing as has been represented." Concluding her argument, she challenged the men who opposed women's economic independence but took advantage of their poverty under existing conditions: "opening to women careers in freely chosen and adequately paid work would mean closing the doors of the brothels. Men, are you ready for this?"[100] Obviously the answer was "no"!

Shortly thereafter, Jules Simon, in his influential study, *L'Ouvrière* (1861), which had earlier been serialized in the influential *Revue des Deux Mondes*, argued for barring women altogether from employment in the manufacturing sector, for encouraging marriage, and for raising men's wages so they could actually support their wives and children. He cast the problem in terms of women *replacing* men in the workplace as mechanization proceeded, to the detriment of their families. "If there is one thing Nature clearly teaches us," Simon reiterated, "it is that woman is made to be protected, to live as a girl with her mother, as a wife under the protection and authority of her husband. To tear her away, from childhood on, from this necessary refuge, to impose on her a sort of public life in a workshop, is to wound her in all her instincts, alarm her modesty, deprive her of the sole milieu in which she can be truly happy."[101]

---

[99] Jenny P. d'Héricourt, *A Woman's Philosophy of Woman, or Woman Affranchised: An Answer to Michelet, Proudhon, Girardin, Legouvé, Comte, and Other Modern Innovators* (New York: Carleton, 1864; reprinted Westport, CT: Hyperion Press, 1981), p. 165. Originally published as *La Femme affranchie* (Brussels: A. Lacroix, Van Meeneen et Cie, 1860) [cf. Chapter 4, n. 106].

[100] Juliette Lamber [pseud. Juliette Lambert Lamessine (Adam)], *Idées anti-proudhoniennes sur l'amour, la femme et le mariage*, 2nd ed. (Paris: E. Dentu, 1861); as translated in *WFF*, vol. 1, doc. 96, p. 333.

[101] Jules Simon, *L'Ouvrière* (Paris: Hachette, 1861; 9th ed., 1891). Quote from my translation in *WFF*, vol. 1 (1983), doc. 126. Much of Simon's book appeared in serial form during 1860–1861 in the *Revue des Deux Mondes*. At least one important British woman reformer shared Simon's critical view of women's absence from the household: see Bessie Rayner Parkes's review of *L'Ouvrière* in *The English Woman's Journal*, 8, n° 43 (1 September 1861), 61–69, and her *Essays on Woman's Work* (London: A. Strahan, 1865), pp. 216–222.

Simon did not oppose women's gainful employment per se, but he did oppose their leaving the household for long hours to gain money elsewhere. *Travail à domicile*, or income-generating homework, however, was quite acceptable in his eyes. Such work still encompassed a highly significant sector of small-scale production, focused on garment making, initially done by hand with needle and thread, then mechanized by the introduction of the sewing machine but only partially centralized in factories. According to historian Judith G. Coffin, "The garment industry was one of the largest employers of industrial labor in France and easily the largest employer of women workers. . . . [it] defies characterization as a traditional trade."[102] But even the use of the labor-saving sewing machine provoked controversy, as physicians began to report cases of genital overexcitement among women operatives that set off a different set of alarm bells among working men.[103]

La Femme pauvre, **or the Feminization of Poverty**

These arguments over women's workforce participation, and their claims to the right to work, set the scene for a remarkable development. In May 1858 – the same year in which Proudhon published *De la Justice* and Juliette Lamber[t] Lamessine blasted back at him in her *Idées antiproudhoniennes*, the Imperial Academy of Lyon announced an essay competition on the subject of women's wages and careers. The prize of 1,200 francs would be awarded to the author who undertook:[104]

> to investigate, above all from the moral point of view, and to indicate to governors, administrators, master manufacturers, and private individuals, what would be the best means, the most practical measures, – 1st, to raise the wages of women to the same level as those of men, where the same amount of service is rendered or labor performed; 2ndly, to open new careers to women, and procure for them work which shall replace those employments necessarily taken from them by the competition of men, and the changes in manners and customs.

---

[102] The Parisian garment trades as a locus for women's paid labor have been astutely analyzed by Coffin, *Politics of Women's Work*; quotes, pp. 5–6.

[103] See Karen Offen, "'Powered by a Woman's Foot': A Documentary Introduction to the Sexual Politics of the Sewing Machine in Nineteenth Century France," *Women's Studies International Forum*, 11:2 (March 1988), 93–101.

[104] Knowledge of this competition was not limited to France. It was reported to England by Mrs. Anna Jameson, one of the principal figures in the early British women's rights movement. *The English Woman's Journal* swiftly translated the call for papers and an accompanying newspaper report from *Le Siècle* and published both in its issue of August 1858, pp. 408–413; quote: pp. 408–409.

The architect of this competition was François-Barthélemy Arlès-Dufour (1797–1872), member of the Academy of Lyon, a self-made millionaire and innovative capitalist who had risen in life from an *enfant de troupe* in the Napoleonic armies to become a highly successful silk merchant and one of the founders of the Crédit Lyonnais. Arlès-Dufour came to the support of women's emancipation as a Saint-Simonian and close friend of the charismatic Prosper Enfantin.[105] As is clear from the above statement, Arlès-Dufour confronted the issue of women's employment with a far different agenda than either his fellow Saint-Simonians of the 1830s or the aggressively antifeminist Proudhon.

The prize in the Lyon academy's competition went to Julie-Victoire Daubié (whom we have already met as the first woman to obtain the *baccalauréat* in France), for a *mémoire* that was subsequently published in 1866 as *La Femme pauvre au XIXe siècle* [The Poor Woman in the Nineteenth Century]. Daubié's lengthy study was not strictly about ways to raise wages or to open new careers to women. Instead she launched an empassioned, no-holds barred attack on a socioeconomic system that increasingly privileged men at women's expense. Tying together the issues of education, law, and economics (so often kept separate in the analyses of others), she blamed the depreciation of women's work on inadequate educational possibilities, on the inequities of civil law that left fathers free of any responsibility for the children they fathered outside marriage, and, not least, on the political powerlessness in French society of single women, be they young working women or widows. Further, Daubié pointed an accusing finger at French society's tendency toward concentration, or centralization (as she called it) in cities, of the rural population, and of commercial and industrial facilities in massive, highly capitalized stores and factories. All this, she believed, was detrimental to women's well-being. She also objected to the accompanying pseudo-professionalization of many

---

[105] François Arlès-Dufour (1797–1872) provided significant financial backing for the women's rights movement during the later Second Empire and early Third Republic. He was one of Prosper Enfantin's testamentary executors, and a principal editor of the multivolume *Oeuvres de Saint-Simon et d'Enfantin*. See in particular the tributes by Léon Richer in *L'Avenir des Femmes*, issues of 4 February 1872 and 5 September 1875. On his life and contributions, see the anonymous biography *Arlès-Dufour* (Lyon, 1874); the entry on Arlès-Dufour by J. Baltean in the *Dictionnaire biographique français*; Jean Bouvier, *Le Crédit Lyonnais de 1863 à 1882*. 2 vols. (Paris: S.E.V.P.E.N., 1961), vol. 1, 129–131; and for personal insights, Juliette (Lambert) Adam, *My Literary Life* (London: T. Fisher Unwin, 1904), *passim*. See also Lucien Jeanmichel, *Arlès-Dufour, un Saint-Simonien à Lyon* (Lyon: Éditions lyonnaises d'art et d'histoire, 1993); unfortunately this study says nothing about his role in promoting women's work or in sponsoring Julie-Victoire Daubié. I have not yet consulted the doctoral thesis, "Un homme d'affaires Lyonnais: Arlès-Dufour 1797–1872," by Jacques Canton-Debat, Université de Lyon-II (2000).

occupations, which placed women at a disadvantage. In particular, she deplored the absence of laws to curb sexual harassment of women on the job and in the streets, laws that might insure women more freedom of movement, a point that had repeatedly been raised, though less forcefully, in the 1830s and 1840s.[106] Daubie's volumes were loaded with facts and figures in support of her arguments.

Refuting the claims of the Proudhons, Comtes, Michelets, Simons, and their supporters, Daubié – like her counterparts Jenny P. d'Héricourt and Juliette Lamber[t] – asserted (once again) that women had a *right* to gainful employment. In line with the arguments of earlier defenders of women's right to work, she cast her analysis in terms of men replacing women in "their" time-honored jobs – and she urged reforms that would permit women to become economically independent.[107] Daubié, too, argued for separate spheres, for a certain sexual division of labor – but, again, in her vision the proper breakdown was not "public/private," with private equated with domestic (and subordinate to the "public"), but rather along the lines of separate but equitable functions for each sex, according to physical capabilities, in the arena of "productive" (i.e., paid) labor.

Reviewing *La Femme pauvre* in the *Journal des Économistes*, Eugène Véron commended the many qualities of the book. But he thought that Daubié's tone, irony, and her vehemence undermined the authority of her argument. Undoubtedly, he would have preferred a more dispassionate analysis, more in keeping with established norms – comfortable norms – of scholarly writing in political economy. Though Véron did not say it in so many words, his review clearly implied that Julie Daubié's book violated the masculine scientific norms of abstraction, of distancing; in his view, it was the product of an emotionally engaged writer – a woman writer fired by a passionate commitment to the betterment of her sex.[108] Which was exactly the case.

Daubié's vehemence seems more understandable when we consider what she had to say. Her multifaceted analysis of what we would now call "the feminization of poverty" came as a shocking revelation in the heyday

---

[106] Julie-Victoire Daubié, *La Femme pauvre* (Paris: Guillaumin, 1866), pp. 1–6. A revised and expanded second edition in three volumes appeared in 1869–1870; this latter edition was republished in 1992–1993 by Éditions côté-femmes in Paris. See also the excerpts from the 1866 edition in English transl. in *WFF*, vol. 1, doc. 127.

[107] Daubié, *Femme pauvre*, pp. 1–6.

[108] See Eugène Véron, in *Journal des Économistes*, 15 August 1867, 300–305, and the earlier review by Paul Lacombe (a friend of Daubié's) in *Le Temps*, 18 July 1866.

of Second Empire prosperity.[109] Her call for equal pay for equal work raised eyebrows.[110] No less shocking to contemporaries was the blame she placed for this phenomenon on the Catholic Church. From the plight of the *institutrices*, crowded out of teaching by the competition of the burgeoning numbers of women joining religious orders, to the seam-stresses displaced and undercut economically both by cheaper convent labor and by prison labor (organized and supervised by nuns), to the revelations of the women who walked the streets in hunger and quiet desperation, Daubié drew a remorseless portrait of urban women's misery. To those who opposed the employment of women, especially married women, in mechanized industry located outside the household, she articulated a challenge of major magnitude. All these issues would remain on the table through the end of the Second Empire, and many would be revisited – and acted upon – by women during the Paris Commune and well into the Third Republic.

Sexual Conflict in the Printing Industry

Daubié's arguments for women's right to work and equal pay arrived at a time when women's employment had again become the subject of great anxiety and protest in the emergent workingmen's movement, particularly among men in the printing trades whose craft was threatened by mech-anization and stagnating pay. To many of them, the possibility of women earning good money – and asserting their right to economic independence by (inadvertently) displacing male breadwinners – seemed abhorrent.

In the early 1860s controversy erupted in Paris over the hiring of women by a major printing firm, that of Paul Dupont, in its annex in Clichy. Paul Dupont was a prominent political figure, a deputy in the Corps Législatif, and a self-styled philanthropist, who insisted he was trying to do right by poor women. However, the male typographers thought otherwise; they petitioned the emperor in an effort to demand a long-overdue increase in the rates at which they were paid and to object, in particular, to the

---

[109] Diana Pearce, a twentieth-century social analyst, coined the term "feminization of poverty." In fact poverty had been feminized for many centuries, as the remarks of Gatti de Gamond (cited in n. 51) and the scholarly investigations of Olwen Hufton and others make abundantly clear.

[110] Daubié's mentor, Arlès-Dufour, seemed optimistic in the mid-1860s that the Empress Eugénie would support a proposal for paying "equal salaries for equal services," or "equal pay for equal work." See his two letters to Daubié, dated 31 July 1865 and 4 June 1866, in Raymonde Bulger, *Lettres à Julie Victoire Daubié (1824–1874): La première bachelière de France et son temps* (New York: Peter Lang, 1992), pp. 91–99.

employers' threat of competition from women, effectively making them *"concurrentes"* or rivals. One of their leaders, a typographer named Coutant, alleged that employers in the printing business were threatening to hire women (and children) as compositors in order to drive down men's wages, which were already too low.[111] "What is certain is that woman is a terrible instrument to wield against man, who can never lower his earnings to that of woman – who has the ultimate resource, if she is not 'honest' or does not wish to die of hunger, to supplement her salary by nocturnal promenades. Ah, Gutenberg, what would you think of your art fallen to the distaff side and supported by prostitution."[112] To be sure, there were other factors at work as well – the introduction of mechanization to the printing industry and its threat to skilled typesetters and compositors, price wars between Parisian and provincial print shops, and the threat of the notion of the law of supply and demand to craftsmen organized in corporate groups that controlled access to their trade. Employers who refused to increase the men's pay and then hired women at substandard rates seemed, to the typesetters, to be the last straw!

The three thousand workingmen employed in the Parisian printing trades were already, without doubt, the most vociferous of all opponents of women's waged labor. Moreover, they considered the printing shop to be a bastion of masculinity. Their attitude cannot be attributed solely to the fact that the antifeminist Proudhon, who was at that time without question the most influential philosopher of working-class activism, happened to be a printer; it is more likely that his own prejudices concerning women's place had been reinforced by the fact that he worked in the printing trades. There was, according to Coutant, a long-standing tradition among French typographers that if any woman entered the *atelier*, the men would stop working.[113] Women, the latter alleged, would agree that if the male breadwinner's wages would go up, their own situation as wives and mothers would also improve; furthermore, he agreed with Daubié that for women who needed work, women's sales positions in *mercerie* (needles, thread, pins, buttons, and other sewing supplies) and novelties should be restored to them and the young men who held such

---

[111] See Coutant, *Du salaire des ouvriers compositeurs* (Paris: Libraire Poulet-Malassis, 1861), in Hoover Archives, Nicolaevsky Collection, Box 705, folder 2: "Lettres à l'Empereur."

[112] Coutant, *Du salaire des ouvriers compositeurs*, p. 23. In French: "tombé en quenouille et soutenu par la prostitution."

[113] Louis Leroy, ouvrier typographe compositeur, "Comment se pose la question," in *Patrons et ouvriers typographes* (Paris: Librairie Poulet-Malassis, 1862), 3rd ed., p. 5. The articles in this brochure all date from February 1862. The quotations below from Coutant appear on pp. 5–6.

jobs redirected toward more "virile" employment. Men, he insisted, are not women's enemies, but "we say that it is up to the father and the husband to be the protectors of daughters and wives, not up to the employers." This threat is really directed against the organization of labor, he insisted. Coutant threatened to take the typographers' case to the Ministry of the Interior, or the Conseil d'État, or to invoke the articles (414, 415, and 416) of the Penal Code that forbade coalitions (of employers in this case), but also to demand that these articles be revised to allow coalitions of workers as well. He also called for a clause in the future wage agreement that would forbid the hiring of women as *compositrices*. Another typographer, Berthelemy, qualified all such moves to employ women (and children) in manufacturing as "immoral and antisocial," and a serious threat to the welfare of the race.[114] The mothers (and future mothers) of the workers, he added, were every bit as important as the mothers of the bourgeoisie. Why should women desert their most important tasks in the household, the welfare of their children, in order to compete for jobs with their husbands and their fathers? Dupont, on the other hand, alleged that creating jobs for women in the printing trades was a philanthropic gesture, destined to aid poor women who had no other means of support.

The "woman question" was central, not only to these debates but also to the typographers' subsequent actions. The hiring of women had already begun in several Parisian print shops, not only at Dupont's Clichy annex but also in the print shop that served the archdiocese of Paris. In March 1862, a group of printers employed in the large Dupont printing plant (rue de Grenelle) organized a strike to protest the employment of women as compositors at the Clichy annex, even though their own rate base of pay had by this time been augmented, by agreement with the employers, to a higher sum per thousand letters.

In May 1862, the Imperial government prosecuted these striking printers in the sixth correctional tribunal for illegally forming a coalition (i.e., unionization), then forbidden under the association laws of the Second Empire. The trial itself became a public forum for debating women's work. The barrister defending them was Maître Armand Lévy who argued that the typographers wanted to feed their wives, not be fed by them. One worker reasoned that women learn the trade quicker than young boys and also expressed the workingmen's fear that women would work for less and

---

[114] Berthelemy, ouvrier typographe, "La Femme dans l'imprimerie," in *Patrons et ouvriers typographes*, pp. 15–16.

thereby undermine men's wages.[115] Maître Lévy argued that the men's action was justified in light of the potential threat to their wages posed by the hiring of women, but the court ruled that they had in fact violated the penal code, their coercive action being contrary to industrial and labor freedoms. The ruling did nothing to resolve the underlying issue – the workers' perceived threat to their wages through female competition at lower rates.[116] Or rather, that they would be paid at piece rates – in this case, by the thousand letters – and that women might work faster (and therefore earn more), much as Flora Tristan's source had reported in 1837. The typographers petitioned emperor Napoléon III in early December 1862, demanding a new law on coalitions, but were refused.[117]

The new generation of liberal economists took a different view of the "woman question," one that strayed from that proposed originally by Roederer and J.-B. Say. One commentator on the typographers' case, Jules Delbrück, writing in *L'Économiste français*, came down on the side of women's right to employment. He acknowledged that in the present state of the economy, some women, including married women, had to find paid work; that was a given. He argued not only that women should be enabled to become compositors, but also that their presence would bring better manners to the print shops. He proposed that instead of protesting, the workers should stand up for the principle of "equal pay for equal work" so that the women workers could not undercut them.[118] A second commentator, Henri Baudrillart, also came to the defense of women's right to work in the leading liberal newspaper, *Le Journal des Débats*. Preventing women from working for a living, he argued, was a thousand times worse than breaking machines; in no way would prohibition of their employment result in their return to the family, but rather it would lead to further public disorder and an increase in prostitution. Women's right to earn their own living was, he insisted (thereby endorsing and extending the analysis of d'Héricourt, Lamber, and Daubié), a "natural right."[119] These progressive liberal economists had begun, in fact, to invoke theories of "natural rights" *in favor* of women's right to employment and fair pay. This signaled a "sea change" in French attitudes toward women's employment.

As prosperity had returned to Second Empire France in the later 1850s, men's wages had greatly improved, in contrast to those of women: the

---

[115] From the account in the *Gazette des Tribunaux*, reprinted in *Le Temps*, 10 May 1862.   [116] *Ibid.*
[117] *Le Temps*, 1 December 1862.
[118] Jules Delbrück, "Les femmes et les ateliers d'imprimerie," *L'Économiste français*, 1:12 (10 June 1862), 153–154.
[119] Henri Baudrillart, untitled articles in the *Journal des Débats*, 30 May and 7 June 1862.

English women's rights activist Jessie Boucherett remarked, in a review of Daubie's *La Femme pauvre*, that "in France the increasing prosperity of the working man is not shared by the working woman, and . . . on the contrary, they are gradually sinking into a more and more miserable condition, . . . This deterioration in their state is caused by legislation."[120] This legislation had, for instance, promoted vocational training for boys at the expense of girls, and gave urban wives no legal recourse if and when on payday husbands managed to dissipate their wages on food and alcoholic drink before returning home to their families (and sometimes compounding the misery by beating their wives and children).

In response to this growing disparity in wages, a small group of older progressive women, earlier associated with the Saint-Simonian and Fourierist movements and also veterans of 1848, took practical steps to address the problem of women's lack of lucrative skills and opportunities for well-paying jobs. They provided young single women with privately sponsored opportunities for substantive formal vocational instruction, thereby countering abuses in extant apprenticeship programs. These schools (part of a European-wide phenomenon that would extend as far away as Russia) would teach young women skills that would prepare their graduates for a *métier* that would allow them to become self-supporting, at least until they married.[121] One such school opened in Lyon in 1857 and several more opened in Paris during the 1860s; their founders were women interested in practical solutions such as Elisa Lemonnier, who established the *Société pour l'Enseignement professionnel des Femmes* [Society for the Professional Instruction of Women] and Caroline de Barrau, both of whom championed women's emancipation.[122] In 1868 one of them issued a "how-to" book to assist other interested persons in founding similar vocational schools.[123] Another such school, the *École Professionnelle de*

---

[120] See Boucherett, "The Condition of Women in France," 98–113, quote, 112–113 (cited, n. 79).

[121] See Karen Offen, *European Feminism, 1750–1950* (Stanford, CA: Stanford University Press, 2000), chapter 5, esp. pp. 122–123, on the general context for founding girls' vocational schools in other European cities, including Berlin, Haarlem, St. Petersburg, and Prague.

[122] On the schools founded by Elisa Lemonnier and the Société pour l'Enseignement professionnel des Femmes, see Charles Lemonnier, *Eliza Lemonnier* (St. Germain: L. Toinon, 1866); Clarisse Coignet, *Biographie de Mme Lemonnier, fondatrice de la Société pour l'Enseignement professionnel des Femmes* (Paris: chez tous les librairies, 1866); Caroline de Barrau, *Elisa Lemonnier, fondatrice de la Société pour l'Enseignement professionnel des Femmes* (Paris, 1868); Eugène de Budé, *Des écoles professionnelles de jeunes filles* (Paris, Geneva, Neuchâtel: Sandoz et Fischbacher, 1879); and Marie Cérati, "Elisa Lemonnier," in *Femmes extraordinaires*, ed. Gilette Ziegler (Paris: Éditions de la Courtille, 1979), pp. 35–84. A comprehensive study of these schools would be very welcome.

[123] Mme Ch. Sauvestre, *Guide pratique pour les écoles professionnelles de jeunes filles* (Paris: L. Hachette, 1868).

Jeunes Filles de Marseille, would open its doors in 1880.[124] An association of employers in the flower-making industry founded a *Société pour l'Assistance paternelle aux Enfants employés dans les Industries des Fleurs et des Plumes*.[125]

The First International Workingmen's Association Condemns Women's Employment and Provokes Angry Responses from Women's Rights Advocates

Controversy over the issue of women working in the Parisian printing trades refused to fade away. A new outburst occurred in 1865, following a banquet sponsored by the printers' mutual aid society.[126] The industrial employment of women was by all accounts becoming even more frequent, thereby raising the level of anxiety among working-class men. One worker set the figures at 3000 printers in Paris, and 180 women compositors (*compositrices*).[127] Fuelled by arguments and figures drawn from the publications by Michelet and Simon, and escalated by Daubié's claims in *La Femme pauvre* for equal pay for equal work, along with job training and new job opportunities, this debate over the employment of women in printing fed into a new eruption of debate on the woman question, a debate that shaped the politics of the newly energized French workers' movement far more than many scholars have seen fit to admit.[128]

This quarrel had a direct effect on French contributions to the debates of the first International Workingmen's Association, established in 1864 in London. Here one finds at least as many echoes of the family-centered views of Michelet, Simon, and Proudhon as of the deterministic and

---

[124] See Phyllis Stock-Morton, "Secularism and Women's Education: The Case of the *École Professionnelle de jeunes filles* of Marseille," *French History*, 10:3 (September 1996), 355–374.

[125] This associational effort is discussed by Marilyn J. Boxer, "Women in Industrial Homework: The Flowermakers of Paris in the Belle Epoque," *French Historical Studies*, 12:3 (Spring 1982), 400–423. It is not clear that this was a woman-inspired initiative, although many young girls and women were employed as flowermakers, a relatively well-paid skill that required a sustained apprenticeship.

[126] See the pamphlets by Edmond About, *La Justice et la liberté dans l'industrie typographique* (Paris: Impr. De J. Claye, 1865), and the response by the typographer Edouard Boutigny, *Du Travail des femmes dans les imprimeries: Réponse à Ed. About et aux journaux L'Opinion nationale, L'Avenir national et Le Temps* (Paris: Jonde, 1865). Boutigny's response squarely links manly dignity with nourishing a wife and family; he blamed speculators and capital for preying on women. Moreover, he argued, the printing workshops were corrupting, insofar as they turned out bad novels, books on syphilis, etc., to which no woman should be exposed.

[127] Boutigny, *Travail des femmes*, pp. 20–21. He was correcting the higher figures put forth by About.

[128] One historian who recognized its importance early on is Marilyn J. Boxer, "Foyer or Factory: Working Class Women in Nineteenth-Century France," *Proceedings of the Western Society for French History*, San Francisco, Nov. 21–23, 1974, 2 (1975), 192–203. For the reprise of this debate in 1879, see Michelle Perrot, "L'Éloge de la ménagère dans le discours des ouvriers français au XIXe siècle," *Romantisme: Revue du Dix-neuvième Siècle*, n° 13–14 (1976), 105–121.

subsequently better-known economic analyses of Karl Marx. At the Association's 1866 congress in Geneva, the Swiss delegate Coullery argued that women must be "emancipated" – emancipated, that is, *from* paid labor and returned to the home, where their development could be completed. French delegates put forth two differing points of view: a thoroughly Proudhonian view represented by Chemalé, Fribourg, and two other workers, and a more liberal, non-interventionist view espoused by Varlin and Bourdon.

At this Geneva congress Chemalé and his group introduced a resolution condemning outright the work of women and children in manufacturing as a major cause of degeneration of the human race and "as one of the most powerful means of demoralization set in motion by the capitalist caste." They called for a full-scale debate on the subject at the following congress. Varlin, of Paris, objected to such a thoroughgoing condemnation of women's work; "to condemn women's work," he argued, "is to ratify charity and to authorize prostitution as well." Fribourg, also from Paris, remarked that widows and orphans ought to be treated as exceptions to the general rule [that women shouldn't work], just as the infirm [men] were excused [from working]. Lawrence, from London, insisted that the work of women and children in industry was a trend in modern industry; condemning it would not change that fact. What workingmen should do, he insisted, "is to protest energetically against such exploitation of woman as is practiced by the capitalist caste." Nevertheless, the congress rejected this attempt to force a class exploitation interpretation. Instead, the delegates endorsed the proposal of Chemalé's group and established a study commission to investigate further the question of women's work.[129]

The following year (1867), in Lausanne, this commission of workingmen produced its report. Invoking the family as "the principal base of the social edifice," the commissioners celebrated paternal authority. "The greatest name on earth is the name of the father; the greatest thing is paternal authority." "[The family] is humanity in miniature. . . . the very source of brotherhood." Woman belonged at the domestic hearth, where

[129] "Compte rendu des débats," Geneva congress, 1866, in *La Première Internationale: Recueil des documents*, ed. Jacques Freymond, I (Geneva: Librairie Droz, 1962); as translated by KO in *WFF*, vol. 1, doc. 130; quotes, pp. 467–468. See also "Compte rendu de J. Card," session of 7 September 1866, in *La Première Internationale*; as transl. in *Victorian Women: A Documentary Account of Women's Lives in Nineteenth-Century England, France, and the United States* (Stanford, CA: Stanford University Press, 1981), doc. 86 (i). This latter account is a compressed version of the same debate. See also J.-J. Blanc, "Congrès ouvrier de Génève," *L'Opinion nationale*, 11 September 1866, who registered the congress's disapproval of women's presence in *ateliers*, and especially in manufacturing.

she could be "the child's first educator, but on the express condition that the father acts as the directing agent." "If the wife of the proletarian is able to become a deputy to the Chamber, the worker's soup may well be inadequately seasoned."[130] As historian Marilyn J. Boxer succinctly summed it up, "any threat to the stability of the traditional patriarchal family encountered Cyclopean resistance."[131]

It was in this same year that the men of the French skilled trades filed their reports for the 1867 Paris Exposition. Jacques Rancière and Patrick Vauday have pointed out that the reports reveal less outright Proudhonism among the workers than might have been expected; instead, they suggest, there is evidence of a definite commitment to a sort of rough parity, an "equality in difference" attitude about the sexual division of labor. But once again this attitude is predicated on women's and men's occupying separate spaces and carrying out different tasks, even in the world of paid labor. Even so, Rancière and Vauday also point to a strong tendency among these workingmen to underscore (along the lines sketched out earlier in the decade by Michelet and Simon) women's "natural vocation" in the home.[132] One thing was certain. Those who wished to emancipate women economically or legally from male authority in the family, or to open access to all professions and careers, could expect little sympathy from the leaders of the French workers' movement who were [now] adamant about raising men's wages to a level that could enable them singlehandedly to support wives and children. Should we be surprised when we recognize that Frédéric Le Play (who, not coincidentally, headed the 1867 Exposition and commissioned the reports) and the *rapporteur* Tartaret, who presented these reports, were both advocates of patriarchal breadwinner solutions?[133]

---

[130] "Rapports lu au Congrès ouvrier réuni du 2 au 8 septembre 1867 à Lausanne," in *La Première Internationale*, I; as translated in *WFF*, vol. 1, doc. 131; quotes, pp. 469–470.

[131] My understanding of this debate has been greatly influenced by the perceptive analysis of Marilyn J. Boxer, in her "Foyer or Factory" article (cited in n. 128); quote, p. 194.

[132] See Jacques Rancière & Patrick Vauday, "En allant à l'Expo: L'ouvrier, sa femme et les machines," *Les Révoltes logiques*, n° 1 (Winter 1975), 5–22; in English as "Going to the Expo: The Worker, His Wife and Machines," in *Voices of the People: The Social Life of "La Sociale" at the End of the Second Empire*, ed. Adrian Rifkin & Roger Thomas. Transl. John Moore (London: Routledge & Kegan Paul, 1988), pp. 23–44.

[133] Alain Dalotel, Alain Faure, & Jean-Claude Freiermuth, *Aux Origines de la Commune: le mouvement des réunions publiques à Paris 1868–1870* (Paris: Maspero, 1980). An analagous viewpoint characterized the German labor movement, among the followers of Lassalle, and predominated in the International, despite extensive efforts by Marx and his associates to counteract it; see Werner Thönnessen, *The Emancipation of Women: The Rise and Decline of the Women's Movement in German Social Democracy 1863–1933*, transl. Joris de Bres (London: Pluto Press, 1973; orig. published in German, 1969), pp. 15–21.

These objections to women's employment became a target the following year at the series of public debates on women's work held in Paris. The enactment of the new law of 6 June 1868 on freedom of public meetings unleashed a plethora of new voices – women's voices. "The question of women's work," insist the authors of a study of the public meeting movement, "was one of those questions that the militants of the public meetings found most divisive." Strange, then, that this "most divisive" question occupies only ten pages in an otherwise remarkable 375-page book.[134]

The series of open meetings on women's work held at the Vauxhall (a meeting hall in the tenth arrondissement, which soon became one of the most prominent settings for public expressions of political dissent) began in late June and continued to the end of August, drawing sizeable crowds that included many women. Thanks to André Léo (pseud. of Léodile Béra, veuve Champceix, 1824–1900), who chronicled the debates in *L'Opinion nationale*, we have a record of the proceedings.[135] Her pungent commentary added to the richness of her report.

Perhaps the most eloquent and forward-looking contributor to these debates was Paule Mink (1839–1901), who spoke on the 13th of July. Her analysis, "Women's Work," was subsequently republished as a pamphlet and as a poster, which could be plastered on the walls of Paris.[136] Paule Mink's speech directly challenged the message of the Lausanne workingmen's congress. Her arguments were impressive. Mink celebrated the ethic of work as good for both sexes, even as she criticized the existing organization of work, which everyone agreed was taking an appalling human toll of ruined health and decimated lives. Speaking "as a woman," she criticized the workingmen who had gathered at Lausanne for wanting to eliminate all work for women except that of reproduction. She argued rather that women's salaries should be raised, that women, like men, could find fulfillment by accomplishing reasonable work. "You claim," she said, "that women are too weak, too delicate for work; you claim that you love them too much to deliver them over to such exhausting and absorbing fatigue."

---

[134] See Dalotel, *et al.*, *Aux Origines de la Commune*, pp. 168–178; quote, p. 175.

[135] See *L'Opinion nationale*, issues of 18 July through 2 September 1868.

[136] Mink's Vauxhall speech, "Le Travail des femmes," has been republished by Alain Dalotel, ed., *Paule Minck [sic]: Communarde et féministe (1839–1901)* (Paris: Syros, 1981), pp. 114–139. For long excerpts in English, see doc. 132 in *WFF*, vol. 1, translated from the *affiche* version in the Bibliothèque Nationale [Microfiche Rp.12236] provided by Marilyn Boxer. Boxer indicates that Mink (not Minck) is Paule Mink's preferred spelling; she alleged that her enemies added the "c" to point to her partially Polish origins.

"It is by such lovely thoughts that ... you have gilded our moral subjection, our social dependence, our intellectual inferiority."[137]

> By denying woman the right to work you degrade her; you put her under man's yoke and deliver her over to man's good pleasure. By ceasing to make her a worker, you deprive her of her liberty and, thereby, of her responsibility ... so that she will no longer be a free and intelligent creature, but merely a reflection, a small part of her husband. ... It is work alone that makes independence possible and without which there is no dignity.

Like Daubié and so many other commentators, she alluded to men's usurping of women's jobs, as well as the converse. "If men were in their proper place," she remarked, "women would be in theirs." Mink opposed the notion that women should do work that was unnatural for them. Women did not want to be like men. "We affirm our individuality, but we want to remain women."[138]

Another spokeswoman, Mlle [Maxime] Breuil, seconded Mink's arguments. To the infamous arguments about the seasoning of the worker's soup, she replied, "Let the woman alone to do as she wishes. . . . she needs something more to fulfill herself than the routine chores of housework to which you wish to condemn her."[139] In assessing the debates and their meaning, André Léo denounced the chauvinism of the ostensibly "democratic" men who were trying to bar women from industrial labor. She charged that "the desire to maintain male supremacy over women has, recently, in our century, pushed the democrats to these conclusions: that industrial labor should be prohibited for women; that they should be nourished by men. Strange social system, this, that would make a woman's very existence the obligation of the man and turn over her life as a *pawn* for the worker's forgetfulness of his duty."[140] No, indeed, this would not do. It would make each man a little despot, with the power of life or death over his wife. "Compared to these theories," she observed sarcastically, "the [Civil] Code begins to look like a monument to liberty and equality."[141]

At the second of these sessions André Léo and her friends presented their "Manifesto for the Rights of Women," based squarely on the human rights of the individual, irrespective of sex, and on liberty and equality for

---

[137] Mink quotes, *WFF*, vol. 1, doc. 132, p. 472.

[138] Mink, in *WFF*, vol. 1, doc. 132, quotes pp. 473–474.

[139] Maxime Breuil, *Deux discours sur le travail des femmes, prononcé aux réunions de la salle de Vauxhall et suivis de quelques réfléxions sur le même sujet* (Paris: A. le Chevalier, 1868); quote, p. 15.

[140] André Léo, *La Femme et les moeurs: Liberté ou monarchie?* (Paris: Au journal Le Droit des Femmes, 1869), p. 131.

[141] André Léo, *La Femme et les moeurs*, p. 132.

all (it will be discussed in Chapter 7).[142] Among its cornucopia of concerns were the economic issues: women's lack of opportunities for decently paid work, the question of their unequal pay, their severely truncated property rights in the laws of marriage. Then, as the Vauxhall meetings concluded in early September, André Léo presented a series of ten resolutions resulting from these meetings.[143] These were widely discussed in the press, and generated responses from around France, especially from Lyon, where a strike of *ovalistes* (skilled silk workers) had just taken place.

By mid-September 1868, the debate on women's economic and human rights had spread well beyond France. In Geneva, the Francophone Swiss reformer Marie Pouchoulin Goegg joined the French women's rights advocates to protest, and asked to speak at the upcoming Brussels congress of the International Workingmen's Association. Its organizers never even acknowledged, much less responded to her request, a rebuke she made public when she spoke in Bern on "Ladies' Day" (26 September) at the more welcoming congress of the *Ligue Internationale de la Paix et de la Liberté* [International League for Peace and Freedom].[144]

There Marie Goegg complained that women still had "no right to work." She invoked (briefly) the limitations on women's ability to earn a living – hampered by a narrow range of employments, deadly competition for positions that cut back earnings for all, and caused "that deplorable immorality" that threatened to overtake society if nothing were done soon.[145] She was speaking, of course, in veiled terms that everyone understood, of the mounting plague of prostitution. She demanded support not only for equal opportunity in work and instruction, but called for "complete equality before the law" on behalf of women. In a subsequent address (1870) to attendees at the first general assembly of the International Association of Women, which Goegg had founded in Geneva, she spoke about the issue of work for women at greater length; again she called for

---

[142] "Manifeste – Revendication des droits de la femme," published in *L'Opinion nationale*, Monday 20 July 1868; reprinted in *Le Progrès de Lyon* and presumably elsewhere in the French provincial press and abroad.

[143] See *L'Opinion nationale*, 2 September 1868, for the text of the resolutions.

[144] *Deux discours de Mme Marie Goegg – 26 sept. 1868, 27 mars 1870 [réédité pour les besoins de la propagande]* (Geneva: Imprimerie coopérative, 1878). Thanks to Sandi E. Cooper for sending a photocopy of this 16-page brochure. I have since consulted two physical copies, one at the BPU-Geneva and another at the Gosteli Archive in Switzerland, which holds Mme Goegg's personal collection of publications, including a bound volume of *La Solidarité* (1872–1880). Goegg's 1870 speech is also published in *Compte-rendu de la Première assemblée générale annuelle de l'Association Internationale des Femmes: le 27 mars 1870* (Geneva: Impr. Pfeffer & Paky, 1870), pp. 3–12. For a contemporary report, see *L'Opinion nationale*, 29 September 1868.

[145] *Deux discours de Mme Marie Goegg.*

women's freedom to work, along with equal pay for equal work; these were the keys women required to be assured of economic independence and "permit [them] to conserve their dignity."[146] Calling for civil equality for wives as well as economic equality and political rights for all women, Goegg tied together the complex of discriminatory structures that shackled women and held them down. "Woman is one [*une*] just as man is one [*un*], and . . . the right of woman is a truth that is just as incontestable, just as sacred as the Right of man."[147] Goegg would work with the Parisian feminists to campaign for women's rights, then went on to spearhead the movement for women's rights in Switzerland. She would also go on to work with the English abolitionist Josephine Butler in her Continental campaigns against government-regulated prostitution and the so-called White Slave Trade, with the ultimate target being the French regulations that authorized governmental licensing of brothels and informally sanctioned the rounding up and licensing of women on the streets by the city morals police (*police des moeurs*).

Prostitution, the "White Slave" Trade, and the Question of the Double Standard of Morality

The subject of prostitution has repeatedly come up in the preceding discussion, and it too became an aspect of debate on the woman question in France that cannot be overlooked, whether in terms of economics or in terms of "morality." French government officials had introduced the regulation of prostitution in France in 1765, and reinstated it under the Napoleonic government (circa 1802). Paris was the first city in the Western world to attempt to regulate prostitution by confining the trade to certain districts, licensing the women involved (whose numbers reputedly increased from 22,000 in 1815 to 52,000 in 1850), and subjecting them to regular – swift, invasive, humiliating, and unsanitary – genital inspections by male physicians. Brothels and brothel keepers also came under government regulation. In particular, the Paris regulations, enforced by the morals police, greatly interested physicians throughout Europe and America, and physicians such as William Acton in England had written about these rules at length in his book on prostitution, first published in 1857. He even provided a translation of the women's registration card which spelled out the rules they had to obey, the areas of the city that were forbidden to

---

[146] *Deux discours*, 2nd speech of 27 March 1870, p. 10.
[147] *Deux discours*, 2nd speech of 27 March 1870, p. 13.

them, and the conditions under which they might solicit customers.[148] Nothing was done to "control" the male clientele.

During the early nineteenth century, physicians, military authorities and government officials had begun to fret over the rising incidence of venereal disease, especially syphilis, among soldiers and sailors, primarily (though not exclusively) in garrison and port cities, and they blamed prostitutes for the growing contagion. Municipal authorities, alarmed by the existence of a seemingly autonomous world of prostitutes, criminals, and thieves within their walls, scrutinized them all with an eye to regulation. In 1836, a pioneering monograph by the French physician A.-J.-B. Parent-Duchâtelet (1790–1836), *De la Prostitution dans la Ville de Paris*, provoked much public attention.[149] Not only did this study provide material for novelists such as Eugène Sue and social reformers but it also served as an international handbook for investigating the trade.[150] The medical establishment thus framed the issue of prostitution as a public health concern, subject to regulation by enlightened [male] government in order to protect *men's* health. Women's rights advocates, both male and female, developed an alternative perspective on prostitution, based in economics, which squarely attributed the epidemic of prostitution to the increasingly desperate economic plight of poverty-stricken urban women workers. They then condemned the double standard of sexual morality, which they sought to eradicate by reining in the aggressive and irresponsible sexuality of the men who frequented brothels or picked up women on the street.

In the 1830s press, the Saint-Simonian women had already raised this issue of sexual morality, encompassing the problem of forced sexuality in marriage along with men's purchase of nonmarital sex in the streets or in brothels.[151] The issue refused to go away. One of the earliest French women to become a social investigator, Flora Tristan, was horrified by

---

[148] See William Acton, *Prostitution Considered in its Moral, Social and Sanitary Aspects in London and other Large Cities, with Proposals for the Mitigation and Prevention of its Attendant Evils* (London: John Churchill, 1857; 2nd ed., 1870; reprinted 1978).

[149] Alexandre-Jean-Baptiste Parent-Duchâtelet, *De la Prostitution dans la ville de Paris, considérée sous le rapport de l'hygiène publique, de la morale et de l'administration: précédé d'une notice historique sur la vie et les ouvrages de l'auteur par Fr. Leuret* (Brussels: Hauman, Cattoir, & cie., 1836). This work was republished in several different editions (2nd ed., 1837; 3rd ed. 1857) and widely translated and circulated. A reprint in French, presented and annotated by Alain Corbin, is available in editions from 1981 and 2008.

[150] One acerbic view of Sue and his influence is Edward R. Tannenbaum, "The Beginnings of Bleeding-Heart Liberalism: Eugène Sue's *Les Mysteres de Paris*," *Comparative Studies in Society and History*, 23 (1981), 491–507.

[151] See the reference concerning the Saint-Simonian women in n. 45.

what she had learned about the extent and depth of commercialized prostitution. She visited England in 1839 and in her book *Promenades dans Londres*, she expressed her outrage and horror at the level of sexual corruption she encountered in a "finish" in London, where alcohol and desire combined forces to allow upper-class men to engage in drunken orgies and savagely mistreat the female prostitutes. She tied this abuse squarely to economic inequalities: "Prostitution," she declared, "is the most hideous of the afflictions produced by the unequal distribution of the world's goods." She blamed the possibility of prostitution squarely on the subordination of women, their lack of education and economic resources, and she condemned the double standard of morality that encouraged it. "One can affirm that, until the day that women are emancipated, prostitution will spread and grow."[152]

By the 1860s, the extent of prostitution in France at every societal level had, by all accounts, become a public scandal. Julie-Victoire Daubié addressed the issue in scathing terms in the second volume (1869) of *La Femme pauvre*, noting how extensively the trade in young girls had spread, even to the countryside (where she cited instances of parents selling their daughters to *procureurs* for hard cash), thanks to the penetration of the railroads, and, via the army, to France's colonies, particularly Algeria, and even into western Africa. "France is no longer anything but a vast field of prostitution," she exclaimed.[153] Like Tristan and unlike the hygienists, she was concerned about the impact of prostitution on the women – most of whom were poor, uneducated women who could not survive on their own – and the social consequences that derived from the trade, such as irresponsible paternity of children born into poverty, incurable diseases, abortions, infanticides, suicides, and other social horrors. Daubié squarely placed the blame on men's unconscionable and profligate sexual behavior and demanded that measures be put in place to curb it.[154]

As the debates on prostitution heated up in France, authorities in other countries enthusiastically imported the French model, including England. Following Parliament's enactment of the Contagious Disease Acts (1864, 1867 and 1869), such government-regulated prostitution began to encounter serious resistance led by outraged women. The English woman

[152] Flora Tristan, *Promenades dans Londres* (Paris & London, 1840); critical edition established by Francois Bédarida (Paris: La Découverte/Maspero, 1983), quotations above pp. 124–125. Joan Moon's translation. For a full translation, see Dennis Palmer & Giselle Pincetl, *Flora Tristan's London Journal, 1840: A Survey of London Life in the 1830s* (London: George Prior, Publishers, 1980).

[153] Daubié, *Femme pauvre*, vol. 2: "Condition morale," quote, p. 14.

[154] Daubié, *Femme pauvre*, vol. 2, p. 21.

Josephine Butler, who spearheaded the campaigns against the Contagious Disease Acts, on the grounds that they violated women's civil rights, would successfully launch a campaign for their repeal. She translated Daubié's exposé of French prostitution into English and published it in 1872 in her *New Era* pamphlet series.[155] In 1874 Butler took her campaign to continental Europe, to garner support for attacking the French regulations, which she identified correctly as the source for the pernicious government regulation of prostitution everywhere else, the "mother" of all governmental regulation systems. This French system had spawned an international network of physicians and public hygienists eager to adopt the regulation system, as well as a robust commercial traffic in underage female flesh, from one city and country to another, to feed men's taste for novelty in the brothels.

The well-educated Butler read and spoke French, and had no hesitation about expanding her campaign. The organization she established in western Switzerland, the "British and Continental Federation against the State Regulation of Vice" (later known as the International Abolitionist Federation) would become a potent lobby for abolishing government-run prostitution and ending the White Slave Trade. It attracted supporters in Francophone Switzerland (especially in Geneva, Lausanne, and Neuchâtel), in Belgium, Italy, and Germany, and also (and most importantly) in France. These activists, many of whom were committed Protestants but, in some cases, freethinkers or socialists, viewed prostitution not as a "necessary evil" but as exploitative of women for the benefit of promiscuous men, and they simultaneously launched a campaign for a single standard of morality for both sexes. Their efforts would be assisted by another association, the *Union des Amies de la Jeune Fille*, also Swiss-based but with branches in France and other countries, which would take practical action to "rescue" young women who were traveling abroad for employment from falling into the hands of pimps and *procureurs*.[156]

Proponents of abolition argued firmly and repetitively that few women would resort to prostitution if they could support themselves

---

[155] Daubié, "French Morality under the Regulation System," (76 pages), in Butler's pamphlet series, *The New Era: A Collection of Twenty-Five Pamphlets Relating to the Contagious Diseases Acts of 1864, 1866, and 1869* (Liverpool: T. Brakell, 1872). See the massive collection of Butler materials reprinted in June Jordan & Ingrid Sharp, *Josephine Butler and the Prostitution Campaigns: Diseases of the Body Politic*, 5 vols. (New York & London: Routledge 2002, Curzon, 2003). Butler's papers can be consulted at The Women's Library @ LSE, in London.

[156] See Emily Machen, "Traveling with Faith: The Creation of Women's Immigrant Aid Associations in Nineteenth and Twentieth Century France," *Journal of Women's History*, 23:3 (Fall 2011), 89–112.

economically. Thus they demanded that major changes be made – on behalf of poor women. The remedies they sought included formal education, skill training, jobs, and adequate pay, which led them quickly into alliance with women's rights activists. In their view, prostitution was not criminal in itself; it was primarily an economic problem, a women's rights issue, and must be addressed as part of the effort to emancipate women. These women and men were talking back to power, condemning its practices in no uncertain terms. Most did not believe that prostitution could ever be completely eliminated, but they intended to eliminate the economic circumstances that forced impoverished women to resort to it in order to survive.

In a subsequent volume, we will see how the French – and now Francophone – debates on the woman question evolved and expanded, and where these campaigns against regulated prostitution would lead during the French Third Republic, when they became increasingly internationalized and intertwined with campaigns for a single standard of sexual morality, based not on male promiscuity but on female virtue, and on efforts to staunch the international trade in women and children.

All these themes – law and politics, medicine, education, economics, and moral standards – coalesced in the 1860s, and we now turn to the later years of France's Second Empire to witness the explosion of the woman question debates into a concerted campaign for women's rights.

CHAPTER 7

Taking Stock: The Woman Question on the Eve of the Third Republic

It was the custom in nineteenth-century Paris to launch new political causes with a flurry of manifestos, banquets, speeches, tracts, and new periodicals. This had been impossible in the period between 1851 and 1868 when, in the aftermath of the 1848 revolution, Napoléon III's authoritarian Second Empire had severely curtailed both freedom of the press and freedom of association. By 1867, however, this situation began to change. Due to a combination of political pressures, the emperor's own ambivalence about authoritarian rule, and no doubt the conclusion of the free trade treaty with England in 1861, Napoléon III and his newly appointed prime minister Émile Ollivier announced that the regime would embark on a liberalization of its institutions.

In early June 1868 the government promulgated a new law on public meetings that greatly increased the possibilities for public discussion of "non-political" issues; in April 1869, it lifted the curbs on the political press. In the wake of these two developments, the partisans of women's emancipation relaunched a campaign for women's rights, the likes of which had not been seen since 1848. Moreover, other countries were moving along the road to progress. The Russian Tsar had just liberated the serfs; the United States had finally emancipated its black slaves after a bloody civil war; and the British Parliament was actually debating the female franchise, after having passed a landmark civil divorce law a few years earlier. Working men were organizing. Liberty was in the air! In these heady days of the newly liberalized Second Empire, as democracy once again marched forward, anything seemed possible. Could women's emancipation be so far away?

Historians of the French women's movement, in their rush to examine the Third Republic, have skipped unevenly over developments during the

Some of the material in this chapter has appeared in a slightly different form in Karen Offen, *European Feminisms, 1700–1950: A Political History* (Stanford, CA: Stanford University Press, 2000), chapter 5.

late Second Empire. Yet the newly revitalized movement for women's civil and political rights and freedoms at this time was dynamic and bears closer examination.[1]

"Decadence," Male–Female Relations, and Foreign Comparisons

A significant new factor weighed on the minds of French men who addressed the woman question – their perception of French "decadence" and the ingredient of male–female relations in contributing to such decadence. Some were deeply impressed with the contrast between their own nation and the new country of promise across the seas – the United States, land of the democratic dream – the "mirage in the West," as one historian referred to it.[2] Most of the men of whom I speak here were social liberals in politics and outward-looking in habit, ready to profit from any wisdom to be gained outside French borders. Some of them had traveled in America; others appear to have taken their cue from the earlier observations of Alexis de Tocqueville concerning women, public morality, and marriage in the United States. Indeed, writer after writer invoked the testimony of Tocqueville who, in one magnanimous flourish, attributed American greatness to the superiority of American women. In particular, they pointed to the extreme (by their own standards) freedom of personal movement and action enjoyed by young American women – in contrast with their

---

[1] A more detailed study of the years 1866–1870, based on primary materials (including a close reading of the political press), is badly needed. Most later accounts derive from the sketch by Hubertine Auclert, "Les Femmes qui agissent et qui écrivent," in her collection of articles, *Le Vote des femmes* (Paris: V. Giard & E. Brière, 1908), pp. 99–114. Other accounts are provided by Jules Tixerant, "Le Mouvement féministe sous le Second Empire," in *Cinquante ans de féminisme, 1870–1920* (Paris: LFDF, 1921), pp. 57–60, and Edith Thomas, *Les Pétroleuses* (Paris: Gallimard, 1963); transl. as *The Women Incendiaries* (New York: G. Braziller, 1966), chapters 1 and 2. A well-documented account (though still too brief) of these groups is Claire Goldberg Moses, *French Feminism in the 19th Century* (Albany, NY: SUNY Press, 1984), chapter 8. Some further information on this period is provided by Laurence Klejman & Florence Rochefort in their joint thesis, "L'Égalité en marche: histoire du mouvement féministe en France, 1868–1914," 3 vols. Thèse de doctorat de 3ème cycle, Université de Paris VII (Jussieu), 1987; see the briefer published version, *L'Égalité en marche; le féminisme sous la Troisième République* (Paris: FNSP & des femmes, 1989), pp. 31–50. See also Maïté Albistur & Daniel Armogathe, *Histoire du féminisme français*, vol. 2 (Paris: des femmes, 1977), chapter 5, and the accompanying documents in Maïté Albistur & Daniel Armogathe, *Le Grief des femmes*, vol. 2 (Paris: Hier et demain, 1978), pp. 6–39. Still briefer versions can be found in Jean Rabaut, *Histoire des féminismes français* (Paris: Stock, 1978), chapter 6, and Rabaut, *Féministes à la Belle Époque* (Paris: France-Empire, 1985), chapter 1. See also the early chapters in Carolyn J. Eichner, *Surmounting the Barricades: Women in the Paris Commune* (Bloomington: Indiana University Press, 2004), who consulted an earlier draft of my chapter.

[2] Durand Echeverria, *Mirage in the West: A History of the French Image of American Society to 1815* (Princeton, NJ: Princeton University Press, 1957). See also the various works of Jacques Portes on French perceptions of the United States.

subordination in marriage.[3] Alfred Assollant, for example, even pondered the thought that "perhaps the freedom of girls before their marriage is the principal cause of the grandeur of the people of Anglo-Saxon origin."[4] Their perception of the American experience caused them to question their own country's aristocratic Latin attitude toward the cloistered upbringing of upper-class women (the production of "demoiselles" or "white geese" referred to earlier). Others tried to envision how far France might move away from this well-entrenched tradition without undermining either women's feminine graces or the foundations of the male-headed, authoritarian family. Then as now, it was not an easy question to answer.[5]

Thinking about the American experience (or more precisely the Frenchmen's perception of the American experience) in providing a stimulant to French thought on the woman question at mid-century certainly deserves further study. It was undoubtedly important in catalyzing the thinking of male reformers, though the degree of its influence is difficult to measure with any precision. It was significant enough, however, to inspire later denunciations of America's adverse influence by antifeminist Frenchmen; one of the most adamant antifeminists would later (1908) characterize America as the "land of milk and honey of feminism."[6] The more moderate critics of feminism would express serious reservations about the effects of too much liberty "*à l'Américaine*" on French women; the social consequences of an overdose of "individualism" or "egotism" administered to the female might cause women to abandon "their place," thereby plunging France's family-centered society into ruins.[7] The leading proponent of women's

---

[3] See Alexis de Tocqueville, *Democracy in America* (orig. ed., 1835 and 1840; Vintage ed., 1959), vol. II, book 2, chapters 9–12, pp. 209–225, and Auguste Carlier, *Le Mariage aux États-Unis* (Paris: Hachette, 1860).

[4] Alfred Assollant, *Le Droit des femmes* (Paris: A. Anger, 1868), p. 173.

[5] At the other extreme, the French invoked the inevitable "Orient," as exemplified by the Turks. But even as some Frenchmen denounced the Orient as despotic and censored the polygamy practiced there by the elites, others such as Napoléon Bonaparte embraced the concept of multiple wives (see his remarks in the *Mémorial de Sainte-Hélène*, quoted in Chapter 2. In the *Communist Manifesto* (1848), the German critic Karl Marx would denounce the hypocrisy of what he viewed, in effect, for the French bourgeoisie, despite the official limitation to one wife, as a de facto system of multiple wives.

[6] See Théodore Joran, *Au Coeur du féminisme* (Paris: Arthur Savaète, 1908), p. 7.

[7] Even the distinguished liberal economist Henri Baudrillart revealed his neo-traditional perspective on womanhood and French family structure when, in a review of the French edition of John Stuart Mill's book, *On the Subjection of Women* (1869), he condemned Mill's arguments for equality of the sexes as the product of an abstract mind and a false idea of equality. See Baudrillart, "L'Agitation pour l'émancipation . . . ," *Revue des Deux Mondes* (1 October 1872), 651–677. A similar wariness of applying abstract thinking to the social relation of the sexes would later characterize the works of Charles Turgeon, *Le Féminisme français* (2 vols. Paris: L. Larose, 1902) – to be discussed in my subsequent volume – and, later, Maurice Bardèche, *Histoire des femmes* (2 vols., Paris: Stock, 1968).

rights, Léon Richer, would invoke the concept of challenge and response; the American experiment represented a challenge to which the older nations of the world must respond – or die. To Richer, the woman question was *the* crucial issue in a mid-nineteenth century version of *le défi Américain*.[8]

Both the American and English situations interested the male-feminists and the feminist organizers in France. If America served them as a model of the future, Anglo-Saxon England provided them with a laboratory nearer to home in which they could observe efforts at cautious reform in a society that was perhaps even more traditional and class-bound than their own. Both were engaged in campaigns for woman suffrage. In the United States, like France (and Switzerland), all men already exercised the vote, without property or income qualification.[9] In England, property ownership was still a precondition for men's eligibility to vote; the property qualification indeed strengthened the case for giving the vote to unmarried property-holding English women, but this was no longer relevant in France.[10]

Both England and the United States had also enacted provisions for civil divorce. With Napoléon III in power, some French liberals anticipated that civil divorce legislation might become possible in their land. After all, the emperor had at one time advocated reestablishing divorce (in his *Idées napoléoniennes*, 1839), and as emperor he had flouted customary French practices by marrying for love and not for status, money, or strategic territorial advantage.[11] But such was not to be. To advocate civil divorce was, in the 1860s, to guarantee the political opposition of the Roman Catholic Church, and Napoléon III had found the support of the clerical party and its authoritarian allies essential to sustaining the regime. Thus it was that advocacy of civil divorce fell to the republican left, where it would remain well into the early Third Republic.

---

[8] See Richer, *La Femme libre* (Paris: E. Dentu, 1877), chapter 10. The allusion here is to J.-J. Schreiber's *Le Défi américain* (Paris: De Noël, 1967). Historian Arnold J. Toynbee is usually given the credit for deploying the paradigmatic "challenge & response" thesis in his multivolume *A Study of History* (Oxford University Press, 1934–1961). Richer anticipates Toynbee's construction by some seventy years.

[9] According to Leduc, French legal reformers had at the time been more immediately interested in the English campaign for a Married Woman's Property Act, which drew in turn on the earlier experience of the Americans in reshaping the common law relative to women, especially in New York state. See Lucien Leduc, *La Femme et les projets de lois rélatifs à l'extension de sa capacité* (Paris: Giard & Brière, 1898), p. 33.

[10] See Clarisse Coignet, *De l'Affranchissement politique des femmes en Angleterre* (Paris: G. Baillière, 1874); an offprint from the *Revue Politique et Littéraire (Revue Bleue)*, n°s 44 & 45 (2 & 9 May 1874).

[11] *Des Idées napoléoniennes* (1839); see the revised translation by Brison D. Gooch, *Napoléon III. Napoleonic Ideas* (New York: Harper & Row, 1967), p. 94.

Among the more controversial restrictions on women's civil rights concerned women's situation in the laws governing the political press. The organic decree of 1851 formally barred women from publishing political newspapers. Under these rules there could never be another *Voix des Femmes* or *Politique des Femmes*. In 1862 Adèle Esquiros – another woman active in 1848 on behalf of women's rights – plaintively beseeched Victor Hugo to found a journal in which women could write concerning the interests of "*la classe féminine*"; the eminent writer was unwilling to help.[12]

Another woman who spoke eloquently against the restrictions on women's publishing in the press law (as an index of her inferior status in French law) was the journalist and travel writer Olympe Audouard (1830–1890). Legally separated from her husband, Mme Audouard was making her living as an author. Unlike a number of other women writers in this time, she published under her own name. She had traveled extensively and had written accounts of her journeys to Russia, Egypt, and Turkey.[13] In 1866 Audouard published an angry little tract entitled *Guerre aux hommes* [War on Men] in which she lashed out against men who disparage women, against the inequality of women in French law, the "double standard" of morality, and a host of related grievances. In 1867, as the press laws were being revised, she founded a periodical revue, *La Revue cosmopolite*, only to be told by the ministry of the interior that she could not be authorized as publisher since she was not an adult French*man* in full possession of her civil and political rights, as demanded by the Organic Decree. In reply, she published an angry "Letter to the Deputies," in which she denounced the absurdity of the situation in which she found herself and demanded that French women be recognized as equal with French men before the law.[14] Prior to 1869 Audouard embarked on an extended tour of the United States, where she visited Mormon communities and met with women's suffrage partisans; the American women's rights advocate Elizabeth Cady Stanton published a translation of her

[12] Esquiros's unpublished letters to Hugo are quoted in Anthony Zielonka, "Le féminisme d'Adèle Esquiros," *Bulletin d'Information des Études Féminines [B.I.E.F.]*, n° 16 (May 1985), 78–81.
[13] Audouard was well-known in her time, as is underscored by her biographical notice in G. Vapereau's *Dictionnaire universel des contemporains*, 5th ed. (Paris: Hachette, 1880), 86. Her substantial corpus of travel writings has been analyzed by Rachel Nuñez, "Between France and the World: The Gender Politics of Cosmopolitanism, 1835–1914," Ph.D. dissertation, Stanford University, 2006, and Rachel Nuñez, "Rethinking Universalism: Olympe Audouard, Hubertine Auclert and the Gender Politics of the Civilizing Mission," *French Politics, Culture & Society*, 30:1 (Spring 2012), 23–45.
[14] See Audouard's *Guerre aux hommes* (2nd ed., Paris: E. Dentu, 1866) and *Lettre aux Députés; les droits de la femme, sa situation que lui fait la législation française* (Paris: E. Dentu, 1867). Portions of the latter text are reprinted by Albistur & Armogathe in *Grief des femmes*, vol. 2, pp. 28–33.

"Letter to the Deputies" in *The Revolution*.[15] Upon her return to France Audouard presented a series of what she called "gynecological" lectures, under the patronage of Alexandre Dumas *fils*, some of which she later published as *Gynécologie; la Femme depuis six mille ans*.[16] Frustrated as a publisher of periodicals, she turned to publishing books, but like Jenny P. d'Hericourt, who was living in Chicago, she seems to have been absent from Paris when the next outburst of women's rights agitation began.

Organizing for Change

In 1868 a small number of activist women founded a new group, known variously to history as the *Société de Revendication des Droits de la Femme*, the *Société de la Revendication du Droit des Femmes*, and simply as *La Revendication*. Its adherents championed a far-reaching program for women's emancipation. At the helm of *Revendication* was Mme André Léo, the pen-name of the novelist and women's rights activist Léodile Béra Champseix (1824–1900).[17] In 1868, André Léo was a widow in her mid-

[15] Audouard's "Letter to the Deputies" was also published in English in *The Revolution* (9 July 1868), translated by Stanton's cousin, Elizabeth Smith Miller. On the American trip, see Audouard's accounts in *A Travers l'Amérique: le Far-West* (Paris: E. Dentu, 1869; subsequent reprints), and *A Travers l'Amérique; North America. États-Unis: constitution, moeurs, usages, lois, institutions, sectes religieuses* (Paris: E. Dentu, 1869; reprinted 1870, 1871).

[16] See Audouard, *La Femme dans le mariage, la séparation et le divorce, conférence faite le 28 février 1870* (Paris: E. Dentu, 1870), and *M. Barbey d'Aurévilly; Réponse à ses réquisitoires contre les bas-bleus. Conférence du 11 avril* (Paris: E. Dentu, 1870). See also Audouard's history of women, *Gynécologie; la femme depuis six mille ans* (Paris: E. Dentu, 1873).

[17] There is still no full-length biographical study of André Léo. The best documented work to date is Fernanda Gastaldello, "André Léo: Quel Socialisme?" (laureate thesis, University of Padua [Italy], 1978–1979), which contains an excellent bibliography of André Léo's widely scattered publications. Some earlier material can be found in a short article by A. Perrier, "Grégoire Champseix et André Léo," *Actualité de l'Histoire*, n° 30 (January–March 1960), pp. 38–39, and in Edith Thomas, *The Women Incendiaries* (New York: G. Braziller, 1966), chapter 9. See also Paule Lejeune, "Une grande journaliste communarde: Léodile Champceix, dite André Léo," *Des Femmes en mouvements*, n° 2 (February 1978), 58–59; and, for an account that emphasizes her socialist commitments over her feminist impulses, *André Léo, une journaliste de la Commune* (*Le Lérot reveur*, n° 44, March 1987). An earlier summary is Karen Offen, "André Léo," in *An Encyclopedia of Continental Women Writers*, ed. Katharina M. Wilson, v. 2 (New York & London: Garland, 1991), 720–721. See also Alain Dalotel, *André Léo (1824–1900): La Junon de la Commune* (Chauvigny: Association des Publications Chauvinoises, 2004), Eichner, *Surmounting the Barricades*, and the Ph.D. dissertation of Alice Primi (cited in my Chapter 2). Aficionados are now republishing some of André Léo earlier works, for example, her treatise, *La Femme et les moeurs: Liberté ou monarchie* (Paris: au journal Le Droit des Femmes, 1869) reprinted with the subtitle reversed (Tusson, Charente: Du Lérot, éditeur, 1990); *André Léo: Écrits Politiques* (Paris: Éditions Dittmar, 2005), and her 1869 novel *Aline-Ali, présenté et annoté par Cecilia Beach, Caroline Granier, & Alice Primi, Cahiers du Pays chauvinois*, n° 41 (2011). A new book, with pathbreaking essays by a team of scholars, is *Les Vies d' André Léo: romancière, féministe et communarde*, ed. Frédéric Chauvaud, François Dubasque, Pierre Rossignol, & Louis Vibrac (Rennes: Presses Universitaires de Rennes, 2015).

forties, the mother of twin sons (André and Léo) and possibly also of a daughter. Returning to Paris in 1860 from Lausanne, where she had married Grégoire Champseix (in exile following the failure of the revolution in 1848), she soon became well-known for her novels on women's issues, in particular *Un Mariage scandaleux* (1862) and *Un Divorce* (1866). Novels (often published serially as feuilletons in the periodical press) provided an important alternative venue for discussing sociopolitical issues that could not otherwise be addressed.

In mid-July 1868, during the series of public meetings on women's work at the Vauxhall (discussed in Chapter 6), André Léo and eighteen other women issued a manifesto for women's rights based squarely on the principles of individual liberty and equality. Departing from the couple-based, or "relational" notion of "equality in difference," which had characterized earlier French feminisms, André Léo and her associates boldly posed the question, "Is woman an individual? Is she a human being?" If so, how could woman then be excepted from the "conditions recognized as indispensable to the dignity and morality of the human being [*personne humaine*]." "Why should woman be obliged to conform to laws which she has neither made nor consented to? Why is she excluded from the recognized right to choose a representative? Why should her property rights be sacrificed to her husband? Why should she be paid half of what a man is paid, and even then not be able to find work? Liberty and the right to justice were surely for women as for men." Calling on all women and all "brave and intelligent" men, they announced that "We are forming a league for a new declaration of rights, not only those of man but those of humanity, and for their social realization."[18] The group demanded equality before the law, equality in marriage, equality in work, and a true fraternity between women and men.

In early 1869 *Revendication* took on a more substantive form. In late January the group, mostly women but including many men (according to André Léo's own account), decided to focus specifically on obtaining civil rights for (married) women and drafting a new manifesto. This document was subsequently published in late April in the new but short-lived *Journal des Femmes*, based in Geneva, Switzerland, and edited by Alfred Bouyon

---

[18]   Their manifesto was published in *L'Opinion nationale*, 20 July 1868. A few days later (23 July 1868) it appeared in *Le Progrès* (Lyon), where it stimulated a public discussion that lasted into September. The Lyon text of the manifesto (which differs slightly from the Paris version) and several published replies by groups of Lyon women are reproduced in appendix to Claire Auzias & Annik Houel, *La Grève des ovalistes: Lyon, juin-juillet 1869* (Paris: Payot, 1982), pp. 169–173.

and Marie Goegg.[19] The women also decided to found a primary school for girls, based on new principles of secular education.[20]

André Léo elaborated the *revendication* program with the publication in 1869 of her book, *La Femme et les moeurs: Liberté ou monarchie.*[21] Setting the French movement for women's rights squarely in a historical perspective, she called for sweeping changes in the legal, educational, and economic status of women. In the wake of slave and serf emancipation in the United States and Russia, she drew unflinchingly on natural rights arguments and boldly criticized the men who represented France's most advanced democratic thinking – the leaders of the reemerging worker's movement – for ignoring or shunting aside women's rights (as they had just done at the congress of the First International) in order to defend their little domestic monarchies, charging them with only pretending to love liberty and with conniving to maintain male supremacy by dispossessing women and confining them to the home.[22] This was a strong indictment of the motives of ostensibly progressive men. André Léo's unequivocal language and her unqualified emphasis on individual human rights was not to everyone's taste; nevertheless she set the tone and agenda for subsequent interventions. Even as she wrote, other constituencies had begun to emerge.

In November 1868 Maria Deraismes (1828–1894), the wealthy, well-educated, and articulate new star of the Parisian lecture circuit, launched a series of lectures on the theme, *"Les ouvrières de l'avenir"* (women workers of the future). This was Deraismes's third season of public lectures, but her first to address the woman question. Her topics included "Woman and the Law," "Woman and Society," "Woman and Morals," "Woman and Reason" – some of which were published at the time in the *Revue des Cours littéraires.*[23]

[19] *Le Journal des Femmes* (1868–1869) can be consulted at the BNF, côte Lc².3205. Following a specimen issue in March 1868, it published just seven numbers (1 March 1869 – 5 June 1869) before disappearing. Thereafter, Marie Goegg published several articles in *Le Droit des Femmes* as well as in *Les États-Unis d'Europe* (published in Geneva).

[20] André Léo, "La Ligue des femmes en France," *Le Journal des Femmes*, n° 2 (26 March 1869); republished from *Les États-Unis d'Europe*. The new manifesto appeared as "Revendication des droits civiles refusés à une moitié de la nation," *Le Journal des Femmes*, n° 4 (20 April 1869). Besides André Léo, the cosigners included Clara Ranvier, Noëmie Reclus, Maria Deraismes and her sister Mme Feresse-Deraismes, Caroline de Barrau, Nelly Lieutier, Mme Léon Richer, and Louise Michel.

[21] *La Femme et les moeurs; Liberté ou monarchie* (1869; cf. note 17). There was also an undated edition in Dutch. Excerpts in English translation were published in *The Revolution* (New York), beginning with the issue of 30 September 1869. See the review by X. Feyrnet, "Chronique," *Le Temps*, 4 July 1869.

[22] *La Femme et les moeurs*, p. 128; this section of chapter 5 of André Léo's text is reprinted in Albistur & Armogathe, *Grief des femmes*, vol. 2, pp. 34–37.

[23] The series announcement appeared in *L'Opinion nationale*, 4 November 1868. One lecture, "La femme et la raison," was published in the *Revue des Cours littéraires*, 6:14 (6 March 1869), 221–224. The entire sequence of lectures can be accessed in Deraismes, *Eve dans l'humanité* (Paris, 1891). For a

The talented Deraismes had been launched as a public lecturer by Léon Richer (1824–1911), who was best known to the French public as a journalist for *L'Opinion nationale* (where André Léo also published) and a staunch anticlerical. The story of Deraismes and Richer has been many times retold, though not in the detail it deserves. Out of their efforts came a second approach to the problem of women's rights, focused around a publication and an association.

In April 1869, following the promulgation of the new press law, the newspaper *Le Droit des Femmes*, edited by Richer, made its first appearance.[24] The group gathered around Deraismes and Richer at *Le Droit des Femmes* focused specifically on improving women's civil (legal) rights, adhering to the program of "equality in dissimilarity" [*égalité dans la dissemblance*],[25] a slightly different emphasis than in Legouvé's earlier program of "equality in difference" or André Léo's brand of individual autonomy. In early July this group held its first banquet. X. Feyrnet, reporting on the banquet in *Le Temps* a few days later, reassured his readers that this program for women's civil rights should not scare anyone and urged them to support it.[26]

As of April 1870, Richer and Deraismes founded an associated group, known as the *Association pour le Droit des Femmes*. This group, under various labels, evolved into the *Ligue Française pour le Droit des Femmes*, which lasted well over fifty years and has to date monopolized the historiography of the French women's movement during the last half of the nineteenth century.[27] The group's April manifesto invoked, perhaps for the first time, the progress made for women's emancipation in other

good resumé of Deraismes's career in English, see Patrick Kay Bidelman, *Pariahs Stand Up! The Founding of the Liberal Feminist Movement in France, 1858–1889* (Westport, CT: Garland, 1982), pp. 75–91. See also Klejman & Rochefort, *L'Égalité en marche*, pp. 34–39.

[24] The history of this publication is traced by G. Lhermitte, "En Feuilletant Le Droit des Femmes, 1869–1891," in *Cinquante ans*, pp. 61–74. Most other accounts rely on this one. See also Li Dzeh-Djen, *La Presse féministe en France de 1869 à 1914* (Paris: Librairie L. Rodstein, 1934), chapter 4, and Bidelman, *Pariahs*, passim. There is no comparable treatment of the *Journal des Femmes* (see n. 4).

[25] *Le Droit des Femmes*, n° 1 (10 April 1869); n° 64 (17 July 1870). See also Léon Richer's preface to his *Livre des femmes* (Paris: Librairie de la Bibliothèque démocratique, 1872), vii–xi; his other books are *La Femme libre* (Paris: E. Dentu, 1877), and *Le Code des femmes* (Paris: E. Dentu, 1883). These will be discussed in my subsequent volume.

[26] Banquet of 11 July 1869, reported by X. Feyrnet, "Chronique," *Le Temps*, 13 July 1869. It was also mentioned by Jules Tixerant, "Le Mouvement féministe sous le Second Empire," in *Cinquante ans*, p. 59. Bidelman, *Pariahs* (p. 78) incorrectly dates this "first feminist banquet in France" as 11 July 1870.

[27] See Moses, pp. 187–189 for an English translation of the *exposé* and statutes of the *Association pour le Droit des Femmes*, founded in April 1870; the French text can be found in *Le Droit des Femmes*, 24 April 1870; it was reprinted in *Cinquante ans de féminisme, 1870–1920*, pp. 129–135.

countries – America, England, Germany, Switzerland, Italy, Holland, "but particularly in England and America," and insisted that France "can no longer remain behind the times." "Woman, as a human person, should be free and autonomous," the group proclaimed, at the same time insisting not on identity to man, but "equality in dissimilarity."[28] Meanwhile the group clustered around André Léo, which included Clarisse Coignet and other women interested in girls' education, undertook to promote a secular educational program, focused on moral and ethical values and, in particular, an entire system of lay primary schools.[29]

Thus, within only a few months, many issues concerning women's status, women's civil and political rights, and emancipation more generally had sprung back onto the agenda for public discussion in France. These topics included closely interlinked concerns with the political and legal status of women, both within and beyond the family: girls' education, women's disadvantaged economic situation and its consequences, and – not least – women's history. All these concerns were part and parcel of an emerging transnational debate with many shared characteristics, both in terms of women's overall experience and the ideologies and quarrels that enveloped it. This debate spanned the English Channel, traversed the Alps and the Caucasus, and crossed the Atlantic Ocean. However, within each nation it crossed, forms of resistance and approaches to reform developed that were culturally specific.

In France, the question of political rights for women quickly reemerged during this period. Well into the Second Empire, leading Frenchmen representing all points of the political spectrum had persistently reiterated the necessity of separate spheres, asserting their right to control political matters. Various statements by monarchists and republicans – and by conservatives, liberals, and radicals within each of those traditions – confirm this view. Take, for instance, the editor of *Le Temps*, Auguste Nefftzer, who could hardly be accused of being a political reactionary. Nefftzer heartily favored educating women and letting them contribute in a private manner to the advancement of the arts and sciences. But he, like so many nineteenth-century liberals, adamantly opposed women's entrée into the hallowed sanctuary of political life. In an 1862 editorial he asserted that:[30]

---

[28] Manifesto, in *ibid.*, p. 187.

[29] Cf. Chapter 4 and the publications of Barry Bergen on this group of women, particularly Clarisse Coignet.

[30] Nefftzer in *Le Temps*, 6 December 1862. In the early 1870s, however, Nefftzer (who had by then retired and moved to England) would do an about-face on this issue, based on his favorable

It is as impossible for women to vote as it is for men to be mothers. The division of social functions between the two sexes is clean and total. The political and social action of woman, which can be great and beneficial, can only be exercised in indirect fashion – not in a public place nor at the tribune but in the home [*foyer domestique*]. That is where woman reigns: it is there she should radiate a strength and virtue which will find their political expression in the virile acts of [male] citizens. Equality of rights and political functions would subvert both nature and reason.

The radical republican Eugène Pelletan similarly envisioned marriage in political terms; he characterized it as a constitutional monarchy, with the husband as minister of foreign affairs, and the wife serving as minister of the interior.[31] The legal and political principle that designated the male-headed family, not the individual, as the primary sociopolitical unit was still overwhelmingly endorsed by men in nineteenth-century France.[32] Few men – even the most radical critics of liberalism – were willing to go further.

Such convictions, however, could not silence the continuing demands for political and civil rights for women, which were now reemerging from the dustbin of history to which they had been consigned following the revolutionary turbulence of 1848–1849. In particular, the reopening of the French debate on woman suffrage was stimulated by British agitation for further extension of the vote to working-class men of property-based suffrage, which had led to the introduction of the Second Reform Bill in March 1865. English women gathered signatures for a huge pro-suffrage petition, which they presented to Parliament in 1866; they organized the London National Society for Woman Suffrage in 1867.[33] The francophile

impressions of participation in municipal suffrage by single property-owning women. On this, see Richer, *Femme libre*, pp. 267–271.

[31] Eugène Pelletan, *La Femme au XIX siècle* (Paris: Pagnerre, 1869), p. 29. Cf. also Assollant, *Droit des femmes*. On Camille Pelletan, the equally radical republican son of Eugène who also had a great deal to say on the woman question, see Judith F. Stone, *Sons of the Revolution: Radical Democrats in France 1862–1914* (Baton Rouge: Louisiana State University Press, 1996).

[32] See Katherine Auspitz, *The Radical Bourgeoisie: The Ligue de l'Enseignement and the Origins of the Third Republic, 1866–1885* (Cambridge, UK: Cambridge University Press, 1982), who concurs: "Above all, radicals repudiated passive or involuntary subordination. They believed in the free individual and the democratic nation, and these two fidelities underlay their *civisme*. Concern for solidarity marked them no less than secularism. They were not individualists, nor indeed, liberals, in any simple sense. None imagined that society could be maintained by the transactions of self-regarding actors" (p. 4). Obviously the balancing act between advocating for the free individual and not becoming "individualists" in the abstract sense, is a difficult one, especially when it came to considering women's rights. Remarkably, in the section of this book that addresses girls' education (pp. 38–46), the speakers are entirely male, despite the fact that a number of prominent women (Daubié, André Léo, Clarisse Coignet) were simultaneously addressing this issue in print.

[33] See A. P. W. Robson, "The Founding of the National Society for Women's Suffrage 1866–1867," *Canadian Journal of History*, 8:1 (March 1973), 1–22.

political economist John Stuart Mill, (whose views on the woman question were extremely liberal), had been elected to Parliament on a pro-woman suffrage platform, and in May 1867 he delivered his celebrated speech on woman suffrage in the House of Commons. On behalf of unmarried property-holding women, he argued that the word "person" be substituted for "man" wherever it appeared in the bill.[34] The British women's rights activist Jessie Boucherett, the founder of the Society for Promoting the Employment of Women, spelled out the implications of this debate for France in a published commentary on Simon's *L'Ouvrière* and Daubié's *La Femme pauvre*:[35]

> The moral we draw from these facts is that [government] centralization when united to manhood suffrage is not advantageous to women, but the contrary, and that wherever large numbers of working men are admitted to the suffrage, unmarried working women ought to be admitted to its exercise also, as the possession of the suffrage then becomes necessary for their protection.

The author of *La Femme pauvre* (1866), Julie-Victoire Daubié, announced her strong support of the vote for single adult women, along the lines being proposed in England.[36]

Further stimulus for the French revisiting of the women's suffrage cause came from the concurrent agitation in the United States, where following the abolition of slavery, black men had been granted the vote, but the women were shut out. The new state of Wyoming in the American West, however, did grant the vote to women (suffrage granting and qualifications were a state prerogative, which could only be overruled by a federal constitutional amendment). This provoked American women's rights

---

[34] The essential parts of Mill's speech and the ensuing debate are reprinted from *Hansard* in *Women, the Family, and Freedom*, vol. 1, docs. 135 and 136. Mill's tactic would have consolidated the effects of Lord Romilly's and Lord Brougham's law of 1850, which stated that "In all Acts [of Parliament] words importing the masculine gender shall be deemed and taken to include females unless the contrary . . . is expressly provided," as had been the case in the 1832 Reform Act. A thorough study is needed of the reception in France of Mill's suffrage speech and the French translation (cited in n. 47) of his book, *On the Subjection of Women*.

[35] Jessie Boucherett, "The Condition of Women in France," *The Contemporary Review*, 5:1 (May 1867), 98–113; quote, 106.

[36] Julie-Victoire Daubié, first in *La Femme pauvre*, pp. 240–253, then in *L'Émancipation de la femme en dix livraisons* (1871). On the other hand, Juliette Lambert Lamessine Adam did not endorse woman suffrage in the 1860s; she was concerned about the fact that the all-male suffrage had contributed to the failure of the Second Republic and the advent of the Second Empire; by the 1890s, however, she would support Jeanne Schmahl's *Avant-Courrière* campaigns, which fostered single-issue reforms in women's legal status.

activists to take action; for many years thereafter they would organize massive campaigns at the state level, but most were unsuccessful.[37]

In France, one of the most heated confrontations over the question of women's public role issued from the Paris Faculty of Law, where for decades prominent French legal scholars, inspired by the work being done in German universities (Savigny school) on the history of law and institutions, had developed the first "scientific" approach to the history of women and the family.[38] Disputes among faculty professors over the question of women's rights generally and over the vote in particular enlivened academic debate during the later Second Empire.[39] In fact, in 1866 a commission was appointed to study revision of the Code and associated laws.[40]

No Frenchman during the Second Empire could have accurately opposed woman suffrage by claiming that women had never voted and were, therefore, not meant to do so. This simply was not true. As mentioned earlier, in Chapter 2, in the Middle Ages, when property took precedence over the individual, French women of the nobility represented their land by voting in the provincial estates (indeed, as historians pointed out, their participation had even won the approval of Pope Innocent IV); as late as the seventeenth century, the illustrious letter writer Madame de Sévigné had voted in the estates of Brittany. These historical facts were verifiable and served to support the pro-suffrage position.[41] There was one

---

[37] See Ellen Carol DuBois, *Feminism and Suffrage: The Emergence of an Independent Women's Movement in America, 1848–1869* (Ithaca, NY: Cornell University Press, 1978).

[38] For the earlier works of Laboulaye, Koenigswarter, and Rathery, and the role of the Académie des Sciences Morales et Politiques as a sponsor of women's history, see Chapter 5 in this volume.

[39] See Karen Offen, "Women, Citizenship, and Suffrage in the French Context, 1789–1993," *Suffrage And Beyond: International Feminist Perspectives*, ed. Melanie Nolan & Caroline Daley, (Auckland: Auckland University Press; copublished with New York University Press & Pluto Press, London, 1994), pp. 151–170.

[40] On the Commission's debates, see Anselme-Polycarpe Batbie, "'Révision du Code Napoléon,' mémoire lu à l'Académie des Sciences Morales et Politiques, 23 et 30 December 1865," *Revue Critique de Législation et de Jurisprudence* (hereafter *RCLJ*), 28:2 (Paris, 1866), 125–162. See also A[lexandre] Duverger, "Observations sur le mémoire de M. Batbie, intitulé 'Révision du Code Napoléon,'" *RCLJ*, 28:4 (April 1866), 308–364; 29:2 (August 1866), 116–167; 30:2 (February 1867), 128–148; and 30:4 (April 1867), 322–346; and Batbie's "Réponse à M. Duverger," *RCLJ*, 30:1 (January 1867), 50–64; and 30:3 (March 1867), 213–231. See also the study by Paul Gide, *Étude sur la condition privée de la femme* (Paris: Durand et Pédone-Lauriel, 1867; 2nd ed., Paris: Larose et Forcel, 1885); his earlier *mémoire* had been crowned by the Académie des Sciences Morales et Politiques in 1866.

[41] See Laboulaye, *Recherches*, and Paul Viollet's subsequent studies of France's public and private laws and institutions. The findings to date would later be popularized by Eliska Vincent in a series of articles, "La Femme et la législation," in the *Revue Féministe*, beginning in 1895; by Hubertine Auclert in articles reprinted in *Le Vote des femmes* (previously cited in n. 1), and by Ferdinand Buisson, *Le Vote des femmes* (Paris: H. Denot & E. Pinat, 1911), pp. 5–11.

hitch; in those times the vote represented landed property, not the embodied individual – which was the form taken in 1848 by the democratic notion of suffrage.

Nevertheless, in the wake of the findings of the Commission, Alexandre Duverger, one of nineteenth-century France's most respected authorities on civil law, concluded decisively against giving the vote to women on the grounds that previous instances of women "meddling" in French political life had proved unfortunate (he may also have been thinking of the empress Eugénie). Learned adversaries like Duverger appealed to the long-standing prejudice against women's political activism by pointing to historical cases, deftly selected from the period of the Renaissance on, in which women's actions were deemed to have adversely affected the fate of the French nation.[42] In the spirit of John Knox, Jean Bodin, and the Jacobins, he reminded his readers of the pernicious political role of queens and queen mothers such as Catherine de Médicis and Anne of Austria, who had served as regents for their sons, the "true" heirs to the French throne under now-concretized Salic Law; he dredged up titillating stories of royal favorites from Madame de Maintenon to La Pompadour.[43] In short, Duverger too sought to slay the "monstrous regiment of women." His selective choice of time period and of examples was no doubt dictated by the necessity of excluding Jeanne d'Arc, who did not vote even though she had saved the kingdom and was already well on the way to reinstatement as a national heroine – and sainthood. Duverger's authoritative essay, *De la Condition politique et civile des femmes*, which contained his earlier published articles, would be published in 1872 and would often be quoted by opponents of women's suffrage during the Third Republic.[44]

The influence of Duverger and those who agreed with him about keeping women out of political life was, for the moment, decisive. With

---

[42] On the sustained opposition to women rulers, cf. Chapter 2. Duverger's particular nemesis, however, was the "excesses" ostensibly committed by women during the revolution of 1789. See Louis Frank, *Essai sur la condition politique de la femme; étude de sociologie et de législation* (Paris: A. Rousseau, 1892), p. 86.

[43] Duverger had very likely been reading (and cribbing from) the Goncourt brothers' influential book on the influence of women in the eighteenth century, published in 1862.

[44] A. Duverger, *De la Condition politique et civile des femmes. Réponse à quelques critiques de nos lois; modifications admissibles. 1e partie (seule publiée)* (Paris: Marescq, 1871). According to the cover, this material was initially published in vols. 26–29 of the *Revue Pratique de Droit Français*. More likely, it reprints the pieces in the *RCLJ*, cited in n. 40. For a contemporary discussion of Duverger's ideas, see Baudrillart, "L'Agitation pour l'émancipation des femmes en Angleterre et aux Etats-Unis," *Revue des Deux Mondes* (1 October 1872), 651–677. For a subsequent assessment of Duverger's influence and discussion of the controversy within the law school, see Frank, *Essai sur la condition politique de la femme*, pp. 53–58.

the enactment of the *Sénatus-Consulte* of 1870, new rules for preserving the Imperial succession exclusively through the male line were implemented. This did not go unnoticed by French women's rights activists. In an angry exchange over the subject of the regency in June 1870, Angélique Arnaud claimed that "Women's inferiority is decreed forever, by the Constitution of the Empire."[45]

Arnaud's dismay over what she considered the new Salic Law is understandable. But not everyone agreed with Arnaud's condemnation of the Second Empire. In the late 1860s especially, the imperial regime had taken quite a few constructive steps as concerns women, just as it had concerning workers. In an article of May 1869, Jenny P. d'Héricourt insisted that the Emperor was by no means women's adversary; she castigated the republican representatives of 1848 for turning against the women's cause and pointed to everything that the Second Empire had done for women. Empress Eugénie had awarded the medal of the Legion of Honor to Rosa Bonheur, and the regime had given women employment in the state telegraph offices, the post offices, and the tobacco and tax stamp concessions. Moreover, in the face of strenuous opposition from the Catholic clergy, Napoléon III had undertaken the reform of girls' secondary education. The Emperor, d'Héricourt said, "has done more for us than the republicans," and "it is because women have not forgiven" them "that the Second Empire has lasted." It is surprising that d'Héricourt did not also mention the admission of women to the study of medicine in the university faculties, a cause so dear to her own heart, or the endorsement of the employment of women in the state printing firms. If the republicans were to do better on women's behalf, they would have to rethink their legacy.[46]

The appearance in 1869 of John Stuart Mill's treatise *The Subjection of Women* ranks among the major publishing events of the Western world. This study, on which Mill had worked (with his wife Harriet Taylor) for many years, was immediately translated into French as *L'Assujetissement des femmes* (as well as many other European languages) and quickly became the mirror for French reassessments of their own views on what Mill called "the social relation of the sexes."[47] If Mill had characterized his 1867 speech in Parliament on behalf of woman suffrage as one of expediency, his essay

---

[45] A. Arnaud, "La loi salique," *Le Droit des Femmes*, 5 June 1870.

[46] See "Woman's Rights in France: Letter from Madame Jenny d'Héricourt," *The Agitator* (Chicago), 1 May 1869.

[47] See John Stuart Mill, *L'Assujetissement des femmes*, transl. by E. Cazelles (Paris: Guillaumin, 1869; 2nd ed., 1876). In 1975 Payot published a translation by Marie-Françoise Cachin mistitled *L'Asservissement des femmes*, reprinted 2005 by Payot/Rivages.

on women's subjection was purposefully devoted to promulgating the theoretical principle of equality. In particular, he argued against the medical men and prominent biological determinists such as Auguste Comte (with whom Mill had quarreled and broken off contact in the early 1840s because of the French *philosophe's* stubborn commitment to biological determinism), insisting that women's "nature" could never be known until all the socially imposed legal and cultural restraints on women's full development as human beings were removed.[48] In addition, he made a breathtaking case for marriage between equals that still resonates today.

The reception and impact of *L'Assujetissement des femmes* in France has never, to my knowledge, been adequately studied. It must have had a profound impact, judging from the comments laced through publications of all kinds, both at the time and during the next four decades – and beyond.[49] Even in the 1920s, the feminist lawyer Suzanne Grinberg would attribute enormous influence to Mill in her *Historique du mouvement suffragiste depuis 1848*, to the point of obscuring the indigenous French arguments for women's vote.[50] In Jules Ferry's celebrated speech on education in April of 1870, for instance, he referred to Mill's book as the "beginning of wisdom" and recommended it enthusiastically.[51] The Fourierist Edouard de Pompéry similarly praised Mill's work, but went on to criticize the author for "an error that prejudices his cause." Pompéry insisted, *pace* Mill, that "it is not in the name of equality of faculties between man and woman that the rights of woman should be demanded, but in the name of human justice, which should assure to each member of society the fullest and most complete expansion of his being."[52]

---

[48] For a thoughtful analysis of the break between Comte and Mill over the woman question, see Mary Pickering, *Auguste Comte: An Intellectual Biography*, vol. 2 (Cambridge, UK: Cambridge University Press, 2009), pp. 72–113. Comte's letters to Mill were published in 1877, but the exchange with Mill was not published in French until the late 1890s; see the *Lettres inédites de John Stuart Mill à Auguste Comte; publiées avec les réponses de Comte et une introduction par L. Lévy-Bruhl* (Paris: Alcan, 1899). The entire correspondence is now available in English.

[49] I have established a working file on the reception of Mill's French edition of 1869.

[50] Suzanne Grinberg, *Historique du mouvement suffragiste depuis 1848* (Paris: H. Goulet, 1926). In her study of the feminist press in France, Li Dzeh-Djen asserts that "the [suffrage] movement was strongly influenced by the agitation of women in England, and by the worldwide stir provoked by Mill's book." ("Ce mouvement [suffragiste] a été fortement influencé par l'agitation des femmes en Angleterre, et par le retentissement mondial qu'a provoqué le livre de Stuart Mill.") See Dzeh-Djen, *Presse féministe en France* (previously cited, n. 24), p. 201.

[51] See Jules Ferry, "Discours sur l'égalité d'éducation (10 avril 1870, Salle Molière)," in *Discours et opinions de Jules Ferry*, vol. 1 (Paris: A. Colin, 1893); as translated in *WFF*, vol. 1, doc. 119, p. 441.

[52] Pompéry, "L'Assujetissement des femmes," *La Philosophie positive*, 6:5 (March–April 1870); as transl. in *WFF*, vol. 1, doc. 108, pp. 405–406. He added that "Slavery, serfdom, the subjection of

The woman question had been central to Mill's thinking since the early 1830s, and he remained convinced that there was no reason to admit the "necessary subordination of one sex to the other." Extending the principle he had developed in his powerful and influential tract *On Liberty* (1859), Mill suggested that all artificial or socially constructed barriers to the flourishing of the female personality should be eliminated, thereby allowing the question of "woman's nature" to be answered once and for all. Women, he argued, should be allowed the same opportunity for personal liberty, the same freedom to acquire individual dignity, as was allowed to men. He sustained his focus on the possible benefits that the development of female capacities might have for society as a whole. "The anxiety of mankind to interfere in behalf of nature, for fear lest nature should not succeed in effecting its purpose," he insisted, "is an altogether unnecessary solicitude." Confronting the deep reservations of those who opposed women's emancipation, Mill threw out a challenge:[53]

> I should like to hear somebody openly enunciating the doctrine (it is already implied in much that is written on the subject) – 'It is necessary to society that women should marry and produce children. They will not do so unless they are compelled. Therefore it is necessary to compel them.' The merits of the case would then be clearly defined.

This line of reasoning effectively authorized women's rights advocates to take the offensive in demanding emancipatory reforms in women's legal status and education without having to justify those demands on the basis of women's special nature.

Opponents, elaborating the societal implications of the new evolutionary theory proposed by Charles Darwin's celebrated *Origin of Species* (1859; in French translation, 1862), asserted that even if women's legal subordination were ended, as Mill proposed, they could never reach the heights of creativity and intellect established by men. Mill's book thus launched a new round of debate in France (and in many other countries) on the woman question, with opponents arguing that there were, in fact, evolutionary constraints on women's capacity for freedom, as suggested by

---

women have been passing necessities, along with war, theocracies, despotism, and that paternal power which extends to the right of life and death over every member of the family; but none of these institutions can find justification in rights or stand firm in the face of reason."

See also Pompéry's earlier treatise, *La Femme dans l'humanité, sa nature, son rôle et sa valeur sociale* (Paris: Hachette, 1864).

53 John Stuart Mill, *The Subjection of Women* (New York: Appleton, 1869), p. 50. Mill equated this argument from "necessity" with the arguments (in his view, specious) used to defend the enslavement of Negroes and the impressment of sailors.

renewed scientific inquiries into brain size, cranial capacity, and the relation of both to body mass, a research thrust that would greatly expand during the Third Republic.

Intermission: The Franco-Prussian War and the Paris Commune, and the Woman Question

France went to war with Prussia in later 1870 and was vanquished, leading to the fall of the Second Empire and the proclamation of a Republic. The former opposition took power and concluded a highly unpopular, even humiliating peace with Bismarck's Germany. One key result of that defeat was an uprising in Paris known as the Commune, which began in mid-March 1871, only to be crushed by the troops from Versailles on the 28th of May. One of the most striking features of the Commune during the ten weeks of its existence was the vigorous insistence on full participation – in decision-making and every other activity – voiced by the women of Paris, and the resistance they encountered from the Commune's male leadership. Historian Edith Thomas has eloquently told the tale of the women's history of the Commune, documenting their exploits, their concrete and intended contributions. She also recounted in detail the ways in which women activists were scapegoated following the defeat by the Versaillais forces. Meanwhile Eugene Schulkind has reclaimed the program and actions of one group, the *Union des Femmes*, for the history of socialism. More recent studies by Kathleen Jones, Françoise Vergès, and Gay Gullickson have addressed the political implications of representation of the Communardes. Odile Krakovitch has studied the fate of the Communardes, and Carolyn Eichner has retold the story of the Commune through the lives of three Communard women – André Léo and Paule Mink, whom we have already encountered, and the Russian-born Elisabeth Dmietrieff.[54] The negative impact of the stories about the women

---

[54] The *ouvrage de base* on women and the Commune remains Thomas, *Les Pétroleuses*; transl. as *The Women Incendiaries* (cited in n. 1). Much additional research was done by Eugene Schulkind, who combed the French archives in search of further evidence to supplement his article, "Le Rôle des femmes dans la Commune de 1871," *1848, Revue des Révolutions Contemporaines*, 42 (February 1950), 15–29; see especially Schulkind's subsequent article, "Socialist Women in the 1871 Paris Commune," *Past and Present*, n° 106 (February 1985), 124–163, which provides a class analysis of the activities of the *Union des Femmes pour la Défense de Paris et les Soins aux Bessés*. See also Richard Cobb's review of Thomas's study (from the *Times Literary Supplement*, 1965), reprinted in his collection, *A Second Identity; Essays on France and French History* (London: Oxford University Press, 1969), pp. 221–236; Persis Hunt, "Feminism and Anticlericalism under the Commune," *Massachusetts Review*, 12:3 (Summer 1971), 418–420, 429–431. For a feminist reinterpretation, see Albistur & Armogathe, *Histoire du féminisme français*, vol. 2, chapter 6, and the accompanying documents in *Grief des*

Communardes, especially the urban legends and myths that developed around the "*petroleuses*" – women who were accused of setting fires all around Paris – would seriously inflect the later debates on the woman question.[55]

My purpose here is not to retell that tale, but rather to insist on the ways in which several women of the Commune repeatedly raised their voices, *speaking as women* on many sociopolitical subjects, highlighting their own disadvantaged situation, and showing how they attempted to resist marginalization. In addition to their active efforts to organize ambulance and nursing services, their initiatives to establish crèches for childcare, lay primary schools, vocational schools for girls, and producers' cooperatives for working women, the Communard women critiqued the existing organization of marriage, clerical control over the education of children, and their own occupational exploitation, due to the wage-undercutting competition of church-sponsored *ateliers* and prisons and to inadequate social services. What is more, their leaders cast an increasingly skeptical eye on what can only be called the male chauvinism of their fellow Communards; the Paris Commune had a sexual politics of its own that can profitably be compared both to its predecessors in 1789–1793 and

femmes, vol. 2, pp. 40–63. See also Paule Lejeune, "Le donne della Comune de Parigi," in *Esistere come donna* (Milan: Mazzotta, 1983), pp. 97–108. Recent English-language scholarship includes: Kathleen B. Jones & Françoise Vergès, "Women of the Paris Commune," *Women's Studies International Forum*, 14:5 (1991), 491–503; Jones & Vergès, "'Aux Citoyennes!' Women, Politics, and the Paris Commune of 1871," *History of European Ideas*, 13:6 (1991), 711–732; and Gay L. Gullickson, *Unruly Women of Paris: Images of the Commune* (Ithaca, NY: Cornell University Press, 1996). The latest study in English, which builds on the post-Thomas publications and archival materials, is Carolyn Eichner's impressive work, *Surmounting the Barricades: Women in the Paris Commune* (cited in n. 1). In French, see Marisa Linton, "Les Femmes et la Commune de Paris de 1871," *Revue Historique*, n° 603 (July–September 1997), 23–47; Jacques Rougerie, "1871: La Commune de Paris," in *Encyclopédie Politique et Historique des Femmes*, ed. Christine Fauré (Paris: PUF, 1997), 405–431, which provides further background on the preceding 1867–1870 period; Alain Dalotel, "Les Femmes dans les clubs rouges, 1870–1871," in *Femmes dans la Cité*, ed. Alain Corbin et al. (Paris: Créaphis, 1997), pp. 293–304, and Alain Dalotel, "La Barricade des femmes," *La Barricade, Actes du colloque. ... 1995*, ed. Alain Corbin & Jean-Marie Mayeur (Paris: Publications de la Sorbonne, 1997), pp. 340–355. See also Odile Krakovitch, *Les femmes bagnardes* (Paris: O. Orban, 1990), and Odile Krakovitch, "Violence des communardes: une mémoire à revisiter," *Revue Historique*, n° 602 (April–June 1997), 521–531.

Two English-language documentary collections on the Commune, published in the wake of the May 1968 events in France and with an eye to the centennial of the Commune itself, contain translations of some of the texts concerning women's participation and concerns: see *The Paris Commune of 1871: The View from the Left*, ed. Eugene Schulkind (London: Cape, 1972), and *The Communards of Paris, 1871*, ed. Stewart Edwards (Ithaca, NY: Cornell University Press, 1973).

[55] See Robert A. Nye, *The Origins of Crowd Psychology: Gustave LeBon and the Crisis of Mass Democracy in the Third Republic* (London & Beverly Hills: Sage, 1975), and Susanna Barrows, *Distorting Mirrors: Visions of the Crowd in Late Nineteenth Century France* (New Haven, CT: Yale University Press, 1981).

1848 and to subsequent obstacles to participation women on the Left have since encountered from their male counterparts. Controversy over the woman question lay at the heart of this tension-riddled situation. Of particular interest here is the women's sense of their own entitlement, as expressed in print, to participate as *citoyennes* and their invocation of historical memory concerning the revolutionary role of their predecessors to legitimate their demands and participation in 1871.

The appeal to history was pronounced in the actions of the Parisian women during the first days of April, when a group of them proposed reenacting the celebrated women's march on Versailles, but were dissuaded from actually doing so.[56] It was subsequently underscored in the manifesto of Elizabeth Dmitrieff, issued on behalf of "the women citizens of Paris":[57]

> *Citoyennes de Paris*, we, descendants of the women of the Great Revolution, who in the name of the people and justice marched on Versailles, took Louis XVI captive, we, mothers and sisters of the French people – can we tolerate any longer the fact that misery and ignorance make enemies of our children ... ? *Citoyennes*, the hour of decision is here; the old world has had it! We want to be free!

This manifesto was followed up a few days later by the formation of the *Union des Femmes*, whose leaders insisted that women be included in the political decision-making of the Commune. It is, argued the women of the Union, "the duty and the right of everyone to fight for the sacred cause of the people, that is, for the Revolution." The signatories called on the Commune to "consider all legitimate grievances of any section of the population without discrimination of sex, such discrimination having been made and enforced as a means of maintaining the privileges of the ruling class." They then called on the government of the Commune to provide the women with headquarters and meeting space, and subsidies for printing notices, posters, etc., that would serve the common cause.[58]

---

[56] "Une véritable citoyenne," manifesto published in *Le Cri du Peuple*, 4 April 1871, under the heading "Les femmes." The following issue (5 April) of Vallès's paper reported that a procession of some hundred women, headed by a young woman carrying a huge red flag (which, according to an earlier notice, was to have formed at noon at the Place de la Concorde, next to the statue of Strasbourg) had reached the pont de Grenelle before being turned back.

[57] "Appel aux citoyennes de Paris par un groupe de citoyennes," 11 April 1871, in *Journal Officiel de la République française sous la Commune* (Paris, 1871); also in *La Sociale*, n° 13 (12 April 1871). Reprinted in *Journal des journaux de la Commune* (Paris, 1871), 336–339. In translation in Schulkind, *Paris Commune*, pp. 171–172.

[58] From the *Journal Officiel ... sous la Commune*, 14 April 1871; as translated by Schulkind in *Paris Commune*, pp. 172–173.

The events of the next few weeks suggest that these privileges would not be easily forthcoming and that some women were becoming disenchanted with the inaction and attitudes of the all-male leadership of the Commune. Even Jules Vallès, who published several small notices concerning the women's activism in *Le Cri du Peuple*, highlighted but also effectively marginalized it by lumping each disparate item under the heading "les femmes." In early May another group of women, speaking as wives and mothers, issued a call for peace and conciliation with Versailles. To this, the women of the *Union des Femmes* replied with a ringing call for all-out defiance of Versailles and the establishment of a social republic.[59]

Perhaps the most eloquent spokeswomen for women's rights to participate fully in the Paris Commune was André Léo, who wrote in and helped to publish *La Sociale* during the Commune.[60] It is unclear whether she was an active member of Dmitrieff's *Union des Femmes*, yet she was equally displeased with the cool response to women's initiatives by the male leaders of the Commune. Already in early April, in the editorial entitled "*Toutes avec tous,*" she had argued that Paris was far from having too many combatants and that women's help was needed. On 22 April, a group of *citoyennes* from Montmartre (André Léo was one of those who signed the petition) offered their services to the government of the Commune to form ambulance units that could deal with the mounting casualties.[61]

The Commune's establishment of a Committee on Public Safety on the 1st of May did nothing to alter the authorities' resistance to women's participation. Then, responding to the refusal of the women's offers of assistance by certain generals and doctors in the Commune's employ, André Léo queried them sharply: "Do they think they can accomplish the revolution without women?"[62]

---

[59] From the *Journal Officiel*, 8 May 1871; as transl. by Schulkind, *Paris Commune*, pp. 174–175. See also Thomas, *Pétroleuses*, pp. 81–82.

[60] On André Léo's role in the Commune, see Thomas, pp. 141–152; *André Léo, journaliste de la Commune*, no. 44 of *Le Lérot reveur* (March 1987); Eichner, *Surmounting the Barricades*, especially chapters 2, 4, and 6. See also Dalotel's book (cited in n. 17). A number of André Léo's articles from *La Sociale* are republished in her *Écrits politiques*, also cited in n. 17.

[61] See *La Sociale*, n° 13 (12 April 1871); also cited in Schulkind (1950), p. 25. The women's offer of services was also published under the rubric "Les Femmes" in *Le Cri du Peuple*, 26 April 1871.

[62] André Léo, "La Révolution sans la femme," *La Sociale*, n° 39 (8 May 1871); reprinted in Albistur & Armogathe, *Grief des femmes*, vol. 2, pp. 47–48. See also her account, "Aventures de neuf ambulancières à la recherche d'un poste de dévouement," *La Sociale*, n° 37 (6 May 1871). Both these editorials are also reprinted in *André Léo, journaliste* (n. 17) and in *Écrits politiques*. See also Thomas, *Petroleuses*, pp. 162–163. The most thorough study of André Léo is Fernanda Gastaldello, "André Léo: Quel Socialisme?" (Laureate thesis, University of Padua, 1978–1979; I have a personal copy).

For eighty years they've been trying, and haven't yet succeeded. Certainly the first revolution bestowed on women the title of *citoyenne* but not the rights. It left them excluded from liberty, from equality. . . . From one point of view our history since '89 could be written under the title, "History of the Inconsequences of the Revolutionary Party." The woman question would be the longest chapter.

Such a condemnation might be taken as mere circumstantial rhetoric, a means of invoking history to chastise the reluctant Communards. Indeed, this critique was frequently repeated by women critics and their allies both before and during this short-lived revolt. What the women perceived – and they were historically correct – was a systematic, deliberate, and repetitive pattern of exclusion from political affairs, an exclusion that had set back republicans and, more generally, democrats. Already in 1860, Jenny P. d'Héricourt had invoked that history, arguing that the reason women had abandoned the Revolution in 1793 and again in 1848 was because their rights had been repeatedly sacrificed by male partisans of democracy. "I tell you truly; all your struggles are in vain, if woman does not go with you. An order of things may be established by a *coup de main*, but it is only maintained by the adhesion of majorities; and these majorities, gentlemen, are formed by us women, through the influence that we possess over men, through the education we give them with our milk."[63] A few years later Maria Deraismes reiterated the point: "If the democrats don't have the women on their side, their triumphs will only be superficial and transitory."[64] These women fully understood the power of this appeal and used it time and again. Rossel, the Commune's delegate for war, responded publicly to André Léo, offering to do whatever he could to enable the women to serve. Several days later, the Commune's Committee on Public Safety arrested Rossel and stripped him of his functions.[65]

Other women of the Commune acted on their strong sense of women's importance to the common endeavor by breaking with prescribed behavior. Some women appropriated the uniforms of the Communards, red sashes and the rest; some carried revolvers and rifles – and learned how to use them to good effect! If there were no *pétroleuses*, as was charged in the

---

[63] Jenny P. d'Héricourt, *La Femme affranchie* (Brussels: A. Lacroix, 1860). In English translation as *A Woman's Philosophy of Woman* (New York: Carleton, 1864), p. 222; see also *WFF*, vol. 1, doc. 98, p. 347.

[64] Maria Deraismes, "Nos principes et nos moeurs" (1868) in *Oeuvres complètes de Maria Deraismes*, vol. 3 (Paris, 1896); as quoted in Thomas, *Pétroleuses*, p. 40.

[65] See the published exchange between André Léo and Rossel in *La Sociale*, n°s 38 (7 May), 40 (9 May), and 45 (14 May 1871). Only three more issues of *La Sociale* were published.

trials that followed the Commune's defeat, there were certainly armed women, some of whom were killed or wounded in combat.[66]

Indeed, the presence of a sizeable number of armed women was (as has often been the case in European history) deeply disturbing to many men, whatever their political persuasions. The ferocity against the women that one encounters in the testimonies of Maxime du Camp, and in the trials of the women of the Commune, serves as irrefutable proof of this. Indeed, the exaggerated eloquence of their prosecutor (Captain Jouanne, at the military tribunal in September 1871), blaming the very downfall of civilization on the doctrines of women's emancipation and on women's ostensible refusal to serve as legitimate spouses, seems – in the retrospective light of the actual evidence of their behavior – to be absurdly overdrawn. Yet it captured perfectly the spirit of a deeper social fantasy and fear of unruly, disruptive – and powerful – women who must be controlled and kept in a different, more marginal place, by orderly male rule, and chastised if they stepped beyond its boundaries. For such men, women's activism embodied danger and disorder.

Anxieties such as these would not be allayed by the implacable challenge put forth in the name of the social revolution by one of the most politically radical of the Communardes, Louise Michel, at her trial before the military tribunal the following December. "Why should I defend myself? I have already told you I refuse to do it. You are the men who are going to judge me.... You are men, and I, I am only a woman. Nevertheless, I am looking you straight in the face.... If you are not cowards, kill me ...!"[67] If this woman and her peers were the products of a French effort to subordinate, humble, and marginalize women, then clearly the system was not working effectively! The remedy: death sentences! Even when commuted to lives of forced labor, deportation, and lengthy imprisonment, these were harsh sentences – comparable to the sentences meted out to the male Communards. That seems particularly ironic, given that the condemned were women whose participation had not even been welcomed by the Commune's male leadership and whose claims to civil and political rights remained deliberately unrecognized.

The phantasms evoked by the women of the Commune would cast a long shadow; throughout the 1870s support for political rights for women

---

[66] On the armed women, see Thomas, *Pétroleuses*, pp. 163 ff. See also the brief eulogy to the female casualties on the barricades in *La Sociale*, n° 18 (17 April 1871).

[67] Louise Michel's words of defiance, as quoted in *The Red Virgin: Memoirs of Louise Michel*, ed. and transl. by Bullitt Lowry & Elizabeth Ellington Gunter (University [Tuscaloosa], AL: University of Alabama Press, 1981), pp. 86–87.

in France would remain virtually a dead letter. There had, of course, been some efforts made during the late Second Empire to promote women's suffrage in France. Following the defeat of the Empire, in late September 1870 the ubiquitous Julie-Victoire Daubié had petitioned the mayor of her Paris arrondissement to be added to the voter rolls. Single adult and widowed women taxpayers, she argued, should be allowed to vote. Following the defeat of the Commune, Daubié organized a petition to that effect. But only a few years later, Daubié died prematurely and her suffrage agitation ground to a halt. In 1874, the year of her death, the National Assembly debated a new electoral law; the deputies virtually ignored the woman suffrage issue, except for some sarcastic humor on the subject.[68] In this time of transition from Empire to Republic, of Bonapartist threat, republican paranoia (the word is not too strong), and the government of "moral order," the very thought of mixing women into an already turbulent and unstable political situation inspired fear and anxiety, even among those most likely to support women's rights. Henry Baudrillart summed up many men's views in 1872, examining the question of women's emancipation in France (in the *Revue des Deux Mondes*) with an eye to the British and American examples, and explicitly to the arguments of John Stuart Mill and André Léo:[69]

> If one accepts the terms in which [the woman question] is posed [i.e., in terms of individual liberty], one can see in it the germ of perhaps the greatest revolution the world has yet experienced. It would be nothing less than the coming into its rights of an entire sex – that is to say – half of the human species – which until now has been unjustly dispossessed. Even abolitionism, which has been devoted to eradicating the servitude of several million poor blacks from the face of the earth, would amount to little in comparison to this.

Throughout the 1870s advocates of women's suffrage would maintain a low profile. The story of how the woman's suffrage issue was barred from the agenda of the First International Congress on Women's Rights, held in 1878 in Paris, and how, in protest, Hubertine Auclert relaunched the

---

[68] For retrospective views on this matter, see Richer, *Femme libre*, pp. 255–263, and Theodore Stanton, ed., *The Woman Question in Europe* (New York: G. P. Putnam's Sons, 1884), p. 247. Daubié's suffrage efforts are discussed by A. Henry-Nathan, "Un ancêtre du suffragisme, Julie Daubié," *Revue Politique et Parlementaire* (September 1918), 290–296, and by Paulette Bascou-Bance, "La Première femme bachelière, Julie Daubié," *Bulletin Budé*, 4th ser., n° 1 (March 1972), esp. 111–112. Excerpts from Daubié's letter to the mayor and her suffrage petition are translated in Moses, *French Feminism*, pp. 212–213.

[69] Henri Baudrillart, "L'Agitation pour l'émancipation des femmes," *Revue des Deux Mondes*, (1 October 1872), 652.

question in France, has featured in the historical literature on the period.[70] What is less well-known is the way in which, in the 1870s, the debate on the woman question shifted to highlight other significant issues. It is to consideration of these issues and their supporters that we will turn in the subsequent volume, which will treat the debates on the woman question during the Third Republic from 1872 to 1920.

* * *

In the Introduction to this book, I proposed five salient and peculiarly French characteristics of the debates on the woman question in France, over the course of several centuries and across the customary chronological divide of the French Revolution. They include: 1) the extraordinary importance the French attributed to women's influence (and the correlate fear of envisioning them in positions of political authority or even as equals); 2) the growing propensity for biomedical thinking that permeated every debate, particularly in the counterrevolutionary context of the early and mid-nineteenth century; 3) the ongoing significance of the population issue; 4) the bitter quarrels over women's intellect and educational potential; and finally, 5) the specific forms in which French nationalism would express itself (this characteristic becomes far more significant during the Third Republic). In the chapters of the subsequent volume, I will examine in greater chronological depth and in considerable detail the specific issues that composed the woman question during the early Third Republic with reference to this cluster of particularities. My challenge will be to further explicate these culturally distinctive features, even as I attempt to cast them in relief by developing comparisons with other national-cultural situations. I will also attempt to show how each specific issue was connected with every other issue and with the whole, and how each fed into a broader, increasingly transnational campaign for major changes in the status and condition of women that transcended France's national boundaries.

---

[70] See Bidelman, *Pariahs*, chapter 3; Moses, *French Feminism*, chapter 9; and Steven C. Hause, *Hubertine Auclert* (New Haven, CT: Yale University Press, 1987), chapter 2.

Important Dates for the Woman Question Debates in France, 1400–1870

1399	Christine de Pizan writes *Épître au Dieu d'Amour*, in defense of women from men's insults in *Le Roman de la Rose*
1405	*La Cité des Dames* [The Book of the City of Ladies] by Christine de Pizan; she draws on Boccacio's *De Mulieribus claris* (1355) but probably on the 1401 French translation, and deliberately reinterprets his accounts of famous women
1408–1409	Jean de Montreuil "invents" a Salic law tradition that bars women from the French throne
1429–1431	France at war with the English; Joan of Arc leads the French troops. Christine de Pizan composes a poem in her praise. Joan is captured by the English and burned at the stake in Rouen in 1431
1440	Martin Le Franc writes *Le Champion des Dames*, a defense of the female sex, dedicated to the duke of Burgundy, Phillip II
1452	Johannes Gutenberg (resident of Mainz) puts his press with moveable type to commercial use
1470	Jeanne Hachette leads a troop of women armed with hatchets against the Burgundians, during the siege of Beauvais, and captures their flag

1479   Spain is united through the marriage of Ferdinand of Aragon and Isabelle of Castille

1486   Sprenger's *Malleus Maleficarum* [Hammer of Witches] provides a primer on witchcraft and how to prosecute witches

1491   The French crown acquires the duchy of Brittany, through marriage of the king to the last heir, Anne de Bretagne; by this date Anne already owns a six-piece set of tapestries based on Pizan's *City of Ladies*

1492   The Spanish crown (Isabelle of Castille) finances Christopher Columbus's expedition to find the route to the Indies; expulsion of the Moors from Spain

1517   Martin Luther posts his 95 Theses against the Roman Catholic Church and kicks off the European Reformation

1520–1522   *Le Débat de l'homme et de la femme* (1520) and *Apologie du sexe féminin* (1522)

1528   Baldassare Castiglione publishes his *Il libro del cortegiano* [The Book of the Courtier]; several French editions published in Paris and Lyon, 1537–1538 (features debates between the Aristotelians and the Platonists)

1529   Louise of Savoy and Margaret of Austria conclude the Peace of Cambrai, putting an end to war between France's Valois dynasty and the Habsburgs (Holy Roman Empire)

1533–1536   England's Henry VIII sheds his first wife (of twenty years), Catherine of Aragon, then marries Anne Boleyn, with whom he has daughter Elizabeth; breaks with Rome over question of divorce; assumes headship of the Church of England (Protestant) in 1534; Anne Boleyn beheaded in 1536

1534   *Controverses des sexes masculin et féminin*

1537	First French edition of H.-C. Agrippa de Nettesheim's *Sur la noblesse et l'excellence du sexe féminin, de sa prééminence sur l'autre sexe* [On the nobility and excellence of the feminine sex, and her preeminence over the other sex]; originally written (1509) and published in Latin (1529)
1547	Henri II succeeds his father François I as king of France; Catherine de Médicis is his consort and mother of the dauphin and, later, gives birth to nine other children (she will serve as regent for three sickly sons)
1553	Mary Tudor succeeds her father Henry VIII, then her brother, as Queen of England (she is married to Phillip II of Spain – and a Catholic – which leads to severe persecution of Protestants)
1555	Jeanne d'Albret becomes Queen of Navarre; strong Protestant ties Francois de Billon publishes a long reply to Rabelais: *Le Fort inexpugnable de l'honneur du sexe féminin* Publication of the *Oeuvres* [Works] of Louise Labé, poet and writer from Lyon, who urges women to develop their talents
1558	17 November: in England, Mary I dies (after losing Calais) and is succeeded by her half-sister Elizabeth, who is Protestant Mary, Queen of Scots (whose mother is Marie de Guise, married to James V of Scotland) marries the French dauphin François II (who dies shortly thereafter) From Geneva, the Calvinist John Knox issues his *First Blast of the Trumpet against the Monstrous Regiment of Women*
1558–1559	The *Heptameron* by Marguerite d'Angoulême, Queen of Navarre, published posthumously
1560–1563	Regency of Catherine de Médicis; Mary Stuart and Guise conspiracies provoke opposition of Protestant reformers to women's rule; Mary, Queen of Scots, returns to Scotland to rule and confronts John Knox

262 *Appendix: Important Dates, 1400–1870*

1563	Council of Trent affirms marriage as a sacrament and stipulates conditions for the performance of marriage by a priest – consent of the man and the woman. Parental consent not required
1566	Birth of Infanta Isabella, potential claimant to the French throne through her mother Elisabeth de Valois, should all her uncles (the sons of Henry II and Catherine de Médicis) die (which they eventually all did)
1572	St. Barthelemy's Day massacre of French Protestants, which was blamed on the queen-mother Catherine de Médicis and her allies
1577	Jean Bodin publishes his *Six Livres de la République*, insisting on the subordination of women and their exclusion from political authority
1578–1586	Publications of the dames des Roches (mother and daughter) of Poitiers, who debate the woman question
1587	8 February: Mary Queen of Scots beheaded by order of Elizabeth I of England
1588	*La guerre des mâles contre les femelles*
1593	28 June: the Parliament of Paris confirms the principle of "male right," reinventing the "Salic Law" as "Public Law" that formally excludes women from succession to French throne. Henry IV renounces Protestantism for Catholicism to accede to the throne
1598	April: Edict of Nantes ended the religious wars and granted French Protestants religious toleration and civil rights
1617	*Alphabet de l'imperfection et malice des femmes*, by the Franciscan monk Alexis Trousset
1622	*Sur l'Égalité des Hommes et des Femmes* [On the Equality of Men and Women] by Marie Le Jars de Gournay

1639   French Royal ordinance requires parental (paternal) consent for marriages (not required by the Catholic Church since the Council of Trent)

1640   Louis XIII calls for the suppression of coeducation in schools, male teachers for boys, and female teachers only for girls

1647   Pierre Le Moyne publishes *La Galerie des femmes fortes*

1648–1653 "La Fronde" – civil war, in two parts 1648–1649 and 1649–1653. Two powerful noblewomen played major roles in the opposition to the young king Louis XIV (b. 1638) and his mother, Anne d'Autriche, the Spanish princess who served as regent from 1643 on: Anne-Geneviève de Bourbon-Conde, duchesse de Longueville; and Anne-Marie-Louise d'Orléans, duchesse de Montpensier, known as "La Grande Mademoiselle," a cousin of the king and, not incidentally, the richest woman in France

1654–1660 *Clélie* (1654–1660), a long, serial novel by Madeleine de Scudéry, denounces women's position in marriage as "slavery" and invokes on women's behalf a rhetoric of "liberty" and "breaking chains"

1656–1658 Michel de Pure publishes a novel, *La Prétieuse; ou le mystère des ruelles*, in two volumes: a critique of marriage as slavery and call for the freedom of women

1662   Moliere's comedy *École des femmes* is produced. The playwright Molière satirizes the *prétieuses* and learned women and their critiques of marriage and girls' education

1664   Mlle Clément publishes *Dialogue de la princesse sçavante et de la dame de famille, contenant l'art d'élever les jeunes dames dans une belle et noble éducation*

1666   Edict on Marriage from Colbert, Louis XIV's minister of finance, to promote early marriage and population growth (revoked 1683)

1673–1674   *De l'Égalité des deux sexes* [On the Equality of the Two
                Sexes] by François Poullain de la Barre

1675   Seamstresses' guild founded in Paris

1686   *Entretiens sur la pluralité des mondes*, by Bernard le Bovier de
                Fontenelle – a best seller on science and astronomy, in
                dialogue with a woman student, the Marquise

1687   Fénelon's *Traité de l'éducation des filles* [Treatise on the
                Education of Daughters]; Mme de Maintenon (morganatic
                wife of king Louis XIV) founds St. Cyr, a secular school for
                daughters of the so-called impoverished nobility

1693   G. S. [Gabrielle Suchon, religieuse de Saumur] publishes her
                Traité de la Morale et de la Politique ... in which she argues
                that women are deprived of Liberty, Science, and Authority

1715   Death of Louis XIV; succeeded by his underage great-
                grandson Louis XV; Regency

1721–1722   Montesquieu publishes the *Lettres persanes* [The Persian
                Letters] a critique of French society as seen by two
                Persian travelers to France; the woman question is
                addressed in a later chapter, raising issues about women's
                subordination

1723   First publication of the letters of Madame de Sévigné

1726   Another French translation of Henri Corneille Agrippa de
                Nettesheim, *Sur La Noblesse Et Excellence du Sexe Féminin*
                (1726; orig. 1509, published 1529 in Latin; 1537 in French)

1748   Montesquieu publishes *De l'Esprit des lois;* he traces the
                relationship between the condition of women and types
                of political regimes

1750   Marivaux's comedy *La Colonie* explores women's sense of
                "oppression," their quest for rights, and their revolt against
                masculine efforts, on an island where both sexes are
                refugees, to make laws that reestablish their domination

1750s   Population issue again becomes important; beginning of
                 men's worries about perceived decline in the birth rate

1751–1766   Publication of *L'Encyclopédie* by Denis Diderot and his
                 team of writers

1758   The Catholic apologist Pierre-Joseph Boudier de Villemart,
                 publishes *L'Ami des femmes*, emphasizes women's role as a
                 civilizing force, tamers and inspirers of men; widely
                 translated and republished
                 Lettre de J.-J. Rousseau, citoyen de Genève, à
                 M. d'Alembert . . . sur son article "Genève". . .

1759   *Lettre de M. d'Alembert à M. J.-J. Rousseau sur l'article*
                 "Genève" tiré du VIIe volume de l'Encyclopédie

1760s   Articles and debate on women, education, citizenship,
                 sexuality, and social order in Diderot's *Encyclopédie*, by
                 Jean-Jacques Rousseau, and others. Publication of *Le*
                 Journal des Dames under three women editors

1761–1762   Rousseau publishes his *Julie, ou la Nouvelle Héloise* (1761)
                 and *Émile, ou de l'Éducation* (1762)

1769   Publication of *Histoire littéraire des dames françoises, ou*
                 Lettres historiques et critiques contenant un précis de la vie et
                 une analyse raisonnée des ouvrages des femmes qui se sont
                 distinguées dans la littérature françoise, par un Société des
                 gens de lettres (Joseph de La Porte, Jean-Francois de La
                 Croix, & Jean Maineau) in five volumes
                 Publication of *Dictionnaire historique portatif des femmes*
                 célèbres in 2 vols. by Jean-François de La Croix (de
                 Compiègne)

1771   The naturalist Buffon publishes vol. 2 of his *Histoire*
                 naturelle, générale et particulière . . . He blames the
                 subjection of women on differential in physical strength,
                 but speaks to women's use of beauty and sentiment as
                 means to equalize their condition among the "civilized"
                 as opposed to their lot among the savages

1772, 1774   A. Thomas, of the Académie Française, publishes his *Essai sur le caractère, les moeurs, et l'esprit des femmes dans les différens siècles* (1772), published in English translation (Philadelphia) in 1774 as *Essay on the Character, Manners, and Genius of Women in Different Ages*

1774–1779   The jurist Robert Pothier publishes his *Traité de la puissance maritale* (1774) and *Traité de la puissance du mari sur la personne et les biens de la femme* (1779)

1776   Louise d'Épinay applies the term "gender" to beings of the male and female sexes, insisting that she does not refer to grammar

1778   Jean-François Fournel publishes his *Traité de l'adultère*, arguing that only *women* [wives] can commit adultery

1783   The Academy of Art admits Elisabeth Vigée-Lebrun; Mme d'Épinay beats out Mme de Genlis for the Prix Montyon of the Académie Française

1785   Mme de Coicy publishes *Les Femmes comme il convient de les voir, ou aperçu de ce que les femmes ont été, de ce qu'elles sont, et de ce qu'elles pourraient être*

1786–1789   Louise-Félicité (Guinement de Kéralio; later Robert) publishes *Collection des meilleurs ouvrages françois, composés par des femmes, dédiée aux femmes françoises.* 6 vols.

1787   In his *Lettres d'un Bourgeois de New Haven à un citoyen de Virginie* (1787), the Marquis de Condorcet argues that women should vote in the Estates-General
Mme Gacon-Dufour publishes her *Mémoire pour le sexe féminin contre le sexe masculin*
Le President Roland lays out his *Recherches sur les prérogatives des dames chez les Gaulois*

1789   Outbreak of French Revolution. Many women's petitions to the National Assembly demanding civil and political rights and equal citizenship, economic rights, etc.

Cahier des Doléances et Réclamations de Femmes by Madame B*** B***

Requête des Dames à l'Assemblée Nationale – perhaps the most radical text attributed to women

August: National Assembly decrees the Declaration of the Rights of Man, and the next day reaffirms the exclusion of women from succession to the French throne

5–6 October: women's march on Versailles; the royal family is "escorted" back to Paris

1790   Condorcet publishes *Sur l'Admission des femmes au Droit de Cité* [On the Admission of Women to Citizenship]

Vues législatives pour les femmes, adressées à l'Assemblée nationale, presented by Mlle Jodin

12 July: Civil Constitution of the Clergy

1791   April: Equal division of inheritance property; daughters can inherit as well as sons

21 June: the King and Queen attempt to flee France; they are arrested and returned to Paris and imprisoned

July: "*Adresse des citoyennes françoises à l'Assemblée Nationale*" [Address of French Women Citizens to the National Assembly] by Etta Palm d'Aelders in her *Appel aux Francoises sur la régénération des moeurs et nécessité de l'influence des femmes dans un gouvernement libre*

27 August: Marriage becomes a civil contract

3 September: Constitution of 1791 defines marriage as a civil contract; prescribes civil register of births, marriages, deaths

September: Talleyrand argues that women should be educated for household role, not for active citizenship

Déclaration des Droits de la Femme [Declaration of the Rights of Woman] by Olympe de Gouges

1792   August–September: Abolition of parental authority over grown children (over age 25; then age changed to 21). Single adult women obtain full civil (property) rights

2 September: Massacres of prisoners, including many former religious authorities

Decree of 20 September: establishes *état civil* [civil registry]; the French state takes over registration of births, marriages, deaths from the Catholic Church

Law of 20 September: secularizes marriage and authorizes
civil divorce. Age of majority set at 21 for girls as well as
for boys
Decrees of 21–22, 25 September: abolish the monarchy in
France; announce the Republic as "one and indivisible"
October: Legislative Assembly convened
The Englishwoman Mary Wollstonecraft responds to
Talleyrand's invocation (1791) of "public utility" to
disqualify women with her *Vindication of the Rights of
Woman*, which is quickly published in French translation

1793   21 January: execution of the King
January–February: Louis Prudhomme in his *Révolutions de
Paris* rants against women's clubs and activities
April: Pierre Guyomar pens his defense of women's right to
political equality, *Le Partisan de l'égalité politique entre les
individus, ou problème très important de l'égalité en droits et
de l'inégalité en fait*
April: *Société des Républicaines révolutionnaires* forms
30 October: the Jacobins ban women from clubs and
political activity
Olympe de Gouges executed, along with Marie-Antoinette
and Madame Roland

1793–1794   The Terror

1795   Condorcet's *Sketch for the Progress of the Human Mind*
condemns the inequality of rights between the two sexes
21 February: Separation of church and state

1797   Constance de Théis Pipelet (later princess du Salm-
Reifferscheid-Dyck) publishes her *Épître aux femmes*

1799   Charles Theremin publishes *De la Condition des femmes
dans les républiques*; insists that the husband must
represent the family in public life

1800   Constance de Théis Pipelet responds to Theremin with her
*Rapport sur un ouvrage du C^en Theremin, intitulé De la
Condition des Femmes dans une République*

1801	Controversy over Sylvain Maréchal's proposed law prohibiting women from learning to read Fanny Raoul contests women's exclusion from public life
1802	Louis DuBroca publishes *Les Femmes célèbres de la Révolution*
1803	*Les femmes : leur condition et leur influence dans l'ordre social chez différents peuples anciens et modernes* [Women: Their Condition and Influence in Society], is published by the Vicomte de Ségur
1804	French Civil Code, Napoléon's "gift" to French women, imposes severe restrictions on the rights of married women, etc. *Recherche de la paternité* forbidden. Laws on adultery favor husbands 18 May: *Sénatus consulte organique* reaffirms male succession for the line of the emperor, Napoléon Bonaparte 2 December: Napoléon crowns himself emperor Napoléon sanctions registration and health checks for prostitutes; tolerated brothels begin to appear
1807	*Corinne*, novel by Madame de Staël, praises women's genius
1808	*Théorie des Quatre Mouvements*, 1st ed., published by Charles Fourier
1814–1815	Defeat(s) of Napoléon; restoration of the Bourbon monarchy; Napoléon exiled for life to the island of St. Helena under British authority
1816	Law of 8 May 1816 forbids civil divorce
1820s	Mme Campan, Mme de Rémusat, Mme Guizot, the comtesse de Fleselles, and Fannie de Mongellaz all publish books on the education and influence of women in France
1830	Revolution and installation of the July Monarchy (house of Orléans)
1830–1832	Saint-Simonian debates on women; founding of *La Femme libre*; the Saint-Simonian women prioritize the question

of women's work over that of sexual liberty; Publication by Eugénie Niboyet of *Le Conseiller des Femmes*

1832–1833   *Indiana* (1832) and *Lélia* (1833), novels by George Sand (Aurore Dudevant), take up the woman question under the July Monarchy

1833   Law of 28 June: establishes national network of public schools for boys only

1834   *The Education of Mothers; or, the Civilization of Mankind* by Louis Aimé-Martin

1836   Parent-Duchâtelet's *On Prostitution in the City of Paris*, the first of a number of landmark studies on social questions, including the woman question, resulting from competitions sponsored by the *Académie des Sciences Morales et Politiques*
23 June: Royal ordinance establishing girls' primary education at two levels ("*élémentaire*" and "*supérieure*"), based on 1833 law that also established conditions and credentials for teaching and opening schools, both private and public
Hortense Allart publishes *La Femme et la démocratie de nos temps*
La Gazette des Femmes: Journal de législation et de jurisprudence, ed. by Poutret de Mauchamps and others, begins publication

1830s–1840s   Publications of Flora Tristan, other women novelists, essayists
Tocqueville, in volume 2 of his *Democracy in America* (1840), points to freedom of young American women before marriage and their subordination afterward

1838   4 September: Henriette d'Angeville summits Mont Blanc
Publication of Flora Tristan's *Pérégrinations d'une Paria* (2 vols.) and novel *Méphis*

1840s   P.-J. Proudhon, Étienne Cabet, Jules Michelet, Auguste Comte, and many socialists publish works that discuss or prescribe women's place in the sociopolitical order

1843   Flora Tristan publishes *L'Union Ouvrière*

1845   Jules Michelet publishes *Le Prêtre, la femme, et la famille*

1848   February: revolution breaks out; Louis-Philippe flees to
             England; Provisional Government for a republic formed
             in Paris
             March: Outburst of women's activity in Revolution of 1848;
             quarrel over whether, in the Provisional Government's
             electoral rules, "*tous les français*" includes women – or not
             22 March: Committee for Women's Rights protests,
             petitions the Provisional Government
             Founding of women's newspapers: *La Voix des Femmes*, ed.
             Eugénie Niboyet; begins publication in late March;
             Jeanne Deroin spells out women's "mission"
             Women's clubs open and after two months are declared illegal
             Ernest Legouvé lectures on the moral history of women at
             Collège de France
             April: Elections held for a Constituent Assembly, which will
             decide on an electoral law
             15 May: riots in Paris; 22–26 "June Days"
             July: closing of the women's clubs and their exclusion from
             public life; closing of the newspaper; Jeanne Deroin
             defies this order by publishing one issue of *La Politique
             des Femmes* in August
             20 December: Louis-Napoléon Bonaparte elected president
             of the Second Republic

1849   Jeanne Deroin's candidacy for National Assembly; efforts to
             form mixed sex workers' unions in Paris led by
             revolutionary women; Legouvé publishes his *Histoire
             morale des femmes* [Moral History of Women]

1850   Marie d'Agoult, *Histoire de la Révolution de 1848* (2nd ed. 1862)

1851   Law of 15 March 1851 (Falloux Law): mandates girls' schools
             in each commune; places education of girls into hands of
             the church
             Deroin and Pauline Roland arrested and jailed for breaching
             the laws against association; Roland deported; Deroin in
             exile; 15 June: their "Appeal to the Women of America"

November: Pierre Leroux attempts a modification of the electoral law that would include single adult women; he is unsuccessful

1852   Opening of the *Bon Marché*, Paris's first department store

2 December: Louis-Napoléon's *coup d'état*; Second Empire proclaimed

Organic Law on the Press forbids women from publishing "political" periodicals

1853   In his tribute to Louise Julien, "Sur la Tombe de Louise Jullien," Victor Hugo predicts that the nineteenth century will proclaim the "rights of woman"

1854   Dogma of the Immaculate Conception [of Mary] proclaimed in Rome by the Vatican

1855   15 May – 15 November: First Paris Universal Exposition

1858–1860   Proudhon, Jenny P. d'Héricourt, Michelet, and Juliette Lamber(t) debate the woman question; great influence on Russians, Italians. Michelet publishes *L'Amour* (1858) and *La Femme* (1859)

1859   Julie-Victoire Daubié wins *concours* in Lyon for her thesis on the plight of poor women.

1861   Julie-Victoire Daubié, first woman to pass the *baccalauréat* exam, required for university entrance; *L'Ouvrière* [The Workingwoman] published by Jules Simon

Women typographers hired by Parisian publishers

1862   Elisa Lemonnier establishes vocational schools for girls in Paris; Clémence Royer's French translation of Darwin's *Origin of Species* appears

1865   June: Artist Rosa Bonheur awarded the *Légion d'Honneur* by the Empress Eugénie

1866   *La Femme pauvre* published by Julie-Victoire Daubié

3–8 September: The First Congress of the
International Workingmen's Association meets in
Geneva, debates women's employment;
Proudhonians versus Marxists

Olympe Audouard publishes her *Guerre aux Hommes*

Government Commission appointed to study revision of
the Civil Code

1867   1 April–3 November: 2nd Paris Universal Exposition

Law of 10 April 1867 sets up parity in primary education
of girls

May: The British House of Commons debates women's
suffrage; John Stuart Mill advocates replacing the word
"man" with "person"

2–8 September: The First International Workingmen's
Association. 2nd Congress in Lausanne, again debates
women's employment

30 October 1867: Duruy's ministerial circular establishes the
Cours d'enseignement secondaire pour les filles – 1st course
opens in Paris, 5 December

1868   June: Second Empire grants freedom of association, public
meetings

July: Lecture series on women's work at the Vauxhall; Paule
Mink defends women's work

mid-July: André Léo (Léodile Béra Champseix) founds
Société de Revendication des Droits de la Femme [Society
for the Revendication of Women's Rights]

26 July: Marie Pouchoulin Goegg founds the *Association
Internationale des Femmes* in Geneva

As temporary regent, Empress Eugénie facilitates the entry
of women to the Paris Faculty of Medicine, which then
accepted four women as candidates for the doctorate;
Madeleine Brès, the first Frenchwomen admitted to
study of medicine in Paris Faculty of Medicine, finishes
her M.D. degree in 1875

November: Maria Deraismes launches her lecture series on
women workers of the future; insists that women's
inferiority is a human invention, a social fiction

1869   Liberalization of laws on press; founding of women's rights
associations, publications

La Femme et les Moeurs: Liberté ou Monarchie [Women and
Morals: Liberty or Monarchy] by André Léo

Maria Deraismes and Paule Mink become movement
orators

Thanks to Jenny P. d'Héricourt in Chicago, ties develop
with American women's rights organizations

April: Léon Richer founds paper *Le Droit des Femmes*;
Deraismes and Richer found Society for Amelioration of
Women's Condition

Publication of John Stuart Mill's *The Subjection of Women*,
and immediate translation into French as
L'Assujetissement des Femmes

1870   March: First meeting of *Association Internationale des
Femmes*, in Geneva

April: Richer and Deraismes found the *Association pour le
Droit des Femmes*, which eventually becomes the *Ligue
Française pour le Droit des Femmes*

Olympe Audouard publishes *La Femme dans le mariage, la
séparation et le divorce*

Franco-Prussian war: France defeated by Germany; end of
Second Empire; 4 September: Proclamation of the
Republic

1871   Unification of Germany proclaimed at Versailles, early 1871;
treaty very punitive to France

March–May: Paris Commune; women's efforts to take
leadership positions thwarted, many women's rights
leaders flee into exile; others are arrested and tried in
military courts

Period of reaction, political uncertainty, and cautious
activity for women's rights advocates until 1875

1872   9 June: Banquet for *Le Droit des Femmes* (Léon Richer)

Index